THE PEOPLING OF EAST ASIA

One of the most dynamic research areas in the prehistory of the East Asian region is the synthesis of archaeology, linguistics and genetics. Several countries have only recently been opened to field research and highly active local groups have made possible a raft of collaborative studies which would have been impossible a decade ago. This book presents an overview of the most recent findings in these fields. New proposals on the relationships of the language phyla of East Asia can now be tested against the findings of geneticists and archaeologists. Recent results on the domestication and spread of rice and millet, in particular, are taken up both in the archaeological and linguistic chapters. Hypotheses discussed in the linguistic section include the validity of the Austric hypothesis, the nature of the links between the Daic languages and Austronesian, and the overall relations between the language phyla of East Asia. The chapters on genetics focus particularly on the genetic structure of East Asian populations and the origins of the Austronesian peoples of Taiwan and the minorities of China. Physical anthropology is also considered with a multivariate analysis of East Asian and Pacific populations. The archaeological chapters take a broad view of East Asia and the potential of the 'farming dispersals' hypothesis, as well as the more specific archaeology of Taiwan. The book should be of great interest to scholars of all disciplines working on the reconstruction of the past of East Asia.

Laurent Sagart is Senior Researcher with the Centre National de la Recherche Scientifique, Paris, France. He is the author of three books and numerous articles on Chinese dialectology, Old Chinese phonology and morphology, comparative Chinese linguistics and the Austronesian languages.

Roger Blench is an independent scholar and consultant working in international development but also on language and prehistory. He has edited Language and Archaeology Vols I–IV (Routledge) as well as a book on the history of African livestock.

Alicia Sanchez-Mazas is Professor of Population Genetics and Anthropology at the University of Geneva, Switzerland. Her main research interest is the evolution of modern humans. She has published several articles on worldwide genetic diversity and its relation to human peopling history.

THE PEOPLING OF EAST ASIA

Putting together archaeology, linguistics and genetics

Edited by
Laurent Sagart, Roger Blench
and Alicia Sanchez-Mazas

LONDON AND NEW YORK

First published 2005
by RoutledgeCurzon

Published 2014 by Routledge
2 Park Square, Milton Park, Abingdon, Oxfordshire OX14 4RN
Simultaneously published in the USA and Canada
711 Third Avenue, New York, NY 10017

First issued in paperback 2014

Routledge is an imprint of the Taylor & Francis Group, an informa business

Transferred to Digital Printing 2005

© 2005 Editorial matter and selection, Laurent Sagart, Roger Blench and Alicia Sanchez-Mazas; individual chapters, the contributors

Typeset in Times New Roman by
Newgen Imaging Systems (P) Ltd, Chennai, India

All rights reserved. No Part of this book may be reprinted or reproduced or utilised in any form or by any electronic, mechanical, or other means, now known or hereafter invented, including photocopying and recording, or in any information storage or retrieval system, without permission in writing from the publishers.

British Library Cataloguing in Publication Data
A catalogue record for this book is available from the British Library

Library of Congress Cataloging in Publication Data
A catalog record of this book has been requested

ISBN 978-0-415-32242-3 (hbk)
ISBN 978-1-138-86223-4 (pbk)

CONTENTS

List of plates   viii
List of figures   ix
List of maps   xi
List of tables   xii
List of contributors   xvi
Preface   xxi
Acknowledgements   xxiii

Introduction   1
LAURENT SAGART, ROGER BLENCH AND ALICIA SANCHEZ-MAZAS

PART I
Archaeology   15

1. Examining the farming/language dispersal hypothesis in the East Asian context   17
PETER BELLWOOD

2. From the mountains to the valleys: understanding ethnolinguistic geography in Southeast Asia   31
ROGER BLENCH

3. The origin and dispersal of agriculture and human diaspora in East Asia   51
TRACEY L.-D. LU

4. Recent discoveries at the Tapenkeng culture sites in Taiwan: implications for the problem of Austronesian origins   63
TSANG CHENG-HWA

CONTENTS

PART II
Linguistics 75

5 The contribution of linguistic palaeontology to the homeland
    of Austro-Asiatic 77
    GÉRARD DIFFLOTH

6 Tibeto-Burman vs Indo-Chinese: implications for population
    geneticists, archaeologists and prehistorians 81
    GEORGE VAN DRIEM

7 Kra-dai and Austronesian: notes on phonological
    correspondences and vocabulary distribution 107
    WEERA OSTAPIRAT

8 The current status of Austric: a review and evaluation of
    the lexical and morphosyntactic evidence 132
    LAWRENCE A. REID

9 Sino-Tibetan–Austronesian: an updated and improved
    argument 161
    LAURENT SAGART

10 Tai-Kadai as a subgroup of Austronesian 177
    LAURENT SAGART

11 Proto-East Asian and the origin and dispersal of
    the languages of East and Southeast Asia and the Pacific 182
    STANLEY STAROSTA

PART III
Genetics and physical anthropology 199

12 The physical anthropology of the Pacific, East Asia and
    Southeast Asia: a multivariate craniometric analysis 201
    MICHAEL PIETRUSEWSKY

13 Genetic diversity of Taiwan's indigenous peoples: possible
    relationship with insular Southeast Asia 230
    MARIE LIN, CHEN-CHUNG CHU, RICHARD E. BROADBERRY,
    LUNG-CHIH YU, JUN-HUN LOO AND JEAN A. TREJAUT

CONTENTS

14 Genetic analysis of minority populations in China and its implications for multiregional evolution 248
JIAYOU CHU

15 Comparing linguistic and genetic relationships among East Asian populations: a study of the RH and GM polymorphisms 252
ESTELLA S. POLONI, ALICIA SANCHEZ-MAZAS, GUILLAUME JACQUES AND LAURENT SAGART

16 HLA genetic diversity and linguistic variation in East Asia 273
ALICIA SANCHEZ-MAZAS, ESTELLA S. POLONI, GUILLAUME JACQUES AND LAURENT SAGART

17 A synopsis of extant Y chromosome diversity in East Asia and Oceania 297
PETER A. UNDERHILL

Index 315

PLATES

Colour plates I–IV appear between pages 72–73 and plates V–VIII appear between pages 280–281

- I Cord-marked pot from Nan-kuan-li
- II Shouldered adz from Nan-kuan-li
- III Pearl shell reaping knife from Nan-kuan-li
- IV (a) Carbonised rice grains from Nan-kuan-li and
  (b) carbonised millet grains from Nan-kuan-li East
- V (a) RH frequency distributions and (b) GM frequency distributions
- VI Distributions of M174, M130*(RPS4Y*), M38, M217, M4 and M9* defined chromosome in 74 populations
- VII Distributions of M89, M122, M119, M268, M214 and M45 related chromosomes in 74 populations
- VIII HLA-DRB1 allele frequencies in 48 Asian populations ordered by linguistic families

FIGURES

5.1	AA phylogenetic tree	79
6.1	Klaproth's TB	82
6.2	The Indo-Chinese or ST theory	84
6.3	Schematic geographical representation of TB subgroups	87
6.4	Linguistically inspired archaeological interpretation of the geographical dispersal of TB groups	89
7.1	Kra-Dai language family	109
7.2	AN language family	109
9.1	Higher AN subgrouping	162
11.1	PEA and the origin and dispersal of the languages of East and Southeast Asia and the Pacific	183
12.1	Plot of 63 group means on the first two canonical variates resulting from the application of stepwise discriminant function analysis	208
12.2	Plot of the first 35 groups on the first three canonical variates resulting from the application of stepwise discriminant function analysis	209
12.3	Plot of the last 28 groups on the first three canonical variates resulting from the application of stepwise discriminant function analysis	209
12.4	Dendrogram showing the relationship of 63 groups resulting from cluster analysis (UPGMA) of Mahalanobis' D^2	210
13.1	Normalised deviates of the homozygosity statistic (Fnds) for HLA-A, B, C and DR loci in Taiwan	234
13.2	Neighbour-joining population dendrogram of Taiwan's indigenous peoples	241
15.1	(a) Geographic location of 61 population samples tested for RH polymorphism and (b) geographic location of 102 population samples tested for GM polymorphism	255

FIGURES

15.2	MDS of Reynolds et al. (1983) genetic distances among 61 population samples computed on RH frequency distributions	256
15.3	MDS of Reynolds et al. (1983) genetic distances among 102 population samples computed on GM frequency distributions	257
15.4	Three hypotheses on the phylogenetic relationships among East Asian languages	262
15.5	Partial correlation coefficients of genetic with linguistic distances, controlled for geography. (a) RH data. (b) GM data	263
16.1	MDS analysis of Asian populations based on the HLA-DRB1 allelic polymorphism	279
16.2	The 'least controversial' phylogeny of the 40 East Asian languages used in the correlation analysis	281
16.3	Genetic diversity within (h) and among (F_{ST}) populations and mean number of HLA-DRB1 alleles detected (n) within the main East Asian linguistic groups	283
17.1	Phylogenetic relationships of East Asian and Oceanian Y chromosome binary lineages	303

MAPS

1.1	Approximate distribution of early Neolithic cultures in China and Southeast Asia	26
3.1	Cereal-yielding archaeological sites in and around China	53
4.1	Distribution of Tapenkeng sites in Taiwan	70
6.1	Geographical centres of primary subgroups of the TB family	90
6.2	Lower Brahmaputra basin and surrounding hill tracts colonised by western Tibeto-Burmans	92
6.3	The establishment of the early Neolithic Péilígǎng-Císhan and Dàdìwan civilisations in the Yellow River basin by northern Tibeto-Burmans	93
6.4	Two offshoots of the late Neolithic Mcjiayáo cultural complex	94
6.5	Exodus of deep southern Tibeto-Burmans into peninsular Southeast Asia	95
7.1	Current geographical distribution of Kd languages	127
12.1	Approximate locations of the cranial series used in Chapter 12	205
13.1	Geographical distribution of Taiwan's indigenous peoples	231
13.2	Map of Southeast Asia and Oceania prior to 12,000 BP when Taiwan was connected to the continent	243

TABLES

0.1	Five East Asian phyla	2
0.2	Proposed macrophyla encompassing East Asian languages	5
2.1	Nations of Southeast Asia with role of dominant ethnolinguistic group	33
2.2	Selected radiocarbon dates for rice in Southeast Asia	36
2.3	Rice terms in Proto-Sinitic	39
2.4	Rice terms in PMY	40
2.5	Rice terms in Daic	40
2.6	Rice terms in PAA	41
2.7	PAN reconstructions of rice terminology	42
2.8	Rice terms in Proto-Chamic	43
2.9	Proto-Japonic rice terminology	44
2.A1	Rice in Munda languages	46
2.A2	Rice vocabulary in Chamorro	46
3.1	Remains of millet and rice in the Neolithic Yellow and Yangzi Valleys	55
3.2	Remains of millet and rice in the Yellow and Yangzi Valleys during the Xia and Shang dynasties	55
3.3	Sites with both millet and rice	57
3.4	Cultural comparison between the foxtail millet cultivators in the Yellow Valley and Taiwan	60
5.1	Reconstructed rice terms in PAA	78
5.2	Faunal reconstructions in PAA	78
7.1	A core list of Kd vocabulary	110
7.2	Kd-related AN etyma	111
7.3	Kd reflexes for 'to fart', AN *qe(n)tut	112
7.4	Kd reflexes for 'head louse', AN *kuCu	113
7.5	Kd reflexes for 'live, raw', AN *qudip	114
7.6	Kd reflexes for 'head', AN *qulu	114
7.7	Development of Kd syllables with initial vowel *-u- in the Hlai languages	115
7.8	Kd reflexes for 'fire', AN *Sapuy	115

7.9	Kd reflexes for 'tooth', AN *nipen	116
7.10	Kd reflexes for 'hand', AN *(qa)lima	116
7.11	Kd reflexes for 'water', AN *daNum	117
7.12	Kd reflexes for 'bird', AN *manuk	118
7.13	Kd reflexes for 'eye', AN *maCa	118
7.14	Main AN–Kd correspondences of final consonants	119
7.15	Contrast between *-C and *-t in Kd and AN	119
7.16	Kd correspondences for AN final *-q	119
7.17	Kd correspondences for AN final *-s	120
7.18	Kd correspondences for AN final -R and -N	120
7.19	A special Kd development corresponding to AN -R	120
7.20	Kd correspondences for AN voiced stop endings	121
7.21	A possible correspondence for AN final *-l	121
7.22	Summary of PAN and PKd final correspondences	121
7.23	Examples of AN–Kd medial correspondences	122
7.24	AN comparanda for Kd words in tone B	123
7.25	AN–Kd kinship terms showing tone B in Tai	124
7.26	AN–Kd roots in Kd tonal category *C	124
7.27	Tone C from *-c in some Kd groups	125
7.28	Abbreviations of language names in Kd reflex charts	129
8.1	Proposed lexical correspondences between PAA (and PEAA) and PAN (79)	135
8.2	Morphological reanalysis of PAN reconstructions (implied in Hayes 2000) (26)	137
8.3	Hayes' proposed PA affixes in PAN reconstructions	137
8.4	Potential PAA–PAN comparisons (31)	138
8.5	Potential PEAA–PAN comparisons (19)	139
8.6	Hayes' PAA–PMP comparisons (36)	140
8.7	Potential PAA–PMP comparisons (13)	141
8.8	Potential PEAA–PMP comparisons (13)	141
8.9	PAN and PMP phonemic systems	141
8.10	AN–AA phonological correspondences (based on Hayes' complete set of proposed lexical correspondences)	142
8.11	Results of the evaluation of Hayes' basic vocabulary comparisons	146
9.1	Sixty-one basic vocabulary comparisons between AN, Chinese and TB	163
9.2	Fourteen cultural vocabulary comparisons between AN, Chinese and TB	165
9.3	Correspondences of syllable-initial consonants (PAN final syllable initial: Chinese root initial: TB)	166
9.4	Correspondences of syllable-final consonants	166
9.5	Preservation by PAN and TB of a contrast in consonant endings lost by Chinese	167

TABLES

9.6	Vowel correspondences (PAN last vowel: Chinese root vowel)	167
9.7	Correspondences of Chinese syllable type and manner of articulation in PAN penultimate syllable initial consonant	167
10.1	A sound correspondence between AN and Tai-Kadai	178
10.2	PAN second-person pronoun (endings) compared with PKT	179
13.1	Samples and sampling locations	232
13.2	Summary of alleles with extremely high frequencies found in Taiwan indigenous tribes	233
13.3	HLA B-DRB1 haplotype frequencies among Taiwan's indigenous tribes and other populations	236
14.1	Officially recognised populations in China and in Yunnan	249
15.1	Representation of the linguistic families by numbers of population samples (and numbers of individuals) in the analyses	254
15.2	Proportion of the total genetic variation that is due to differences between populations	258
15.3	Levels of genetic structure among populations within linguistic groups and mean expected heterozygosity in linguistic groups	258
15.4	Proportion of the total genetic variation that is due to differences between linguistic groups, and between populations within linguistic groups	259
15.5	Proportion of the total genetic variation that is due to differences between linguistic groups compared two by two	260
15.6	Proportion of the total genetic variation of the GM system that is due to differences within (above diagonal) and between (below diagonal) ST groups compared two by two	260
16.1	Populations considered in this study	274
16.2	Main patterns of population genetic diversity and their possible explanations in terms of genetic evolutionary mechanisms	277
16.3	Correlation coefficients among genetic, geographic, and linguistic distances in East Asia	282
16.4	Amounts of HLA-DRB1 genetic diversity observed among (F_{ST}) and within (h) populations within each East Asian linguistic group	282

TABLES

16.5	Amounts of HLA-DRB1 genetic diversity observed among linguistic groups (F_{CT}), and among populations within linguistic groups (F_{SC}) in East Asia	283
17.1	Populations considered in this study	299
17.2	Cross reference of various haplotype designations between published data sets and the combinations used to collapse data into 12 chromosome group summary	302

CONTRIBUTORS

Peter Bellwood is Professor of Archaeology at the Australian National University. He has written three books: Man's Conquest of the Pacific (Collins, 1978), The Polynesians (2nd edn, Thames and Hudson, 1987) and Prehistory of the Indo-Malaysian Archipelago (2nd edn, University of Hawaii Press, 1997). His latest book, entitled Ancient Farmers, is about to go to press with Blackwell. He has also edited The Austronesians (with James Fox and Darrell Tryon, Australian National University, 1995) and Examining the Farming/Language Dispersal Hypothesis (with Colin Renfrew, McDonald Institute, Cambridge, 2003). His latest edited book, Southeast Asia: from Prehistory to History (edited with Ian Glover), is about to be published by RoutledgeCurzon. Peter Bellwood's current archaeological research is in the Northern Philippines, Taiwan and Indonesia, excavating early Neolithic sites relevant for questions of Austronesian cultural origins.

Roger Blench (born 1953) is Managing Director of Mallam Dendo, a consultancy company specialising in natural resources. He was educated at Cambridge University where he completed a PhD in social anthropology. He has previously worked mainly in Africa but began a more global approach with the publication of the four edited volumes of Archaeology and Language (Routledge 1997–99). He has published numerous articles on the interpreting of linguistic data for historical purposes, as well as historical papers on the spread of agriculture.

Richard E. Broadberry was born in Dublin, Ireland in 1953. He grew up and was educated in Southampton, England. He worked in Taiwan at the Mennonite Christian Hospital (1979–83) and Mackay Memorial Hospital (1983–97) where he specialised in Transfusion Medicine. He also worked at the Blood Centre in Tianjin, China (1997–98). He is the author of more than 90 publications in journals such as Transfusion, Vox Sanguinis, British Journal of Haematology and Transfusion Medicine. He is also co-author of God's Promise to the Chinese and The Beginning of Chinese Characters which compare the Bible with ancient Chinese writing and religion.

CONTRIBUTORS

Tsang Cheng-hwa was educated at National Taiwan University at Taipei, Taiwan and Harvard University at Cambridge, Massachusetts, USA. He is currently the Director of National Museum of Prehistory at Taitung and a Research Fellow of the Institute of History and Philology, Academia Sinica at Taipei, Taiwan. He is the author of The Archaeology of the P'enghu Islands (Taipei: Institute of History and Philology, Academia Sinica 1992) and The Archaeology of Taiwan (Taipei: Council for Cultural Affairs 2001). He has edited or co-edited eight monographs, and published a number of articles. Since 1995 he has been directing a salvage archaeology project at the Tainan Science-based Industrial Park at Xinshi City, Tainan County, rescuing 13 prehistoric sites so far and making major discoveries in Taiwan archaeology.

Chen-Chung Chu is a Research Associate in the Department of Medical Research at the Mackay Memorial Hospital in Taiwan. He received his PhD degree in biochemistry from Taiwan University. As a molecular geneticist, his main interest focuses on the study of the genetic association of the major histocompatiblity complex with diseases. He is the author of several articles, of which 'Diversity of HLA among Taiwan's indigenous tribes and the Ivatans in the Philippines' (Tissue Antigens 2001) brought new insights about the settlement of populations in Taiwan.

Jiayou Chu is the Director of the Institute of Medical Biology, Chinese Academy of Medical Sciences and a professor at the same institution. He conducted his postdoctoral research at the Oncology Institute, Chinese Academy of Medical Sciences after obtaining his PhD from Tongji Medical College. He is currently engaged in research on the human genome, and is the principal investigator of the Chinese genomic diversity and Chinese nationalities gene bank project (DNA bank and cell bank), which is part of the Chinese Human Genome Project. He is the author of a number of articles on the impact of human genomic diversity and disease gene investigation. He is an editor of such journals as Acta Genetica Sinica, National Medical Journal of China , Chinese Journal of Medical Genetics etc.

Gérard Diffloth was born in Chateauroux, France, and educated in linguistics at the University of California, Los Angeles. He taught for many years at the University of Chicago and at Cornell University. He has written a number of articles on Mon-Khmer languages, and two books: The Wa Languages, 1980, LTBA, University of California, Berkeley and The Dvaravati Old-Mon language and Nyah-Kur, 1984, Chulalongkorn University, Bangkok. He is a Member of the Ecole Française d'Extrême-Orient, in Siem-Reap-Angkor, Cambodia, and is currently working on an Introduction to Comparative Mon Khmer and on a Mon-Khmer Etymological Dictionary.

Guillaume Jacques (born in 1979) is a PhD candidate at the Department of Linguistics, University of Paris. He received his education in Paris and

Amsterdam. He has conducted two field trips to Sichuan where he has investigated the rGyalrongic languages. He is the author of several articles on Old Chinese, Tibetan and rGyalrong.

Marie Lin , born in Taiwan, is the Director of the Immunohaematology Reference and Transfusion Medicine Laboratory of the Mackay Memorial Hospital in Taiwan; she is also a professor at the National Taiwan University and at the Taipei Medical Schools. She helped Taiwan develop her national blood programme. She pioneered and conducted extensive research on blood groups, as well as several anthropological studies of the Taiwan populations.

Jun-Hun Loo was born in Taiwan and educated at Tunghai University in Taiwan and at the University of California, Los Angeles, in the USA. She is a Junior Research Scientist in the Transfusion Medicine Research Laboratory, Mackay Memorial Hospital, Taiwan, focusing on Population Genetics and Statistics. She is also the co-author of 'The origin of Minnan and Hakka, the so-called "Taiwanese", inferred by HLA study' Tissue Antigens (2001: 57).

Tracey L.-D. Lu was born in China and educated at Beijing University and the Australian National University. She teaches Archaeology and Museology at the Chinese University of Hong Kong. She is the author of The Mausoleum of the Nanyue King and the Nanyue Kingdom (Guangzhou Culture Press 1990), and The Transition from Foraging to Farming and the Origin of Agriculture in China (Oxford: BAR International Series 1999). She has published articles in Antiquity, Asian Perspectives and Asian Anthropology. Her major research interest is on the interaction dynamics between natural environment, resources and prehistoric subsistence strategies in China.

Weera Ostapirat was born in Bangkok and received his PhD from the University of California, Berkeley. He is currently Visiting Associate Research Fellow at the Institute of Linguistics, Academia Sinica, Taiwan. He has published several articles on Tai, Kra-Dai, and Tibeto-Burman languages and is the author of Proto-Kra (Berkeley 2000). His current work focuses on the interaction among languages of southern China and mainland southeast Asian area, including Chinese, Tai, Miao-Yao and Mon-Khmer. He is currently preparing a book on Chinese and Kra-Dai lexical comparison.

Michael Pietrusewsky is Professor of Anthropology at the University of Hawai'i. His most recent book is Ban Chiang, a Prehistoric Site in Northeast Thailand. I: The Human Skeletal Remains. University Monograph 111 (Philadelphia: University of Pennsylvania Museum of Archaeology and Anthropology, 2002, M.T. Douglas, co-author). He is also the author of chapter in books and of numerous journal articles, most recently in American Journal of Physical Anthropology, Anthropological Science, Asian Perspectives, Bulletin of the Indo-Pacific Prehistory Association, Current Anthropology, Homo, Oceanic Linguistics, Man and Culture in Oceania, Micronesica, Journal of Forensic

Sciences, New Zealand Journal of Archaeology and Records of the Australian Museum. His major research interests include topics in bioarchaeology, skeletal biology and biodistance studies using cranial morphology. His regional focus is the Pacific, Southeast Asia and East Asia.

Estella S. Poloni teaches and conducts research at the Laboratory of Genetics and Biometry of the University of Geneva. She is a population geneticist mainly interested in anthropology and evolution. Her research focuses on the variability of gender-specific molecular markers in human populations, and the relationships between genetic and linguistic differentiation in human populations. Her recent journal articles have appeared in American Journal of Human Genetics (1997), Annals of Human Genetics (1999), European Journal of Human Genetics (2000) and American Journal of Physical Anthropology (2003).

Lawrence A. Reid is a Researcher Emeritus with the University of Hawai'i where he was a member of the Social Science Research Institute and taught linguistics for more than thirty years. He now lives in Japan. He is the author of An Ivatan Syntax (1966); Philippine Minor Languages: Word Lists and Phonologies (1971); Bontok-English dictionary (1976); Guinaang Bontok Texts (1992) and over 60 articles on Philippine and Austronesian descriptive and comparative linguistics.

Laurent Sagart (born in 1951) is a senior researcher with the Centre National de la Recherche Scientifique, Paris, France. He received his education in Bordeaux, Paris and Nanjing and his PhD from the University of Aix-Marseille in 1990. He is the author of three books and numerous articles in Chinese dialectology, Old Chinese phonology and morphology, comparative Chinese linguistics, and the Austronesian languages. He has been a Visiting Scholar in Hawai'i, Melbourne and Beijing and a Visiting Professor in Taiwan. He has organised research projects in phonetics, historical phonology and language contact. His most recent book is The Roots of Old Chinese, published by John Benjamins in 1999.

Alicia Sanchez-Mazas (born in 1962) is a professor at the Laboratory of Genetics and Biometry of the University of Geneva. After obtaining a PhD in biological sciences in 1990, she specialised in human population genetics, biostatistics and molecular anthropology, with a special interest for the major histocompatibility complex in humans (HLA). She took part in a field expedition to Western Africa investigating the molecular genetics of a Senegalese population in 1990, and published numerous articles on African and worldwide genetic diversity. She is involved in several research projects aiming at reconstructing human peopling history (e.g. of East Asia) based on genetic and linguistic data.

Stanley Starosta was a professor at the Department of Linguistics of the University of Hawai'i until his untimely death on 18 July 2002, aged 62. He was the author of a theory of grammar, outlined in his 1988 book The Case for

Lexicase (1988, Pinter), and of many articles on grammar in general, and specifically of languages of South and Southeast Asia and the Pacific. His research interests also included 'seamless morphology', of which he was a major promoter, and the prehistory, history and classification of the languages of Asia and the Pacific.

Jean A. Trejaut is a senior research fellow in the Transfusion Medicine Research Laboratory of Mackay Memorial Hospital in Taiwan. Born in French Morocco, he studied Biochemistry in Paris and Sydney. During his 20 years of service with the Australian Red Cross and the Kidney and Bone marrow transplant programme, he published several articles relating to the major histocompatibility complex (MHC). He wrote his dissertation on the HLA polymorphism among aboriginal populations of Australia, Papua New Guinea and Southeast Asia. His present research interests include the contribution of recent and ancient DNA data to the phylogeography of Asian populations and the prehistory of Taiwan.

Peter A. Underhill is a senior research scientist in the Department of Genetics at Stanford University. His research involves the molecular analysis of human genetic variation in human populations. In 1995, he co-invented DHPLC technology, which greatly accelerated the discovery of genetic markers on the human Y chromosome. This pioneering work has led to the development of a phylogeny which exquisitely defines numerous Y-chromosome lineages with distinctive geographic appellation providing considerable transparency concerning paternal biogeographical ancestry (Nature Genetics 2000, 26: 358–61). He has co-authored numerous peer-reviewed publications, most of which provide genetic perspectives to human population structure and history.

George van Driem, Professor of Linguistics at Leiden University, writes grammars of previously undocumented languages in the Himalayas. He directs the Himalayan Languages Project and conceived the research programme Languages and Genes of the Greater Himalayan Region. In addition to several reference grammars, he wrote a two-volume handbook on The Languages of the Himalayas (Brill, Leiden, 2001). He is currently completing grammars of the three most endangered languages of Bhutan.

Lung-Chih Yu was born and educated in Taiwan. He worked in the Department of Medical Research at the Mackay Memorial Hospital in Taiwan (1993–2002) and is currently Associate Professor in the Institute of Biochemical Sciences at the National Taiwan University and Assistant Research Fellow in the Institute of Biological Chemistry, Academia Sinica, Taiwan. He specialises in the molecular genetics of the human red cell antigens and is the author of several papers published in journals such as Blood, Transfusion, Vox Sanguinis, etc.

PREFACE

This volume arose out of a workshop on the phylogeny of East Asian languages, organised by Laurent Sagart and the much missed Stanley Starosta in Périgueux, SW France, 29–31 August 2001. Thirty-two linguists, geneticists, physical anthropologists and archaeologists participated, either as authors of invited papers, discussants, or authors of summations. The aim was to have specialists of the other disciplines critically evaluate the linguists' theories on the formation of East Asian language phyla. The principal advocates of some of the main linguistic theories had been invited to present the current state of their proposals: Lawrence A. Reid (Austric), Weera Ostapirat (Austro-Tai), George van Driem (Tibeto-Burman), Laurent Sagart (Sino-Tibetan–Austronesian), Stanley Starosta (East Asiatic).[1] Gérard Diffloth presented his own, less positive, evaluation of the evidence for Austric, and some considerations on the location of the Austroasiatic homeland. Archaeologists Peter Bellwood, Tracey L.-D. Lu, Tsang Cheng-hwa, archaeolinguist Roger Blench, physical anthropologist Michael Pietrusewsky, geneticists Cheng-Chung Chu, Jiayou Chu, Marie Lin, Estella Poloni, Alicia Sanchez-Mazas and Peter A. Underhill each discussed the formation of East Asian populations and cultures, with direct or indirect reference to language. In return, statements by archaeologists and geneticists were critically addressed by linguists. Finally, archaeologist Charles Higham, linguist William Baxter III and geneticist Mark Stoneking each summarised the debates from their particular point of view.

After the workshop, participants were invited to modify their paper so as to take into account the observations and remarks made at the workshop, and after the workshop, by the editors. The important finding of carbonised millet and rice grains in an early Neolithic context in Nan-kuan-li, Taiwan, by a team of archaeologists led by Prof. Tsang Cheng-hwa, after the workshop, in 2002–03 (Tsang, Chapter 4, this volume) was also taken into account by some linguists and archaeologists in rewriting their papers. This volume presents the workshop papers after modification by their authors.

The preparation of this volume was saddened by the passing away of Stanley Starosta, one of the organisers of the workshop and a contributor to this volume, on 18 July 2002, in Honolulu, of heart complications; he was 62. His reworked paper was sent to us on 6 July 2002, only twelve days before he died. As dialogue between editor and author was not possible in this case, Starosta's paper is here accompanied with a few editorial notes.

Note

1 Unfortunately Sergei A. Starostin (Sino-Caucasian) did not receive his travel documents from the Russian authorities in time and had to cancel his participation.

ACKNOWLEDGEMENTS

The Périgueux workshop was held, and this volume was published, with the generous assistance of the Chiang Ching-Kuo Foundation for International Scholarly Exchange, the French Centre National de la Recherche Scientifique and its Origine de l'homme, origine du langage, origine des langues programme, the French Ministry of Research, the French Ministry of Foreign Affairs and the Dordogne region council. The organisers and editors gratefully acknowledge the financial help of these institutions.

Photographs showing artefacts and cereal grains from the Nan-kuan-li excavations were kindly provided by Professor Tsang Cheng-hwa, to whom the editors express their gratitude.

INTRODUCTION

Laurent Sagart, Roger Blench and Alicia Sanchez-Mazas

In the past ten years or so, important advances in our understanding of the formation of East Asian populations, historical cultures and language phyla have been made separately by geneticists, physical anthropologists, archaeologists and linguists. In particular, the genetics of East Asian populations have become the focus of intense scrutiny. The mapping of genetic markers, both classical and molecular, is progressing daily: geneticists are now proposing scenarios for the initial settlement of East Asia by modern humans, as well as for population movements in more recent times. Chinese archaeologists have shown conclusively that the origins of rice agriculture are to be sought in the mid-Yangzi region around 10,000 BP and that a millet-based agriculture developed in the Huang He Valley somewhat later. Linguists have been refining their reconstructions of the proto-languages of the main phyla of the region, and proposing evidence for genetic links to relate these phyla. The period of time they are considering is, by and large, the same period which saw the spread of domesticated plants. General hypotheses are being tested on East Asia: how congruent are languages and genes? and is the formation of language phyla linked with the beginnings of agriculture? Archaeologists, linguists and geneticists are attempting to unravel different aspects of the East Asian problem, sometimes proceeding independently, more often attempting to account for advances in other disciplines. It is important to emphasise that there are conflicting hypotheses in each field and to clarify for other disciplines the significance of these hypotheses for their own interpretations.

Five building blocks

Before introducing the individual chapters, we review current ideas on the classification of East Asian languages for the benefit of non-linguist readers. Excluding Japanese, Korean, Ainu and the Altaic languages (Mongolic, Turkic and Tungusic) spoken in the north and east of the region, there is near-universal agreement that the languages of East Asia fall into five phyla (Table 0.1), whose membership, by and large, is beyond dispute: Sino-Tibetan, Hmong-Mien, Tai-Kadai, Austro-Asiatic and Austronesian.

Table 0.1 Five East Asian phyla

Phylum	Alternative name	Representative languages	Principal locations	Approximate date of ancestor
Sino-Tibetan	Tibeto-Burman (van Driem)	Chinese, Tibetan, Burmese, Jingpo	China incl. Tibet, Burma, Nepal, Bhutan, Northeast India	7,000–6,000 BP
Hmong-Mien	Miao-Yao	Hmong, Mien, Ho Nte	South China, North Vietnam, Laos	2,500 BP
Tai-Kadai	Kra-Dai (Ostapirat), Daic	Thai, Lao, Kam, Li, Gelao	South China, Indochina, Burma	Earlier than 4,000 BP
Austro-Asiatic		Vietnamese, Khmer, Mon, Khasi, Munda	Indochina, Central Malaysia, Northeast India	7,000 BP
Austronesian		Atayal, Rukai, Paiwan, Tagalog, Malay, Malagasy, Hawaiian, Maori	Pacific islands except Australia and parts of NewGuinea, Madagascar	5,500 BP

Sino-Tibetan is a large phylum of some 365 languages,[1] including Chinese and its 'dialects' (Sinitic), Tibetan, Burmese and Jingpo, and spoken over a vast unbroken area, mainly in China (including Tibet), Laos, Burma, India, Nepal and Bhutan. Its internal classification is disputed (see van Driem, Chapter 6, this volume). Morphemes are mono- and iambisyllables (i.e. a major syllable preceded by a minor, unstressed syllable); many languages are tonal, but tones arose secondarily out of final laryngeal consonants; morphology is predominantly derivational and prefixal, with some suffixes and even infixes; word order is mostly Subject-Object-Verb but Chinese and Karen are Subject-Verb-Object. Chinese has also evolved in the direction of monosyllabicity, and loss of morphological alternations. The Sino-Tibetan proto-language is generally estimated to have been spoken around 6,000 or 7,000 BP, but the location of the homeland is disputed, with arguments variously made for northern India, Sichuan, the Tibetan plateau and the Yellow River Valley in northern China.

Hmong-Mien (also Miao-Yao) is a small and relatively coherent phylum of 32 languages, including the various Hmong 'dialects' and Ho Nte, Bunu, Mien etc. Hmong-Mien languages are spoken in scattered pockets, mainly in South China, but also in Laos, Thailand and Vietnam, by farming communities specialising in the exploitation of upland resources. Two branches: Hmongic (Hmong, Ho Nte, Bunu) and Mienic are usually recognised, but other phylogenies have been proposed. Hmong-Mien has been very much influenced by Chinese, to which it is now typologically very close. Only the most basic portion of the reconstructed Hmong-Mien vocabulary is not of Chinese origin. Some Chinese loanwords were already part of the Hmong-Mien proto-language; their phonological shape and cultural content suggest a date around 2,500 BP for Proto-Hmong-Mien. The homeland was most likely in the middle and lower Yangzi Valley. It has been suggested that Proto-Hmong-Mien was the language of the state of Chu, a southern neighbour of China during the Zhou dynasty.

The 70 Tai-Kadai languages are spoken mainly in South China (including Hainan Island), Thailand, Laos, Burma and Vietnam by communities of lowland rice farmers. Its most representative member and oldest literary language is Thai. Like Hmong-Mien, Tai-Kadai (and especially its Kam-Tai subgroup) has received much Chinese influence, and has come to resemble Chinese typologically, with monosyllables, tones and little overt morphology: it has also borrowed numerous Chinese loanwords. However, Benedict (1942) showed that a few languages spoken by small communities conserve more of the original vocabulary of the phylum. He referred to these conservative languages collectively as 'Kadai'. The internal subgrouping of Tai-Kadai is disputed. South China (Guangxi-Guizhou-Hainan) is the area of highest diversity and most Tai-Kadai languages outside of South China belong to southern and Central Tai, two subgroups of Tai, itself a subgroup of Kam-Tai. The Tai-Kadai homeland was most likely in South China and the historically documented expansion of southern and central Tai occurred towards the end of the first millennium CE. Evaluations of the age of Tai-Kadai vary considerably but a date earlier than 4,000 BP appears plausible (Ostapirat, Chapter 7, this volume). Another name for Tai-Kadai is Kra-Dai, used by Weera Ostapirat (2000, Chapter 7, this volume) whose analysis of the internal subgrouping and age of the phylum differ from Benedict's.

Austro-Asiatic is a very diverse phylum of 168 languages whose original geographical unity has been lost, due to migration and intrusion of other languages in its midst. It is mainly spoken in Southeast Asia where the most representative languages are Khmer, Mon and Vietnamese, and also in northern India (Khasi, Munda). Austro-Asiatic is often regarded as comprised of two branches, a western branch (Munda) and an eastern one (the remainder, including Khasi), but Diffloth (Chapter 5, this volume) proposes a different phylogeny, with a central branch consisting of Khasi and Khmuic. Austroasiatic speakers tend to be rice farmers, but some communities in Central Malaysia, Nicobar and elsewhere maintain a foraging lifestyle. Austro-Asiatic languages have monosyllabic and iambisyllabic morphemes, with prefixal and infixal derivational morphology, Subject–Verb–Object and head-modifier word order. Estimates of the age of the proto-language fall in the range 7,000–6,000 BP, with a homeland presumably in the East, where diversity is highest (but see Diffloth, Chapter 5, this volume).

Austronesian is a very large phylum of 1,262 languages covering the entire Pacific, excepting parts of New Guinea and surrounding islands, and Australia, plus Madagascar and parts of South Vietnam. Some of the larger Austronesian languages are Malay, Javanese, Tagalog and Malagasy. Words typically have one, two or three syllables, with disyllables predominating. Syllables tend to be of a simple Consonant Vowel type. Morphology is predominantly derivational, with prefixes, infixes and suffixes; in many languages, word order is verb-initial and head-modifier. There is growing agreement that the proto-language was spoken c.5,500 BP in Taiwan, by a population of millet and rice farmers who were skilled navigators adept at exploiting marine resources. By this view, Austronesian expansion occurred first in Taiwan, where diversity is highest. All the Austronesian languages outside of Taiwan have been shown by Robert Blust to share a few innovations exclusively, and are therefore considered to form a monophyletic taxon within Austronesian: Malayo-Polynesian. Whether Malayo-Polynesian is a primary branch of Austronesian, or merely a subgroup within one primary branch, is a matter of dispute.

An East Asian complex of phylogenies

While the monophyletic status of the five phyla discussed in the preceding section is generally accepted, a number of proposals to integrate them into larger constructs, or macrophyla, have been put forward (Table 0.2). We will only be concerned here with theories currently defended by living linguists. For an overview of the early history of ideas on East Asian linguistic classification, the reader is referred to van Driem (2001).

A view that the Sino-Tibetan and Tai-Kadai languages together form a large East Asian language macrophylum,[2] sometimes also including Hmong-Mien, was prevalent among students of East Asian languages under the name 'Sino-Tibetan' well into the second half of the twentieth century. This theory (here Macro-Sino-Tibetan) was based on the observation that these languages share important traits, such as mono- or iambisyllabicity, tonality, and, for many of them, lack of overt morphology, as well as significant amounts of shared lexicon. Shafer (1966–74) and Li Fang-kuei (1976) among others have been influential advocates of this theory, which is still popular in mainland China (Xing 1999). In a recent development Zhengzhang (1993, 1995) and Pan (1995) accept Sagart's view of a genetic relationship between Chinese and Austronesian but (unlike Sagart) make the Austronesian languages part of Macro-Sino-Tibetan under the name Pan-Sino-Austronesian.

Complementary with Macro-Sino-Tibetan, the idea that the Austronesian and Austro-Asiatic phyla are the two primary branches of a larger Austric macrophylum is due to Schmidt (1906). Much of the lexical evidence presented by Schmidt is no longer valid but the morphological evidence continues to be suggestive. Today, Austric is defended by Reid (1994, Chapter 8, this volume), Blust (1998) and Higham (1996: 71) among others, but in a significant development, Reid (Chapter 8, this volume) stresses that the Austronesian–Austro-Asiatic relationship need not be monophyletic, and that while he regards a genetic relationship of Austronesian and Austro-Asiatic as secure, Sino-Tibetan may be part of that relationship and stand closer to Austronesian than to Austro-Asiatic. Reid's position is close to that in Sagart (1994: 303 and see later).

Table 0.2 Proposed macrophyla encompassing East Asian languages

Name of macrophylum	Main advocates	Proposed membership
Macro-Sino-Tibetan	Shafer (1966–74), Li (1976), Xing (1999)	Chinese Tibeto-Burman Tai-Kadai (Hmong-Mien)
Austric	Schmidt (1906), Reid (1994), Blust (1998), Higham (1996)	Austronesian Austro-Asiatic
Austro-Thai	Benedict (1942)	Austronesian Tai-Kadai
Yangzian	Davies (1909), Haudricourt (1966), Peiros (1998), Starosta (Chapter 11, this volume)	Austro-Asiatic Hmong-Mien
Sino-Caucasian	Starostin (1991/1984)	Sino-Tibetan North Caucasian Ket
Sino-Tibetan-Austronesian	Sagart (2001)	Sino-Tibetan Austronesian including Tai-Kadai
Greater Austric	Benedict (1942), Ruhlen (1991), Peiros (1998)	Austro-Thai Austro-Asiatic
Macro-Austric	Schiller (1987)	Austronesian Austro-Asiatic Sino-Tibetan Hmong-Mien Tai-Kadai
Pan-Sino-Austronesian	Zhengzhang (1993, 1995), Pan (1995)	Austronesian Austro-Asiatic Sino-Tibetan Hmong-Mien Tai-Kadai
East Asiatic (conjecture)	Starosta (Chapter 11, this volume)	(Sino-Tibetan Yangzian) Austronesian
East Asiatic (conjecture)	Sagart (Chapter 15, this volume)	Sino-Tibetan-Austronesian Yangzian

In the early 1940s Paul Benedict approached the classification of East Asian languages with the premise that the principal type of evidence for genetic relationships must come from basic vocabulary. He noticed lexical resemblances between Thai and Austronesian in lower numerals, personal pronouns and other basic vocabulary. At the same time, he argued that the strong typological resemblances between Thai and Chinese were not accompanied by significant amounts of shared basic vocabulary: he accordingly removed Thai from Sino-Tibetan, treating the relationship between Thai and Chinese as one of contact, with Chinese being on the receiving side. At first, Benedict (1942) simply transferred Thai from Macro-Sino-Tibetan to the Austronesian side of Austric, which he then accepted, but in his later works, he eliminated Austro-Asiatic from the ensemble of Thai and Austronesian, these two now forming Austro-Thai. The result was a new overall configuration of East Asian linguistic classification, with three separate entities: a restricted Sino-Tibetan phylum in the north, consisting of just Chinese and Tibeto-Burman, an isolated Austro-Asiatic phylum in the south-west, and an Austro-Thai phylum in the south-east, to which he eventually added Hmong-Mien (1975) and Japanese (1990).

Accepting Benedict's idea that the Sino-Tibetan languages are unrelated to any of the other languages of East Asia, Sergei Starostin (1991 [1984]), citing agreements in basic vocabulary with sound correspondences, sought to find their relatives in the languages of the north Caucasus and in Ket of the Yenisei Valley. This is the Sino-Caucasian hypothesis (see also Peiros 1998). Starostin envisions a proto-language spoken 10,000 BP in a location west of East Asia, with Sino-Tibetan, and especially Chinese, being intrusive in East Asia.

Starting in 1990, Sagart cited sound correspondences and agreements in vocabulary, basic and non-basic, as well as in morphology, to argue for a genetic relationship between Chinese and Austronesian – the Sino-Austronesian theory. In its first version (1993), Chinese was more closer to Austronesian than to Tibeto-Burman, but more recently (2001), Sino-Austronesian has two branches, Sino-Tibetan and Austronesian. To reflect this change, Sagart now calls the resulting macrophylum Sino-Tibetan-Austronesian. The proto-language is identified with the speech of the first rice and millet farmers in the Huang He Valley around 8,000 BP. Sagart also claims that Tai-Kadai is a branch of the Austronesian phylum (Chapter 10, this volume), rather than a separate phylum. Sino-Tibetan-Austronesian thus unites Sino-Tibetan, Austronesian and Tai-Kadai into one macrophylum.

Complementary with Sino-Tibetan-Austronesian, a theory claiming that Austro-Asiatic and Hmong-Mien are two branches of a larger macrophylum has its origin in Davies (1909); it was later defended by Haudricourt (1966), Pejros and Shnirelman (1998: 155 ff.), who cite Yakhontov as another precursor, and Starosta (Chapter 11, this volume). It relies on shared elements of basic vocabulary. As there is no accepted term for this construct we will use Starosta's 'Yangzian' (so named because Starosta places the homeland in the Yangzi Valley).

Benedict's fleeting consideration of a macrophylum consolidating Austric and Austro-Thai, soon abandoned by him, was taken up by Ruhlen (1991) and Peiros (1998). The name they use is 'Austric', but clearly this is different from Schmidt's Austric (limited to Austronesian and Austro-Asiatic). We will use the term 'greater Austric' to refer to this construct. Pejros and Shnirelman (1998) date its disintegration to the ninth to eighth millennium BCE.

Then come global proposals which aim at unifying all of the five language phyla of East Asia: both Schiller's Macro-Austric (Schiller 1987) and Zhengzhang's Pan-Sino-Austronesian (Zhengzhang 1993) consolidate Sino-Tibetan, Austro-Tai, Hmong-Mien and Austro-Asiatic into a macrophylum without an explicit subgrouping. Sagart (1994: 303), acknowledging the validity of some of Reid's morphological arguments, argues speculatively for a higher level unity between his Sino-Austronesian (then including Tibeto-Burman) and Austro-Asiatic, a view close to that expressed by Reid (Chapter 8, this volume). A further version of this conjecture, in which Hmong-Mien is added as a third primary branch, is subjected to genetic testing in Chapter 15 of this volume under the name East Asiatic. Starosta's East Asiatic (Chapter 11, this volume) is a conjecture consolidating Sino-Tibetan and Yangzian, and Sino-Tibetan-Yangzian further with Austronesian. Starosta's and Sagart's versions of East Asiatic differ in their internal subgrouping, despite having the same name.

The chapters

This volume consists of three sections: Archaeology (Chapters 1–4), Linguistics (Chapters 5–10), Genetics and Physical Anthropology (Chapters 12–17) which all address the general issues of the peopling of East Asia and the formation of its populations, material cultures and language phyla.

Part I – Archaeology

Chapter 1 by Peter Bellwood considers the general hypothesis that many language phyla dispersed as a consequence of the adoption of agriculture in the light of recent archaeological evidence from East Asia. New dates for rice in Taiwan provide additional support for agriculture as the engine of expansion for Austronesian while the dates for the Yangzi Valley allows us to explore the interface between different phyla. The time difference between the earliest dates for rice and for foxtail millet in northern China led Bellwood to formulate a scenario in which only one transition to agriculture occurred in East Asia when rice was domesticated in the Yangzi Valley: under this scenario, foxtail millet is a secondary domesticate, brought into cultivation in the Huang He Basin as the earliest domesticated rice economy expanded beyond its natural limits. This scenario is alternative to that presented by Tracey Lu in Chapter 3.

Roger Blench (Chapter 2) discusses the ethnolinguistic geography of the East Asian region and in particular the imbalance between the single dominant group in each country and a scatter of numerically small minorities, a pattern not found in other continents. It attributes this to the spread of paddy rice agriculture and looks at linguistic reconstructions of rice terminology to support this. Wet and dry rice turn out to have very different modes of dispersal and it is clear that dry rice had only a limited impact on linguistic diversification.

In Chapter 3, Tracey Lu presents a discussion of the archaeological dates for millets and rice in East Asia, with emphasis on the Chinese mainland. She argues that there are two distinct foci for the transition to agriculture: one in the mid-Yellow River region, based on millet, with early antecedents in the final Palaeolithic of Xiachuan culture of Shanxi; and another in the mid-Yangzi for rice, with antecedents in Jiangxi and Hunan. The question of millet cultivation in Taiwan is given special consideration. The chapter includes a map of cereal-yielding sites with dates.

Taiwan archaeologist Tsang Cheng-hwa reports in Chapter 4 on the recently excavated Ta-Pen-Keng site in Southwest Taiwan which has yielded the earliest dates for cultivated rice (3,000–2,000 BCE) on the island so far, and the first findings of cultivated grains of millet ever, also dated c.3,000–2,500 BCE. These remarkable findings indicate that the earliest Austronesian communities engaged in rice and millet agriculture, as pointed out by Bellwood in Chapter 1. Based on similarities in the material culture, Tsang argues that the most probable homeland of the Austronesians is in the Pearl River delta in Guangdong Province in China. The chapter is accompanied by clear photographs of rice and millet grains, as well as of artefacts found at Nan-kuan-li.

Part II – Linguistics

Austro-Asiatic is one of the least-known language phyla in the world and many of its languages remain inaccessible and unmapped. Using new reconstructions based on unpublished fieldwork, Diffloth argued in his oral presentation for an early-period dispersal of shifting cultivators using hillsides along the watersheds of Southeast Asia and Northeast India river valleys. The present short contribution in Chapter 5 sets out the Austroasiatic reconstructed forms for terms related to rice cultivation and faunal terms as a contribution towards eventually locating the homeland of Austro-Asiatic speakers as well as his latest 'tree' of the internal structure of Austro-Asiatic.

George van Driem has published a series of papers challenging the conventional internal classification of Sino-Tibetan and suggests that the whole phylum must be rethought, arguing in particular for an incorporation of Sinitic and Bodic in the same subgroup. He presents 'an informed but agnostic picture of Tibeto-Burman subgroups' in Chapter 6 and uses both recent archaeological and genetic data to make an argument for the homeland of Sino-Tibetan in Sichuan.

Weera Ostapirat has been at the forefront of gathering new data on the Tai-Kadai languages in China and has recently published a new reconstruction of 'Proto-Kra (Kadai)'. Using this material, in Chapter 7 he makes a convincing case for a genetic link between Tai-Kadai and Austronesian, using sound correspondences from lexical cognates. He shows that Tai-Kadai preserves early distinctions in the Austronesian languages, typical of the West and Central Formosan languages, such as the distinction between PAN *t and *C, and between PAN *n and *N. He concludes that if, as Sagart argues in Chapter 10, the Tai-Kadai languages are a subgroup within Austronesian, rather than being a related phylum, then they are more likely to be outside the clade which includes the languages of the Formosan east coast and Malayo-Polynesian.

Chapter 8 by Lawrence Reid, currently the most prominent advocate of the Austric theory, critically examines the supporting lexical evidence presented by L.V. Hayes, concluding that limited parts of it are admissible. He also reviews the morphosyntactic evidence presented to date and answers some criticisms of earlier publications. Reid reiterates the validity of the Austronesian–Austro-Asiatic genetic connection but, in an important development, concludes, in view of the evidence presented by Sagart linking Sino-Tibetan and Austronesian, that the relationship between Austro-Asiatic and Austronesian may turn out to be more remote than earlier considered, and the Austric phylum as traditionally defined not monophyletic, but could include Sino-Tibetan as well.

Sagart first proposed a genetic link between Sinitic and Austronesian in 1990, based essentially on shared lexicon, sound correspondences and shared morphology. In Chapter 9 he presents an improved argument for Sino-Tibetan–Austronesian, a theory which claims the Sino-Tibetan and Austronesian families are related. The proposed proto-language (PSTAN) would originate in the millet culture of northern China in the mid-Huang He Valley between 8,500 and 7,500 BP, and the Taiwan millet culture would thus be a retained feature from this epoch.

Chapter 10, also by Sagart, presents a new theory of the origin of Tai-Kadai. Instead of being a coordinate with Austronesian, as Benedict argues, it is viewed as an offshoot of Proto-Austronesian, belonging to the clade which includes several of the languages of the Formosan east coast and Malayo-Polynesian. Evidence comes from lexical and morphological features in the vocabulary Thai (broadly speaking) shares with Austronesian: in particular Tai-Kadai shares with Malayo-Polynesian some characteristic innovations in the second-person pronouns.

Under the name 'Proto-East-Asian' the late Stanley Starosta presents a conjecture in Chapter 11 unifying all five-language phyla of East Asia, accompanied by an explicit scenario linking linguistics with archaeology. Starosta's conjecture involves an ancestral language spoken around 8,500–8000 BP on the North China plain by an expanding population of millet farmers identified with the Cishan-Peiligang culture. The first to break off was a group identified as the pre-Austronesians, who were located on the eastern seaboard of China (Dawenkou and Hemudu cultures): one subgroup reached Taiwan, acquiring rice agriculture along the way. In Taiwan these people became the Proto-Austronesians and started diversifying into the various Austronesian branches, including Tai-Kadai (Starosta accepts Sagart's view, presented in Chapter 10, that the Tai-Kadai phylum is a subgroup of Austronesian, rather than a distinct phylum). Meanwhile, those who stayed at home in the North China Plain expanded South towards the Yangzi region, forming a southern, or Yangzian branch, later to diversify into Hmong-Mien and Austro-Asiatic, while the others still in the northern China plain evolved into the Tibeto-Burman phylum (Starosta accepts Driem's understanding of this phylum, with the associated terminology). Some linguistic characteristics of each proposed node in the tree are outlined.

Part III – Genetics and physical anthropology

In Chapter 12, physical anthropologist Michael Pietrusewsky analyses the available craniometric data of modern and near-modern indigenous inhabitants of East Asia and Oceania using multivariate analyses on a total of 2,805 male crania. The study suggests a major subdivision into an East Asian/Pacific group and an Australo-Melanesian group, supporting the hypothesis of two separate colonisation events involving morphologically distinct populations. An early differentiation of

Southeast and East/Northeast Asian populations also emerges from the data. On the other hand, the results challenge views based on archaeology and historical linguistics by proposing a homeland for Pacific peoples in island Southeast Asia rather than China/Taiwan.

The other chapters in this section focus on genetics. In Chapter 13, immunogeneticist Marie Lin and co-workers present a large synopsis of classical and HLA polymorphisms in aboriginal people of Taiwan. Very peculiar genetic traits and a high intertribal diversity are observed in this island, suggesting long isolation of small populations. Although Taiwanese people are genetically related to insular Southeast Asians, the authors also suggest a possible link between the Ami of the east coast of Taiwan and Australo-Melanesians. Overall, they argue, present Taiwanese differentiations indicate a complex peopling history possibly starting before 12,000 BP when the island was still connected to the continent.

The significance of DNA markers in the reconstruction of East Asian prehistory is addressed by geneticist Chu Jiayou, whose chapter (Chapter 14) describes the remarkable diversity of Chinese populations (especially in Yunnan Province) and summarises two recently published works on microsatellite and Y chromosome polymorphisms in China. His main conclusion supports a unique origin of all modern humans rather than a multiregional model of Homo sapiens' origins.

Chapters 15 and 16 are two contributions by geneticists Estella Poloni and Alicia Sanchez-Mazas in collaboration with linguists Guillaume Jacques and Laurent Sagart. They compare the genetic structure of East Asian populations to the linguistic structure observed in this continent by analysing large sets of genetic data for two blood polymorphisms (RH and GM) and the HLA-DRB1 locus of the major histocompatibility complex. Using an analysis of variance framework, both studies indicate a significant correspondence between linguistic and genetic differentiation in East Asia, although the genetic landscape of human populations is closely related to geography showing a pattern of continuous differentiation along a north-to-south axis. In Chapter 15, Poloni and her collaborators also compare the RH and GM variation against three competing linguistic phylogenies, that is, Sagart's hypothesis of a main East Asian macrophylum, a combination of the greater Austric and Sino-Caucasian hypotheses, and a null hypothesis, assuming no genetic relationships with the main East Asian phyla. The authors conclude that the data do not yet permit us to discriminate between the three hypotheses.

In Chapter 16, Sanchez-Mazas et al. also discuss the observed HLA-DRB1 genetic diversity in each East Asian linguistic phylum in relation to several models of human differentiation based on the variation of two genetic diversity indexes, the diversity among and within populations, respectively. A main difference is observed between continental East Asians and the insular populations represented by Austronesians who probably experienced rapid genetic differentiations. Based on the frequencies of peculiar HLA-DRB1 alleles, a close historical relationship is also tentatively proposed between extra-Formosans and populations from the east coast of Taiwan, in particular the Amis. This view is alternative to that presented by Marie Lin et al. in Chapter 13.

Geneticist Peter Underhill presents a complete overview of Y chromosome diversity in East Asia and Oceania in Chapter 17 by synthesising the data of 3,702 samples from 73 populations analysed by different authors to produce a broad phylogeny. East Asian lineages are derived from a unique ancestor that developed into three main branches. The author relates these lineages to different migration events, notably a first migration from Africa into southern Asia via a coastal route, and an early settlement of Asia by successful colonisers displaced to the geographic margins by pressure from more recent migrations. On the other hand, the two complementary graphs of Y chromosome frequencies in Asia/Oceania presented by Underhill reveal intricate genetic relationships which suggest a highly complex history of the peopling of these continents.

Broad themes

Deep similarities between the language phyla of East Asia have led scholars to believe that they reflect genetic connections and proposals for macrophyla have a long history. However, these proposals are themselves highly diverse and certainly some similarities must be explained by early contacts, for example, the ancient strata of Sinitic lexemes in Hmong-Mien. It is also true that a history of intense bilingualism has caused some phyla to undergo dramatic morphological restructuring thereby concealing similarities; witness the encapsulation of Tai-Kadai within Sinitic. A proposal that has had particular longevity is the Austric proposal, uniting Austronesian and Austro-Asiatic. Originally put forward by Schmidt, it has had a significant revival in the 1990s in the publications of Reid and La Vaughn Hayes. Blust is now a supporter and archaeologists such as Higham have adopted it to explain patterns of East Asian prehistory. Others, such as Diffloth and Sagart, oppose it and a consensus may be emerging that the relationship is not as neat as a single clade, but rather that Austro-Asiatic and Austronesian fit together in a larger macrophylum that includes all the phyla under discussion in different configurations. Similarly, Austro-Thai, first put forward by Benedict, is now gathering support from Ostapirat and Sagart, although they differ in their interpretations of the structure of this relationship. The key to disentangling such high-level relationships is more complete reconstruction of proto-languages, a particularly urgent task in the case of Sino-Tibetan.

Peter Bellwood has been an active promoter of the notion that language expansions have been driven by agriculture, a hypothesis that has itself expanded out of the Austronesian region to cover much of the world (for a recent restatement see Diamond and Bellwood 2003). This has been a major stimulus to the field and has gathered much support in various areas. Some language phyla do demonstrate such a wealth of reconstructions in the field of agriculture that it is economical to suppose that its introduction was the engine of their expansion. This is true, for example, in Austronesian and Tai-Kadai. However, in other phyla, such as

Sino-Tibetan and Austro-Asiatic, reconstructions are fewer and appear to reflect principally cereal cultivation. It is also important to emphasise that reconstructions of single crop names can simply reflect the presence of wild forms; for agriculture to be given this starring role more breadth is required. What is stimulating is that archaeology and linguistics can come together to throw up hypotheses and test each other's models; and the pace at which new archaeobotanical material is appearing will surely change the picture of agriculture in East Asia rapidly in the coming decade.

Macrophyla proposals have a venerable history in the field, but the comparison of genetic variation and linguistic classification, pioneered by the teams of Luca Cavalli-Sforza, Robert Sokal and André Langaney among others is less than two decades old (Cavalli-Sforza et al. 1988, 1992; Excoffier et al. 1987, 1991; Sokal et al. 1988, 1992). The potential of both classical and DNA polymorphisms for assessing the historical relatedness or level of admixture between human populations appears to be enormous, but it is clear from the analyses both here and in related texts that their interpretation should be kept within reasonable limits. Genetic studies allow us to offer major narratives of the peopling of East Asia, but not to decide between specific transphylic hypotheses. This is partly a matter of sampling: because the indigenous populations of Taiwan have been so intensively studied, observations such as the special status of the Amis (Lin and colleagues, Chapter 13) can be made. But this is also a matter of evolution; genes and languages, even when deriving from a common origin, do not evolve at the same rate, and the levels of gene flow across linguistic boundaries may also vary greatly around the world. While keeping such limitations in mind, we believe that our understanding of human peopling history can be considerably improved by putting together the three disciplines, archaeology, linguistics and genetics.

Notes

1 Numbers of languages per phylum cited here are from the Ethnologue http://www.ethnologue.com/family_index.asp (accessed July 2003).
2 The position of the then little-known Hmong-Mien languages was a question mark, but recent versions of the theory, especially in China, make Hmong-Mien a part of Macro-Sino-Tibetan.

Bibliography

Benedict, P.K. (1942) 'Thai, Kadai and Indonesian: a new alignment in Southeastern Asia', American Anthropologist, n.s., 44, 576–601.
—— (1975) Austro-Thai: language and culture, New Haven: HRAF Press.
—— (1990) Japanese/Austro-Tai, Ann Arbor: Karoma.
Blust, R. (1998) 'Beyond the Austronesian homeland: the Austric hypothesis and its implications for archaeology', in Ward H. Goodenough (ed.) Prehistoric Settlement of the Pacific. Philadelphia: American Philosophical Society.

Cavalli-Sforza, L.L., Piazza, A., Menozzi, P. and Mountain, J. (1988) 'Reconstruction of human evolution: bringing together genetic, archaeological, and linguistic data', Proceedings of the National Academy of Science USA 85: 6002–6.

Cavalli-Sforza, L.L., Minch, E. and Mountain, J.L. (1992) 'Coevolution of genes and languages revisited', Proceedings of the National Academy of Science USA 89: 5620–4.

Davies, H.R. (1909) Yunnan: the link between India and the Yangzi, Cambridge: Cambridge University Press.

Diamond, J. and Bellwood, P. (2003) 'Farmers and their languages: the first expansions', Science 300: 597–603.

van Driem, G. (2001) Languages of the Himalayas. An ethnolinguistic handbook of the Greater Himalayan Region, (2 vols), Leiden: Brill.

Excoffier, L., Harding, R., Sokal, R.R., Pellegrini, B. and Sanchez-Mazas, A. (1991) 'Spatial differentiation of RH and GM haplotype frequencies in Sub-Saharan Africa and its relation to linguistic affinities', Human Biology 63, 3: 273–97.

Excoffier, L., Pellegrini, P., Sanchez-Mazas, A., Simon, C. and Langaney, A. (1987) 'Genetics and history of sub-Saharan Africa', Yearbook of Physical Anthropology, 30: 151–94.

Haudricourt, A.-G. (1966) 'The limits and connections of Austroasiatic in the Northeast', in Norman H. Zide (ed.) Studies in Comparative Austroasiatic Linguistics, 44–56, The Hague/Paris: Mouton.

Higham, C. (1996) The Bronze Age of Southeast Asia, Cambridge: Cambridge University Press.

Li, F.K. (1976) 'Sino-Tai', Computational Analyses of Asian and African Languages 3: 39–48.

Ostapirat, W. (2000) 'Proto-Kra', Linguistics of the Tibeto-Burman Area 23: 1.

Pan, W.Y. (1995) 'Dui Hua-Ao yuxi jiashuo de ruogan zhichi cailiao', in W. Wang (ed.) The Ancestry of the Chinese language, Journal of Chinese Linguistics Monograph Series no. 8, 113–44.

Peiros, I. (1998) Comparative Linguistics in Southeast Asia. Canberra: Pacific Linguistics.

Peiros, I. and Shnirelman, V. (1998) 'Rice in Southeast Asia: a regional interdisciplinary approach', in R. Blench and M. Spriggs (eds) Archaeology and Language, Archaeological Data and Linguistic Hypotheses, Vol. II: 379–89, London: Routledge.

Reid, L. (1994) 'Morphological evidence for Austric', Oceanic Linguistics 33, 2: 323–44.

Ruhlen, M. (1991) A guide to the world's languages Vol 1: Classification, Stanford University Press.

Sagart, L. (1993) 'Chinese and Austronesian: evidence for a genetic relationship', Journal of Chinese Linguistics 21, 1: 1–62.

—— (1994) 'Old Chinese and Proto-Austronesian evidence for Sino-Austronesian', Oceanic Linguistics 33, 2: 271–308.

—— (2001) 'Connections across the south Pacific: a personal synthesis', paper for Pacific Neighborhood Consortium conference, Hongkong, January.

Schiller, E. (1987) 'Which way did they grow? (Morphology and the Austro-Tai/(Macro)-Austric debate)', Proceedings of the 13th Annual Meeting of the Berkeley Linguistic Society, 235–46.

Schmidt, W. (1906) Die Mon-Khmer Völker, ein Bindeglied zwischen Völkern Zentralasiens und Austronesiens, Braunschweig: Friedrich Vieweg und Sohn.

Shafer, R. (1966–74) Introduction to Sino-Tibetan, Wiesbaden: Otto Harrassowitz.

Sokal, R.R., Oden, N.L. and Thomson, B.A. (1988) 'Genetic changes across language boundaries in Europe', American Journal of Physical Anthropology 76: 337–61.

Sokal, R.R., Oden, N.L. and Thomson, B.A. (1992) 'Origins of the Indo-Europeans: genetic evidence', Proceedings of the National Academy of Science USA89: 7669–73.

Starostin, S. (1991 [1984]) 'On the hypothesis of a genetic connection between the Sino-Tibetan languages and the Yeniseian and North-Caucasian languages', translation and introduction by William H. Baxter III, in V. Shevoroshkin (ed.) Dene-Sino-Caucasian, Bochum: Brockmeyer.

Xing, G.W. (1999) Han-Tai yu bijiao shouce, Beijing: Shangwu.

Zhengzhang, S.F. (1993) 'The root of Austro-Tai languages is in Sino-Austronesian', Paper presented at the Conference on Asia-Mainland/Austronesian connections (CAMAC) Honolulu, May 10–13.

—— (1995) 'Hanyu yu qinshu yu tongyuan genci ji fuzhui chengfen bijiaoshang de zedui wenti', in W. Wang (ed.) The Ancestry of the Chinese language, Journal of Chinese Linguistics Monograph Series no. 8, 269–82.

Part I

ARCHAEOLOGY

1

EXAMINING THE FARMING/ LANGUAGE DISPERSAL HYPOTHESIS IN THE EAST ASIAN CONTEXT

Peter Bellwood

Introduction

The Farming/Language Dispersal Hypothesis (Bellwood 2001a; Bellwood and Renfrew 2003; Renfrew 1996) suggests that the foundation dispersals of many of the major language families of tropical and temperate latitudes (e.g. Indo-European, Afro-Asiatic, ST, AA, AN, Uto-Aztecan) occurred consequent upon the establishment of reliable agricultural (and especially agropastoral) economies and increasing population densities in and around agricultural homeland areas. As a result of these increasing population densities, some degree of centrifugal movement would have been inevitable in non-circumscribed situations. The hypothesis has been applied to the geographical region termed 'China' on several occasions (e.g. Bellwood 1994, 1995, 1997a,b; see also Higham 1996, 2003; Reid 1996), especially for the ST, AA, Tai (Thai-Kadai, Daic, Kd), HM (Miao-Yao) and AN language families. Suffice it to say that recent developments in linguistics and archaeology do not seem to negate the hypothesis in any major way, insofar as it applies to the agricultural homeland regions of China – Manchuria, Mesoamerica or Southwest Asia. However, like all good historical hypotheses which attempt to integrate data from archaeology, linguistics and genetics, this one is not and probably never will be subject to positive proof or disproof. In the following text, the hypothesis will be qualified with respect to certain aspects which sometimes give false impressions of absolutism; it is not intended to explain all language distributions in all periods of the human past and it is highly sensitive to situational factors.

The rationale behind the hypothesis is as follows:

1. Situations of early agricultural development will have tended to encourage outflows of languages, cultures and genes in situations where early farmers had a demographic advantage over surrounding and contemporary populations of hunters and gatherers.

2   The foundation spreads[1] of language families, in many cases occurring long before history and over vast extents, and in sociocultural situations of small-scale preliterate farming societies, required population movement as their major driving force. Language shift doubtless worked to a degree on a local scale, but it could never have propelled foundation Indo-European languages across the vast stretch of territory from Anatolia or the Ukraine to Western Europe and Bangladesh, or AN languages across the even vaster extent of ocean and islands from Taiwan to Madagascar and Easter Island. The corpus of recorded language-spread situations in history is extremely large, and supports this perspective strongly (discussed to some degree in Bellwood 2001b, 2003). There are no recorded situations of language shift, whether through elite dominance or any other mechanism, that could conceivably explain such large-scale dispersals in the absence of any substantial factor of population movement

3   Such outward flows from agricultural heartland areas will have tended to continue as long as demographic gradients falling off centrifugally were maintained, even though

- antecedent populations, whether hunter–gatherers or other preceding groups of less numerous/less aggressive farmers, can always be expected to have given rise to at least some substratum effects.
- antecedent hunter–gatherers sometimes adopted agriculture and the languages of incoming farmers, and then might have undergone expansion in their own right. Preceding groups of agriculturalists could also have adopted the languages of different incoming farming populations, as must presumably have happened amongst some lowland Melanesian Papuan-speaking populations who adopted AN languages (such populations could have been either gardeners or hunter–gatherers). In this regard it is important to note the high degree of biological variation amongst populations who belong to some of the major language families, for example northern Indians and Scandinavians (Indo-European), Filipinos and Solomon Islanders (AN), Arabs and Ethiopians (Afro-Asiatic), Mongolians and Turks ('Altaic', if one accepts the existence of this grouping). It seems most unlikely that such variation could be due to natural selection alone working on common base populations in the short time spans available since the Neolithic or since the relevant proto-languages existed, and obviously one needs to incorporate concepts of language shift and contact-induced change in any global class of explanation, such as that represented by the farming/language dispersal hypothesis. But these concepts alone cannot explain everything.
- following on from the earlier text, we cannot expect genetic outcomes to mirror exactly those of archaeology and linguistics (people intermarry, but languages find it difficult to do so on the 50:50 level characteristic of recombining chromosomes, at least not anew in every generation!).

However, current tendencies within the anthropological literature to state that geographical patterns in languages, cultures and genes always vary completely independently of each other are not helpful for historical understanding and seem to reflect more an ethical statement about how our present troubled and ethnically-divided world should function, rather than any informed wisdom about how it might have functioned in the past.

- the actual spreads of ancestral languages within specific families have been layered through quite long time spans (4,000 years in the case of AN and doubtless longer in the case of Indo-European). Our interest in this article is mainly in the primary and very extensive foundation layers of language family dispersal.

I should also add three provisos. First, no claim is being made here that only agriculturalist language families ever spread; we also have several language families which originated and spread amongst hunter–gatherers, such as Uralic, Eskimo-Aleut, Athabaskan, Algonquian in Canada, and maybe even the much debated Pama-Nyungan. These need to be explained too, and population movement is doubtless as significant here as in the spreads of the agriculturalist language families. Second, I do not wish to suggest that agriculturalist dispersal goes back to the very roots of all language families which are currently agriculturalist. It is possible, for instance, that both Niger-Congo and Afro-Asiatic had already undergone some dispersal prior to the development of agriculture, although in both these cases the evidence is by no means clear since it is difficult to reconstruct with absolute certainty the economic basis of the period represented by the basal proto-language (e.g. Ehret 2003 vs Militarev 2003 for Proto-Afro-Asiatic). Third, not all agriculturalist language families/subgroups underwent spread – the list of stay-at-homes, doubtless for reasons connected with circumscription and successful intensification of production, is long (Egyptian, Sumerian, Mixe-Zoque, the Caucasian language families...).

If we are to explain the genesis of language families coherently, we must offer reconstructions which tie language spreads to language speakers, and language speakers to archaeological horizons. I see no benefit in simply proposing scenarios for language family origins and dispersal histories in vacuo, with no reference to an explanatory background cultural context. Since one of the most significant archaeological horizons, in most temperate and tropical regions where agriculture is/was possible, is represented by the Neolithic (or Formative in the Americas) spread over a background of Mesolithic or Archaic hunting societies, then it makes logical sense to regard this horizon as a major one for language family expansion.[2] In my view, language families and major subgroups such as Bantu (Phillipson 2003), Indo-European (Renfrew 1999), Afro-Asiatic (Militarev 2003) and Uto-Aztecan (Hill 2003) reflect in their foundation dispersals this 'farmer-over-hunter' replacement/assimilation reconstruction very well, allowing of course for continuing expansion in post-Neolithic times in most cases. How does East Asia fit this hypothesis?

East Asia in closer focus

The first matter I would note is that linguists, over the years, have suggested so many links of a putative genetic nature between two or more of the East Asian language families, all in considerable disagreement and cross-cutting each other, that I see a high likelihood that all are related to some degree (e.g. Benedict 1975; Blust 1996; Reid 1996, and of course many of the other chapters in this volume, especially Sagart, Starosta, Reid and Ostapirat). However, I would not be so unwise as to claim that all relationships are genetic; arguments for early borrowing also are numerous. The suggestion here is that early forms of the major southern families – AA, HM, AN and Tai – were at one time located sufficiently close together for some degree of sharing of heritage, both genetic and areal. The questions of ST and 'Altaic' I will leave aside for the moment, although these seem to form the northern pieces of a coherent East Asian early agricultural jigsaw.

I think it should be noted, in addition, that the majority of origin hypotheses for these southern language families see them moving outwards from the general region of Central and southern China rather than inwards. Central and southern China are also the only regions, if we include Taiwan, where ST, AA, HM, AN and Tai all overlap in distribution (see e.g. Bellwood 1994, 1995; Blench 1999; Blust 1996; Peiros 1998; Reid 1996). Furthermore, glottochronology, whatever one might think of the overall merits of this technique, has tended in the past to give dates for major family-founding proto-languages that fall well within the date range of early farming societies in both the Old and New Worlds, including East Asia (see discussion in Bellwood 2000).

My main aim in the remainder of this chapter is to summarise my thoughts on two questions:

- How and where (and when) did agriculture develop in East Asia and how many different cultural populations were involved in the process?
- What were the main expansion trends of the relevant language families?

Early agriculture in China

In her very thorough recent summary of the Chinese evidence, Tracey Lu (1999) suggests a dual origin for Chinese agriculture – one in the middle Yangzi Valley involving Oryza sativa, the other in the middle (and lower?) Huanghe involving Setaria italica (Foxtail millet). As she points out, there is good evidence for interaction between these two zones, particularly via the site of Jiahu in the Huai basin, where rice occurs with a Peiligang type of material culture (Zhang and Wang 1998). The Peiligang Culture of the middle Huanghe Valley and adjacent regions is normally associated with remains of the two types of millet to be discussed below, so the dominance of rice, a middle Yangzi domesticate according to current archaeological knowledge, at Jiahu is of obvious significance. As far as the middle Yangzi zone is concerned, the evidence for an indigenous transition to agriculture is now quite strong, particularly in terms of the rice phytolith records from cave sites in Hunan and Jiangxi (Chen Xingcan 1999; Higham and Lu 1998; Pei Anping 1998; Zhang Chi 1999). The appearance of villages with evidence for domesticated rice and pottery occurred in this area between 7,000 and 6,500 BC.

In the Huanghe Basin, however, the picture is less clear. Here too, villages with Neolithic material culture (Cishan, Peiligang, Jiahu) are present by 6,500 BC, but phytolith and macrofossil records for the millets ultimately to be cultivated along the latitude of the Yellow River are so far missing prior to this date. This situation means that the independent domestication of foxtail millet is not so well documented for the Huanghe as is the parallel case for rice in the Yangzi Basin. I detect in this the germs of a scenario, that would run as follows.

By 7,000 BC, the domestication of rice had occurred in the middle Yangzi Basin, a region at that time on the northern edge of the range for reliable growth of wild rice (Bellwood 1996; T.T. Chang 1983: 73; Yan 1992: 121–2). Perhaps the northern edge proper lay a little further north in the Huai Basin, but it evidently did not occur as far north as the Huanghe, where Neolithic finds of rice exist but are rare and equivocal (Wu Yaoli 1996). The result of this middle Yangzi transition to rice cultivation and domestication, together presumably with the domestication of the pig and chicken, was to promote some degree of population expansion. Those populations who attempted to move north of the Huai valley would rapidly have found their rice yields below expectation. In such circumstances, it is not hard to visualise how attention could have turned to local hardier annual cereals, particularly the wild foxtail millet Setaria viridis.

This scenario thus regards foxtail millet as a secondary domesticate, brought into cultivation somewhere in the Huanghe Basin as the earliest domesticated rice economy expanded beyond its natural limits, but brought in sufficiently early to be present by at least 6,500 BC in Cishan and Peiligang and perhaps by 6,000 BC further north in southern Manchuria (Shelach 2000). The scenario would, of course, be weakened if older finds of Neolithic cultivated millet can be made in the Huanghe drainage, or if use-wear analyses of microblades from late Palaeolithic sites such as Xiachuan can reveal traces of millet harvesting (Lu 1998, 1999), and hence possibly a genuinely independent Huanghe trajectory of domestication.

Attention now turns to that other millet species, the broomcorn or common millet Panicum miliaceum. This also occurs in the earliest sites of the Huanghe Neolithic, being present according to Yan (1992: Table 1) in Peiligang and Dadiwan. To judge from Yan's table, it is commonly found in the Gansu Neolithic. This could be a matter of considerable importance, since Zohary and Hopf (2000) describe common millet as a plant of hot dry climates with poor soils, with wild and weedy forms reported from the region between the Aral and Caspian Seas across to Xinjiang and Mongolia. Its occurrence in many European Neolithic sites is quite early, presumably from at least 5,500 BC in terms of its presence in the Linearbandkeramik (Danubian), Trichterbecker (Funnel Beaker), Vinca and Tripolye cultures, also at Tepe Yahya in Iran and by a similar date in Georgia (Wasylikowa 1991). It is reported from Neolithic Argissa in Greece (c.6,500 BC: Dennell 1992: 77). Exactly where common millet was first domesticated is unclear, but there is no compelling reason to suspect that it was in the vicinity of sites such as Cishan or Peiligang. Was it introduced into Neolithic China from the steppes of Central Asia, via Xinjiang and Gansu?

The same suggestion is less likely for foxtail millet, which does seem to have its oldest dates as a domesticated cereal in China if we accept the much younger dates for its presence elsewhere, as presented by Jane Renfrew (1973) and by Zohary and Hopf (2000). However, Renfrew (1973: 101) also notes that Setaria viridis grows wild in western Asia and around the Mediterranean, and that it occurs in Neolithic deposits in Hungary. There may be scope here for some palaeobotanical sleuthing.

The upshot of all of this is that the domestication of the millets in China remains something of a mystery. The possibility of contacts with Central Asia involving the movement of common millet, perhaps at a remarkably early date of 6,500 BC, must remain open. There is a possible implication of directionality here in that the move is most likely to have been into the middle and lower Huanghe basin from the west, perhaps via Xinjiang and Gansu. It is this general implication of contact so far to the west which is striking at such an early date. Chang Kwang-chih (1986: 143) extends the distribution of the early Neolithic in China to as far west as eastern Gansu, in the form of the Laoguantai culture (6,000 BC). The possibility of a cultural exchange here, with populations extending into the steppelands which extend westwards right across Central Asia north of the Tarim Basin, might be entertained. Unfortunately, the relevant archaeological record from Central Asia seems to be rather thin prior to the Bronze Age, although the non-reporting of millets from the very rich macrobotanical deposits from Neolithic Jeitun in Turkmenistan (Harris and Gosden 1996) suggests that the contacts did not proceed this far south of the steppes.

Despite the absence of any positive archaeological evidence for farmers and pastoralists in the general vicinity of the Altai Mountains and Central Asian steppes before the Bronze Age, commencing during the third millennium BC (Afanasievo culture: Dergachev 1989, and see papers in Mair (ed.) 1998), there is a quantity of linguistic evidence which is a little more suggestive of earlier, possibly Neolithic, contacts. Some of this is concerned with relationships so remote that they are unlikely, given present knowledge, to throw much direct light on population relationships during pre-Bronze periods. Such include the suggestion by Pulleyblank (1995) for links between Proto-Indo-European and PST, and Starostin's[3] (1991 [1984]) suggestion that the ST and North Caucasian languages belong to a Sino-Caucasian macrofamily. The status of such suggested links is unclear; if real, do they reflect genetic or borrowing relationships, and at what approximate date? More mileage is perhaps to be gained from a consideration of the Tocharian subgroup of languages within Indo-European.

Even though the Tocharian languages, now extinct, are not attested around the Tarim Basin in Xinjiang until the first millennium AD, questions of their ancestry have recently come into prominence with the discovery of Caucasoid mummies in the Tarim Basin, some dating back into the second millennium BC (Barber 1999;

chapters in Mair (ed.) 1998). A number of archaeologists (in Mair (ed.) 1998) appear content to equate the Tocharian dispersal with the eastward movement of Bronze Age cultures along the steppes, particularly with the Afanasievo culture of the late fourth and third millennia BC, although Renfrew (1999: 275) has recently suggested a much earlier, fifth millennium BC, dispersal from the Ukraine with an economy adapted to steppe lands. Such an economy presumably had both pastoral and cereal cultivation components, given that the Tarim Basin and surrounding regions supported agricultural populations in later times (e.g. Chang and Tourtellotte 1998 for a presence of wheat, barley, millets and domesticated animals in the Talgar region after 400 BC).

Arguing in the face of negative evidence can be dangerous, but given the paradigm-changing significance of some recent discoveries of deeply buried early agricultural sites beneath the alluvial plains of western Taiwan (Tsang, Chapter 4, this volume) or southern Arizona (Muro 1999), one is forced to ask if such problems of deep burial and inaccessibility to archaeologists could also occur in the alluvial basins of Central Asia. Is there a deeply-buried Tarim Basin Neolithic which dates from 6,000 BC?

The most suggestive current evidence for this could be the linguistic evidence for the Tocharian subgroup. Even though this subgroup is not diverse within itself and the Proto-Tocharian entity may have been quite recent in time, the initial separation of Pre-Tocharian from its Indo-European root evidently occurred very early in relative terms. As Ringe et al. (1998: 407) state

> What is very clear is that Tocharian, like Anatolian and Italo-Celtic, is a peripheral member of the IE family that began its independent history earlier than most other surviving branches of the family.

Renfrew (1999) also points to an early separation of Tocharian from the other Indo-European languages, second in time only to the Anatolian languages. If we apply the farming/language hypothesis to Indo-European and associate its foundation spread with Neolithic cultures from Anatolia at about 7,000–6,500 BC (Renfrew 1996, 1999), then the commencement of Pre-Tocharian dispersal eastwards towards Xinjiang could certainly have commenced as early as 6,000 BC.

All of this may be deemed idle speculation, fuelled purely by a very early Neolithic presence of common millet in both Europe and China. Perhaps common millet was domesticated more than once, independently, although in the absence of genetic evidence for such an eventuality it is more economical to argue for a single domestication. I find it unlikely that the Neolithic cultures of China and western Asia should have evolved in absolute isolation from each other until some budding Bronze Age Marco Polo introduced bronze working, horses, wheeled vehicles, sheep and other wonders of the Western World during or just before the Shang dynasty. It is more likely that the steppeland environments of Central Asia were indeed settled by small pockets of farmers, emanating mainly from the west. These farmers, Pre-Tocharians perhaps, could have interacted with early Chinese farmers in Gansu as early as 6,000 BC. Any surviving and direct traces of an early Indo-European trail eastwards, apart from the Tocharian languages themselves, will have been erased by the subsequent expansions of the Indo-Iranian and Turkic languages.

Neolithic language geography in Central China

Current language geography and comparisons at the family level suggest that, of the southern Chinese and Southeast Asian families extant today, the HM family is the one most likely to have originated closest to the central Yangzi early rice zone. Although the extant HM languages do not in themselves have an antiquity anything like as great as 8,500 years, I note here Peiros' suggestion (1998: 160) that a combined AA/HM grouping may well do so. Peiros offers a date for this in the sixth millennium BC, based on glottochronology. Whether AA and HM are indeed related genetically is a matter for linguists to decide, but AA geography suggests a homeland somewhere south of the Yangzi, probably in the northern reaches of the Southeast Asian mainland (Higham 2003). At the Périgueux meeting, Diffloth suggested a glottochronological date of about 5,000 BC for PAA.

The Tai languages are, as a group, not of great antiquity, with a diversification history dating within the past 4,000 years according to Peiros. I am not aware of any really strong evidence to place their homeland outside the zone of greatest diversity today, this being the southern Chinese provinces of Guangxi and Guizhou, with a possible pre-Han extension into Guangdong (Ostapirat, Chapter 7, this volume). AN is of a greater antiquity at possibly 6,000 years (4,000 BC), and has a generally-accepted homeland in Taiwan. Remoter relationships of AN are variously presented, with cases argued for Austro-Thai (Benedict 1975), Austric (Reid, Chapter 8, this volume; Blust 1996) and Sino-Austronesian (Sagart, Chapter 9, this volume).

For a non-linguist to attempt to referee these opinions on the deep relationships of AN would be presumptuous, but the archaeological picture has changed recently in Taiwan with the discovery of both rice and foxtail millet in carbonised form from two sites at Nanguanli in the Tainan Science-Based Industrial Park (Cheng-hwa Tsang, Chapter 4, this volume). The Nanguanli sites belong to the Dabenkeng culture, c.3,500–2,500 BC, and represent the oldest Southeast Asian discoveries of both rice and foxtail millet made so far outside the borders of modern China. Until recently, many archaeologists believed that the DBK people were either hunter–gatherers or growers of root crops, not cereals. It is now clear that the Taiwan Neolithic was fully agricultural from the beginning and could have either Huanghe or Yangzi homelands (or both), although the cultural relationships of the DBK Culture, the earliest Neolithic in Taiwan, are generally believed to be with adjacent parts of southern China, especially Fujian and Guangdong, at least in terms of pottery and adzes, rather than with anywhere north of the Yangzi (Tsang, Chapter 4, this volume). Despite this, the new finds at Nan-kuan-li certainly re-open the issue of Taiwan early Neolithic origins for further debate.

Perhaps we can hypothesise that, at around 6,000 BC, ancestral HM languages were located to the immediate south of the middle Yangzi, with early AA languages further to the southwest and early Tai languages to the south. PAN was ultimately to be located in Taiwan, with Pre-Austronesian forebears in southeastern coastal China. Naturally, these language families did not all begin to expand at the same time and we need to reckon with chain-reaction (or domino) effects, whereby certain populations in the course of their expansion unleashed similar tendencies in others. Naturally also, it would be ridiculous to state that, for instance, all AN or all AA speakers emanate from southern China – such would be unacceptable for Solomon Islanders or Malaysian Orang Asli. The focus here is on the formative regions wherein commenced the early stages of Neolithic and language family expansion, and in this regard we can see the outlines of an expanding network with a focus in the Yangzi and Huanghe Valleys. Indeed, the Huanghe brings us to our next topic – the ST homeland mystery tour.

In recent years, linguists have given some remarkably divergent opinions on the homeland for the ST family (or TB; see van Driem, Chapter 6, this volume). Peiros (1998) prefers a northern South Asian homeland, van Driem (1999) prefers Sichuan, Matisoff (1991) prefers the Himalayan Plateau. Janhunen (1996: 222) presents in my view the most likely homeland hypothesis by associating the early ST languages with the Huanghe Neolithic (Yangshao culture). Norman (1988: 17) merely states that the homeland is unknown, but notes that, on the way to the Huanghe, the early ST languages borrowed from early HM and early AA languages, thus implying a slightly southerly origin.

Of all the recent hypotheses, that of van Driem (1998, 1999, Chapter 6, this volume) is perhaps the most detailed and lucid. Van Driem refers to the whole language family as TB and sources it to Sichuan, from where the oldest movements took place into the Himalayas and northern India, at that time settled by 'indigenous Austroasiatic populations' (1999: 50). Soon after this, other groups (Northern TBs) spread with Neolithic cultures into the Yellow River Basin, to Dadiwan (Gansu), Peiligang and Cishan. The Sinitic languages later developed from the more easterly of these populations. Van Driem refers to evidence of early millet cultivation in Sichuan, but does not specify where this evidence comes from (note that Bagley 2001, for instance, does not refer to any early Neolithic assemblages in Sichuan). Since Sichuan contains the basin of the Yangzi immediately above its middle course, and immediately above the area where evidence for early rice cultivation has been found, it follows that this province could one day produce sites belonging to a Neolithic dating from 6,000 BC. The problem, so far, is that it has not done so; again, perhaps the relevant sites are buried. The alternative is to apply the reasoning behind the Farming/Language Dispersal Hypothesis and to place the homeland of ST in the agricultural heartland area of Central China. Whether this heartland extended into Sichuan is a matter for future archaeologists to decide.

Van Driem's reconstructions bring up questions for both archaeologists and linguists to consider. The linguists need to consider the effects on ST (or TB) geography of the historical fact of Sinitic expansion. Language families, during the courses of their evolution, can sometimes automatically erase the evidence of their origins as their component native-speaker populations shuffle and reshuffle across the landscape. ST surely suffers in a major way from this problem, such that much of the diversity that might have derived from Neolithic foundation spread in Central China will have been masked by subsequent Sinitic expansion since Shang and Zhou times.

My intention is not to challenge van Driem's hypothesis of a Sichuan homeland for TB. But, at present, such westerly origins leave unanswered the question of mechanisms for the dispersal of the language family. My own preference would be for the region between the Yangzi and Huanghe. Did the rice growers of Jiahu speak Proto-Tibeto-Burman, within reach of early speakers of the HM languages? We will never know for certain, but we do need to weigh up all the options.

My current conclusions on the homelands of the East and Southeast Asian language families are presented in Map 1.1. Admittedly, there are no absolutely

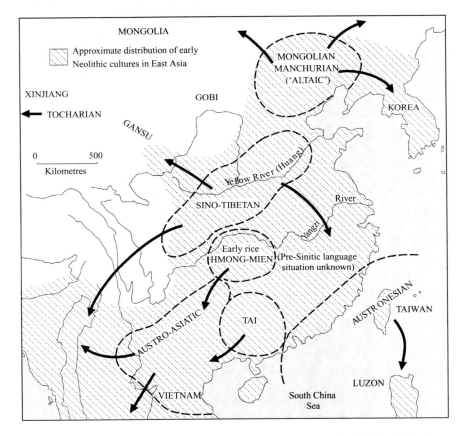

Map 1.1 The approximate distribution of early Neolithic cultures in China and Southeast Asia, with suggested approximate homelands for language families.

Note
The Neolithic cultures are oldest in the Huanghe-Yangzi regions and become progressively younger as one moves south and southwest.

positive linguistic homeland identifications which give this map full support. Indeed, linguists seem to be quite unable to offer solid reconstructions concerning the homelands of any of these major families, with the possible exception of AN. This circumstance reflects the erosion of the original phylogenetic linguistic patterns established as these families began their expansions, and it also reflects the inability to reconstruct precise family trees back to the roots of these families, except possibly for AN, where the sheer extent of the primary dispersal means that backtracking and eradication of earlier language horizons was a fairly rare event. So Map 1.1 is a hypothesis, based in part on the archaeological and linguistic logic behind the Farming/Language Dispersal Hypothesis. The next step is to test it against those portions of the growing archaeological and genetic records that relate to the dispersal of human populations and agriculture.

Abbreviations

AA	Austro-Asiatic
AN	Austronesian
HM	Hmong-Mien
Kd	Kra-Dai
PAA	Proto-Austro-Asiatic
PAN	Proto-Austronesian
PST	Proto-Sino-Tibetan
ST	Sino-Tibetan
TB	Tibeto-Burman

Notes

1 The emphasis here on foundation spread is intentional. Obviously, some Indo-European languages have been spreading very successfully in historical times, as have other languages such as Chinese and Bahasa Indonesia. But the fact remains that the Indo-European family had spread across a vast range of territory from Ireland to Bangladesh, excluding some regions of the Middle East and the northern Mediterranean hinterland, prior to any recorded (e.g. Greek, Roman) history. Later spreads can therefore be noted, but they are not relevant for the issues discussed in this chapter.
2 Just as, for instance, the Roman, early Islamic and European colonial periods were also 'horizons' of major language spread in more recent historical times.
3 I wish to thank Laurent Sagart for bringing this reference to my attention.

Bibliography

Bagley, R. (2001) Ancient Sichuan, Seattle: Seattle Art Museum.
Barber, E. (1999) The Mummies of Ürümchi, London: Macmillan.
Bellwood, P. (1994) 'An archaeologist's view of language macrofamily relationships', Oceanic Linguistics 33: 391–406.
Bellwood, P. (1995) 'Early agriculture, language history and the archaeological record in China and Southeast Asia', in Yeung Chun-tong and Li Wai-ling (eds) Archaeology in Southeast Asia, Hong Kong: University of Hong Kong Museum and Art Gallery.

Bellwood, P. (1996) 'The origins and spread of agriculture in the Indo-Pacific region', in D. Harris (ed.) The Origins and Spread of Agriculture and Pastoralism in Eurasia, London: UCL Press.
—— (1997a) Prehistory of the Indo-Malaysian Archipelago, Honolulu: University of Hawaii Press.
—— (1997b) 'Prehistoric cultural explanations for widespread language families', in P. McConvell and N. Evans (eds) Archaeology and Linguistics, Melbourne: Oxford University Press.
—— (2000) 'The time depth of major language families: an archaeologist's perspective', in C. Renfrew, A. McMahon, L. Trask (eds) Time Depth in Historical Linguistics, Vol. 1, Cambridge: McDonald Institute for Archaeological Research.
—— (2001a) 'Early agriculturalist population diasporas? Farming, languages and genes', Annual Review of Anthropology 30: 181–207.
—— (2001b) 'Archaeology and the historical determinants of punctuation in language family origins', in A. Aikhenvald and R. Dixon (eds) Areal Diffusion and Genetic Inheritance: Problems in Comparative Linguistics, Oxford: Oxford University Press.
—— (2003) 'Farmers, foragers, languages, genes: the genesis of agricultural societies', in P. Bellwood and C. Renfrew (eds) Examining the Farming/Language Dispersal Hypothesis, Cambridge: McDonald Institute for Archaeological Research, pp. 17–28.
Bellwood, P. and Renfrew, C. (eds) (2003) Examining the Farming/Language Dispersal Hypothesis, Cambridge: McDonald Institute for Archaeological Research.
Benedict, P. (1975) Austro-Thai Language and Culture, New Haven: HRAF Press.
Blench, R. (1999) 'Language phyla of the Indo-Pacific region', Bull. Indo-Pacific Prehistory Assn. 18: 59–76.
Blust, R. (1996) 'Beyond the Austronesian homeland: the Austric hypothesis and its implication for archaeology', in W. Goodenough (ed.) Prehistoric Settlement of the Pacific, Philadelphia: American Philosophical Society.
Chang, K.C. (1986) The Archaeology of Ancient China, 4th edn, New Haven: Yale University Press.
Chang, T.T. (1983) 'The origin and early cultures of the cereal grains and food legumes', in D.N. Keightley (ed.) The Origins of Chinese Civilization, Berkeley: University of California Press.
Chang, C. and Tortellotte, P. (1998) 'The role of agropastoralism in the evolution of steppe culture in the Semirechye area of southern Kazakhstan', in V. Mair (ed.) The Bronze Age and Early Iron Age Peoples of Eastern Central Asia, Vol. 1, Washington DC: Institute for the Study of Man.
Chen, X.-C. (1999) 'On the earliest evidence for rice cultivation in China', Bull. Indo-Pacific Prehistory Assn. 18: 81–94.
Dennell, R. (1992) 'The origins of crop agriculture in Europe', in C.W. Cowan and P.J. Watson (eds) The Origins of Agriculture, Washington DC: Smithsonian.
Dergachev, V. (1989) 'Neolithic and Bronze Age cultural communities of the steppe zone of the USSR', Antiquity 63: 793–802.
Ehret, C. (2003) 'Language family expansions: broadening our understandings of cause from an African perspective', in P. Bellwood and C. Renfrew (eds) Examining the Farming/Language Dispersal Hypothesis, Cambridge: McDonald Institute for Archaeological Research 17–28: 163–76.

Harris, D.R., Gosden, C. and Charles, M. (1996) 'Jeitun: recent excavations at an early neolithic site in southern Turkmenistan', Proc. Prehistoric Society 62: 423–42.

Higham, C. (1996) 'Archaeology and linguistics in Southeast Asia', Bull. Indo-Pacific Prehistory Assn. 14: 110–8.

—— (2003) 'Languages and farming dispersals: Austroasiatic languages and rice cultivation', in P. Bellwood and C. Renfrew (eds) Examining the Farming/Language Dispersal Hypothesis, Cambridge: McDonald Institute for Archaeological Research 17–28: 223–32.

Higham, C. and Lu, T. (1998) 'The origins and dispersal of rice cultivation', Antiquity 72: 867–77.

Hill, J. (2003) 'Proto-Uto-Aztecan cultivation and the Northern Devolution', in P. Bellwood and C. Renfrew (eds) Examining the Farming/Language Dispersal Hypothesis, Cambridge: McDonald Institute for Archaeological Research 17–28: 341–56.

Janhunen, J. (1996) Manchuria: An Ethnic History, Helsinki: Suomalais-Ugrilainen Seura.

Lu, T. (1998) 'Some botanical characteristics of green foxtail (Setaria viridis) and harvesting experiments on the grass', Antiquity 72: 902–7.

—— (1999) The Transition from Foraging to Farming and the Origin of Agriculture in China, Oxford: BAR International Series 774.

Mair, V. (ed.) (1998) The Bronze Age and Early Iron Age Peoples of Eastern Central Asia, Washington DC: Institute for the Study of Man.

Matisoff, J. (1991) 'Sino-Tibetan linguistics: present state and future prospects', Annual Review of Anthropology 20: 469–504.

Militarev, A. (2003) 'Prehistory of dispersal: the Proto-Afrasian (Afroasiatic) farming lexicon', in P. Bellwood and C. Renfrew (eds) Examining the Farming/Language Dispersal Hypothesis, Cambridge: McDonald Institute for Archaeological Research 17–28: 135–50.

Muro, M. (1999) 'Not just another roadside attraction', American Archaeology 2/4: 10–15.

Norman, J. (1988) Chinese, Cambridge: Cambridge University Press.

Pei, A.-P. (1998) 'Notes on new advancements and revelations in the agricultural archaeology of early rice domestication in the Dongting Lake region', Antiquity 72: 878–84.

Peiros, I. (1998) Comparative Linguistics in Southeast Asia, Canberra: Pacific Linguistics Series C-142.

Phillipson, D. (2003) 'Language and farming dispersals in Sub-Saharan Africa, with particular reference to the Bantu-speaking peoples', in P. Bellwood and C. Renfrew (eds) Examining the Farming/Language Dispersal Hypothesis, Cambridge: McDonald Institute for Archaeological Research 17–28: 177–90.

Pulleyblank, E.G. (1995) 'The historical and prehistorical relationships of Chinese', in W.S.-Y. Wang (ed.) The Ancestry of the Chinese Language, Berkeley: Journal of Chinese Linguistics Monograph 8.

Reid, L. (1996) 'The current state of linguistic research on the relatedness of the language families of East and Southeast Asia', Bull. Indo-Pacific Prehistory Assn. 15: 87–92.

Renfrew, C. (1996) 'Language families and the spread of farming', in D. Harris (ed.) The Origins and Spread of Agriculture and Pastoralism in Asia, London: UCL Press.

—— (1999) 'Time depth, convergence theory, and innovation in Proto-Indo-European', Journal of Indo-European Studies 27/3–4: 257–93.

Renfrew, J. (1973) Palaeoethnobotany, London: Methuen.

Ringe, R., Warnow, T. and Taylor, A. (1998) 'Computational cladistics and the position of Tocharian', in V. Mair (ed.) The Bronze Age and Early Iron Age Peoples of Eastern Central Asia, Washington DC: Institute for the Study of Man.

Shelach, G. (2000) 'The earliest Neolithic cultures of northeast China', in Journal of World Prehistory 14: 363–414.

Starostin, S. (1991 [1984]) 'On the hypothesis of a genetic connection between the Sino-Tibetan languages and the Yeniseian and North-Caucasian languages', translation and introduction by William H. Baxter III, in V. Shevoroshkin (ed.) Dene-Sino-Caucasian, Bochum: Brockmeyer.

van Driem, G. (1998) 'Neolithic correlates of ancient Tibeto-Burman migrations', in R. Blench and M. Spriggs (eds) Archaeology and Language II, London: Routledge.

—— (1999) 'A new theory on the origin of Chinese', Bull. Indo-Pacific Prehistory Assn. 18: 43–58.

Wasylikowa, K., Carciumaru, M., Hajnalova, E., Hartyanyi, B., Pashkevich, G. and Yanusevich, Z. (1991) 'East-Central Europe', in W. van Zeist, K. Wasylikowa, K.-E. Behre (eds) Progress in Old World Palaeoethnobotany, Rotterdam: Balkema.

Wu, Y. (1996) 'Prehistoric agriculture of rice in the Yellow River Valley', Bull. Indo-Pacific Prehistory Assn. 16: 223–4.

Yan, W. (1992) 'Origins of agriculture and animal husbandry in China', in C.M. Aikens and S.-N. Rhee (eds) Pacific Northeast Asia in Prehistory, Pullman: Washington State University Press.

Zhang, C. (1999) 'The excavations at Xianrendong and Diaotonghuan, Jiangxi', Bull. Indo-Pacific Prehistory Assn. 18: 97–100.

Zhang, J. and Wang, X. (1998) 'Notes on the recent discovery of ancient cultivated rice at Jiahu, Henan Province', Antiquity 72: 897–901.

Zohary, D. and Hopf, M. (2000) Domestication of Plants in the Old World, 3rd edn, Oxford: Oxford University Press.

2

FROM THE MOUNTAINS TO THE VALLEYS

Understanding ethnolinguistic geography in Southeast Asia

Roger Blench

Introduction

The worldwide distribution of ethnolinguistic diversity is highly uneven and concentrated in particular regions; sub-Saharan Africa from Nigeria to Chad, Melanesia, much of the New World and Southeast Asia. Although the question is frequently posed as if explaining such diversity was the problem, it is better reformulated in terms of models to explain uniformity. The underlying pattern is diversity, but ethnic homogeneity has developed in particular regions usually by the expansion of one group and the assimilation of its neighbours.

The causes of such expansions are by no means obvious; why have the Kikuyu expanded to over a million while their closely related neighbours have remained in the thousands, or the Khalkh Mongols overwhelmed the other speakers of Mongolic languages? In many cases the answer is undoubtedly military; the Romans eliminated diversity in Europe by conquest and enforced a distinctive culture everywhere they conquered. Even so, military cultures do not come out of a vacuum, but are born in appropriate social and environmental conditions. Apart from the expansion of particular ethnic groups, there is the related question as to what distinguishes these from the expansion of a phylum. Polynesian, Turkic, Bantu and Berber all represent subphylic expansions without any individual language becoming dominant.

One pattern dramatically illustrated in Southeast Asia is the expansion of a single ethnolinguistic group to outnumber all related languages in its region. The interest of this pattern is that it seems to be quite ubiquitous in the region and not elsewhere replicated. This chapter will argue that this type of expansion is linked quite specifically to lowland rice cultivation and the conjunction of mountainous terrain with flooded lowlands, that is, to geography. Much of the archaeological debate on rice systems focuses on the genesis of states or otherwise. But the evidence is that the agronomic system can override socio-political considerations, that whatever the surface social organisation, the expansion of rice and associated habitat conversion continues relentlessly.

Since the majority of these expansions took place in eras without historical documentation, they are accessible principally via archaeology and historical linguistics. The second part of the chapter examines the reconstruction of terminology associated with rice in the various language phyla of Southeast Asia. It uses comparative vocabulary sets, particularly those collected in Revel (1988) to gauge the extent to which rice-associated words can help interpret the ethnodemographic pattern described. It is striking how many claims about the links between phylic and agrarian expansion are framed in terms of general hypotheses and do not examine the lexical evidence in enough detail to ascertain whether it really provides the expected support.

The chapter largely excludes island Southeast Asia with the exception of Taiwan. Rice is dominant in much of the Philippines and as far as Java and Bali in the Indonesian chain. East of this region, other types of swamp agriculture takeover, based on taro and other tubers, and rice becomes insignificant in subsistence terms. There is probably no good agronomic reason for this; it is rather a reflection of the original history of domestication of these species of tuber and the limits of their historical spread. Once tuber-based swamp agriculture is predominant, the ethnodemographic pattern of a single group taking control of a whole ecozone disappears and linguistic fragmentation becomes the norm.

Historical demography of Southeast Asia

Southeast Asia is, broadly speaking, a region of great ethnic diversity. Unlike the colder regions of inner Asia, numbers of languages in relation to geographical area are very high, as are human population densities. In contrast to other regions of high diversity such as South America, New Guinea or Nigeria-Cameroun, the absolute size of minorities is also large; China has 'minorities' of several million. Southeast Asia also displays an unusual pattern of extreme numerical imbalances between a dominant group and minorities within a region, as the analysis of human population figures in the modern nation-states shows. Table 2.1 shows the countries of Southeast Asia with absolute numbers and populations of minorities and dominant groups as well as the percentages these represent.

Obviously the nation-state is not an ideal analytic tool, since many international boundaries are quite recent. However, more than elsewhere in the world, present-day nation-states do represent the approximate sphere of influence of large ethnic groups and these may be incorporated into the name of the country. Moreover, many states are defined significantly by river basins, either by dividing the basin of one large river (in the case of the Mekong) or encompassing a series of parallel rivers as in Myanmar. The figures fall within a limited range with minorities representing 0.1–4.5 per cent of the modern-day state and dominant groups up to 99 per cent of the population. The large size of minorities in

Table 2.1 Nations of Southeast Asia with role of dominant ethnolinguistic group

State	Total population	No. minorities	Dominant group	No. speakers in dominant group	% Total	Mean size minority	Minorities as % of dominant
Cambodia	10,716,000	19	Khmer	5,932,800	55.4	265,733	4.48
China	1,262,358,000	201	Han	1,033,057,000	81.8	1,146,505	0.11
Laos	5,163,000	82	Lao	3,000,000	58.1	26,704	0.89
Malay Peninsula	10,115,000	39	Malay	7,181,000	47.0	77,211	1.08
Myanmar	44,497,000	108	Burmese	21,553,000	48.4	214,430	0.99
Taiwan	21,507,000	22	Han	21,157,880	98.4	16,625	0.08
Thailand	60,300,000	75	Thai	45,815,000	76.0	195,743	0.43
Vietnam	77,562,000	93	Vietnamese	65,051,000	83.9	135,989	0.21
Total	1,492,218,000	639		1,202,747,680			
Means	186,527,250	80		150,343,460	68.6	259,867	1.03

Source: Figures from Grimes (2001).

China and their small size in Taiwan somewhat distorts the figures; otherwise for mainland Southeast Asia the figures would be even more homogeneous.

The geographical pattern is almost equally clear-cut; the great majority of the river basins and floodplains are occupied by a single ethnic group; the same one dominant in individual states. Such groups live by a single system, lowland rice cultivation, partly irrigated, partly capture of natural flooding. The remainder of the population, almost all, inhabits the mountainous regions and depends mainly on slash-and-burn agriculture. The broad assumption is that mountain agriculture and high levels of ethnic diversity were the norms in prehistory. Surprisingly, there is an almost complete absence of evidence for hunter–gatherer sites in the swampy lowlands and lacustrine flood plains of Southeast Asia (Higham 1989: 90). Pre-agricultural sites seemed to be confined to limestone rock shelters and coastal sites inhabited by fishing-peoples and aquatic produce collectors; the mangrove site of Khok Phanom Di is a striking example of the richness of this habitat. Only when rice was developed, with its high yields, high digestibility and potential for multiple annual crops, did the lowlands become attractive to inhabit. Even then, irrigation was limited; natural flooding and dry-season recession rice predominated.

Southeast Asia represents a major confluence of language phyla and recent research has tended to show that these phyla are all distinct. Hypotheses that used to link several phyla together are now regarded with some scepticism as much that was thought to be cognate vocabulary now appears to be ancient loanwords. Nonetheless, there may be arguments for higher order linkages as some chapters in this volume suggest (cf. Starosta (Chapter 11), Sagart (Chapters 9 and 10), Reid (Chapter 8)). The relative antiquity of these phyla is also under discussion; older research tended to assume that Sinitic (Chinese) was very ancient because of the continuity of material culture from the Neolithic; but it now seems that a greater ethnolinguistic diversity, previously characterised the region and has been assimilated by Sinitic culture and language.

One thread through this complex story of movement and interaction is the spread of rice cultivation; it can also connect past and present and help interpret the synchronic pattern of languages. Archaeology and linguistics combine to tell a story based on current evidence, acknowledging that archaeology is highly dynamic and that new finds may well alter our perception of chronology quite profoundly. This is not the first attempt to develop this narrative. Spencer (1963) describes the initial movement of rice into Indonesia and Snow et al. (1986) into the Philippines. Hanks (1972) and Watabe (1985) present overviews of rice ecology and dispersal in Southeast Asia. Zide and Zide (1976) reconstructed rice vocabulary in Munda while Hill (1977), Glover (1985) and Sorensen (1986) explored the issue from a historical point of view. Pejros and Shnirelman (1998) summarise some of the recent archaeological literature, as well synthesising the literature in Russian. Vovin (1998) used Japonic reconstruction to build hypotheses about the origin of rice cultivation in the Japanese islands.

Rice cultivation

Oryza is a worldwide genus with edible seeds that must have been collected in the wild since the evolution of hominids. It is often considered to have been domesticated twice,[1] once in the Southeast Asian region and once in India (see discussion in Crawford and Chen Shen 1998, Khush 1997, also Oka 1988). Sato (1996) has argued that the perennial Oryza rufipogon is ancestral to japonica and the annual O. navira gave rise to indica. Chen and Jiang (1997) report on rice remains before 8,000 BP at Jiahu in Henan in Central China.

Whether or not double domestication occurred, rice has developed a remarkable phenotypic diversity. Cambodia, for example, is considered to have over 2,000 rice varieties that are unique to the country. There are also two key groups of cultivars in terms of cooking quality, sticky and non-sticky rices. Sticky, glutinous rice appear to be more archaic and are still preferred in rural areas, but non-sticky rices are more widespread and more saleable (Roder et al. 1996).

Rice is also highly adapted to different agronomic strategies. Dry, upland or hill rice is extremely widespread throughout the region despite being very low-yielding compared with paddy rice. White (1995) argues that upland rice is a secondary development from wetland rice, although this perception may simply be an artefact of the sites for early rice. The deepwater rices are adapted to sudden flooding and can grow very quickly to outpace a rising river. Bangladesh is known for these cultivars but they occur throughout the region, albeit in small numbers. However, most common are the lowland rices, either irrigated or fed by rain and natural or managed flooding. These are often cultivated in association with ducks or fish and occasionally mixed with taro or lotus. Naturally flooded rice still predominates throughout the region, although irrigation is providing a growing percentage of all output. Even within floodland rice there are divisions between those who use bunded fields (where yields are relatively low) and dry-season flood recession rice (with much higher yields). Irrigated cultivars have been the major focus of attention for the IRRI, which has transformed rice agriculture throughout the region over the last 40 years. Less than 5 per cent of the rice production in Asia is traded in the international market, and China, India and Indonesia account for three-fourths of the global rice consumption. In 1993, rice represented some 88 per cent of all crops grown in Cambodia.

There has been considerable work attempting to date the domestication and spread of rice, most recently reviewed in Crawford and Shen (1998) and for China in Lu (Chapter 3, this volume). The website http://www.carleton.ca/~bgordon/Rice/paper_database.htm provides translations of all the most recent works on archaeological rice in China. Bellwood et al. (1992) review dates for Asian rice obtained from pottery temper. They note that it is not possible to be certain that these are domestic rice plants, although the cultural context of each makes this likely. Surprisingly, if it is the case that rice was domesticated twice, once in Northeast India and once in the Yangzi Valley, the grains of both seem to have

Table 2.2 Selected radiocarbon dates for rice in Southeast Asia

Country	Site	Location	Date	Type*	Reference
China	Xianrendong	Jiangxi Province	10,000 to 7,000 BC	I	Yan (1997) (quoted in Sagart 1999)
China	Pengtoushan	N. Hunan Province	6,000 BC	D	Yan Wenming (1991)
China	Hemudu	Zhejiang Province	5,000 BC	D	Chang (1989)
China	Lijiacun	Jiangxi Province	5,500 to 5,000 BC	D	Wu Yaoli (1996)
Taiwan	Ta-p'en-k'eng culture		c.3,000 BC	D	Tsang (1992) but see discussion in Bellwood (1997: 213)
India	Khairadih		2,404 BC	?	Bellwood et al. (1992)
Malaysia	Gua Sireh	Sarawak	1,950 BC	?	Bellwood et al. (1992)
Marianas	Chalan Piao	Saipan	1,733 to 1,263 BC	D	Hunter-Anderson et al. (1995)
Indonesia	Sembiran	Bali	790 BC	?	Bellwood et al. (1992)

Notes
* D Direct
  I Indirect
See Crawford and Shen (1998) and Lu (Chapter 3, this volume) for much greater detail on the Chinese sites.

spread and interchanged remarkably quickly. Both subspecies are found in Taiwan. Table 2.2 is a composite of recent sites and dates for rice.

Claims by Yan (1997) for finds of intermediates between wild and cultivated rice in Hunan and Jiangxi have yet to be widely accepted. Nonetheless, barring new findings, a pattern of rice domesticated first in the Yangzi Valley and spreading out from there seems credible.

States and debates

Debates about the prehistory of rice cultivation in Southeast Asia focus on two main issues, the link with language expansion and the role it has played in the rise of state systems. To look at a text like Spencer (1966) is to realise how much our analyses have moved on in recent decades. Spencer realised that there was a correlation between slash and burn agriculture and high ethnic diversity, but he conceptualised this in terms of 'remnant' and 'simpler cultural groups' even though he argued against the pejorative term 'primitive' (op. cit. 19).

Terwiel (1994) has shown the widespread role played by rice in myths of origin through Southeast Asia. Rice irrigation techniques are believed to have been introduced into Cambodia from India c.500 AD (Chandler 1993; Mabbett and Chandler 1995). One of the more well-known correlations between state-building and the spread of irrigated rice, the rise of the Angkor between the ninth and Fourteenth centuries, was associated with the construction of reservoirs and irrigation canals along rather Indian lines (Chandler 1993; Grunewald 1992). Fox and Ledgerwood (1999) have argued that the key innovation was dry-season flood recession rice both in Angkor and along the Mekong as far as the delta. This type of rice production is both high-yielding and sustainable. Revisionist historians have proposed that these public works were symbolic and ceremonial but this is more to do with the dynamics of the discipline; once the Angkor kingdom began to fold from the fifteenth century onwards the hydraulic works fell into decay and the Khmer rice farmers, who represented the backbone of the economy, moved to the southeast where production conditions were less labour-intensive.

It may be that to understand the present-day ethnographic pattern, the model must be inverted. Typically, rice production is associated with the spread and diversification of a phylum or subphylum. But the reverse may be the case; diversity is the background noise, the Brownian motion of language. Diversification occurs within any production system where population densities are low and techniques of restoring soil fertility restricted. Lowland rice cultivation drives the expansion of individual ethnic groups and accentuates their cultural divergence from the main body of a phylum. The typical output is then the single/numerous: many/few pattern observable across the region. Such divergence may then be at the root a state construction, whether a single state (as in Angkor) or a multistate system (as in the Malay Peninsula) (e.g. Allen 1997).

Higham (1998: 74) has a diagrammatic representation of the spread of rice, based on the assumption that it was first domesticated in the Yangzi Valley. This largely follows the view of Blust (1996a,b) and Diffloth (Chapter 5, this volume) that rice may underlie the expansion of Austro-Asiatic (AA). In this model, rice spreads out from the Pengtoushan area both south to the China coast and west to the highlands of Laos, where it begins to power the expansion of AA speakers. Four arrows, marked Proto-Munda, Proto-Mon, Proto-Khmer, and Proto-Viet carry the rice East, South and West. The following section discusses whether such a model is appropriate in the light of the linguistic evidence. However, it is enough to notice at present that such an approach mixes phylic branches with individual languages, a highly problematic approach in terms both of chronology and interpreting linguistic data.

One of the more surprising aspects of the geography of rice is its diffusion to the Marianas at a very early period (Craib and Farrell 1981). Hunter-Anderson et al. (1995) report the site of Chalan Piao on Saipan dated to c.3,500 BP. The presence of non-Hispanic rice vocabulary in Chamorro points to an AN source, apparently specifically the Philippines (Appendix Table 2.A1). The isolated occurrence of rice in this otherwise sea of vegetative farming systems suggested to the authors that rice was a 'prehistoric valuable' used in exchanges and ceremonial transactions.

Certainly its failure to spread to other regions of Micronesia argues for some type of specialised and location-specific use.

Linguistics and the history of rice cultivation

General

The principle of using the names of cultivated plants to trace their likely routes of introduction has been used within West Africa (Blench 1998; Blench et al. 1997) and South Asia (Southworth 1976). In Southeast Asia, Revel (1988) is a major compilation of rice terminology which attempts to lay out both the geography of rice names and to make historical deductions from them. Given the importance of this document it is more than somewhat surprising that it has not been used in the major texts on Southeast Asian prehistory published subsequently. Revel and her collaborators list seven terms for rice-associated vocabulary by language phylum and analyse the results as well as plotting these terms on an extensive series of maps. Only Japonic and Sino-Tibetan (ST) languages other than Sinitic are omitted. These data compilations are the basis of many of the observations that follow, although my interpretations sometimes differ sharply from those in the text.

Evidence for individual phyla

Although there are a variety of hypotheses concerning the higher order or macrophylic relationships of East Asian languages, these remain controversial and there are few crop reconstructions relevant to the present argument (although Sagart, this volume, proposes cognate forms for 'paddy', 'husked rice' and 'Setaria millet' in ST-AN). Recognised and uncontroversial phyla therefore remain the unit of analysis. Blench (1999) reviews the recent literature on the classification of the language phyla of the Indo-Pacific region and this will not be repeated here. The principal independent phyla of the region are:

Tibeto-Burman inc. Sinitic
Miao-Yao, also Hmong-Mien
Daic, also Tai-Kadai
Austro-Asiatic
Austronesian
Japonic

The linguistic data available for each phylum and subphylum is analysed below.

Sinitic

The Sinitic languages have a wide variety of terms reconstructible to PS, suggesting knowledge and cultivation of rice at the period of their dispersal. This

Table 2.3 Rice terms in Proto-Sinitic

Transplanted rice-seedling	秧 ya⁻₁	Not recorded in OC and perhaps a borrowing from Miao-Yao #¤ w i ˘_A
Rice-plant	稌 tu₂	OC
Paddy	稻 dao₄	Possibly originally a word for 'husked grain'. Only occurs in scattered modern lects.
Hulled rice	米 mi₃	Applies to millet in northern lects and perhaps
Cooked rice	飯 fan₄	Derived from a verb 'to eat'
Rice soup	粥 zhou₁	OC
Food, hulled rice	粲 can₄	OC. A regular nominal derivation from a verb 'to eat', closely resembling Miao-Yao and likely to be a loan into Miao-Yao

Source: Haudricourt (1988) and Sagart (1999: 180–2); Sinitic forms are cited in modern mandarin pin-yin transcription.

represents no major deduction, since the archaeology of rice in China suggests dates older than the likely initial break-up of Sinitic. Typical items either reconstructible or attested in OC are given in Table 2.3.

Unless our understanding of the dating of OC is very inaccurate, rice cultivation must have preceded Sinitic expansion throughout much of this region. This supports the scenario outlined by Haudricourt and Strecker (1991: 336) who posited that wet rice cultivation was already in place when the Sinitic expansion began and the Chinese, originally a nomadic pastoralist society, came into contact with and adopted rice early in their career. Haudricourt and Strecker (1991) propose that the incoming Chinese borrowed wetfield agriculture (including 'wet rice-field', 'young rice plant' and 'unhulled rice' and 'flour') from the in situ Miao-Yao speakers, but Sagart (1995) has argued that the loans proposed do not stand up under further analysis.

Tibeto-Burman

The phylum conventionally known as ST was characterised as a conjunction of Chinese and the TB languages, that is, all others, of which Tibetan is the most well-known. However, van Driem (1999, 2001) has recently argued that this is a cultural classification and that Chinese should be treated as coordinate with the Bodic languages, that is within TB. This is now called the 'Sino-Bodic' hypothesis. Without passing judgment on this hypothesis, the Sinitic languages, that is, Chinese and its dialects, can be treated as a group, since the Han certainly represent the main numerous, lowland rice-growing population.[2] Sinitic is treated later, but for the rest of TB, the analysis of rice terminology is problematic in the absence of any comparative source.

Miao-Yao

The Miao-Yao are today scattered across the south-central regions of China and into Northeast Thailand and look very much like a refugee population, nearly

Table 2.4 Rice terms in PMY

Rice-plant	#ɤ w i ˜ ₐ	Corresponds to OC 秧 *ᵇɤa˜ 'rice seedling'
Unhulled rice/sticky rice	#mbl t	Corresponds to OC 秫 *ᵇm-lut 'glutinous millet'
Hulled rice	#tshui˜ ᵦ	Corresponds to OC 粲 *ᵃtshan-s 'fine grain, food'
Cooked rice	h˜ a˜ ᴄ	Corresponds to OC 饟 *ᵇs-hna˜ ᵟ-s 'food as brought to labourers in the field, soldiers etc.'

Source: PMY forms are given in the reconstructions of Wang and Mao (1995); Chinese forms in the reconstruction of Sagart (1999).

a,b Syllable types in OC. See Sagart (1999) for possible interpretations of their significance.

Table 2.5 Rice terms in Daic

| Rice-plant | #ka/ca | Found in AA, notably Palaungic and Khmuic |
| Rice hulled, unhulled, cooked | #xau | Found throughout much of AA, notably Vietnamese gạo |

Source: Lévy (1988).

overwhelmed by the incoming Sinitic speakers. Miao-Yao languages are relatively homogeneous, leading most scholars to assume their diversification is relatively late (cf. Purnell 1970). However, their geographic fragmentation would be better explained by assuming an early date.

The Miao-Yao languages have several roots for rice that appear to be reconstructible to PMY, according to Wang and Mao (1995). These are shown in Table 2.4.

This also suggests that the PMY were familiar with wetfield rice cultivation rather than simply wild rice. Given their location and the clear evidence for rice cultivation in Miao-Yao culture, it may be that they were the original domesticators of rice.

Daic

Daic represents all the languages related to Thai – sometimes referred to as Tai-Kadai in standard sources. Ostapirat (2000) has recently proposed reconstructions for the 'Kra' languages, that is, Kadai, which are evidently rich in agricultural terminology. Table 2.5 shows the Daic rice terminology.

A very distinctive feature of Daic not shared elsewhere in the region is that hulled, unhulled and cooked rice are usually called by the same name. The lack of any very ramified terminology and the astonishing homogeneity between Daic lects argues very strongly that Proto-Daic speakers were not originally rice cultivators and that they borrowed rice from their AA neighbours during an early period of expansion.

Table 2.6 Rice terms in PAA

Rice (general)	*ɓa:	
Rice (general)	*sro:	Irregular reflexes make this less certain
Husked rice	*riˇ ko:	
Rice-grain	*sˇ~:	Reconstructs only to Proto-Mon-Khmer
Also:		
Swidden	*sre:	
Pestle	*ji nre:	

Source: Diffloth (p.c.).

Austro-Asiatic

AA lexemes for rice are much more complex than the other phyla so far discussed. Ferlus (1988) does not include the Munda and Nicobarese languages, but fortunately his data can be supplemented by the tables in Zide and Zide (1976). AA is important in the rice debate, because claims have been made for the reconstructibility of rice to PAA (notably in Zide and Zide 1976) and for the role of rice cultivation in the expansion of AA. Gerard Diffloth (p.c.) has kindly made available rice-related reconstructions from his extensive database which give a fuller picture than any published data (Table 2.6).

Ferlus (1988: 87 ff.) notes the high levels of diversity for rice terminology in AA. Zide and Zide (1976) first proposed a 'bimorphemic' reconstruction for Proto-Munda of #ruˇ and #kug for 'hulled rice', combined in some witnesses such as Khmu rˇ ko, Brou rakáw and Lawa li ko. Some of the words for 'rice-plant' seem to be borrowed into Daic, for example #ka, but many have no obvious etymology.

The absence of reconstructions for terms relating to wetfield rice and the presence of terms indicating pounding and swidden agriculture are surely significant. Rice was probably familiar to early AA speakers as a trade good, an opportunistic crop or as a valuable but was not the basis of subsistence. It was only when the wetfield cultivators such as the Viet and the Khmer split off from the main branch of AA that rice became dominant.

Austronesian

Whether the speakers of PAN had rice and if so of what type, is controversial. Most writers accept that AN languages were once spoken in Southeast China (see Chang and Goodenough (1996) for a summary of the arguments) and this has led to the idea that rice cultivation was the engine of early AN expansion (e.g. Bellwood 1985: 223). Blust (1976; 1995: 496 ff.), Mahdi (1994), Li (1994) and Wolff (1994) have all discussed the reconstruction of rice terminology in PAN. Three words are reconstructed as PAN (Table 2.7).

At least one cognate set (*Semay 'rice as food') is irregular in Formosan languages and *pajay 'rice plant' may be irregular too, possibly due to interaction

Table 2.7 PAN reconstructions of rice terminology

	Rice-plant	Husked rice	Cooked rice
Blust (1976)	*pajay	*beRas	*Semay
Li (1994)	*pag'ey	*beRat	*sem[ae]y
Mahdi (1994: 434)	*paji i	*Bi Ras	*Sumai/Hi mai
Wolff (1994)	*págey	*beʔ ás	*semáy

with Philippine languages (Li 1994). Formosan rice terminology is thus variable and uncertain. Mahdi's doublet reconstruction *Hi mai, not accepted by other writers, allows him to connect this PAN form with Miao-Yao. However, the only Miao-Yao forms cited in Haudricourt (1988) that resemble *Hi mai are the isolated Mien Úi i and Mun mei, both of which are more likely to be borrowings from Sinitic #mi. Sagart (Chapter 9, this volume) notes OC ^{b}mi-rat-s and presumably cognate Tibetan 'bras, which he links to AN *beRas.

Once down the AN family tree as far as PMP, words associated with rice become very numerous and reconstruction more certain. This situation would be best explained by supposing that the early AN migrants to Formosa had both upland rice and millets, but that the millets were central to their agriculture and indeed their ritual calendar (Arnaud 1974, 1988). There would be nothing very surprising about this; hill-rice is a minor opportunistic crop among many mountain peoples in Southeast Asia up to the present. The earliest rice occurs archaeologically at 2,500 BC,[3] first in the Taiwan straits and then in Taiwan proper, rather late for rice to be a key AN crop.

Reid (1994) in a detailed investigation of rice terminology among the Cordilleran languages of the northern Philippines, shows that all the terms associated with rice cultivation reconstruct to Proto-Cordilleran, suggesting very strongly that rice cultivation in the northern Philippines was contemporaneous with the first AN settlement. This includes the 'pondfield' construction typical of the region that underlies the extraordinary and apparently ancient terraces. Reid (1994: 372) also notes that few terms relating to pondfield construction have external cognates, leading to the conclusion that it was locally developed technology specific to the area.

The 'inland Austronesian' or Chamic languages in Vietnam, such as Jorai, Rhade and Roglai, seem to have largely borrowed their rice terms from Malay (Table 2.8).

Although Moken and the other sea-nomad languages of the Mergui archipelago are AN, they have borrowed heavily from non-AN languages. The term for 'rice-plant' pai/pie etc. is probably AN.

Rice is not generally cultivated in Oceania, but appears to have reached the Marianas as early as 3,500 BP (Hunter-Anderson et al. 1995). Nonetheless, Chamorro rice terminology is something of a puzzle. Although the archaeological evidence for ancient rice production on the Marianas appears to be solid, the

Table 2.8 Rice terms in Proto-Chamic

Gloss	Proto-Chamic	
Rice-plant	*paday	Malay padi
Glutinous rice	*ɟiip	No external cognates
Husked rice	*bra:s	PMP *beRas also widespread in ST (Sagart, Chapter 9, this volume)
Rice wine	*alak	Arabic perhaps via Malay
Cooked rice	*lasɟy	cf. Malay nasi

Source: Thurgood (1999).

affiliations of its rice vocabulary appear to be anything but archaic. Appendix Table 2.A2 shows these terms and those cognates that have been so far identified; these are suspiciously similar to Ilocano, suggesting not an ancient AN link, but rather lexical innovation or replacement from the sixteenth century onwards through contact with the Philippines. Reid (1998) has discussed the evidence for contact between Chamorro and Philippine languages; although the level of contact is significant, its date is hard to determine.

Austric

The Austric hypothesis, a proposed macrophylum that would unite AA and AN, although first proposed in 1906, remained largely in limbo until the 1990s when the work by Reid (1996, Chapter 8, this volume) and Blust (1996b) placed it back into serious consideration. Blust (op. cit) has put forward a scenario for the early expansion and spread of these two phyla, emerging from 'the area in which the Salween, Mekong and Yangzi run parallel at their narrowest watershed'. Blust believes that rice domestication is possible at this period but that the extensive exploitation of wild rice is equally likely. Higham (1996a: 71) says quite unambiguously 'the development of rice cultivation in the Yangzi valley took place among people who spoke languages of the Austric phylum' and he reaffirms this view in his interpretation of the archaeological evidence (Higham 1996b, 1998). It is certainly true that there is strong lexical evidence for AA loans into OC (Norman and Mei 1976) but this shows only that now-assimilated languages were once widespread in South China. This is not the place to evaluate the overall hypothesis, but it is important to state that there is no linguistic support for the place of rice in the diversification of Austric. A complete absence of similarities in the rice terminology of the two phyla suggests that rice cultivation emerged only after the two phyla diverged (cf. Tables 2.6 and 2.7).

Japonic

Japan is a pre-eminent rice culture, but Japan is notable for its lack of ethnic diversity, the only other language in the Japanese islands being the now-extinct

Table 2.9 Proto-Japonic rice terminology

Gloss	Reconstruction	Possible etymology
Rice-plant	*(z)ina-Ci/ *(h)ina-Ci 2.4	
Unhulled rice	*momi 2.1	
Hulled rice	*dona-Ci 2.1	
(Hulled) rice	*koma-Ci 2.3	Vovin compares to #com, Proto-Viet-Muong for 'cooked rice' but this seems unlikely because of the change in meaning and the isolation of this term within AA
Cooked rice	*ipi 2.3	cf. Palaungic # i p- 'cooked rice'
Ear of grain	*pwo 1.3a	
Ricefield	*ta 1.3a	
Rice bran	*nuka ?2.3	
Flour	*kwo 1.3a	
Starch rice Glue	*nori 2.3	

Source: Adapted from Vovin (1998: 368).

Notes
Numerical notations represent different PJ noun accent classes (H – high pitch, L – low pitch, X – number of moras in a word): 1.1: H-H, 1.2: H-L, 1.3a: L-L, 1.3b: L-H, 2.1: HH-H, 2.2a: HH-L, 2.2b: HL-L, 2.3: LL-L, 2.4: LH-H, 2.5: LH-L.

Ainu (Hudson 1994). Japanese rice terminology has been investigated by Vovin (1998: 366–78). Japanese lects are extremely homogeneous and indicate that the migrants who brought rice to Japan had fully established wetfield rice. Table 2.9 shows Vovin's reconstructions of Proto-Japonic and some etymological speculations on their external affiliations.

Vovin argues for AA links, but the truth is that most Japonic terms seem to have no external cognates at all. What parallels there are could as easily be early loans as evidence of any cultural affiliation.

Summary of linguistic evidence

The main points emerging from the linguistic analysis are as follows:

1 There are definite similarities between OC and Miao-Yao wet rice vocabulary and there was early interaction between the groups. The direction of loans is debated, but it seems possible that the Miao-Yao or their predecessors were the original domesticators of rice in the Yangzi Valley and were forced into their present-day hill locations by Sinitic expansion.
2 Daic languages show little diversification of rice terminology and clear similarities with their AA neighbours. The homogeneity of Daic suggests an expansion much later than AA and early borrowings into Daic of rice terms.

3   PAA speakers were familiar with rice but it is unlikely that their expansion was initially driven by the adoption of rice cultivation, which may have been an upland crop or even simply a traded valuable. However, AA speakers such as the Khmer and Viet became major rice cultivators as part of the process of diverging from the main body of the phylum. Munda speakers probably also had rice when they began to move westward.
4   The Austronesians seem to have had some form of rice when they began to colonise Taiwan, although evidence for wetfield systems is lacking and they probably cultivated upland rice. Rice systems today in Taiwan have apparently borrowed elements from the Philippines. Rice cultivation really develops once the migrating Austronesians reach the Philippines; the linguistic evidence appears to point to a largely indigenous development of agronomic techniques.
5   Although there is evidence for ancient rice cultivation in the Marianas, the rice vocabulary in use today seems to come from Philippine languages, notably Ilokano, probably pointing to a major influence of early migrants on a rather marginal crop.
6   Japanese rice systems are largely sui generis: few external parallels seem to indicate links with other rice systems. This suggest that however the original mainland Japanese acquired rice agriculture, it was from a now-vanished source.

Building a model

The ethnodemography of Southeast Asia presents a strongly realised pattern of single groups developing irrigated or rain-fed cultivation and expanding into lowland regions previously sparsely populated. The resident groups, presumably fishing-peoples, were driven out or assimilated and marked population increases occurred. Ethnolinguistic diversity was then confined to mountainous regions. It is doubtful if mountains were refuge areas as was supposed in earlier literature; their diversity is 'natural' and the ethnic homogeneity of the lowlands a later development. Modern rice cultivation techniques have tipped this balance still further towards the rice cultivators.

Rice may not have been the direct engine of expansion of any of Southeast Asia's language phyla, despite its dominant role today. In the early period, the two millets, Panicum and Setaria, were probably the dominant crops with upland rice a minor part of the cultigen repertoire. However, once experience was gained with rice in lowland areas, it functioned as a localised driver of demographic expansion. Hence the pattern of homogeneity in the river basins and coastal wetlands of Southeast Asia. Much archaeological debate has evolved around state formation and irrigated cultivation evidently makes state formation more feasible. But the two are not necessarily connected, as several studies have shown; populations can increase slowly but inexorably within any sort of political context; what counts is the techno-environmental conditions.

Much further work remains to be done, both archaeologically and linguistically, to clarify the picture. In particular, much more rice vocabulary relating to different production systems could help elucidate what type of rice agronomy was adopted by which ethnic group and how such systems spread.

Appendix

Rice vocabularies

Table 2.A1 Rice in Munda languages

Language	Raw, husked	Paddy, unhusked
Sora	ro l ko	sYŕo kond ‡m
Gorum	rũ l k (-aja l)	kundem (-ar)
Gta¤	rko ¤ /-ro	condia ¤, kia, ya
Remo	ru l ku /l kuk'	ker ~l /-ker
Gutob	rukug	kero l /-ker
Kharia	rumkub	ba ¤a, bag
Juang	ru l kub	bua
Mundari	cauli	baba
Santali	here (but ru rul 'to husk')	hurhu, horo
Ho	ruu l 'to husk'	n.a.
Korku	rum 'to husk'	baba
Asuri, Turi	n.a.	hu ru ('paddy plant')
Birhor	n.a	hu ru ('paddy plant')

Source: Zide and Zide (1976).

Table 2.A2 Rice vocabulary in Chamorro

Chamorro	Meaning	External cognates
alaguan	Rice soup	cf. Philippines/Borneo languages, for example, Timugon linagas
bibenka	Rice-pudding	cf. Ilokano bib íngka,
fa'i	Growing rice	reflex of the *pari , *padi forms found throughout much of the Philippines and Borneo
fama ayan	Ricefield	?
hineksa	Cooked rice	?
potu	Rice-cake	cf. Ilokano púto
pugas	Uncooked rice	cf. Philippines/Borneo languages, for example, Ilokano, Timugon bag ás
timulo	Pile of rice stalks	
tinitu	Hulled rice	cf. Ilokano forms for 'cooked rice' ¤inutu although the initial t- is a problem

Source: Hunter-Anderson et al. (1995) and Rubino (2000).

Acknowledgements

The first version of this chapter was given as a paper at the Perigueux meeting, and a revised version was presented at the Institute of Archaeology, London on 11 October 2001. Many thanks to Laurent Sagart, George van Driem, Peter Bellwood, Ian Glover, Victor Paz, Janice Stargardt, Waruno Mahdi, Gerard Diffloth and Dorian Fuller, who have all commented on a preliminary version. I have tried to respond to their comments although they should not be held responsible for my interpretations.

Abbreviations

AA	Austro-Asiatic
AN	Austronesian
IRRI	International Rice Research Institute
OC	Old Chinese
PAA	Proto-Austro-Asiatic
PAN	Proto-Austronesian
PMP	Proto-Malayo-Polynesian
PMY	Proto-Miao-Yao
PS	Proto-Sinitic
ST	Sino-Tibetan
TB	Tibeto-Burman

Notes

1 Africa also domesticated rice quite separately, and Oryza glaberrima is a widespread staple in the west of West Africa. However, it is not interfertile with the high-yielding Asian rices, hence these have become dominant in West Africa over the last 50 years.
2 Van Driem (p.c.) notes that there appears to be little in common between Sinitic and other TB rice terminology.
3 A date later than 2,500 BC for alluvium near Tainan has just been reported (Tsang, Chapter 4, this volume).

Bibliography

Allen, J. (1997) 'Inland Angkor, coastal Kedah: landscapes, subsistence systems and state development in early Southeast Asia', Bulletin of the Indo-Pacific Prehistory Association 16: 79–87.
Arnaud, V. (1974) 'La culture du millet chez les Yami, population austronésienne de Botel Tobago', Journal d'Agriculture Traditionnelle et de Botanique Appliquée 10–12: 275–311.
Arnaud, V. (1988) 'Les langues de Formose', in N. Revel (ed.) Le riz en Asie du sud-est, Vol. I, 101–12, Paris: EHESS.
Bellwood, P., Gillespie, R., Thompson, G.B., Vogel, J.S., Ardika, I.W. and Ipo Datan (1992) 'New dates for prehistoric Asian rice', Asian perspectives 31, 2: 161–70.
Blench, R.M. (1998) 'The diffusion of New World Cultigens in Nigeria', in M. Chastenet (ed.) Plantes et paysages d'Afrique 165–210, Paris: Karthala.

Blench, R.M. (1999) 'Language phyla of the Indo-Pacific region: recent research and classification', Bulletin of the Indo-Pacific Prehistory Association 18: 59–76.

Blench, R.M., Williamson, K. and Connell, B. (1997) 'The diffusion of maize in Nigeria: a historical and linguistic investigation', Sprache und Geschichte in Afrika XIV: 19–46.

Blust, R.A. (1976) 'Austronesian culture history: some linguistic inferences and their relations to the archaeological record', World Archaeology 8, 1: 19–43.

—— (1995) 'The Prehistory of the Austronesian-speaking peoples: a view from language', Journal of World History 9, 4: 453–510.

—— (1996a) 'Austronesian culture history: the window of language', in Ward H. Goodenough (ed.) Prehistoric Settlement of the Pacific (Transactions of the American Philosophical Society, Vol. 86, Pt. 5), 28–35, Philadelphia: American Philosophical Society.

—— (1996b) 'Beyond the Austronesian homeland: the Austric hypothesis and its implications for archaeology', in Ward H. Goodenough (ed.) Prehistoric Settlement of the Pacific (Transactions of the American Philosophical Society, Vol. 86, Pt. 5), 117–60, Philadelphia: American Philosophical Society.

Chandler, D.P. (1993) A History of Cambodia, 2nd edn, Colorado: Westview Press.

Chang, Kwang-chih and Ward H. Goodenough (1996) 'Archaeology of south-eastern coastal China and its bearing on the Austronesian homeland', in Ward H. Goodenough (ed.) Prehistoric Settlement of the Pacific (Transactions of the American Philosophical Society, Vol. 86, Pt. 5), 36–56, Philadelphia: American Philosophical Society.

Chang, T.T. (1989) 'Domestication and the spread of the cultivated rices', in D.R. Harris and G.C. Hillman (eds) Foraging and Farming: The Evolution of Plant Exploitation, 408–17, London: Unwin Hyman.

Chen, B. and Jiang, Q. (1997) 'Antiquity of the earliest cultivated rice in central China and its implications', Economic Botany 51: 307–10.

Craib, J. and Farrell, N. (1981) 'On the question of prehistoric rice cultivation in the Mariana islands', Micronesica 17, 1: 1–9.

Crawford, S.W. and Chen Shen (1998) 'The origins of rice agriculture: recent progress in East Asia', Antiquity 72: 858–66.

Ferlus, M. (1988) 'Les langues austroasiatiques', in N. Revel (ed.) Le riz en Asie du sud-est, Vol. I, 81–94, Paris: EHESS.

Fox, J. and Ledgerwood, J. (1999) 'Dry-season flood-recession rice in the Mekong Delta: two thousand years of sustainable agriculture?', Asian Perspectives 38, 1: 37–50.

Glover, I.C. (1985) 'Some problems relating to the domestication of rice in Asia', in V.N. Misra and P. Bellwood (eds) Recent Advances in Indo-Pacific Prehistory, 265–74, Leiden: Brill.

Grimes, Barbara F. (2001) Ethnologue Language Family Index (14th edition), Dallas: Summer Institute of Linguistics.

Grunewald, F. (1992) Essai d'analyse historique de l'évolution de l'agriculture cambodgienne, Phnom Penh: GRET.

Hanks, L.M. (1972) Rice and Man. Agricultural Ecology in Southeast-Asia, Chicago & New York: Aldine.

Haudricourt, A.G. (1988) 'Les dialectes chinois', in N. Revel (ed.) Le riz en Asie du sud-est, Vol. I, 35–42, Paris: EHESS.

Haudricourt, A.G. and Strecker D. (1991) 'Hmong-Mien (Miao-Yao) loans in Chinese', T'oung Pao, LXXVII, 4–5: 335–41.

Higham C. (1989) The Archaeology of Mainland Southeast Asia, Cambridge: Cambridge University Press.
—— (1996a) The Bronze Age of Southeast Asia, Cambridge: Cambridge University Press.
—— (1996b) 'Archaeology and linguistics in Southeast Asia: implications of the Austric hypothesis', in Bulletin of the Indo-Pacific Prehistory Association 14: 110–18.
—— (1998) 'Archaeology, linguistics and the expansion of the Southeast Asian Neolithic', in R.M. Blench and M. Spriggs (eds) Archaeology and Language II, 103–14, London: Routledge.
Higham, C. and Thosarat, R. (1998) Prehistoric Thailand: From Early Settlement to Sukothai, Bangkok: River Books.
Hill, R.D. (1977) Rice in Malaya: A Study in Historical Geography, Kuala Lumpur: Oxford University Press.
Hudson, Mark (1994) 'The linguistic prehistory of Japan: some archaeological speculations', Anthropological Science 102, 3: 231–55.
Hunter-Anderson, R.L., Thompson, G.B. and Moore, D.R. (1995) 'Rice as a prehistoric valuable in the Mariana Islands, Micronesia', Asian Perspectives 34, 1: 69–89.
Khush, G.S. (1997) Origin, dispersal and variation of rice, Plant Molecular Biology 35: 25–34.
Lévy, A. (1988) 'Les langues Thai', in N. Revel (ed.) Le riz en Asie du sud-est, Vol. I, 47–80, Paris: EHESS.
Li, Paul Jen-Kuei (1994) 'Some plant names in Formosan languages', in A.K. Pawley and M.D. Ross (eds) Austronesian Terminologies: Continuity and Change, 241–66, Pacific Linguistics C-127. Canberra: ANU.
Mabbett, I. and Chandler, D. (1995) The Khmers, Oxford: Blackwell.
Mahdi, W. (1994) 'Some Austronesian maverick protoforms with culture-historical implications-II', Oceanic Linguistics 33, 2: 431–89.
Norman, J. and Mei, T. (1976) 'The Austroasiatics in ancient south China: some lexical evidence', Monumenta Serica 32: 274–301.
Oka, H.I. (1988) Origin of Cultivated Rice, Amsterdam: Elsevier.
Ostapirat, W. (2000) Proto-Kra, Linguistics of the Tibeto-Burman Area 23, 1.
Pejros, I. and Shnirelman, V. (1998) 'Japanese rice agriculture terminology and linguistic affiliation of Yayoi culture', in R.M. Blench and M. Spriggs (eds) Archaeology and Language II, 379–89, London: Routledge.
Purnell, H.C. Jr (1970) Towards a Reconstruction of Proto-Miao-Yao, unpublished Ph.D., Cornell University.
Reid, Lawrence A. (1994) 'Terms for rice agriculture and terrace-building in some Cordilleran languages of the Philippines', in A.K. Pawley and M.D. Ross (eds) Austronesian Terminologies: Continuity and Change, 363–99, Pacific Linguistics C-127, Canberra: ANU.
—— (1996) 'The current state of linguistic research on the relatedness of the language families of East and South-East Asia', Bulletin of the Indo-Pacific Prehistory Association 15: 87–91.
—— (1998) 'On linguistic evidence for early Philippine contact with Chamorro,' Paper presented at the 16th Congress of the Indo-Pacific Prehistory Association.
Revel, N. (ed.) (1988) Le riz en Asie du sud-est (3 vols), Paris: EHESS.
Roder, W., Keoboulapha, B., Vannalath, K. and Phouvaranh, B. (1996) Glutinous rice and its importance for hill farmers in Laos, Economic Botany 5: 401–08.
Rubino, C.R.G. (2000) Ilocano Dictionary and Grammar, Hawai'i University Press.

Sagart, L. (1995) 'Chinese "buy" and "sell" and the direction of borrowings between Chinese and Hmong-Mien: a response to Haudricourt and Strecker', T'oung Pao, LXXXI, 4–5: 328–42.

—— (1999) The Roots of Old Chinese, Amsterdam: John Benjamins.

Sato, Y. (1996) Origin of Rice and Rice Cultivation Based on DNA Analysis, Tokyo: NHK Books.

Snow, B.E., Shutler, R., Nelson, D.E., Vogel, J.S. and Southon, J.R. (1986) 'Evidence of early rice cultivation in the Philippines', Philippine Quarterly of Culture and Society 14: 3–11.

Sorensen, P. (1986) 'On the problem of early rice in Southeast Asia', in I. Norlund, S. Cederroth and I. Gerdin (eds) Rice Societies: Asian Problems and Prospects, 267–79, London: Curzon Press.

Southworth, F.C. 1976. 'Cereals in South Asian prehistory: the linguistic evidence', in K.A.R. Kennedy and G. Possehl (eds) Ecological Backgrounds of South Asian Prehistory, 52–75, Ithaca: Cornell University Press.

Spencer, J.E. (1963) 'The migration of rice from mainland southeast Asia into Indonesia', in J. Barrau (ed.) Plants and the Migration of Pacific Peoples, 83–89, Honolulu: Bishop Museum Press.

—— (1966) Shifting Cultivation in Southeastern Asia, Berkeley & Los Angeles: University of California Press.

Terwiel, B.J. (1994). 'Rice legends in mainland Southeast Asia: history and ethnography in the study of myths of origin', Contributions to Southeast Asian Ethnography 10: 5–36.

Thurgood, G. (1999) From Ancient Cham to Modern Dialects, Honolulu: University of Hawai'i Press.

Tsang, C.-H. (1992) Archaeology of the P'eng-hu Islands, Taipei: Academia Sinica.

van Driem, G. (1999) 'Sino-Tibetan', Bulletin of the Indo-Pacific Prehistory Association 18: 59–76.

—— (2001) Languages of the Himalayas: An Ethnolinguistic Handbook, Handbuch der Orientalistik, Leiden: Brill.

Vovin, A. (1998) 'Japanese rice agriculture terminology and linguistic affiliation of Yayoi culture', in R.M. Blench and M. Spriggs (eds) Archaeology and Language II, 366–78, London: Routledge.

Wang, F.S. (1994) Reconstruction of the Proto-Miao Language, [In Chinese and English] Tokyo: Institute for the Study of the Languages and Cultures of Asia and Africa.

Wang, F.S. and Mao, Z.W. (1995) Miao-yao yu guyin gouni, Beijing: Zhongguo Shehui Kexue.

Watabe, T. (1985) 'Origin and dispersal of rice in Asia', East Asian Cultural Studies 24, 1–4: 33–9.

White, J.C. (1995) 'Modelling the development of early rice agriculture: ethnoecological perspectives from northeast Thailand', Asian Perspectives, 34, 1: 37–68.

Wolff, John U. (1994) 'The place of plant names in reconstructing proto-Austronesian', in A.K. Pawley and M.D. Ross (eds) Austronesian Terminologies: Continuity and Change, 511–40, Pacific Linguistics C-127, Canberra: ANU.

Wu, Y.L. (1996) 'Prehistoric rice agriculture in the Yellow River Valley', Bulletin of the Indo-Pacific Prehistory Association 15: 223–4.

Yan, W.M. (1991) 'China's earliest rice agriculture remains', Bulletin of the Indo-Pacific Prehistory Association 10: 118–26.

Zide, A.R.K. and Zide N.H. (1976) 'Proto-Munda cultural vocabulary: evidence for early agriculture', in P.N. Jenner, L.C. Thompson and S. Starosta (eds) Austro-Asiatic Studies, Part II, 1295–334, Honolulu: University of Hawai'i.

3

THE ORIGIN AND DISPERSAL OF AGRICULTURE AND HUMAN DIASPORA IN EAST ASIA

Tracey L.-D. Lu

Archaeological data suggest that millet and rice were domesticated indigenously in the Yellow and the Yangzi Valleys by 8,500 BP (Lu 1999). Prosperous Neolithic and historical cultures developed in the Yellow and the Yangzi Valleys based on millet and rice farming. Current archaeological data suggest that Chinese civilisation was founded on both these cereals, as remains were found in Zaojiaoshu of the Xia dynasty, and in Anyang of the late Shang dynasty in the middle Yellow Valley (Chen 1993, 2000; Ye et al. 2000). Foxtail and broomcorn millets as well as rice were sacred cereals in Bronze Age China, used for ancestor worship and other ritual activities (Chen 1993).

Once the transition to farming had occurred, millet and rice quickly spread to adjacent areas in East and Southeast Asia. Such expansion might also be related to prehistoric human diasporas in these regions. Although the exact routes and the timing of these expansions are still under debate, it is certain that millet or rice production was also the foundation of many ancient civilisations in East and Southeast Asia.

Research progress on the origin of agriculture in the Yellow and Yangzi Valleys

Farming societies in both the Yellow and the Yangzi Valleys seem to have made their appearance quite suddenly. Archaeological discoveries dated to between 12,000 and 9,000 BP in these two river valleys are very scanty. Yet many farming societies dated after c.8,500 BP have been located in both regions. My survey of archaeological data published to date (Table 3.1) indicates that remains of foxtail millet occur in 50 Neolithic sites while remains of broomcorn millet are reported from 7 Neolithic sites. Rice has been recovered from 130 Neolithic sites, including the well-known Pengtoushan, Bashidang and Jiahu assemblages.

Archaeological and experimental research suggests that there must have been a period of intensive gathering of grass seeds before the beginning of grass cultivation, which eventually led to domestication (Anderson 1999). Archaeological evidence for such gathering activities now seems to have emerged in two regions. In the Yellow Valley, the second season of excavation at the Nanzhuangtou site in 1997 yielded more than 47 potsherds, seven grinding slabs and rollers, bone artefacts, as well as plant and animal remains (Guo and Li 2000). It is reported that the pottery vessels found at Nanzhuangtou consist of round-bottom and flat-bottom pots, the former still bearing charcoal on the surface, indicating their use as cooking utensils. Potsherds were also found at Hutouliang, another site in Hebei Province, during the excavation in 1995–97, but only flat-bottom vessels are present there, and it is inferred that they were used for storage. Both Nanzhuangtou and Hutouliang are dated to approximately 10,000 BP (Guo and Li 2000). It has been argued that the origin of pottery might have related the human gathering and consuming of substantial quantities of grass seeds (Lu 1999). The grinding slabs and rollers found in Nanzhuangtou in association with pottery seem to suggest the possibility of seed gathering during the period 10,000 9,000 BP, although further research will have to confirm this. In addition, both round- and flat-bottom vessels are found in Nanzhuangtou. These pottery vessels, grinding slabs and rollers are typical artefacts of the succeeding Neolithic cultures in the same region, namely the Cishan and Peiligang cultures (Lu 1999).

In addition, use-wear research conducted in 1999 on artefacts found in the Xiachuan assemblage, middle Yellow Valley, indicates that the prehistoric residents gathered wild grasses between 18,000 and 13,000 BP (Lu 2000). The polish on several flint flakes of the Xiachuan assemblage is identical to those on replicas used for reaping panicles of green foxtail. If people gathered only the panicles, the purpose of this gathering could only be for the grains as food resources. It seems that gathering wild grass for food did exist in the Yellow Valley prior to the beginning of millet cultivation.

In the Yangzi Valley and adjacent areas, phytolith analysis and analysis of macro-remains now suggest that wild rice was gathered at Xianrendong and Diaotonghuan (Zhao 1998), at Yuchanyan which is at the southern edge of the middle Yangzi Valley (Yuan 2000), and at Niulandong cave, Guangdong Province, at the northern edge of South China (Yingde Museum and Zhongshan University 2000) (Map 3.1). All these assemblages are dated to around or before 10,000 BP (Yan 2000; Yingde Museum and Zhongshan University 2000). Early pottery with cord-marking has been found in all these sites, further suggesting the likely causal link between the origin of pottery and gathering activities, although such activities in South China could also include the gathering and cooking of shells (Lu 2001). The stone tools found in the rice-gathering area are basically pebble tools, completely different from the lithic tradition in the Yellow Valley, but similar to the subsequent local Neolithic cultures.

In summary, it seems that there were two centres of grass gathering during the period from the terminal Pleistocene to the early Holocene. Wild rice was gathered in an area between latitudes 24 and 29 N, while other grass seeds were gathered in another area, between latitudes 35 and 40 N (Map 3.1). The toolkits in these two centres are completely different, but the cultural continuity in each centre is quite obvious (Lu 1999).

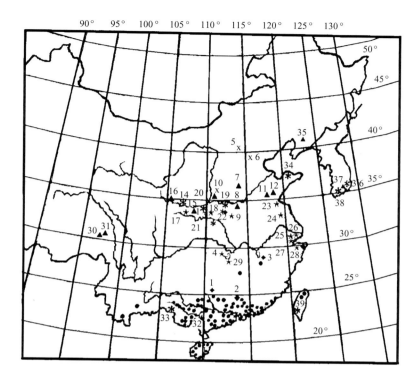

Map 3.1 Archaeological sites in the text.

Legend
- Current loci of common wild rice (O. rufipogon) apart from the major distribution.
  Prehistoric loci of common wild rice.
x Archaeological sites of the upper Palaeolithic.
★ Archaeological sites where cultivated rice (O. sativa) is found.
∗ Archaeological sites where both cultivated rice and millet are found.
▲ Archaeological sites where cultivated millets are found.

Sites
1. Yuchanyan 14,000 to 10,000 BP? 2. Niulian Cave 12,000 to 10,000 BP? 3. Xianrendong/Diaotonghuan 14,000 to 12,000 BP? 4. Pengtoushan/Bashidang 9,500 to 8,000 BP. 5. Hutouliang 11,000 BP . 6. Nanzhuangtou 11,000 to 9,000 BP. 7. Cishan c.8,000 to 7,500 BP. 8. Peiligang c.8,000 to 7,500 BP 9. Jiahu c.8,400 to 7,600 BP. 10. Xiachuan 18,000 to 13,000 BP. 11. Beixin 7,400 to 6,400 BP. 12. Dadunzi c.6,800 to 6,360 BP. 13. Huaxian 5,000 to 4,000 BP. 14. Anban c.4,852 to 4,487 BP. 15. Banpo 6,065 to 5,490 BP. 16. Dadiwan 7,150 to 4,900 BP. 17. Lijiancun c.7,179 to 6,796 BP. 18. Xiawanggang c.7,210 to 4,490 BP. 19. Dahecun c.5,500 to 4,400 BP. 20. Xiyincun 7,000 to 5,000 BP. 21. Qinglongquan c.5,350 to 4,148 BP. 22. Lilou c.4,142 to 3,725 BP. 23. Lianyungang about 7,000 BP. 24. Longqiuzhuang 7,000 to 5,500 BP. 25. Xudun 5,605 to 4,610 BP. 26. Songze 5,330 to 4,550 BP. 27. Luojiajiao 6,220 to 6,080 BP. 28. Hemudu c.7,200 to 6,400 BP. 29. Chengtoushan 6,500 to 4,500 BP. 30. Chengdou Karuo 5,555 to 4,750 BP. 31. Changguogou 3,370 BP. 32. Dingsishan 6,500 BP. 33. Gantuoyan approximately 4,000 BP. 34. Qixia cal. 4,873 to 3,780 BP. 35. Xinle 6,620 to 6,150 BP. 36. Daundong 2,510 to 2,000 BP. 37. Tongsamdong 4,590 BP. 38. Nam River localities 4,060 to 2,800 BP. 39. Nan-kuan-li approx. 5,000 BP.

Sources: Crawford and Lee 2003: The Institute of Archaeology CASS 1991 C14 dates in Chinese Archaelogy (1965–91). Beijing: Cultural Relics Publishing House; Lu 1999; Fu 2001; Tsang 2003, Chapter 4, this voulume.

By 8,500 BP rice and millet were cultivated in the Yellow and the Yangzi Valleys respectively. Jiahu, the oldest and most advanced archaeological assemblage of the Peiligang culture found to date, is a rice-farming society. It has been proposed that the Jiahu population might have been farmers expanding from the middle Yangzi Valley towards the Yellow Valley who were forced to become millet cultivators due to the drier and colder climate there (Bellwood, Chapter 1, this volume). This could certainly be so if the Jiahu archaeological assemblage was similar to the Pengtoushan-Bashidang assemblage in the Yangzi. However, the artefacts, and in particular the toolkit of Jiahu are completely different from those of the rice farmers in the middle Yangzi Valley (Lu 1999). Such differences clearly show that the Jiahu and Pengtoushan-Bashidang rice farmers were two distinct groups.

Biological research suggests that the progenitor of foxtail millet is green foxtail (Setaria viridis) (Gao and Chen 1988; Li et al. 1945), and that of broomcorn millet is wild broomcorn grass (Panicum spp.) (Chai 1999). The ancestor of domesticated rice is still under debate, as some scholars suggest the perennial wild rice (Oryza rufipogon), while others argue for the annual wild rice, Oryza spp. (Lu 1999). All these wild grasses are widely found in Eurasia. Green foxtail is found today in both the Yellow and Yangzi Valleys, as well as in South China. Wild rice is mainly found in South China, with a few stands in the Yangzi Valley (The National Survey Group of Wild Rice 1984). But wild rice was reported from the Lilou site in the middle Yellow Valley at around 4,000 BP and from Hemudu, in the lower Yangzi Valley at around 7,000 BP (Chen 1993) (Map 3.1). Given the warmer climate between 7,000 and 4,000 BP, such a distribution is not surprising. It is also claimed that wild rice was present in Xianrendong and Diaotonghuan prior to 10,000 BP (Zhao 1998).

How were the progenitors of millets and rice domesticated? What techniques would have been required for initial cultivation of wild grasses? Was sedentarisation a necessary condition for the cultivation, human selection and eventual domestication of these grasses? To obtain data to answer these questions, a cultivation experiment on green foxtail (Setaria viridis) was conducted from 1999 to the present. A cultivation experiment on perennial wild rice began in the spring of 2001. The location of the millet experiment is a small village in the loess area of the middle Yellow Valley. Seeds of green foxtail were broadcast, then left unattended until harvesting time after four months. The preliminary outcome suggests that it is possible for foragers to cultivate green foxtail initially, and that sedentarisation is not a necessary condition for the beginning of cultivation, as green foxtail requires little attention after sowing, and the production can be more than 15 times that of the seeds sown if the climate is balanced (Lu 2002a). However, association with a particular area or territory is required if the so-called 'first farmers' are to return to harvest their plants (Lu 2002a).

In summary, we now know that grass seeds were gathered in the Yellow and Yangzi Valleys, as well as in South China. We also know that cultivation would have meant only limited efforts as long as the first farmers did not rely upon cultivated grass seeds as their only food resource. The cultural continuity and sequence in the Yangzi Valley now seems clearer than that in the Yellow Valley. However, we still cannot be certain at this stage whether millet and rice farming originated in one or two centres.

Table 3.1 Remains of millet and rice in the Neolithic Yellow and Yangzi Valleys

	Yellow Valley		Yangzi Valley		South China		Other areas		Total
	Sites	%	Sites	%	Sites	%	Sites	%	
Foxtail millet	43	86.00	1	2.00	0		6	12.00	50
Broomcorn millet	5	71.43	0		0		2	28.57	7
Rice	21	16.15	98	75.38	6	4.62	5	3.85	130

Source: Chen 1993, 2000.

Table 3.2 Remains of millet and rice in the Yellow and Yangzi Valleys during the Xia and Shang dynasties

	Yellow Valley		Yangzi Valley		South China		Other areas		Total
	Sites	%	Sites	%	Sites	%	Sites	%	
Foxtail millet	3	42.86	0		0		4	57.14	7
Broomcorn millet	3	100.00	0		0		0		3
Rice	4	44.44	3	33.33	0		2	22.22	9

Source: Chen 1993, 2000.

The expansion of farming and human diasporas in East and Southeast Asia

The expansion of farming and its relation to human diasporas in East and Southeast Asia, particularly with respect to the origin and migration of the Austronesians in this region, has been a topic of lively debate since the 1960s or even earlier (Bellwood 1997; Blench, Chapter 2, this volume; Tsang, Chapter 4, this volume). Archaeological discoveries have continuously provided new data, while at the same time also raising new questions.

A summary of remains of foxtail and broomcorn millets and rice in Neolithic and early bronze age sites of the Yellow and Yangzi Valleys as well as in South China to this date is given in Tables 3.1 and 3.2. Of course, these discoveries cannot be taken as an accurate representation of early millet and rice farming in these areas, as the preservation and discovery of organic materials in archaeological sites are subject to many conditions, such as proto- and post-depositional conditions, prehistoric human behaviour, archaeologist's skill, etc. However, some indications on the expansion of millet and rice agriculture in this vast area can still be derived from these data.

The spread of millet cultivation

Current data seem to suggest that the first wave of expansion of millet cultivation went along the Yellow River, from the middle to the lower Yellow Valley, and then expanded south from the Yellow Valley. Domesticated foxtail millet is found in the Beixin assemblage, lower Yellow Valley, c.7,000 BP; in the Dadunzi assemblage between the lower Yellow and the lower Yangzi Valley by c.6,800 BP, in the Qinglongquan assemblage in the Yangzi Valley by c.5,000–4,100 BP, and in the Gantuoyan site in South China by 4,000 BP (Wei et al. 2001; Map 3.1).

The second dispersal wave of millet cultivation went beyond present-day mainland China. Millet cultivation may have reached South Korea by c.5,000 BP (Crawford and Lee 2003), and Taiwan by 4,500 BP (Tsang, Chapter 4, this volume). Linguistic analysis suggests that the speakers of PAN were 'growing rice and millet, with domesticated pigs and dogs' (Bellwood 1997: 9). Ethnographic data suggests that millet is perceived as a sacred grain, and is used ceremonially by the AN-speaking ethnic groups of Taiwan (Fogg 1983). Does the special status of millet among Taiwan's indigenous peoples indicate that they have received cultural influences from the Yellow Valley, which is the heartland of millet domestication? Yet recent archaeological discoveries suggest that they were from South China (Ferrell 1966; Tsang, Chapter 4, this volume). When and how was millet cultivation brought to Taiwan? This is a question relating to the dispersal of PAN.

Ethnographic data suggested that millet cultivation was brought to Taiwan before rice farming (Fogg 1983). Further, foxtail millet was cultivated by 'slash and burn' until the 1970s in Taiwan. On the other hand, taro and yam were also cultivated by the indigenous populations. As taro and yam are plants from subtropical to tropical areas, not from temperate areas such as the Yellow Valley, their cultivation indicates a cultural connection between the indigenous populations of Taiwan and the prehistoric populations of South China. Further, recent discoveries made in Nan-kuan-li, Taiwan show that both rice and millet were cultivated there by 4,500 BP (Tsang, Chapter 4, this volume). It seems that we are dealing with apparently conflicting ethnographic, linguistic and archaeological data.

The spread of rice farming

The first wave of rice farming expansion started approximately 7,000 BP. Rice was cultivated by the Lijiacun and Xiawanggang populations in the upper and middle Yellow Valley at around 7,000–6,000 BP respectively, and by the Qixia population in the lower Yellow Valley around 4,800–3,700 BP (Map 3.1). The southward expansion of rice farming seems slower, as current archaeological data suggest that rice was not cultivated in South China until around 6,000 BP (Fu et al. 1998).

Rice farming then further expanded to areas outside present-day mainland China. It seems to have reached the Japanese Archipelago around 3,000 BP (Yasuda 2000) and Taiwan by around 4,500 BP (Tsang, Chapter 4, this volume). The Taiwan discovery, along with pottery and stone tools similar to those found in Hong Kong, has been cited as supporting evidence of a possible human migration from South China to Taiwan (Tsang, Chapter 4, this volume). But, as mentioned above, this hypothesis seems inconsistent with ethnographic data regarding the sacred status of millet among Taiwan's indigenous people.

Table 3.3 Sites with both millet and rice

	Yellow Valley	Yangzi Valley
Neolithic	5	1
Xia and Shang dynasties	2	

Source: Chen 1993, 2000.

Discussion: human diasporas and replacement and/or cultural contact?

Based upon the archaeological data presented in this paper, a few points can be made. First, the Neolithic Yellow Valley was the core area for millet farming, while the contemporary Yangzi Valley was the same for rice farming, as the majority of millet remains are found in the Yellow Valley, and the majority of rice remains in the Yangzi (Tables 3.1 and 3.2).

Second, it seems that rice agriculture had expanded to the Yellow Valley by 7,000 BP, only some 1,500 years after its first occurrence in the middle Yangzi and Huai Valleys. Rice remains have been found in 21 Neolithic sites in the Yellow Valley, of which five have yielded both rice and foxtail millet (Table 3.3). On the other hand, millet expansion seems to have been much more constrained, as only one site in the middle Yangzi Valley has yielded millet remains, with rice also found in the same site (Table 3.3).

However, as mentioned above, it would be prudent to view this pattern as a trend rather than a precise representation of the actual distribution of millet and rice farming. Millet grains, being particularly small, are less likely to be preserved and/or discovered. The under-representation of millets in the archaeological record is further underlined by the recent discovery at Nan-kuan-li in Taiwan (Tsang, Chapter 4, this volume). If the Nan-kuan-li people were from the Pearl River Delta, they presumably were local residents there before moving to Taiwan. Current archaeological research indicates that rice was cultivated in South China about 6,000 BP, but there is no evidence for millet farming in this region until around 4,000 BP. If the Nan-kuan-li people were rice and millet farmers when they arrived in Taiwan, then there must have been millet farming in the Pearl River Delta before 4,500 BP. If they were only rice farmers when arriving in Taiwan, developing millet farming only afterwards, then we are facing the possibility of multiple origins of millet farming. However this may be, much more research is required on this topic.

The dates of these cereal remains in different areas should also be noticed. Rice cultivation occurs in the Jiahu assemblage in the Huai Valley around 8,500 BP, then expands northwards to the upper and lower Yellow Valley by 7,000 BP. Rice was probably cultivated there on-and-off up to the Shang dynasty (sixteenth to eleventh century BC). Pollen profiles, animal remains, sea level analysis and isotopic analysis all indicate that the time span between 7,000 and 4,500 BP was warm and humid in East Asia, with higher precipitation and higher temperatures; after this period the climate gradually became cooler and drier (Lu 1998). This climatic pattern may have facilitated the rapid and large-scale spread of rice cultivation in the Yellow Valley during this period. As rice grains are much larger than millet grains, the yield of rice is also much higher, on the basis of current agronomic data. Therefore, prehistoric populations would have found rice an attractive crop, and cultivated it wherever they could. On the other hand, millet, with its smaller grain and lower yield, may have been perceived as less attractive, so that its expansion was limited to areas where rice would not grow well. Because both foxtail and broomcorn millets are very drought-resistant, they remained major crops in the dry loess area.

Finally, the archaeological cultures of the farming societies in the Yellow and Yangzi Valleys differ significantly, as indicated by different toolkits, dwelling styles and pottery assemblages. However, whether these different populations can be defined as particular ethnic groups is another question. Many Chinese scholars have been identifying the prehistoric farming societies in the Yellow and Yangzi Valleys as the ancestors of the Pre-Han and Miao-Yao or Pre-Chu groups respectively (e.g. Xiang 1995). But whether current ethnic identity and linguistic classification can be so directly applied to prehistoric populations around 8,000 BP, and whether the sense of group identification existed in prehistoric times in the way we have inferred, are questions requiring further study.

Despite these cultural differences, rice and millets were cultivated by many Neolithic groups. The millet cultivators at Qinglongquan were members of the Yangzi Valley cultural cluster. On the other hand, the rice cultivators at Jiahu clearly belonged to the Peiligang culture of the Yellow Valley; those at Lijiacun in the upper Yellow Valley belonged to the Dadiwan Culture, while those further east at Qixia, Shandong Province, belonged to the Dawenkou Culture. Further, the prehistoric rice farmers in South China belonged to local cultural traditions such as the Dingsishan culture, which differs from other Neolithic cultures in China.

This trans-cultural cultivation of rice and millet seems to suggest two things. First, the expansion of rice and millet farming in this vast area seems to be the result of prehistoric cultural contacts, exchanges and adoption, although the movement of certain groups migrating into new areas is also visible in a few archaeological sites, such as that in the Dahecun site in the central Yellow Valley, where cultures from the Yellow and Yangzi valleys were present, but at different periods (Lu 1998). In other words, human diaspora and population replacement were not the only format accounting for the expansion of rice and millet farming in the area of present-day mainland China.

Second, it seems that there was little cultural resistance to the introduction of new cultivars. While the toolkit they used to farm, and the pottery vessels they used to store and cook cereals were all different, many prehistoric populations in the landmass from the Yellow Valley to South China accepted and practiced cereal farming within approximately 3,000 years of its origination. This is different from the situation among Taiwan indigenous populations, who regard only millet as their sacred grain, and display a certain resistance towards rice (Fogg 1983).

Archaeological evidence seems to suggest that the prehistoric populations in Taiwan around 5,000 and 3,000 BP were migrants from South China (e.g. Bellwood 1997; Tsang, Chapter 4, this volume). Yet ethnographic data say that millet, not rice, was the first cultivar among Taiwanese indigenous populations (Fogg 1983). Apparently there are inconsistencies between archaeological and ethnographic data. The key question is that of the cultural connection between the Nan-kuan-li people and the indigenous peoples of modern Taiwan; in other words, the question is whether the former were the cultural 'ancestors' of the latter, or whether there were significant cultural changes over a long period of time, in which case the ethnographic data on millet would be the result of late developments. If the latter were the case, this would be alarming to archaeologists and ethnologists who seek to understand past society through modern ethnographic data.

Fogg reported that it was 'taboo' to harvest foxtail millet 'en masse as with a sickle' (Fogg 1983: 108). If this reflects prehistoric practice, then sickles would not have been used for millet harvesting in prehistoric Taiwan. Sickles have been found in Neolithic Taiwan, but we don't know yet whether they were used for millet or rice cultivation (Tsang Cheng-hwa, p.c, 2001). Fogg also reported that the cultivar of foxtail millet grown by the Taiwanese has many panicles, which seems to indicate that the domestication process is not complete. Fully-domesticated foxtail millet in the Yellow Valley often has only one to two robust panicles. Further, indigenous Taiwanese farming techniques also seem to be at an early stage compared to those in the prehistoric mainland (Table 3.4). All these indicate that foxtail millet cultivation by the indigenous peoples of Taiwan either was at a very early stage of farming when it was introduced and that it has changed little since then, or that it was a modified subsistence strategy, again at an early phase of development, resulting from a relatively recent change in their environment.

This technical issue also raises questions about the cultural relationship between the prehistoric and the modern indigenous peoples of Taiwan. If the Nan-kuan-li residents were culturally related to the modern indigenous peoples of Taiwan, or if millet had been cultivated in Taiwan since 4,500 BP, the presence of fully-domesticated millets should be expected after such a long period of time, as well as the progress of farming techniques similar to those found in the Yellow Valley (Table 3.4). Yet neither are present. Why, then, did millet farming techniques and millet cultivars remain basically unchanged for so long? If rice and millet farming were present at the same time (Tsang, Chapter 4, this volume), why is only millet perceived as sacred, and not rice? If the Nan-kuan-li residents were not the cultural 'ancestors' of the Taiwan indigenous peoples, then who were they, and where have they gone?

In summary, to investigate the subsistence strategies in prehistoric Taiwan in relation to the origin and dispersal of the pre-Austronesian, more detailed study

Table 3.4 Cultural comparison between the foxtail millet cultivators in the Yellow Valley and Taiwan

Development of millet cultivation techniques	Time and tools used in the Yellow Valley	Diet structure and religion related to foxtail millet	Time and tools used by the Central Mountain Tribes	Diet structure and religion related to foxtail millet	Time and tools used by the Yami group	Diet structure and religion related to foxtail millet
Incipient stage	At least before 8,000 BP. Possibly digging stick and stone flakes (knives) or hand reaping for harvesting.				Until the 1970s. Digging stick and iron knife (from later cultural contact).	Millet is only minor item for food but still is sacred grain for ceremonies, but no wine.
Early stage	8,000–5,000 BP. Slash and burn but with sickle and knives for harvesting.	Millet was staple food and used for ceremonies. Also to make wine.	Until the 1970s. Hoe, and bamboo knives or hand-reaping for harvesting.	Millet supplies 50% of farmed food. Sacred grain for ceremonies and to make wine.		
Middle stage I	Around 5,000–4,000 BP. Hoe and knives for harvesting.					
Middle stage II	After 4,000 BP. Plough and other tools.					

is required. For example, ethnographic and archaeological study of the origin of millet and rice cultivation in Taiwan is fundamental, as well as an in-depth investigation of the behaviours and taboos relating to millet farming techniques. It is also necessary to investigate the complete subsistence strategies and material cultures of the Taiwan indigenous peoples and to compare these data with those in mainland China and the archaeological cultures found in Taiwan, in order to locate their original homeland in the mainland, and to trace the approximate time and route of their migration to Taiwan.

Abbreviations

AN   Austronesian
PAN Proto-Austronesian

Bibliography

Anderson, P. (ed.) (1999) *Prehistory of Agriculture*, Los Angeles: The UCLA Institute of Archaeology.
Bellwood, P. (1997) 'The Austronesian dispersal', *Newsletter of Chinese Ethnology* 35: 1–26. Taipei: Ethnological Society of China.
Chai, Y. (ed.) (1999) *Mizi*, Beijing: Chinese Agronomy Press.
Chen, W. (1993) *Zhongguo Nongye Kaogu Tulu*, Nanchang: Science and Technology Press.
—— (2000) 'Zhongguo Nongye Kaogu Ziliao Suoyin', *Nongye Kaogu* 1: 304–34.
Crawford, G. and Lee, G.-A. (2003) 'Agricultural origins in the Korean peninsula', *Antiquity* 77, 295: 87–95.
Ferrell, R. (1966) 'The Formosan tribes: a preliminary linguistic, archaeological and cultural synthesis', *Bulletin of the Institute of Ethnology* 21: 97–130.
Fogg, W.H. (1983) 'Swidden cultivation of foxtail millet by Taiwan Aborigines: a cultural analogue of the domestication of *Setaria italica* in China', in D. Keightley (ed.) *The Origin of Chinese Civilization*, Berkeley: University of California Press.
Fu, X.-G. et al. (1998) 'Guangxi Yongning Dingsishan Yizhi Fajue', *Kaogu* 11: 11–33.
Gao, M.-J. and Chen, J.-J. (1988) 'Zaipeisu Qiyuan de Tonggongmei Yanjiu', *Zuowu Xuebao* 14, 2: 131–6.
Guo, R.-H. and Li, J. (2000) 'Cong Nanzhuangtou Yizhi kan Huaibei Diqu Nongye he Taoqi de Qiyuan', in W.M. Yan and Y. Yasuda (eds) *Daozuo, Taoqi he Dushi de Qiyuan*, Beijing: Cultural Relics Publishing House.
Li, H.W., Li, H. and Pao, W.K. (1945) 'Cytological and genetical studies of the interspecific cross of the cultivated foxtail millet (*Setaria italica*) and the green foxtail (*S. viridis*)', *Journal of the American Society of Agronomy* 9: 32–54.
Lu, T.L.-D. (1998) 'The mid-Holocene climate and cultural dynamics in China', Paper presented at International Conference on the Mid-Holocene, Maine, USA, Oct. 1998.
—— (1999) *The Transition from Foraging to Farming and the Origin of Agriculture in China*, Oxford: BAR International Series No. 774.
—— (2000) Use-wear analysis on flint flakes found in Xiachuan, the middle Yellow Valley, unpublished data.

Lu, T.L.-D. (2001) 'Early pottery in South China', Paper presented at Conference on The Oldest Pottery in the World, Cambridge, Oct. 2001.

—— (2002a) 'A Green Foxtail (Setaria viridis) cultivation experiment in the Middle Yellow River Valley and some related issues', Asian Perspectives 41: 1–14

—— (2002b) 'Les outils de récolte de céréales néolithiques de la vallée du Fleuve Jaune' (Harvesting tools in the Neolithic Yellow River Valley), Annales de la Fondation Fyssen: 103–14.

The Institute of Archaeology CASS (1991) C14 Dates in Chinese Archaeology (1965–1991), Beijing: Cultural Relics Publishing House.

The National Survey Group of Wild Rice (1984) 'Zhongguo Yeshengdao Ziyuan Diaocha', Zhonguo Nongye Kexue6: 27–34.

Wei, J., He, A.Y., Zhang, X.W., Huang, F. and Huang, X. (2001) 'Discovery at Gantuoyan provides new data for Guangxi prehistory', Chinese Antiquity News front page, 19th October.

Xiang, A.-Q. (1995) 'Zhongguo Daozuo Qiyuan Wenti zhi Tantao', Dongnan Wenhuai 1: 44–58.

Yan, W.-M. (2000) 'The origins of rice agriculture, pottery and cities', in W.-M. Yan and Y. Yasuda (eds) The Origin of Rice Agriculture, Pottery and Cities, Beijing: Cultural Relics Publishing House.

Yasuda, Y. (2000) 'Rice agricultural crescent in Eastern Asia and wheat agricultural crescent in Western Asia', in W.-M. Yan and Y. Yasuda (eds) The Origin of Rice Agriculture, Pottery and Cities, Beijing: Cultural Relics Publishing House.

Ye, W.-S. et al. (2000) 'Zaojiaoshu Yizhi Guhuanjing yu Guwenhuai Chubu Yanjiu', in K.-S. Zhou and Y.-Q. Song (eds) Research on Environmental Archaeology, Beijing: Science Press.

Yingde Museum and the Dept. of Anthropology, Zhongshan University (1999) Archaeology Discovery in Yingde County (translated version). Guangdong: People's Press (in Chinese).

Yuan, J.-R. (2000) 'Rice and pottery dated to 10,000 BP at Yuchanyan, Daoxian County, Hunan Province', in W.-M. Yan and Y. Yasuda (eds) The Origin of Rice Agriculture, Pottery and Cities, Beijing: Cultural Relics Publishing House.

Zhao, Z.-J. (1998) 'Daogu Qiyuan de Xin Zhengju', Nongye Kaogu 1: 394.

4

RECENT DISCOVERIES AT THE TAPENKENG CULTURE SITES IN TAIWAN

Implications for the problem of Austronesian origins

Tsang Cheng-hwa

Introduction

The TPK culture, also known as the Corded Ware culture, is the earliest Neolithic cultural stratum ever found in Taiwan. As early as the 1940s, Kano Tadao suggested that the earliest cultural stratum on the island of Taiwan was characterised by cord-marked pottery. The clarification of its characteristics and its formal establishment as an archaeological culture, however, was not achieved until the excavations of the sites of TPK in Taipei and Fengpitou in Kaohsiung by Kwang-chih Chang in 1964–65. The new culture was named TPK by Chang, after the site he had studied in most detail. On the basis of discoveries made at TPK and Fengpitou and other relevant data, Chang (1969) suggested the following as the specific characteristics of this culture:

1   The TPK is characterised by pottery made of coarse paste and decorated with cord-marked impressions. The stone inventory includes pecked river pebbles, net sinkers, stone adzes, points and bark beaters.
2   TPK is unquestionably the oldest Neolithic cultural horizon thus far found in Taiwan. It apparently antedates the subsequent prehistoric culture, which began round 2,500 BC, by a considerable amount of time.
3   The subsistence base of the TPK people was hunting, fishing and collecting, but some form of farming, such as root and fruit cultivation, was also carried out.
4   TPK settlements were located on marine and river terraces, not far from water.
5   TPK evolved in a humid and warm subtropical–tropical environment, and shows adaptations to marine, estuarine, riverine and lacustrine micro-environments.

6   Possible cultural affinities for the TPK culture of Taiwan include the Jomon culture of Japan; South China (Hsien-jen-tung and other sites), and Southeast Asia (the Kalanay complex in the Philippines).

These characteristics led Chang (1969) to suggest that the people of the TPK culture were among the earliest horticulturalists in Southeast Asia. Since then, scholars like Ferrell (1969), Shutler (1975), Bellwood (1979) and Blust (1985) realised that the TPK culture presumably represents the PAN population, which extended from the Southeast coast of China to Taiwan. Based upon this, the region of the Southeast coast of China, including Taiwan, has been proposed to be the AN homeland. In fact, in the past, the evidence for TPK culture, which drew mainly from the two sites of TPK and Fengpit'ou, upon which important inferences were primarily made, is scanty and insufficient. For a better understanding of this important culture in Taiwan and its significance, more information and studies are required.

In the last two decades, some new sites of the TPK culture have been discovered on the island of Taiwan and the nearby Peng-hu archipelagos. The archaeological evidence yielded from these sites is of great significance and importance. The purpose of this chapter is to present a brief introduction to the new archaeological data of the TPK culture and discuss their implications for the problem of AN origins.

The Tapenkeng culture and the problem of Austronesian origins

The earliest inhabitants of Taiwan, as the current evidence has revealed, are represented by the pre-ceramic assemblages, dated from 15,000 to 5,000 BP or even earlier, uncovered from the cave site at Ch'ang-pin on the eastern coast and the sites of O-luan-pi II and Lung-K'eng on the southern coast (Li et al. 1985; Sung 1969). These assemblages have been named as 'Changpin Culture', characterised by a lithic industry consisting of chipped pebble and flake tools, as well as by the absence of pottery and a lack of evidence of farming. Compared with the stone industries of the adjacent regions, archaeologists in Taiwan have generally believed that this culture came from South China during the late Pleistocene when Taiwan was still a part of the Asian continent. Since there is no clear developmental relationship between the pre-ceramic assemblages and the later Neolithic cultures in Taiwan, it is difficult to argue that the Changpin Culture represents the earliest incursion of AN people onto Taiwan. Current evidence seems to suggest that traces of the earliest AN speakers on Taiwan are to be found at the sites of Neolithic cultures on the island.

In order to identify the earliest AN speakers on Taiwan, scholars tried to classify the modern aboriginal cultures and linguistic divisions and to correlate them with the variations and developments of archaeological cultures. But this has proved difficult. Several attempts have been made to classify the AN languages of Taiwan, such as Asai (1936), Nikigawa (1953) and Loukotka and Lanyon-Orgill (1958). But a more scientific study was not made until 1963, when Isidore Dyen conducted a lexicostatistical study on several of the aboriginal languages of Taiwan. He first provides a linguistic hierarchy by making a three-division classification of these languages, with F1 including Atayal and Sedeq of northern Taiwan, F2 including Tsouic of Central Taiwan, and F3 containing the remaining languages of Bunun, Rukai, Paiwan, Ami, Puyuma, Pazeh and Kavalan.

Ferrell (1966), based on cultural assessment, tried to correlate a tentative classification of Taiwan aboriginal cultures of three major groups: Atayalic, Tsouic and Paiwanic, with three linguistic divisions. He then compared these major groupings with the three major archaeological cultures known thus far and made the following conclusions:

> Archaeological data point clearly to a direct South China derivation for the overwhelming majority of the Formosan peoples and cultural traits. Close examination of cultural and linguistic data, which show the present-day tribes to fall into three distinct groupings, also gives surprisingly explicit clues as to the possible affinity of each of the major groupings with one of the three prehistoric cultural traditions on the island. This in turn permits us to assign a tentative area of origin on the South China mainland for the speakers of the various present-day Formosan languages. The Atayalic/Cord-Marked Pottery Horizon shows clear affinities with the South and Southwest China region, and the Tsouic/North Formosan Proto-Lungshanoid (Yuanshan) Culture has unmistakable northern elements, and may represent the more northerly of the Austronesian mainland peoples who earlier occupied the entire eastern coastal region of China and probably extended as far northward as modern Japan and Korea. The Paiwanic/South Taiwan Lungshanoid-Geometric Horizons are probably from an area between the Atayalic and Tsouic areas on the mainland. Their culture was basically that of pre-Han Southeast China, and their spread to Formosa was part of the large-scale movements of Lungshanoid agricultural peoples from the Northwest China nuclear area into mainland Southeast Asia and the Pacific islands during the first and second millennia BC.
>
> (Ferrell 1966: 124)

This is the first time that the association between the Corded Ware culture and the early radiation of PAN was hypothesised.

In 1969, Kwang-chih Chang made a comprehensive synthesis of Taiwanese prehistory based on his excavations of Ta-pen-k'eng and Feng-pi-t'ou. He pointed out a remarkable coincidence of the archaeological picture with the reconstructed separation of the ancestral groups of the Taiwan AN languages.

> At about 2,500 BC two major cultures emerged in the Taiwan scene – the Yuan-shan in the north and the Lungshanoid in the south. At about the same time, moreover, the Lungshanoid culture had already experienced several divergent phases, each one of which could be traced to a cultural

group on the mainland. Since the glottochronological results suggest that at exactly this same time the ancestral Atayalic and Paiwanic had just begun to separate, whereas the two prehistoric cultures already showed sharp contrasts, it would not be possible to identify the two ancestral linguistic groups with the two prehistoric cultures. It appears more likely that both Atayalic and Paiwanic split from a single prehistoric ancestor.

(Chang 1969: 246)

Based on this, Chang (1969) concluded that the majority of the modern ANs of Taiwan probably descended from two major prehistoric cultures, Lungshanoid and Yuan-shan, and that the ancestral ANs on Taiwan were presumably related to the Lungshanoid cultures from the southeastern coasts of the mainland. Clearly, Chang neglected the possible association between the TPK culture and PAN.

In the same year, 1969, however, Ferrell changed his earlier hypothesis and argued that the diversity of the Taiwan aboriginal languages was not necessarily indicative of separate waves of migration. He suggested that 'Four to five thousand years in situ would be ample time to produce the difference seen in the present-day languages, even had the ancestral Formosan all arrived at once and spoken one single language' (Ferrell 1969). In consideration of the archaeological evidence to date, however, he further suggested that:

> If the archaeological evidence were not what it is and indicated more uniformity in the early stages of Taiwan's prehistory, we might indeed believe that present linguistic difference could be merely the result of divergence from a single ancestral language after its arrival in Taiwan. However, the archaeological pictures of Taiwan, after the very early period characterized by the Cord-marked Pottery Horizon, indicate the fairly sudden appearance of not one but perhaps three main cultural complexes.
> (Ferrell 1969: 73)

Ferrell was apparently in a dilemma of deciding which archaeological culture or cultures would have been related with the ancestor(s) of the present AN languages in Taiwan. In order to take care of both linguistic and archaeological evidence, he could not but suggest four possibilities that could be used to explain the present-day aboriginal language situation:

1   all of the Formosan languages developed from one common ancestor in Taiwan;
2   two separate migrations, Proto-Atayalic and Proto-Paiwanic-Tsouic;
3   three movements, Proto-Atayalic, Proto-Tsouic and Proto-Paiwanic; and
4   four migrations, Proto-Atayalic, Proto-Tsouic, Proto-Paiwanic I and Proto-Paiwanic II (Ferrell 1969: 74).

Ferrell's explanation reveals clearly that he does not necessarily mean that all of the Formosan languages developed from one common ancestor on Taiwan. He does indicate, however, that the bearers of the Corded Ware culture were very likely among the earliest ancestral ANs on the island.

Hereafter, the association between the TPK culture of Taiwan and the early expansion of the ANs became a commonplace. In 1975, Shutler and Marck were for the first time in an attempt to set up a hypothetical framework for explaining the dispersal of AN. Based upon the archaeological and linguistic data, they suggested that the dispersal of the AN was probably related with movements of horticulturalists. Since the Corded Ware culture in Taiwan represents the earliest horticulturalists' community, Taiwan may have been the AN homeland.

Bellwood (1979) has also noted that 'The Corded Ware Culture may well be associated with speakers of an early AN language ancestral to the present-day Atayalic, which may represent an initial split from the PAN, and which was probably established on the island by 4,000 BC, or earlier' (p. 203). But in subsequent publications (Bellwood 1980, 1983, 1988, 1995, 1997) proposes a theory different from Shutler and Marck, namely that the population of the TPK culture colonised Taiwan probably with a cereal-based economy (rice and millet). Bellwood (1980, 1997) believes that the settlers carrying the TPK culture would have already been rice growers, and their descendants expanded from Taiwan to the Philippines, and by 2,000 BC these AN-speaking people spread into the equatorial islands of eastern Indonesia and gradually replaced the indigenous hunting and collecting Australoid populations.

In 1989, Chang changed his earlier viewpoint that the ancestral ANs in Taiwan were related to immigrating Lungshanoid cultures from the southeastern coast of the mainland. He suggested that 'If there were major radiations of Proto-Austronesians from the Southeast China homeland (including Taiwan), they probably began no later than the period of the Ta-p'en-k'eng culture' (1989a: 95). In order to further explain why and how the TPK culture moved to Taiwan, Chang (1989b) suggested that the PAN population on the southeastern coast of China moved into Taiwan because of pressure from the ST speakers, represented by the Lungshanoid cultures arriving from the North, as at the Tan-shih-san site of Fukien.

Although many scholars believe that the TPK culture represents the earliest ancestral AN-speaking people in Taiwan and was the source of the AN expansion from the Chinese Mainland to the Pacific, this viewpoint has by no means gained unanimous support among archaeologists. For instance, William Meacham (1988) has argued that the TPK culture is clearly distinct in style from the contemporaneous middle Neolithic cultures of Southeast China and therefore 'there were no movement of people or ever significant contact across Formosa Strait during the duration of Tapenkeng' (Meacham 1988: 97). Apparently, the TPK culture and its role in the questions of AN expansion is still, to some extent, a controversial issue. We need to clarify at least four crucial points;

1   The internal relationships of the TPK culture with the subsequent cultures in Taiwan, especially the Lungshanoid cultures, which played an important role in the development of the later prehistoric cultures in Taiwan.

2   The external relationships of the TPK culture with the contemporary cultures in neighbouring areas.
3   The accurate date of the TPK culture.
4   The economic patterns of the TPK culture.

Recent discoveries and new evidence of the TPK culture

In addition to TPK and Fengpitou, only one more site of the TPK culture was discovered in Taiwan prior to 1980. This is the Pa-chia-tsun site, located in Kui-ren Hsiang (township) of Tainan. Huang Shih-chiang and others made surface collections at the site in 1972 and 1974. Potsherds with cord-marked decorations, stone tools including chipped stone axes, polished axes and adzes, as well as bone points were found on the surface of a riverbed. A radiocarbon date of 3,696 60 BC from a sample of shells without provenance was obtained. Because no excavation was conducted at the site, the significance of these materials has not been clear (Huang 1974).

In 1984, a site characterised by coarse cord-marked pottery was found and excavated at the Kuo-yeh Tsun (village) on the Peng-hu Island by the present author (Tsang 1992). Cultural materials excavated from this site consist of pottery and stone artifacts, as well as animal bones, deer antlers, shells and coral artifacts. Compared with the surrounding areas of Peng-hu, the materials from the Kuo-yeh site are strikingly similar to the TPK culture in Taiwan. From the overall similarities in cultural manifestations, there is little doubt that the cultural assemblage of the Kuo-yeh site is a part of the TPK culture of Taiwan. Analyses of the Kuo-yeh materials indicate a shift in settlement patterns from temporary or occasional visits to more permanent habitation and more intensive exploration of the surrounding environment. The major subsistence resources for the Kuo-yeh settlers were the marine resources along the shoreline. Shellfish, fish and pre-sumably seaweed from the intertidal rocks and coral reefs were probably the dietary staples. In addition to the earlier data, the Kuo-yeh materials provide even more important information to a better understanding of the TPK culture in Taiwan.

1   The date of the TPK culture in Taiwan has long been a question. Kwang-chih Chang once suggested a time range from the third to the tenth millennium BC. The antiquity of this date, however, was questioned. Chang suggested later a new date of 5,000–2,500 BC. But this date is still not certain, for only one single Carbon-14 date from Pa-chia-tsun is so far available. The radiocarbon dates, around 3,000–2,500 BC, from the Kuo-yeh site provided important new evidence for dating the TPK culture.
2   The relationship between the TPK culture and the subsequent Red Corded Ware culture was argued among archaeologists in Taiwan. The evidence from Kuo-yeh and its detailed comparison with the Red Corded Ware culture in

Penghu and Taiwan supports the view that the Red Corded Ware culture was essentially a continuous development of the TPK culture.

3   The comparison of the Kuo-yeh materials with the cord-marked pottery assemblages on the southeastern coast of China shows that the most likely source area of the TPK culture of Taiwan is on the coastal areas of Kwangtung.

This new information presumably has implications for the problem of AN origins and expansion.

In recent years, more and more TPK culture sites have been gradually recovered around the southern, north and eastern coasts of Taiwan. In the South, three sites including Fu-te-yie-miao, Liu-he and Kung-chai were discovered on the Fengshan tableland in Kao-hsiung County (Tsang et al. 1994), and Nan-kuan-li and Nan-kuan-li East were found on the flood plain in Hsin-shih Hsiang of Tainan County (Nanke Archaeological team 2002). In the North, remains of the TPK culture were found in the sites of Yuan-shan, Chih-san-yian, and Kuan-tu of the Taipei Basin (Liu et al. 1995; Liu 2002), as well as in a series of sites including Chuang-tsuo, Pei-tao-chiao, Teng-kung Kuo-hsiao, Si-chan-chiao and Kuo-hsi-tzu, etc. on the terraces along the northeastern coast (Chen 2000; Liu 2000). TPK style potsherds have also been found in several sites on the east coast of Taiwan, including Pei-nan (Lien 1986) Chang-kuang (Yeh 2000) and Tung-he-pei (Huang and Liu 1993) (Map 4.1).

Among these newly discovered TPK culture sites, the discoveries from the sites of Nan-kuan-li and Nan-kuan-li East are especially noteworthy. Because the analysis of these materials has just begun, I will only give a brief introduction to the major materials uncovered.

Nan-kuan-li is located on the flood plain of Hsin-shih Hsiang, Tainan County, where the construction of a science-based industrial park is underway. The site was found by Liu Ku-hsiung, an assistant of archaeology, who was examining an area of the construction site when he observed some TPK style potsherds exposed by the bulldozer. The disturbed soil bulldozed from 7 m under the current ground level contained a large number of potsherds of the TPK. For the purpose of rescuing its archaeological remains, an archaeological team led by the author conducted an intensive excavation at the site in September and October of 2000. An area of about 1,000 m^2 was excavated. Two major depositional layers of the TPK culture were observed, and in which archaeological remains are extremely abundant, including pottery, stone tools, and shell and bone tools, as well as animal bones, plant remains and human burials.

The pottery (Plate I) unearthed from Nan-kuan-li are mainly jars and bowls, dark or reddish brown in colour with cord-marked, painted and incised decorations, which are strikingly similar in style and form to the coarse cord-marked pottery of Kuo-yeh and Pa-chia-tsun in many respects. Stone tools are mainly polished adzes, arrowheads and net sinkers. It is noted that polished adzes include both quadrangular and shouldered types (Plate II). One broken stone bark-cloth beater was also found. Instead of stone knives, a large number of reaping knives,

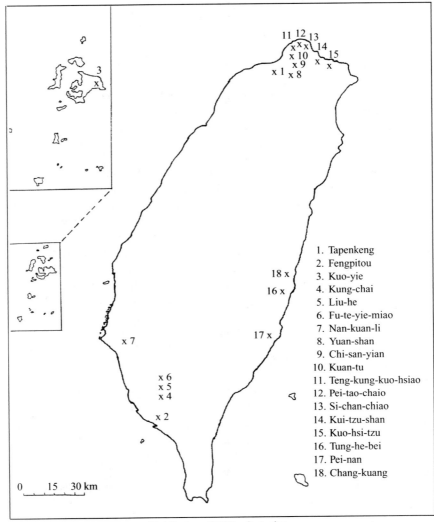

Map 4.1 Distribution of TPK sites in Taiwan.

which were made of pearl shells (Plate III), were recovered. A few bone and antler artifacts were uncovered, including points, chisels and ornaments of beads and pendants. A large number of faunal and plant remains were recovered. Major faunal remains include bones of fish, deer, pigs and dogs. Plant remains consist mainly of seeds of Picrasma quassioides and Celtis sinensis. Especially noteworthy is the discovery of a few carbonised rice grains (Plate IVa). Twelve human burials were recovered at Nan-kuan-li. Six of them belong to infants and youths, and the rest belong to adults. Except one, which was buried in a flexed posture, all of the skeletons were supine and extended. Their heads all point toward the South. Ten radiocarbon-14 age determinations obtained from Nan-kuan-li indicate that the site was occupied by inhabitants in a period between 3,000 and 2,500 BC.

Nan-kuan-li East is located about a few hundred meters east of Nan-kuan-li. This site was also discovered because of the construction of a factory building. Many potsherds of the TPK style were dug out from the soil about seven to eight meters deep under the current ground level. The archaeological team led by the present author conducted a salvage excavation at the site from September 2002 to March 2003. An area of about 2,400 m^2 was excavated. The materials excavated from this site are basically similar to what were uncovered from Nan-kuan-li, except the discovery of thousands of carbonised grains of millet (Plate IVb). Since no millet grains had ever been found archaeologically in Taiwan, this discovery is of great importance and significance. So far, the species of the millet grains has not been genetically identified. But, morphologically, they are similar to foxtail millet (Setaria italica L.), which is still cultivated by the AN-speaking people in Taiwan.

The new archaeological data from the sites of Nan-kuan-li and Nan-kuan-li East show that:

1   The C-14 dates obtained from Nan-kuan-li confirms the upper date of the TPK culture to as late as 2,500 BC.
2   The discovery of carbonised rice in Nan-kuan-li and millet in Nan-kuan-li East, along with a large number of shell reaping knives and stone adzes, provide us with a concrete evidence of rice and millet farming during the TPK period and completely changes our earlier understanding of the subsistence pattern of the TPK culture.
3   The varieties, styles and forms of artifacts uncovered from Nan-kuan-li further support the earlier view based on evidence from Kuo-yeh of Penghu that the TPK culture of Taiwan has close affinities with the Neolithic cultures of Hong Kong and the Pearl River Delta. The Pearl River Delta of Kuangtung is most probably the source area of the TPK culture in Taiwan.

Conclusions

The importance of Taiwan for AN origins lies partly in its role as a bridge between the Mainland and the Pacific, and partly in its potential role in the connection between the prehistoric cultures and its modern AN speakers. Archaeological studies in Taiwan help reconstructing not only prehistoric cultures on the island but also the internal and external relationships of the Formosan languages. The TPK culture has long been hypothesised to represent the initial wave of AN speakers who went across the Taiwan Straits from the Chinese mainland (Bellwood 1997) and the earliest ancestors of the modern AN population on the

Pacific Islands (Chang 1989). In the past, several crucial questions, such as the developmental relationship of the TPK culture with the subsequent cultures, its date, its economic patterns, and its external affinities, could not be clarified due to absence of enough and adequate data. The recent archaeological finds have undoubtedly great potential to solve these questions.

Abbreviations

AN   Austronesian
ANs Austronesians
PAN Proto-Austronesian
ST   Sino-Tibetan
TPK Tapenkeng or Ta-pen-k'eng

Bibliography

Asai, E. (1936) A Study of the Yami Language, an Indonesian Language Spoken on Botel Tobago Island, Leiden: J. Ginsberg.
Bellwood, P. (1979) Man's Conquest of the Pacific, New York: Oxford University Press.
——(1980) 'The peopling of the Pacific', Scientific American 243: 5: 174–85.
——(1983) 'New perspectives on Indo-Malaysian prehistory', Bulletin of the Indo-Pacific Prehistory Association 4: 71–83.
——(1988) 'A hypothesis for Austronesian origins', Asian Perspectives 26, 1: 107–17.
——(1995) 'Austronesian prehistory in Southeast Asia: homeland, expansion and transformation', in P. Bellwood, J.J. Fox and Darrell Tryon (eds) The Austronesians, 96–106, Canberra: The Department of Anthropology, Research School of Pacific and Asian Studies, The Austronesian National University.
——(1997) Prehistory of the Indo-Malaysian Archipelago, Honolulu: University of Hawaii Press.
Chang, K.C. (1969) Fengpitou, Tapenkeng and the Prehistory of Taiwan, Yale University Publication in Anthropology, no. 73, New Haven: Yale University Press.
——(1974) 'Ancient farmers in the Asian Tropics: major problems for archaeological and palaeoenvironmental investigations of Southeast Asia at the earliest Neolithic level', in Asok K. Ghosh (ed.) Perspectives in Palaeoanthropology, 273–86, Calcutta: Firma K.L. Mukhopadhyay.
——(1981) 'The affluent foragers in the coastal areas of China: extrapolation from evidence on the transition to agriculture in affluent foragers' in S. Koyama and D.H. Thomas (eds) Affluent Foragers, Senri Ethnological Studies, no. 9, Osaka: National Museum of Ethnology.
——(1989a) 'Taiwan archaeology in Pacific perspective', in K.C. Chang, C.C. Yin, K.C. Li (eds) Anthropological Studies of the Taiwan area: Accomplishments and Perspectives, Taipei: Department of Anthropology, National Taiwan University.
——(1989b) 'Xinshiqi shidai de Taiwan haixia', Kaogu 541–50.
Chen, Y.P. (2000) Taiwan dianligongsu heneng sichang nei kaogu yizhi shijue baogao (Report on the test excavation in the fourth nuclear power plant of Taiwan Power Company), Taipei: Taiwan Power Company.

Plate I Cord-marked pot from Nan-kuan-li.

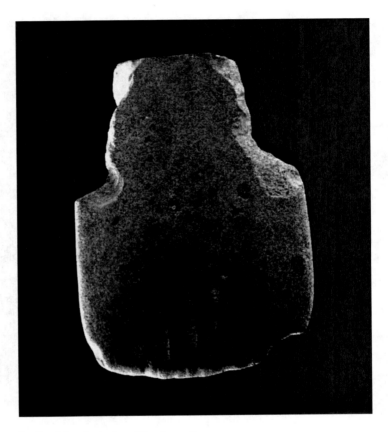

Plate II Shouldered adz from Nan-kuan-li.

Plate III Pearl shell reaping knife from Nan-kuan-li.

Plate IV (a) Carbonised rice grains from Nan-kuan-li and (b) carbonised millet grains from Nan-kuan-li east.

Dyen, I. (1963) 'Position of Malayo-Polynesian languages of Formosa', Asian Perspectives 7, 1–2: 261–71.
Ferrell, R. (1966) 'The Formosan tribes: a preliminary linguistic, archaeological and cultural synthesis', Bulletin of the Institute of Ethnology 21: 97–130.
—— (1969) Taiwan Aboriginal Groups: Problems in Cultural and Linguistic Classification, Institute of Ethnology, Academia Sinica, Monograph series, no. 17.
Huang, S.C. (1974) 'Tainan xian Guiren xiang Bajiacun yizhi diaocha', Bulletin of The Department of Archaeology and Anthropology, National Taiwan University, 35–6: 62–8.
Huang, S.C. and Liu, Y.C. (1993) Taidong Xian Dongheqiao nanbei yindao kaogu yizhi qiangjiu yu pinggu, Taipei: Ministry of Interior Affairs.
Li, K.C., Zheng, Y.S., Chen, W.J., Han, X.D. and Chen, Y.B. (1985) Kending guojia gongyuan kaogu diaocha baogao, Pingtung: Ken-ting National Park.
Lien, C.M. and Sung, W.H. (1986) yizhi duiji cengci ji wenhuaceng chutu yiwu zhi fenxi yanjiu, Beinan yizhi fajue ziliao zhengli baogao Vol. III, Taipei: Ministry of Education.
Liu, Y.C. (2000) Taibei shi shiqianyizhi diaocha yu yanjiu, Taipei: Department of Civil Affairs, Taipei Municipal Government.
—— (2002) Danshui hekou de shiqian wenhua yu zuqun, Taipei: The Shisanhang Museum of Archaeology.
Liu, Y.C., Chen, Y.S., Zhan, S.J. and Chen, L.Q. (1996) Zhisanyan wenhua shiji gongyuan shiqian wenhua renwen lishi shijujingguan deng ziyuan ji jumin ziyuan zhi peiyu, Taipei: Department of Civil Affairs, Taipei Municipal Government.
Loukotka, C. and Lanyon-Orgill, P.A. (1958) 'A revised classification of the Formosan languages', Journal of Austronesian Studies 1, 3: 56–63.
Meacham, W. (1988) 'On the probability of Austronesian origins in South China', Asian Perspectives (1984–85) 26, 1: 89–106.
Nanke Archaeological Team (2002) Jinnian lai nanke kaogu de yixie chengguo ji qi suo yinqi de yixie wenti
Nikigawa, A. (1953) 'A classification of the Formosan languages', Journal of Austronesian Studies 1, 1: 145–51.
Shutler, R. and Marck, J.C. (1974) 'On the dispersal of the Austronesian horticulturalists', Archaeology and Physical Anthropology in Oceania 10: 81–113.
Sung, W.H. (1969) 'Changbin wenhua: Taiwan shouci faxian de xiantao wenhua', Newsletter of Ethnological Society of the Republic of China 9: 1–27.
Tsang, C.H. (1992) Archaeology of the Peng-hu Islands, Special Publications No. 95, Taipei: Institute of History and Philology, Academia Sinica.
Tsang, C.H., Chen, C.Y. and Liu, Y.C. (1994) Taimin diqu kaogu pucha: Gaoxiong Xian he Gaoxiong Shi, Taipei: Ministry of Interior Affairs.
Yeh, M.C. (2000) 'Shiqianguan kaogu shinian gongzuo jianjie', Wenhua Yizhan 10: 1–7.

Part II

LINGUISTICS

5

THE CONTRIBUTION OF LINGUISTIC PALAEONTOLOGY TO THE HOMELAND OF AUSTRO-ASIATIC

Gérard Diffloth

The AA phylum, comprising the Munda family of Eastern India and the Mon-Khmer family of mainland Southeast Asia, is one of the longest-established language families to inhabit this vast region. AA is therefore of crucial importance when discussing ancient population movements in the Asian continent generally. Rather than presenting a detailed review of this question, I will briefly summarise here some recent historical linguistic findings, and spell out the questions which they compel us to ask. The discussion focuses on three issues, the terminology of rice (see also Blench, Chapter 2, this volume), faunal terms and the distribution of languages.

Rice

A rich lexicon for rice terminology is reconstructible to PAA,[1] making it evident that the people who spoke this language were thoroughly familiar with rice agriculture. This is shown in Table 5.1.

Although some writers have argued until recently that rice agriculture was of South Asian origin (Haudricourt and Hédin 1987: 159–61, 176) it is generally accepted to have been domesticated twice, in South Asia and along the middle Yangtze (Khush 1997).

Tropical faunal taxa

In the reconstructed PAA lexicon there are names for animal species which are restricted to the humid tropics. The floral vocabulary would probably lead to the same conclusion, but it is more difficult to reconstruct at present. These words are morphologically opaque, suggesting long-term familiarity with the items in question. Table 5.2 shows the quasi-reconstructions so far available for AA.

The obvious implication is that the AA homeland was located in the tropics. Minor climatic changes are said to have occurred in the East Indian and mainland

Table 5.1 Reconstructed rice terms in PAA

English	PAA reconstruction
Rice plant	#(ki)Ɡaː◻
Rice grain	#ri koː◻
Rice outer husk	#ci kaːm
Rice inner husk	#ki ndi k
Rice bran	#pheː◻
Mortar	#ti mpal
Pestle	#ji nre◻
Winnowing tray	#ji mpii r
To winnow	#guːm
Dibbling-stick	#ji rmui l
Rice-complement (cooked food other than rice)	#ki ntuː◻

Table 5.2 Faunal reconstructions in PAA

Scientific name	English	PAA reconstruction
Varanus bengalensis, or nebulosus	Land, or tree monitor	#ti rkui t
Manis javanica	Ant-eater	#(bi n-)joːl, #j(i rm)oːl
Bubalus bubalus	Buffalo	#ti nriak
Arctitis binturong	Bear-cat	#ti nyuː
Capricornis sumatrensis	Mountain goat	#kiaM
Elephas maximus	Asian elephant	#kacia
Pavo muticus	Peacock	#mraːk
Dicerorhinus sumatrensis	Rhinoceros	#ri maːs
Rhizomys sumatrensis	Bamboo-rat	#di kan[1]

Notes
The forms marked # are not fully reconstructed, but represent reasonable approximations.
1 Malay dekan is a borrowing from AA and indeed Malay has borrowed other faunal terms such as ketam 'crab'.

Southeast Asia area since PAA times, and it is not clear how significant they are. The question then arises: did the faunal landscape in the middle Yangtze environment include these taxa during the relevant period?

Language geography

The geographic distribution of the thirteen branches of AA (Munda plus MK) would imply a centre of greatest historical diversity in the region which encompasses the fertile flood plains of the Irrawaddy in Burma and the plains along the lower Brahmaputra in Assam and Bangladesh. But it is striking that the reconstructed rice vocabulary does not imply wet rice, and it is likely that the first AA speakers were growing dry rice in hilly areas. Even today, the AA languages show their greatest diversity in upland areas and probably they only colonised the plains at a later stage in their expansion, as with other phyla in the region (Blench, Chapter 2, this volume). Our modern perspective of fertile plains giving rise to centralisation and political power postdates the perspective of peoples who had not yet adopted or innovated wet agriculture.

Figure 5.1 shows the most recent form of a possible AA tree. The Pearic languages, spoken in scattered locations across eastern Thailand and Cambodia

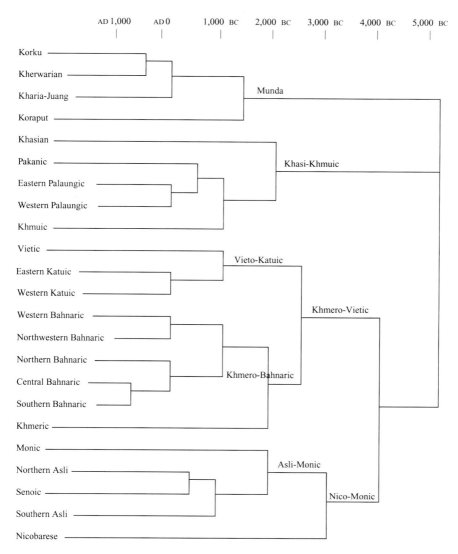

Figure 5.1 AA with a tentative calibration of time-depths for the various branches of the language family.

remain problematic and so have been omitted from the present diagram. Their genetic affinity is uncertain, although they are presumably MK and not Munda. The linking of the Aslian languages with Nicobarese does suggest an ancient westward movement in the Southern part of the AA range of hunting and gathering populations prior to the expansion of Khmero-Vietic

Somatic diversity

What processes of prehistoric language shift and spread can account for the observable physiological heterogeneity of modern AA language communities? The Negritos of the Malay Peninsula and the Mundas of the Koraput Hills in Orissa show obvious somatological contrasts with the Khasi, Khmu' and Khmer, not to mention Hanoi suburbanites. AA has lagged behind many other language phyla in terms of DNA studies, partly because of access problems. However, the time is now ripe for a fine-mesh population genetic study of AA language communities to be conducted in an ethnolinguistically informed and sensitive way.

Abbreviations

AA   Austro-Asiatic
MK   Mon-Khmer
PAA   Proto-Austro-Asiatic

Note

1 The precise linguistic evidence for these and for the animal names cited below will be discussed in my forthcoming 'Introduction to comparative Mon-Khmer', EFEO, Paris.

Bibliography

Haudricourt, A.-G. and Hédin, L. (1987) L'homme et les plantes cultivées, Paris: A.-M. Métailié.

Khush, G.S. (1997) Origin, dispersal and variation of rice, Plant Molecular Biology 35: 25–34.

6

TIBETO-BURMAN vs INDO-CHINESE

Implications for population geneticists, archaeologists and prehistorians

George van Driem

The Tibeto-Burman language family

Inklings of a TB language family first appeared in the eighteenth century, when Western scholars observed that Tibetan was genetically related to Burmese. However, the precise contours of the TB language family were first defined in Paris in 1823 by the German scholar Julius Heinrich von Klaproth, the same man who first coined the term 'Indogermanisch'. In his Asia Polyglotta, Klaproth (1823a,b) defined TB as the language family which comprised Burmese, Tibetan and Chinese and all languages which could be demonstrated to be genetically related to these three. He explicitly excluded Thai (i.e. Daic) as well as Vietnamese and Mon (i.e. AA) because the comparison of lexical roots in the core vocabulary indicated that these languages were representatives of other distinct language phyla.

Julius Heinrich von Klaproth was born on 11 October 1783 in Berlin and died on 28 August 1835 in Paris. As a young man he travelled to China in the years 1805–06 and again in 1806–07. He was widely read and mastered a good number of Oriental tongues. He edited the Asiatisches Magazin in Weimar, became a foreign associate of the Société Asiatique after its founding in 1821 in Paris. He was the first to observe that the root for 'birch', a phytonym which Sanskrit shares with other Indo-European languages, was important to an understanding of the population prehistory of the subcontinent:

> Il est digne de remarque que le bouleau s'appelle en sanscrit भूर्ज bhourtchtcha, et que ce mot dérive de la même racine que l'allemand birke, l'anglais birch et le russe, берe a (bereza), tandis que les noms des autres arbres de l'Inde ne se retrouvent pas dans les langues indo-germaniques de l'Europe. La raison en est, vraisemblablement, que les nations indo-germaniques venaient du nord, quand elles entrèrent dans l'Inde, où elles apportèrent la langue qui a servi de base au sanscrit, et qui a repoussé de la presqu'ile, les idiomes de la même origine que

le malabar et le télinga, que ces nations, dis-je, ne trouvèrent pas dans leur nouvelle patrie les arbres qu'elles avaient connu dans l'ancienne, à l'exception du bouleau, qui croît sur le versant méridional de l'Himâlaya.
(Klaproth 1830: 112–13)

This idea which was later seized upon by the Swiss linguist Adolphe Pictet, who coined the term 'linguistic palaeontology' in his 1859 study Les origines indo-européennes ou les aryas primitifs: Essai de pal éontologie linguistique.

As far as I have been able to trace, Klaproth (1823a: 380) was also the first to state clearly that the Formosan languages were members of the AN family, genetically related to Malay and Malagasy. Klaproth carefully scrutinised the lexical and grammatical data available at the time, and, following the precedents set by Nicolaes Witsen (1692) and Phillip von Strahlenberg (1730), he was the first to be able to present an informed and comprehensive polyphyletic view of Asian languages and language families. In order to reconcile this view with his religious beliefs, Klaproth (1823a: 43) devised a table of correspondence between Hindu and Biblical chronology, dating 'die große Ausbreitung des Indo-Germanischen Völkerstammes' to a prehistoric period 'vielleicht schon vor der Noah'ischen Fluth'. He identified and distinguished 23 main Asian linguistic stocks, which he knew did not yet represent an exhaustive inventory. Yet he argued for a smaller number of phyla because he recognised the genetic affinity between certain of these stocks and the distinct nature of others (Klaproth 1823a,b, 1831).

Klaproth was also the first to identify a family of languages comprising Chinese, the Burmese language of 'Awa', the language of the 'Tübeter' and related tongues, but specifically excluding languages such as Siamese, the Vietnamese language of Annam, the 'Moan' language of the 'Peguer' and so forth. Later German proponents of the TB theory had precocious intuitions about Chinese historical grammar. Scholars such as Carl Richard Lepsius (1861) and Wilhelm Grube (1881) mooted reflexes of TB historical morphology in Chinese. Lepsius even recognised that the tones of Chinese had arisen from the loss of older syllable-final segments and the loss of distinctions between older syllable-initial segments. Figure 6.1 shows a schematic view of Klaproth's model.

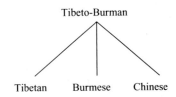

... and all languages which can be demonstrated to be genetically related to these three

Figure 6.1 One of the language phyla identified by Klaproth (1823a) in his polyphyletic view of Asian linguistic stocks.

Yet Klaproth's view of a polyglot Asian continent as the home to many distinct language phyla was not universally well-received. In January 1825, in a letter to Baron Paul Schilling von Canstadt, for instance, August Wilhelm von Schlegel described his distaste for the polyphyletic view of Asia presented by Klaproth (Körner 1930, I: 631), whereas Schlegel evidently found John Leyden's undifferentiated 'Indo-Chinese' view of Asian languages to be more palatable (1832: 21). To scholars in Europe, the two most important language families were what was known in the nineteenth century variously as Indo-European, Indo-Germanic or Aryan, and the Semitic family, later known as Hamito-Semitic and most recently as Afroasiatic. It did not come naturally to everyone to view the many distinct linguistic stocks of Asia as language families on an equal footing with Indo-European and Afroasiatic.

Personalities also played a role, and even the even-keeled Wilhelm von Humboldt made reference to the 'Ätzigkeit' of the brilliant Klaproth (Walravens 1999a). Moreover, between 1826 and 1829, the Société Asiatique in Paris was split apart by the feuding between the group comprising Klaproth, Abel Rémusat, Eugène Burnouf and Julius von Mohl and the 'fleuristes' or 'philologues-poètes', led by the acrimonious Silvestre de Sacy. The lines of animosities drawn in this conflict emanated far beyond Paris. Indeed, the professional perceptions of many a scholar of Oriental languages were shaped by the constellation of likes and dislikes which existed between the linguists of the day as much as they were by substantive arguments, and arguably this is to some extent still the case in TB linguistics today. However, in the nineteenth-century personality conflicts also had the effect of exacerbating unstated but deeply rooted Eurocentric preconceptions.

The Indo-Chinese or Sino-Tibetan view

One sally against Klaproth's polyphyletic view of Asian languages was Friedrich Max Müller's Turanian theory, a putative language family encompassing each and every language of the Old World other than the 'Semitic' or Afroasiatic and 'Arian' or Indo-European languages (van Driem 2001). The Turanian view was highly influential in the British Isles and throughout the British Empire and continued to influence scholars after Müller's death in 1900, even though he had himself abandoned the theory in his lifetime.

Another more enduring challenge to the differentiated view of Asian linguistic stocks was originally named 'Indo-Chinese'. Indo-Chinese has a more chequered history than Turanian and still continues to lead a life of its own under the guise of 'Sino-Tibetan'. This view of languages originated with the Scottish physician and poet John Leyden. Leyden's work on 'Indo-Persic' lacked the profundity and erudition of the great Sanskrit scholar Henry Thomas Colebrooke (1765–1837), but his work on 'Indo-Chinese' was published in Asiatick Researches in 1808. Leyden's 'Indo-Chinese' encompassed Mon, which he called 'the Moan or language of Pegu', Balinese, Malay, Burmese, 'the Tai or Siamese' and 'the Law, or language of Laos', and Vietnamese or 'the Anam language of Cochin Chinese'. These 'Indo-Chinese' languages of the Asian continent shared a more immediate genetic affinity with Chinese in Leyden's conception, but Indo-Chinese also explicitly included 'the inhabitants of the Eastern isles who are not immeadiately [sic] derived from the Chinese nations' (1806b: 1). In fact, Indo-Chinese encompassed all the languages spoken by 'the inhabitants of the regions which lie between India and China, and the greater part of the islanders in the eastern sea', which although 'dissimilar', according to Leyden, 'exhibit the same mixed origin' (1806a: 1).

After Leyden's death, the Indo-Chinese idea began to lead a life of its own. In 1837, the American missionary and linguist Nathan Brown used the term 'Indo-Chinese' to designate all the languages of eastern Eurasia. The fact that Brown's Indo-Chinese even included Korean and Japanese illustrates the appeal and dogged longevity of undifferentiated views in the face of more informed opinions. Later versions of Indo-Chinese excluded Japanese and Korean, and the AA languages were recognised as constituting a separate language family by the American Baptist missionary Francis Mason in 1854, when he saw evidence for a specific genetic relationship between the Mon-Khmer language Mon and the Munda language Kol. This newly recognised language family was known as Mon-Khmer-Kolarian for over half a century until Wilhelm Schmidt renamed it AA in 1906. After AA had been removed from Indo-Chinese, German scholars such as Emile Forchhammer (1882) and Ernst Kuhn (1889) continued to refer to what was left of the pseudophylum by the name 'indochinesisch', and in general the same practice was generally observed in the Anglo-Saxon literature. However, a few British scholars, for example, Sir Richard Temple (1903) and George Whitehead (1925), used the term 'Indo-Chinese' in precisely the opposite sense, to designate the AA or 'Mon-Khmer-Kolarian' language family which had been extracted from the expansive pseudophlyum.

After the removal of other phyla, Indo-Chinese had been whittled down to the original TB plus Daic (Figure 6.2, N.B. Daic has been excluded since the Second World War). However, in the confused Indo-Chinese conception, the putative language family consisted of a 'Tibeto-Burman' branch (i.e. the original TB minus Sinitic) and a 'Sino-Daic' branch, for example, August Conrady (1896), Franz Nikolaus Finck (1909). There was residual uncertainty about the genetic affinity of Vietnamese, particularly in the French scholarly community. André-Georges

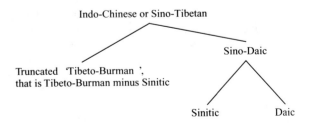

Figure 6.2 The Indo-Chinese or ST theory.

Haudricourt settled the question once and for all in 1954, and Vietnamese has been universally recognised as AA ever since.

Indo-Chinese was renamed 'sino-tibétain' by Jean Przyluski in 1924, and the name entered the English language in 1931 as 'Sino-Tibetan' when Przyluski and the British scholar Gordon Hannington Luce wrote an etymological note on the 'Sino-Tibetan' root for the numeral 'hundred'. A defining feature of the Indo-Chinese or ST theory, very much at variance with Klaproth's original TB theory, was that Chinese was not seen as a part of TB, whilst Daic was seen as the closest relative of Chinese. In the United States, Alfred Kroeber and Robert Shafer adopted the new term 'Sino-Tibetan' for Indo-Chinese. Chinese scholars similarly adopted the term Hàn-Zàng 'Sino-Tibetan', the contours of which are still the same as that of Conrady's 'Indo-Chinese' and Przyluski's antiquated 'Sino-Tibetan'.

Robert Shafer soon realised that Daic did not belong to the Indo-Chinese or ST family and in 1938 'prepared a list of words showing the lack of precise phonetic and semantic correspondence' between Daic and other Indo-Chinese languages. Armed with this list, Shafer travelled to France before the outbreak of the Second World War 'to convince Maspero that Daic was not Sino-Tibetan' (1955: 97–8). Instead, Henri Maspero managed to convince Shafer to retain Daic within ST.

When Paul Benedict moved to Berkeley in 1938 to join Kroeber's ST Philology project, he likewise exchanged the name Indo-Chinese for 'Sino-Tibetan'. Over a century after Klaproth had already identified Daic as a linguistic stock distinct from TB (inc. Chinese), Benedict too in 1942 ousted Daic from 'Sino-Tibetan', but he remained more resolute about this measure than Shafer. The removal of Sinitic from the 'Sino-Daic' branch of 'Sino-Tibetan' resulted in a tree model characterised by the retention of the heuristic artifact that Chinese was a separate trunk of the language family. In fact, this was the sole remaining feature which defined ST as a putative language family and distinguished it from the TB theory. For a brief spate in the 1970s, ST even consisted of a Chinese branch and a Tibeto-Karen construct, which in turn was divided into a Karen branch and an even more mutilated 'Tibeto-Burman' (Benedict 1972, 1976).

The tacit but always untested assumption of Sino-Tibetanists has been that all 'Tibeto-Burman' languages share unitary developments not found in Chinese and Karen. Great significance has been ascribed to superficial criteria such as word order. Though Karen was later put back into truncated 'Tibeto-Burman', adherents of ST have continued to assume the existence of as yet undemonstrated common innovations shared by all TB languages other than Sinitic.

Tibeto-Burman outlives Sino-Tibetan

In the 1990s, the time was ripe for the Indo-Chinese or ST paradigm to be replaced by the original TB theory of Klaproth. Three developments converged to yield insights heralding a return to the TB language family, that is, (1) a better understanding of OC, (2) improved insights into the genetic position of Sinitic and an appreciation of its TB character, and (3) the exhaustive identification of all the TB subgroups.

The first development involved the production of better reconstructions of OC. Major advances in the historical phonology of Chinese were accompanied by new insights into Chinese historical morphology. New insights on the genetic position of Chinese vindicated Klaproth's and Lepsius' views. By the 1990s, the TB character of Sinitic had been amply demonstrated. In the history of the field no uniquely shared innovations have ever been adduced which could define truncated 'Tibeto-Burman' as a separate coherent taxon that would exclude Chinese and be coordinate with Proto-Sinitic. The new face of OC was of a language with a decidedly TB countenance and more closely allied with certain groups like Bodic and Kiranti. In fact, OC is less remote from the mainstream TB point of view than, say, Gongduk or Toto. A second development is that isoglosses possibly representing lexical innovations as well as uniquely shared morphological innovations in Brahmaputran appear to indicate that a more primary bifurcation in the language family is between subgroups such as Brahmaputran and the rest of the TB family whilst other lexical and grammatical features show that Sinitic is a member of a sub-branch, that I proposed, named Sino-Bodic.

The third development which has heralded a return to the original TB theory is the exhaustive charting of TB subgroups. Only recently have all the languages and language groups of the TB language family been identified with the discovery in Bhutan in the 1990s of the last hitherto unreported TB languages, namely Black Mountain and Gongduk. In addition to the identification of all basic subgroups, new members of already recognised subgroups have been discovered and rediscovered in Tibet, southwestern China, northeastern India and Nepal. In 1999, in an enclave around the shores of lake Ba-gsum or Brag-gsum in northern Koṅ-po rGya-mdah in Tibet, Nicolas Tournadre identified the language Bag-skad [bʈkʈ], spoken by an estimated 3,000 speakers and previously erroneously classified as a Tibetan dialect. Tournadre reports that this tongue is related to Dzala and other East Bodish languages of Bhutan. Similarly, Baram or 'Bhrámú', a TB language reported by Hodgson in the mid-nineteenth century, but thought since to have gone extinct, was rediscovered in Gorkha district in central Nepal in the 1990s.

The basic outline of the TB family is shown in Figure 6.3. The model does not have the shape of a family tree, but this is not to claim that there is no Stammbaum. Not only is the branching pattern of the tree not within view, the constituent language subgroups of the family have only finally exhaustively been identified within the past decade. At present, we do not know the higher-order branching, but we have every reason to believe that these branches are there.

This more candid but at the same time more comprehensive view of the language family confronts scholars with the immediate need to search for and identify the evidence which could support empirically defensible higher-order subgroups within TB, analogous to Italo-Celtic and Balto-Slavic in the

TIBETO-BURMAN vs INDO-CHINESE

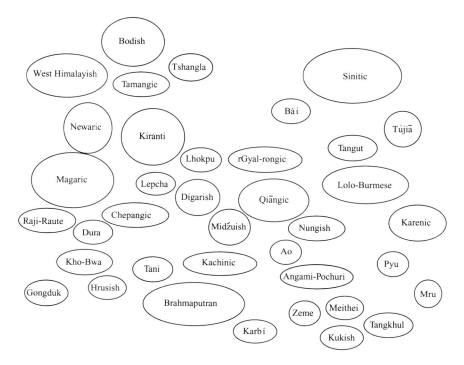

Figure 6.3 Informed but agnostic picture of TB subgroups.

Notes
The extended version of the Brahmaputran hypothesis includes Kachinic, but for the sake of argument this diagram depicts the short variant of Brahmaputran, namely excluding Kachinic. Kachinic comprises the Sak languages and the Jinghpaw dialects. Likewise, Tangut is separately depicted, although Tangut is likely to be part of Qiangic. Digarish is northern Mishmi, and Midźuish is southern Mishmi, that is the Kaman cluster. Bái is listed as a distinct group, whereas it may form a constituent of Sinitic, albeit one heavily influenced by Lolo-Burmese. Tǔjiā is a TB language of indeterminate phylogenetic propinquity spoken in a few villages in northwestern Húnán. The Sino-Bodic hypothesis encompasses at least the groups called Sinitic, Kiranti, Bodish, West Himalayish, rGyal-rongic, Tamangic, Tshangla and Lhokpu and possibly Lepcha. Other hypotheses, such as the inclusion of Chepang and perhaps Dura and Raji-Raute within Magaric, are discussed in van Driem (2001)[1]

Indo-European language family. The burden of proof now lies squarely on the shoulders of Sino-Tibetanists who propagate truncated 'Tibeto-Burman' as a valid taxon to adduce evidence for this construct.

Implications for interpreting prehistory

The Neolithic Revolution and the spread of agriculture are widely thought to have been important factors in the dispersal of ancient populations and the spread of language families. However, the Fertile Crescent itself attests to the fact that agriculture was adopted by ethnolinguistically unrelated populations and that agriculture spread effortlessly across ethnolinguistic boundaries without affecting them in any significant way. Sumerian, Elamite, Akkadian, Hurrian, Hattic and other languages of early agricultural civilisations which have left no surviving linguistic descendants bear witness to the permeability of linguistic boundaries for the dissemination of agriculture. The Neolithic and Bronze Age of Asia Minor and Mesopotamia is characterised by a very long period of incursive population movements into, rather than out of Anatolia and the Fertile Crescent, driven or lured, it seems, by the relative affluence of urban centres supported by agricultural surplus.

Those who secondarily adopt a technique, tradition or cultural institution often improve upon it and excel in its exploitation beyond the attainments of its original innovators. In Dutch this is known as de wet van de remmende voorsprong, that is, the 'law' that the very group which has managed to get ahead of other groups by virtue of an innovation is also more prone to get bogged down at a later stage by shortcomings inherent to the prototypical version of the technology which originally gave them the edge over other groups. Meanwhile, other groups who did not have to invest the resources and effort to develop and implement the technology in the first place forge ahead by introducing a more refined and streamlined version of the innovation and are unhampered by having to replace or revamp an obsolete infrastructure. O'Connor (1995) and Blench (Chapter 2, this volume) have argued that irrigated rice agriculture in the Southeast Asian lowlands does not correlate with a spread at the language family level, but with spreads at a lower phylogenetic level.

By contrast, perhaps what the incursive Indo-Europeans did may have been nothing other than land theft. Nevertheless, the spread of specific, well-defined Neolithic cultural assemblages remains a powerful tool in the reconstruction of ancient population movements and, more particularly, in the possible early dispersal of language families. The hypothesis that an agricultural dispersal may reflect the ancient spread of a language community underlies my reconstruction of the spread of the Sino-Bodic branch of TB (van Driem 1998, 1999, 2001, 2002). Yet the incentive for migration into affluent regions with an agricultural surplus is a factor to be reckoned with in TB prehistory too. The distribution of primary branches of TB suggests that it may be that the urban affluence of pre-TB agricultural populations was what drew the linguistic ancestors of early Sinitic civilisation to the Yellow River and North China Plain in the first place, just as Gutaeans, Kassites, Amorites and Indo-Europeans were drawn to the Fertile Crescent and Anatolia. Benedict once proposed that the Shang may not have been Sinitic at all and that the Zhou, who came from the West, may have been the bearers of the Proto-Sinitic language to the Yellow River basin, where they adopted the Shang ideograms devised by a pre-TB population (1972: 197). Rather, the prosperous agricultural civilisation on the North China Plain may have lured the linguistic forebears of Sinitic, or perhaps Sino-Bodic, to the Yellow River basin long before the Shang period.

Quite often the archaeological record may not directly reflect such linguistic intrusions. Instead, rather than reflecting the spread of language families, archaeology shows the regional discrepancies in technical advancement which may have motivated foreign linguistic intrusions. In particular, this may apply in the case of the early displacement of Sinitic outside of the TB core area as well as in the case of the advent of Indo-European groups to the Near East, such as the Hittites in Anatolia and the Mitanni in the Jazirah. Not only did agriculture spread across linguistic boundaries from the very outset, the direction of linguistic intrusions in many episodes of prehistory may have been diametrically opposed to the direction of the spread of agriculture.

My reconstruction is based on a family tree model of TB, which presumes a clustering of groups and suggests a relative chronology. Yet, the model is not purely a Stammbaum as such. The problem with the TB family tree models proposed to date is that uniquely shared innovations are scarce, and higher-level subgroups are often defined by what later turn out to be shared retentions. The family tree in Figure 6.4 is not just a geographically inspired schema, for it incorporates subgroups which were discerned by Shafer and are still recognised on the basis of phonological and morphological criteria and lexical isoglosses. The model also incorporates Sino-Bodic, a higher-level subgrouping hypothesis involving Sinitic and those languages within TB which appear to be more immediately related to Sinitic than either are to, for example, Brahmaputran, Karbí and other genetically remote groups.

Although Sino-Bodic is associated with me (van Driem 1995, 1997), earlier versions of the Sino-Bodic hypothesis had previously suggested themselves to Walter Simon (1929), Robert Shafer (1955, 1966, 1967, 1968, 1974) and Nicholas Bodman (1980), on the basis of uniquely shared lexical items. In addition to the limited set of lexical isoglosses, I have described morphological features that

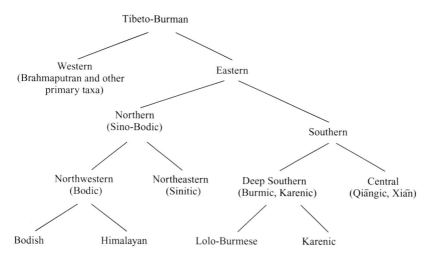

Figure 6.4 Linguistically inspired archaeological interpretation of the geographical dispersal of TB groups.

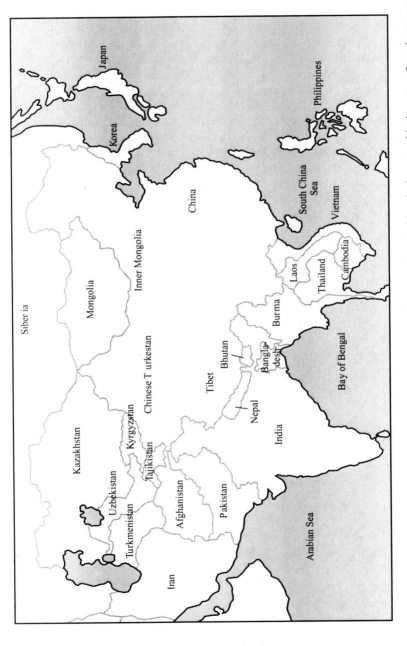

Map 6.1 In this clutch of 39 diamonds, each diamond represents not a language, but the historical geographical centre of a primary taxon or subgroup of languages of the TB family. In order to present a fair picture of the internal diversity of the Brahmaputran branch, the Dhimalish, Bodo-Koch and Konyak subgroups have each been represented by a diamond. Likewise, two separate diamonds indicate Kiranti and Newaric, the two constituent subgroups within the hypothetical and internally highly diverse Mahakiranti branch. The extinct Tangut language, however, is treated as a member of Qiangic.

appear to bolster the identification of Sino-Bodic as a subgroup (van Driem 1997). By contrast, the constellation of subgroups which I collectively name Western TB represents a number of primary branches which I assume had split off at an early stage and settled in northeastern India, originating from a TB proto-homeland which I locate in Sìchuān, as British scholars in the nineteenth century had already proposed, even though they did not have access to modern-day linguistic, archaeological and genetic evidence. Here I shall briefly outline the model again and adduce additional supporting arguments from recent research on haplotypes on the Y chromosome. I shall also point out linguistic and archaeological weaknesses in the model, which leave room for an alternative version of the reconstructed linguistic dispersal.

Though primarily linguistically inspired, my theory represents an interpretation of the archaeological record in light of TB subgrouping hypotheses and the geographical distribution of modern and historically attested communities (Map 6.1). The theory depicted schematically in Figure 6.4 is illustrated in Maps 6.2–6.5. The differences between Figure 6.3 and Figure 6.4 illustrate the linguistic and the archaeological view between which some correlation is sought. Western TB in particular is not just a linguistic hypothesis, but an archaeological theory about the population history of the TB area informed by linguistic insights about the primary nature of subgroups in the Himalayas and northeastern India. From a phylogenetic perspective, Western TB is analogous to the Formosan language groups within AN. Like Formosan, Western TB is not a single taxon, but a collection of primary taxa within the family. Rather, it is the remaining branch, Eastern TB, which may constitute a possible genetic unit, just as Oceanic is a single primary branch within AN. It is therefore more fitting to speak of an Eastern than of a Western TB hypothesis, if there is such a thing as the latter. Brahmaputran is just one of the many taxa collectively referred to as Western TB. The short variant of Brahmaputran consists of the Dhimalish, Bodo-Koch and Konyak subgroups, and the extended version of the Brahmaputran hypothesis includes Kachinic, that is, the Sak languages and the Jinghpaw dialects. Some other Western TB taxa in the northeast of the Subcontinent include the Kho-Bwa cluster, Hrusish, Midźuish, Nungish, Digarish, Tani, Karbí, Ao, Angami-Pochuri, Zeme, Tangkhul and Gongduk.

The various ways of reconstructing prehistory, that is, archaeology, linguistics and genetics, measure three independent quantities which are merely probabilistically correlated and which, moreover, divide into taxa which may correspond to quite different time depths. Discrepancies between the chromosomal and the linguistic pictures of the past indicate that, in some cases, a larger incursive population may have adopted a language of a smaller population already resident in the area which they had settled, as in the case of Bulgarian, whereas some languages borne by ruling élites have been adopted by a larger dominated resident population, as in the case of Hungarian. The racial heterogeneity of TB populations in northeastern India, particularly the phenotypic difference between Brahmaputran language communities and other TB groups in the northeast, has been noted ever since the earliest British accounts of the area.

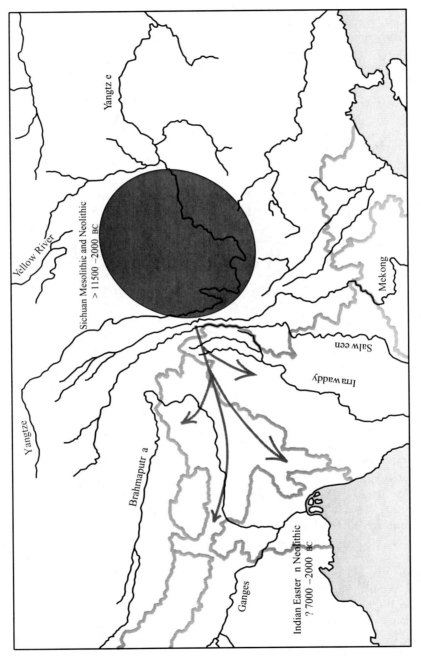

Map 6.2 Lower Brahmaputra basin and surrounding hill tracts colonised by western Tibeto-Burmans bearing the technologies from Sichuan which were to become known as the Indian Eastern Neolithic, an Auswanderung possibly set in motion before the seventh millennium BC.

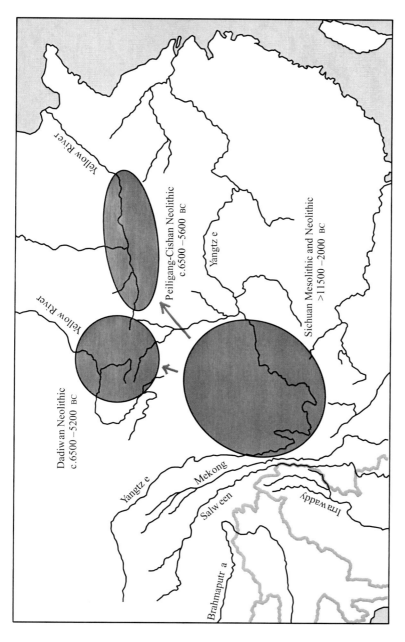

Map 6.3 The establishment of the early Neolithic Péilígɛng-Císhān and Dàdìwān civilisations in the Yellow River basin by northern Tibeto-Burmans before the beginning of the sixth millennium BC.

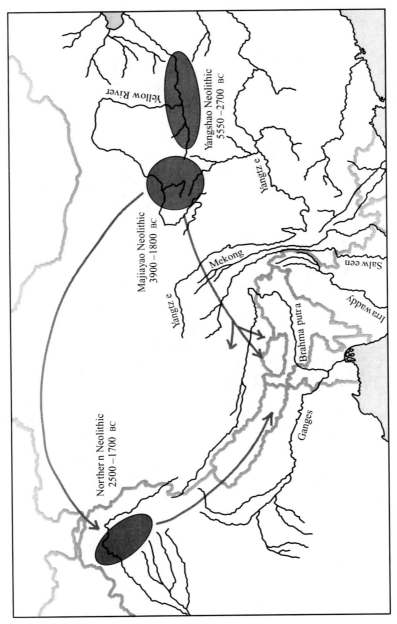

Map 6.4 One offshoot of the late Neolithic Májiāyáo cultural complex migrated south through northern Sichuan and eastern Tibet into Sikkim, whereas another offshoot migrated to the southwest across the Himalayas to establish the northern Neolithic civilisation in Kashmir. Northwestern Tibeto-Burmans peopled the Himalayas, both from the northeast, colonising Sikkim and Nepal, and from the west, colonising the western Himalayas and the Tibetan plateau.

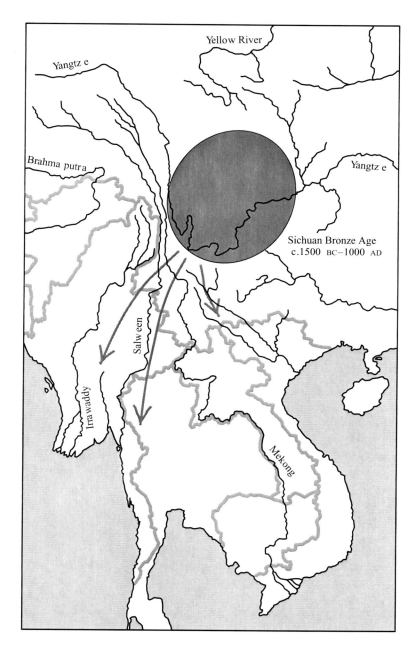

Map 6.5 The exodus of deep southern Tibeto-Burmans into peninsular Southeast Asia had begun by the first millennium BC, and the process seems never to have completely come to a halt, as Lolo-Burmese groups have continued to trickle into Thailand from Yúnnán in recent history.

Modern genetic studies occasionally corroborate old theories of population history which were exclusively inspired by, and based on, language and old-fashioned racial somatology. For example, Basu et al. (2001) recently studied haplotype frequencies of $(CTG)_n$ repeat and three other biallelic markers in and around the myotonic dystrophy locus in 13 ethnolinguistically and geographically diverse populations of India. Their findings support the traditional ethnographical conception that certain tribal groups such as the AA Lodhas and Santhal represent 'the most ancient inhabitants' of the Subcontinent and may be identified as the 'descendants of modern humans who arrived in India on one of the early waves of "out-of-Africa" migration' (2001: 316, 317). Likewise, in keeping with the conceptions of traditional Indian ethnography, their findings suggest that tribal populations have 'remained relatively more isolated than the caste populations', and 'the boundaries of caste populations, especially those of middle and lower ranks, have been more fluid than those of tribal populations' (2001: 316).

Until recently the state of the art was such that the interpretation of the chromosomal picture using classical markers sometimes only provided a limited glimpse of events in prehistory in the absence of supporting archaeological or linguistic evidence. But a spectrum of markers is now available which ranges from slowly evolving biallelic markers to rapidly evolving minisatellites. Binary haplotypes with very low mutation rates represent unique event polymorphisms which occurred at large intervals in human evolution. These are known as 'unique mutation events', abbreviated UME, and include the single-base pair substitutions described by Underhill et al. (1997, 2001). By contrast, some rapidly evolving loci on the Y chromosome, such as the minisatellite locus MSY1 studied by Jobling et al. (1998), exhibit a mutation rate of between 2 per cent to 11 per cent per generation. Intermediate between these two extremes are markers which evolve with moderate rapidity, such as Y chromosome microsatellite loci known as short tandem repeats, abbreviated STR, which Kayser et al. (2001) have shown to be a powerful tool in reconstructing population history. Though still problematic in some respects, the findings of studies on these different types of polymorphisms allow statistical analyses which may be of some utility in evaluating competing models of the peopling of Eurasia reconstructed on the basis of linguistic and archaeological evidence.

Any model of TB prehistory will have to account for the racial affinities of some Western TB groups, for example, Toto, Raji, Raute, Dhimal and some other Brahmaputran groups. The intriguing racial variation of TB and non-TB groups in the Subcontinent, already evident to earlier generations of ethnographers, is being charted in greater detail by current population genetic studies, such as those currently being conducted by Peter de Knijff and myself in the Himalayan region. Both the collection of genetic samples and the interpretation of the results must be conducted in an ethnolinguistically informed way.

In this context, two apparently conflicting sets of findings have recently been obtained by teams of geneticists looking at TB populations in China and the greater Himalayan region. Yet, the discrepancy between these findings may be more apparent than real, and may very well correspond to different realities situated at different time depths. The hypothesis of a TB homeland in Sìchuān has recently found unexpected corroboration in the findings of the Chinese Human Genome Diversity Project, whose ethnolinguistically informed assays of population groups in China have shown that genetically East Asian populations can be derived from Southeast Asian populations and that, therefore, populations ancestral to the Chinese may not have originated in the Yellow River basin but could have migrated to this area in a northeasterly direction from southwestern China (Chu et al. 1998). This information was still unavailable when I first proposed that the TB homeland lay in Sìchuān on linguistic grounds.

Another team of geneticists has found a strong genetic affinity amongst population groups of the TB language family in the form the prevalence of a T to C mutation at Y chromosome locus M122, whereas the extremely high frequency of H8, a haplotype derived from M122C, reflects the results of a genetic bottleneck effect that occurred during an ancient southwesterly migration (Su et al. 2000). The latter group of geneticists attempted to relate the geographical distribution of TB populations with a migration from the middle Yellow River basin about 10,000 years ago, and to conjecture that the earliest Neolithic cultures of this area might have been associated with the putative TB homeland. However, there are two flaws in this interpretation.

First of all, the study by Su et al. (2000) sampled only six populations from the pivotal, ethnolinguistically most heterogeneous TB heartland in northeastern India. The samples from this area were limited to a 'Kachari' individual, a Rabha, a Naga, an Adi, a Nishi and an Apatani. Their study left most key TB population groups untouched. Conjectures were advanced about prehistoric migrations to the Himalayas, but, other than the three sample populations from Arunachal Pradesh, no Himalayan populations were tested. Fifteen samples, constituting half of the test material, were obtained from individuals representing Hàn Chinese populations settled in various provinces of China. The remaining samples were from several TB populations resident in China, that is, Nakhi, Bái, Yí, Jinuò, Jinghpaw, Yúnnán Lahu and T jia. Finally, there were two Tibetan samples, one from Lhasa and one from Yúnnán, and a single Karen sample from Southeast Asia. The assay was therefore limited and did not sample most of the key TB language communities in the Himalayas about whose ancestors inferences were made. The second problem is that the interpretative framework was based on the phylogenetic model presented by Matisoff (1991), in which an Indo-Chinese or 'Proto-Sino-Tibetan' Ursprache at its deepest time depth is presumed to have split east–west into 'Proto-Chinese' and 'Proto-Tibeto-Burman'. Problems with this model have been discussed earlier.

At a far greater time depth, ethnolinguistically informed assays of the population of eastern Asia on the basis of 30 microsatellites made by Chu et al. (1998) have shown that the ethnolinguistic composition of China is reflected in the genetic complexity, and that the peopling of eastern Asia probably occurred in a northward movement from Southeast Asia. These results have been corroborated in a study of 19 biallelic loci on the Y chromosome, which demonstrated that northern populations in eastern Asia only represent a subset of the haplotypes found in southern populations, which show greater polymorphism on the whole than northern populations (Su et al. 1999).

Craniometric and skeletal evidence is still routinely used by archaeologists and palaeontologists to reconstruct population history. For example, Brown (1998) and Demeter (2000) argue for major morphological changes in population in the Far East between various phases of the post-Pleistocene or between the Mesolithic and Neolithic periods. Hopefully, it will be possible in future to make such findings square with the new insights of genomic studies. Particularly in view of the phenotypic variation sometimes observed within single populations, it will hopefully be undertaken to extract DNA from such crania for study. Recent work by Ding et al. (2000) has also shown that northern and southern haplotype clusters blend across a cline without any abrupt change, so that no clear genetic support has yet been identified that might corroborate linguistic theories connecting Chinese to Caucasian, for example, the Sino-Caucasian theory advocated by Starostin, or connecting Chinese genetically with Indo-European, as Pulleyblank does. Yet all these investigations have merely scratched the surface of a vast terrain which lies to be charted and have begun to make possible an integrated vision of the genetic, linguistic, historical, archaeological and anthropological data.

Three arguments support the identification of Sichuan as the TB homeland. The first is the centre of gravity argument based on the present and historically attested geographical distribution of TB language communities. Sichuan encompasses the area where the upper courses of the Brahmaputra, Salween, Mekong and Yangtze run parallel to each other within a corridor just 500 km in breadth. The second argument is that archaeologists identify the Indian Eastern Neolithic, associated with the indigenous TB populations of northeastern India and the Indo-Burmese borderlands, as a Neolithic cultural complex which originated in Sichuan and spread into Assam and the surrounding hill tracts of Arunachal Pradesh, the Meghalaya, Tripura, the Mizoram, Manipur, Nagaland and Chittagong before the third millennium BC (Dani 1960; Sharma 1967, 1981, 1989; Thapar 1985; Wheeler 1959).

Archaeologists have estimated the Indian Eastern Neolithic to date from between 10,000 and 5,000 BC (Sharma 1989; Thapar 1985). If these estimates are taken at face value, it would mean that northeastern India had shouldered adzes at least three millennia before they appeared in Southeast Asia. Whilst some archaeologists may give younger estimates for the Indian Eastern Neolithic, a solid stratigraphy and calibrated radiocarbon dates are still unavailable for this major South Asian cultural assemblage. The Indian Eastern Neolithic appears intrusively in the northeast of the Subcontinent and represents a tradition wholly distinct from the other Neolithic assemblages attested in India. Assuming that the Indian Eastern Neolithic was borne to the Subcontinent by ancient Tibeto-Burmans, then if the younger estimates for this cultural assemblage can be substantiated by solid dating, the linguistic fracturing of subgroups would have to have occurred earlier in Sìchuan before the migrations, as I had suggested previously (1998, 2001).

The third argument for a TB homeland in Sìchuan is that archaeologists have argued that southwestern China would be a potentially promising place to look for the precursors of the Neolithic civilisations which later took root in the Yellow River Valley (Chang 1965, 1977, 1986, 1992; Chêng 1957). The Dàdìwan culture in Gansù and Shcnxi, and the contiguous and contemporaneous Péilígcng-Císhan assemblage along the middle course of the Yellow River share common patterns of habitation and burial, and employed common technologies, such as hand-formed tripod pottery with short firing times, highly worked chipped stone tools and non-perforated semi-polished stone axes. The Dàdìwan and Péilígcng-Císhan assemblages, despite several points of divergence, were closely related cultural complexes, and the people behind these civilisations shared the same preference for settlements on plains along the river or on high terraces at confluences. Whereas the Sìchuan Neolithic represented the continuation of local Mesolithic cultural traditions, the first Neolithic agriculturalists of the Dàdìwan and Péilígcng-Císhan cultures may tentatively be identified with innovators who migrated from Sìchuan to the fertile loess plains of the Yellow River basin. The technological gap between the earlier local microlithic cultures and the highly advanced Neolithic civilisations which subsequently come into flower in the Yellow River basin remains striking. Yet a weakness in this third argument lies in the archaeological state of the art. Just as it is difficult to argue for a possible precursor in Sìchuan in face of a lack of compelling archaeological evidence, neither can the inadequate state of the art in Neolithic archaeology in southwestern China serve as an argument for the absence of such a precursor.

Moreover, agricultural dispersals and linguistic intrusions may be distinct issues altogether. The concentration within a contiguous geographical region of all major high-order TB subgroups other than T jia and Sinitic constitutes a linguistic argument for an early TB linguistic intrusion into the area that today is northern China. If the Dàdìwan culture in Gansù and Shcnxi, and the contiguous Péilígcng-Císhan assemblage along the middle course of the Yellow River are indeed primary Neolithic civilisations, then the eccentric location of Sinitic and T jia may even trace the route of the early migration out of the TB homeland to the affluent and more technologically advanced agricultural societies in the Yellow River basin. In other words, since the linguistic evidence puts the TB heartland in southwestern China and northeastern India, an archaeological precursor in Sìchuan for the Dàdìwan and Péilígcng-Císhan cultures would fit the hypothesis that the displacement of Sinitic to northern China was the result of an early TB archaeological dispersal. The absence of any such precursor in Sìchuan would fit a theory of early migration from the northern end of the ancient TB dialect continuum to the affluent areas of pre-TB agricultural civilisations along the Yellow River.

I collectively refer to the ancient TB populations, who either bore with them from Sìchuan to the loess plateau the technologies of polished stone tools and cord-marked pottery or were enticed to the loess plateau by the affluence of the technologically more advanced agricultural civilisations there, as 'Northern Tibeto-Burmans'. I identify these Northern Tibeto-Burmans as the likely linguistic ancestors of the Sino-Bodic groups. Subsequent technological developments were both innovated and introduced comparatively rapidly in the North, whereas relatively egalitarian small-scale agricultural societies persisted in southwestern China until the Bronze Age. This hypothesis places the split between Northern and Southern TB in the seventh millennium BC, just before the dawn of the Dàdiwan and Péilígcng-Císhan civilisations.

I identify the spread of Bodic groups from Gansù with the dispersal of the Mcjiayáo and Yengsháo Neolithic cultures and the cultivars broomcorn millet (Panicum miliaceum) and foxtail millet (Setaria italica), first domesticated on the North China Plain, into the Himalayan region in the third millennium BC. Sino-Bodic would have split up into Sinitic and Bodic before this date. This dispersal proceeded along two routes. The Mcjiayáo Neolithic culture spread westward along the main ancient Inner Asian trade route across the Himalayas to establish the genetically related Northern or Kashmir Neolithic in Kashmir and Swat. At the same time, the Mcjiayáo cultural assemblage spread southward from Gansù through eastern Tibet into southeastern Tibet, Bhutan and Sikkim to establish the Neolithic cultures of Chab-mdo and northern Sikkim, both of which have been identified as colonial exponents of the Mcjiayáo Neolithic. Moreover, these colonial exponents make their appearance in Kashmir, eastern Tibet and Sikkim in the second half of the third millennium BC, so that the final phase of these movements coincides precisely with the Bànshan phase of the Mcjiayáo cultural assemblage, which covers the period between 2,200 and 1,900 BC and is characterised by a marked geographical contraction of the original Mcjiayáo core territory.

My reconstruction of TB dispersals, presented in greater detail elsewhere (van Driem 1998, 1999, 2001), is outlined here in Maps 6.2 to 6.5. On the whole, this reconstruction still fits the known facts well. Yet the weaknesses in this model must be recognised. First of all, Sìchuan and southwestern China in general remains archaeologically inadequately researched, despite the significance of the area's prehistory. A second problem is that the linguistic state of the art gives us no real relative chronology for the splitting off of the main taxa of the language family, as shown in Figure 6.3. None the less, the sheer number of major language groups in the Himalayan region and the northeast of the Subcontinent provides a good idea of where and when it would be most fruitful to look for likely archaeological correlates for the dispersal of ancient TB populations. The lopsided geographical distribution of most major TB groups in the Himalayas and northeastern India, the likely linguistic affinity of Sinitic with Bodic, and the possible affinity of 'Deep Southern' with 'Central' TB groups have inspired the tree schema outlined in Figure 6.4.

An alternative proposal to a TB homeland in Sìchuan would be to identify the earliest Neolithic cultures along the Yellow River basin and on the North China Plain with the TB homeland. However, if the TB homeland were to have lain in the Yellow River basin, then we would be hard pressed to find a plausible archaeological correlate for the spread of Brahmaputran language communities, which once extended beyond Assam and the Meghalaya and formerly covered much of the area that is now Bangladesh and West Bengal. Furthermore, it must be kept in mind that the early Neolithic civilisation on the Yellow River is distinct from the cultural assemblages of the middle Yangtze basin, the succeeding stages of which ultimately spread as far afield as Oceania in the course of millennia. Both the Yellow River and the middle Yangtze civilisations represent ancient agricultural societies as old as those of the Fertile Crescent.

Clearly, the first and foremost desiderata are that the archaeology of Sìchuān and northeastern India be better understood, that a fine-grid and ethnolinguistically informed genome study of the greater Himalayan region be carried out, and that a new look be taken at subgroups within TB, whereby the same methodological rigour of sound laws and shared innovation is applied which has characterised Indo-European studies. My reconstruction of TB language dispersals will remain sensitive to revision and modification based on new data and new insights.

An intriguing theory involving a remote linguistic relationship with TB is the Sino-Austronesian theory proposed by Laurent Sagart (1994, 2001 and this volume) connecting TB with AN. Because Sagart initially recognised possible Sino-Austronesian correspondences in Chinese material more than in TB, he was originally inclined to identify the Sino-Austronesian unity with the Lóngshān cultural horizon. However, there is an alternative way of viewing the Sino-Austronesian evidence and the archaeological record. The Lóngshān coastal interaction ensued upon a northward expansion of PAN or Austro-Tai culture from its ancient homeland in southern and southeastern China, and this northward expansion of early Austronesians would have brought them into contact with early Northern Tibeto-Burmans. The ensuing contact situations between AN and the Sino-Bodic branch of TB could have involved the ancient exchange of vocabulary between the two language families. The way to test this would be to determine whether items shared by AN and TB are indeed limited to the Sino-Bodic branch of TB, including rice terms such as Malay beras and Tibetan ɦbras, a correspondence already pointed out by Hendrik Kern in 1889. The Lóngshān interaction sphere is an obvious candidate in terms of time and place for early contacts between ancient Austronesians and ancient Tibeto-Burmans, particularly the Dàwènkǒu Neolithic of Shandong with its well-established ties both with the other coastal cultures of the Lóngshān interaction sphere as well as with the ancient Northern TB Yǎngsháo Neolithic civilisation.

However, the archaeological record presents earlier possible correlates for contact between ancient Daic or Austro-Tai and ancient Northern TB culture. For one, impressions of rice contained within the walls of ceramic vessels from the sixth millennium BC indicate that the Yǎngsháo Neolithic maintained some degree of interaction with the probably Daic rice-cultivating civilisations south of the Qínlǐng mountains along the Yangtze. However, the first reported instance of recovery of actual rice remains in the Yellow River basin dates from the beginning of the second millennium BC, associated with the Lóngshan culture of Hénán, though some rice impressions found on potsherds would appear to be of earlier date (Wú 1996). A much later candidate for an archaeological reflection of intense interaction between ancient Northern Tibeto-Burmans on the Yellow River and ancient Daic or Hmong-Mien peoples on the middle Yangtze, some time after the Lóngshan horizon, is the Qwjialkng and Shíjiahé culture, which expanded from the middle Yangtze into peripheral regions rapidly and on a grand scale, even replacing the Ycngsháo culture in southern and southeastern Hénán in the middle of the third millennium BC (Chang 1996).

Abbreviations

AA   Austro-Asiatic
AN   Austronesian
OC   Old Chinese
PAN Proto-Austronesian
ST   Sino-Tibetan
TB   Tibeto-Burman

Note

1 Jackson Sun (Swn Tianxin) of the Academia Sinica argues that Guìqióng, spoken in west-central Sichuan (cf. van Driem 2001: 498), may represent a separate subgroup in its own right, whereas Swn Hóngkai of the Chinese Academy of Social Sciences suspects that Guìqióng is a Qiangic language heavily influenced lexically and phonologically by its Lolo-Burmese neighbours. Conversely, Swn Hóngkai believes that Báimc, spoken in central northern Sichuan, is a separate TB subgroup which has previously been misidentified as a Tibetan dialect, whereas Jackson Sun believes it is a Tibetan dialect. Swn and Swn agree, however, that the solutions to the controversy will only come through the detailed analysis and documentation of both languages. Only linguistic field work leading to the detailed description of undocumented Tibeto-Burman languages will render possible the comparative work which will enable us to build a tree of genetic subgroup relationships.

Bibliography

Basu, P., Majumder, P., Roychoudhury, S. and Bhattacharya, N. (2001) 'Haplotype analysis of genomic polymorphisms in and around the myotonic dystrophy locus in diverse peoples of India', Human Genetics 108, 4: 310–17.
Benedict, P. (1942) 'Thai, Kadai, and Indonesian: a new alignment in southeastern Asia', American Anthropologist 44: 576–601.
—— (1972) Sino-Tibetan: A Conspectus, Cambridge: Cambridge University Press.
—— (1976) 'Sino-Tibetan: another look', Journal of the American Oriental Society 96, 2: 167–97.
Blench, R. (2001) 'From the mountains to the valleys: understanding ethnolinguistic geography in Southeast Asia', paper presented at the Colloque Perspectives sur la Phylogénie des Langues d'Asie Orientales at Périgueux, France, 30 August.

Bodman, N. (1980) 'Proto-Chinese and Sino-Tibetan: data towards establishing the nature of the relationship', in Frans van Coetsem and Linda R. Waugh (eds) Contributions to Historical Linguistics: Issues and Materials, 34–199, Leiden: E.J. Brill.

Brown, N. (1837) 'Comparison of Indo-Chinese languages', Journal of the Asiatic Society of Bengal VI, 2: 1023–38.

Brown, P. (1998) 'The first Mongoloids: another look at Upper Cave 101 and Minatogawa 1', Acta Anthropologica Sinica 17: 260–75.

Chang, K.C. (1965) 'Relative chronologies of China to the end of Chou', in Robert W. Ehrich (ed.) Chronologies in Old World Archaeology, 503–26, Chicago: Chicago University Press.

—— (1977) The Archaeology of Ancient China (3rd edn), New Haven, Connecticut: Yale University Press.

—— (1986) The Archaeology of Ancient China (4th edn), New Haven, Connecticut: Yale University Press.

—— (1989) 'Xīn shíqì shídài de Táiwān hcīxiá', Kǎogǔ 6: 541–50.

—— (1992) 'China' in Robert W. Ehrich (ed.) Chronologies in Old World Archaeology (3rd edn, 2 vols), Chicago: Chicago University Press.

Chêng Tê-K'un (1957) Archaeological Studies in Szechwan, Cambridge: Cambridge University Press.

Chu, J.Y., Huang, W., Kuang, S.Q., Wang, J.M., Xu, J.J., Chu, Z.T., Yang, Z.Q., Lin, K.Q., Li, P., Wu, M., Geng, Z.C., Tan, C.C., Du, R.F. and Jin, L. (1998) 'Genetic relationship of populations in China', Proceedings of the National Academy of Sciences of the United States of America 95: 11763–8.

Conrady, A. (1896) Eine indochinesische Causativ-Denominativ-Bildung und ihr Zusammenhang mit den Tonaccenten, Leipzig: Otto Harrassowitz.

Dani, A. (1960) Prehistory and Protohistory of Eastern India, with a Detailed Account of the Neolithic Cultures in Mainland Southeast Asia, Calcutta: Firma K.L. Mukhopadhyay.

de Knijff, P. (2000) 'Messages through bottlenecks: on the combined use of slow and fast evolving polymorphic markers on the human Y chromosome', American Journal of Human Genetics 67: 1055–61.

Demeter, F. (2000) Histoire du peuplement humain de l'Asie extrême-orientale depuis le pléistocène supérieur récent, thèse de doctorat, Université de la Sorbonne à Paris, 19 décembre.

Ding, Y.C., Wooding, S., Harpending, H., Chi, H.C., Li, H.P., Fu, Y.X., Pang, J.F., Yao, Y.G., Xiang Yu, J.G., Moyzis, R. and Zhang, Y.P. (2000) 'Population structure and history in East Asia', Proceedings of the National Academy of Sciences 97, 25: 14003–6.

D'jakonov, I. (1968) Predystorija Armjanskogo Naroda: Istorija Armjanskogo Nagor'ja s 1500 po 500 g. do n.è., Xurrity, Luvijcy, Protoarmjane. Erevan: Akademija Nauk Armjanskoj Sovetskoj SocialistiTeskoj Respubliki.

Finck, F. (1909) Die Sprachstämme des Erdkreises, Leipzig: B.G. Teubner.

Forchhammer, E. (1882) 'Indo-Chinese languages', Indian Antiquary XI: 177–89.

Grube, W. (1881) Die sprachgeschichtliche Stellung des Chinesischen, Leipzig: T.O. Weigel.

Haudricourt, A.-G. (1953) 'La place du viêtnamien dans les langues Austro-asiatiques', Bulletin de la Société Linguistique de Paris 49, 1: 122–8.

—— (1954) 'De l'origine des tons en viêtnamien', Journal Asiatique 242: 68–82.

Jobling, M., Bouzekri, N. and Taylor, P.G. (1998) 'Hypervariable digital DNA codes for human paternal lineages: MVR-PCR at the Y-specific minisatellite MSY1 (DYF155S1)', Human Molecular Genetics 7: 643–53.

Kayser, M., Krawczak, M., Excoffier, L., Dieltjes, P., Corach, D., Pascali, V., Gehrig, C., Bernini, L., Jespersen, J., Bakker, E., Roewer, L. and de Knijff, P. (2001) 'An extensive analysis of Y-chromosomal microsatellite haplotypes in globally dispersed human populations', American Journal of Human Genetics 68: 990–1018.

Körner, J. (ed.) (1930) Briefe von und an August Wilhelm Schlegel(2 vols), Zürich: Amalthea-Verlag.

Kuhn, E. (1889) 'Beiträge zur Sprachenkunde Hinterindiens', Sitzungsberichte der Königlichen Bayerischen Akademie der Wissenschaften (München), Philosophisch-philologische Classe, II: 189–236.

Lepsius, C. (1861) 'Über die Umschrift und Lautverhältnisse einiger hinterasiatischer Sprachen, namentlich der Chinesischen und der Tibetischen', Abhandlungen der Königlichen Akademie der Wissenschaften zu Berlin, aus dem Jahre 1860: 449–96.

Leyden, J. (c.1806a) Plan for the Investigation of the Language, literature, History and Antiquities of the Indo-Chinese Nations [69-page manuscript held by the British Library, ADD. MSS 26,564; later published with changes as Leyden (1808)].

—— (c.1806b) Plan for the Investigation of the Language, Literature and History of the Indo Chinese Nations. [11-page manuscript held by the British Library, ADD. MSS 26,565].

—— (1808) 'On the languages and literature of the Indo-Chinese nations', Asiatic Researches X: 158–289.

Mason, F. (1854) 'The Talaing language', Journal of the American Oriental Society IV: 277–89.

Matisoff, J. (1991) 'Sino-Tibetan linguistics: present state and future prospects', Annual Review of Anthropology 20: 469–504.

O'Connor, R. (1995) 'Agricultural change and ethnic succession in Southeast Asian states: a case for regional anthropology', Journal of Asian Studies 54, 4: 968–96.

Pictet, A. (1859) Les origines indo-européennes ou les aryas primitifs: Essai de pal éontologie linguistique (première partie), Paris: Joël Cherbuliez.

—— (1863) Les origines indo-européennes ou les aryas primitifs: Essai de pal éontologie linguistique (seconde partie), Paris: Joël Cherbuliez.

Przyluski, J. (1924) 'le sino-tibétain', and 'les langues austroasiatiques', in Antoine Meillet and Marcel Cohen (eds) Les Langues du Monde, Paris, Librairie Ancienne Édouard Champion.

Przyluski, J., and Luce, G. (1931) 'The number "a hundred" in Sino-Tibetan', Bulletin of the School of Oriental Studies VI, 3: 667–8.

Sagart, L. (1990) 'Chinese and Austronesian are genetically related', Paper presented at the 23rd International Conference on Sino-Tibetan Languages and Linguistics (5–7 October), University of Texas at Arlington.

—— (1994) 'Proto-Austronesian and Old Chinese evidence for Sino-Austronesian', Oceanic Linguistics 33, 2: 271–308.

—— (2001) 'Lexical evidence for Austronesian-Sino-Tibetan relatedness', Paper presented at the Conference on Connections across the Southern Pacific, Hong Kong City University, 18 January.

Schmidt, W. (1906) 'Die Mon-Khmer Völker, ein Bindeglied zwischen Völkern Zentral-Asiens und Austronesiens', Archiv für Anthropologie, Neue Folge, V: 59–109.

—— (1966) Introduction to Sino-Tibetan, Part I, Wiesbaden: Otto Harrassowitz.

—— (1967) Introduction to Sino-Tibetan, Part II, Wiesbaden: Otto Harrassowitz.

—— (1968) Introduction to Sino-Tibetan, Part III, Wiesbaden: Otto Harrassowitz.

—— (1974) Introduction to Sino-Tibetan, Part IV, Wiesbaden: Otto Harrassowitz.

Shafer, R. (1955) 'Classification of the Sino-Tibetan languages', Word, Journal of the Linguistic Circle of New York 11, 94–111.

Sharma, T.C. (1967) 'A note on the neolithic pottery of Assam', Man, Journal of the Royal Anthropological Institute (n.s.) 2, 1: 126–8.

——(1981) 'The neolithic pattern of north-eastern India', in M.S. Nagaraja Rao (ed.) Madhu: Recent Researches in Indian Archaeology and Art History, Delhi: Agam Kala Prakashan.

——(1989) 'Neolithic: Eastern region', in A. Ghosh (ed.) An Encyclopaedia of Indian Archaeology (2 vols), Vol. 1, 58–60, New Delhi: Munshiram Manoharlal Publishers.

Simon, W. (1929) 'Tibetisch-chinesische Wortgleichungen, ein Versuch', Mitteilungen des Seminars für Orientalische Sprachen an der Friedrich-Wilhelms-Universität zu Berlin XXXII, 1: 157–228.

Su, B., Xiao, J.H., Underhill, P., Deka, R., Zhang, W.L., Akey, J., Huang, W., Shen, D., Lu, D.R., Luo, J.C, Chu, J.Y., Tan, J.Z., Shen, P.D., Davis, R., Cavalli-Sforza, L., Chakraborty, R., Xiong, M.M., Du, R.F., Oefner, P., Chen, Z. and Jin, L. (1999) 'Y-chromosome evidence for a northward migration of modern humans into eastern Asia during the last Ice Age', American Journal of Human Genetics 65: 1718–24.

Su, B., Xiao, C.J., Deka, R., Seielstad, M., Kangwanpong, D., Xiao, J.H., Lu, D.R., Underhill, P., Cavalli-Sforza, L., Chakraborty, R. and Jin, L. (2000) 'Y chromosome haplotypes reveal prehistorical migrations to the Himalayas', Human Genetics 107, 6: 582–90.

Temple, R. (1903) Census of India, 1901, Vol. III: The Andaman and Nicobar Islands: Report on the Census, Calcutta: Office of the Superintendent of Government Printing, India.

Thapar, B.K. (1985) Recent Archaeological Discoveries in India, Paris: United Nations Educational Scientific and Cultural Organization.

Tsang, C.H. (2001) 'Recent discoveries of the Tap'enkeng culture in Taiwan: Implications for the problem of Austronesian origins', Paper presented at the Colloque Perspectives sur la Phylogénie des Langues d'Asie Orientales at Périgueux, France, 30 August.

Underhill, P., Jin, L., Lin, A., Mehdi, S.Q., Jenkins, T., Vollrath, D., Davis, R.W., Cavalli-Sforza, L. and Oefner, P. (1997) 'Detection of numerous Y chromosme biallelic polymorphisms by denaturing high-performance liquid chromatography', Genome Research 7: 996–1005.

Underhill, P., Passarino, G., Lin, A., Shen, P., Mirazón Lahr, M., Foley, R.A., Oefner, P. and Cavalli-Sforza, L. (2001) 'The phylogeny of Y chromosme binary haplotypes and the origins of modern human populations', American Journal of Human Genetics 65: 43–62.

van Driem, George (1997) 'Sino-Bodic', Bulletin of the School of Oriental and African Studies 60, 3: 455–88.

——(1998) 'Neolithic correlates of ancient Tibeto-Burman migrations', in Roger Blench and Matthew Spriggs (eds) Archaeology and Language II, London: Routledge.

——(1999) 'A new theory on the origin of Chinese', in Peter Bellwood and Ian Lilley (eds) Bulletin of the Indo-Pacific Prehistory Association Bulletin, 18 (Indo-Pacific Prehistory: The Melaka Papers, Vol. 2), 43–58, Canberra: Australian National University.

——(2001) Languages of the Himalayas: An Ethnolinguistic Handbook of the Greater Himalayan Region containing an Introduction to the Symbiotic Theory of Language (2 vols), Leiden: Brill.

——(2002) 'Tibeto-Burman replaces Indo-Chinese in the 1990s: review of a decade of scholarship', Lingua 111: 79–102.

von Klaproth, J. (1823a) Asia Polyglotta, Paris: A. Schubart.

von Klaproth, J. (1823b) *Asia Polyglotta: Sprachatlas*, Paris: A. Schubart.

—— (1830) 'Réponse à quelques passages de la préface du roman chinois intitulé: Hao khieou tchhouan, traduit par M.J.F. Davis', *Journal Asiatique* V: 97–122.

—— (1831) *Asia Polyglotta* (2nd edn), Paris: Heideloff & Campe.

von Schlegel, A. (1832) *Réflexions sur l'étude des langues asiatiques adress ées à Sir James Mackintosh, suivie d'une lettre à M. Horace Hayman Wilson*, Bonn: Weber.

von Strahlenberg, P. (1730) *Das Nord- und Östliche Theil von Europea und Asia, in so weit das gantze Russische Reich mit Siberien und grossen Tatarey in sich begreiffet, in einer Historisch-Geographischen Beschreibung der alten und neueren Zeiten, und vielen andern unbekannten Nachrichten vorgestellet, nebst einer noch niemahls and Licht gegebenen Tabula Polyglotta von zwei und dreyßiglei Arten Tatarischer Völcker Sprachen und einem Kalmuckischen Vocabulario*, Stockholm: In Verlegung des Autoris.

Walravens, H. (1999a) *Julius Klaproth (1783–1835): Leben und Werk*, Wiesbaden: Otto Harassowitz.

—— (1999b) *Julius Klaproth (1783–1835): Briefe und Dokumente*, Wiesbaden: Otto Harassowitz.

Wheeler, R. (1959) *Early India and Pakistan to Ashoka*, London: Thames and Hudson.

Whitehead, G. (1925) *Dictionary of the Car-Nicobarese Language*, Rangoon: American Baptist Mission Press.

Witsen, N. (1692) [2nd impression 1705] *Noord en Oost Tartarye, ofte Bondig Ontwerp van eenige dier Landen en Volken, welke voormaels bekent zijn geweest, beneffens verscheide tot noch toe onbekende, en meest nooit voorheen beschreven Tartersche en Nabuurige Gewesten, Landstreeken, Steden, Rivieren, en Plaetzen, in de Noorder en Oostelykste Gedeelten van Asia en Europa* (2 vols), Amsterdam: François Halma.

Wu, Y.L. (1996) 'Prehistoric rice agriculture in the Yellow River valley', in Ian C. Glover and Peter Bellwood (eds) *Indo-Pacific Prehistory: The Chiang-Mai Papers* (Proceedings of the 15th Congress of the Indo-Pacific Prehistory Association, Chiang Mai, Thailand, 5–12 January 1994), 223–4, Vol. 2, Canberra: Australian National University.

Zhang, C. (1996) 'The rise of urbanism in the middle and lower Yangtze river valley', in Peter Bellwood and Diane Tillotson (eds) *Indo-Pacific Prehistory: The Chiang-Mai Papers* (Proceedings of the 15th Congress of the Indo-Pacific Prehistory Association, Chiang Mai, Thailand, 5–12 January 1994), 63–8, Vol. 3, Canberra: Australian National University.

7

KRA-DAI AND AUSTRONESIAN

Notes on phonological correspondences and vocabulary distribution

Weera Ostapirat

Introduction

A linguistic connection between the Tai and AN languages has been proposed for a century (e.g. Schlegel 1901; Wulff 1942), but the best-known work advocating the hypothesis is undoubtedly that of Benedict (1942, 1975). While the hypothesis itself has proved attractive to some ethno-historians and archaeologists, the supporting linguistic evidence as put forth in Benedict's works has not been received favourably by specialists in the field. As Diller noted:

> Schlegel and Benedict base their arguments on lexical similarities and call attention to some lexical items which do appear common to Tai and Austronesian. Unfortunately for the Austro-Tai case, many additional far less convincing relationships are presented by Benedict (1975, 1990), who not infrequently resorts to loose resemblances, semantic leaps and to a practice known as 'proto-form stuffing' – the making up of maximal earlier forms to account for all desired modern cognate relationships.
>
> Diller (1998: 22)

This is also the view of many specialists in comparative Tai and, probably, in AN linguistics studies as well.

I generally agree with criticisms that rightly point out severe problems in Benedict's works, in terms of linguistic evidence and methodology (especially Benedict 1975, 1990).[1] For decades, the field of Austro-Tai linguistics seems to have had only one main player. It follows that, unfortunately, the weaknesses one finds in Benedict's works have been often taken as reflecting the improbability of the hypothesis itself. To reconsider this issue, therefore, I believe that we need to first distinguish the hypothesis from Benedict's work, or at least not try to equate the two.

In this chapter I will address some issues of phonological development and vocabulary distribution of AN-related etyma in Kd. Recently, Thurgood (1994) asserted that the shared vocabulary items found between the two language groups arose from contact rather than from common origin. Thurgood's conclusion was largely based on his claim that the sound correspondences for those lexical items shared by Kd and AN are irregular within Kd languages. On this point, I will argue that regular correspondences can be established for many of these lexical items, and that some of the irregularities noted by Thurgood result from inadequacy of material and of the proto-forms he cited or reconstructed. Evidence will be presented from a pan-Kra-Dai perspective, including supporting reflexes not only from the more well-known Tai and Kam-Sui languages but also from Hlai and Kra, the lesser-known branches of the family. Some of these materials, especially on the Kra branch (Ostapirat 2000), have not been available until recently.

Whether such linguistic evidence can prove that Kd and AN languages are genetically related or whether they just imply early historical contact between the two groups, however, remains debatable.

Kra-Dai and Austronesian: Lexical connection

The two language families

The Kd languages consist of five well-established groups: Tai, Kam-Sui, Be, Hlai and Kra. The first three are often referred to together as the Kam-Tai branch, based on the high proportion of vocabulary they share. Still, this subgrouping of Kd languages should be taken as provisional. Lexical and phonological evidence exists which suggests the possibility of grouping together Kam-Sui and Kra on the one hand, and Tai and Hlai on the other (Figure 7.1). The issue of internal Kd subgrouping will be elaborated elsewhere.

The higher-order subgrouping of AN languages is shown in Figure 7.2. This is interpreted and simplified from discussions in Blust (1999) and Ho (1998). The AN language family has several primary branches, all of which are spoken on the Taiwan island. The well-known and most widespread AN language subgroup, Malayo-Polynesian, is one of the daughter languages that split from the Eastern Formosan primary branch.

A core list of Kra-Dai vocabulary and Austronesian –Kra-Dai etyma

I shall start with 50 selected Kd etyma, adapted from Ostapirat (2000), as evidence that binds all Kd languages into one stock. The list is selected to cover various semantic fields and to include roots illustrating all four Kd tones. In addition, these etyma can be found in all or most Kd branches, and are thus likely to go back to the PKd stage. This selected core list also contains a number of vocabulary items that belong to the standard basic word lists: 20 items from Yakhontov's

KRA-DAI AND AUSTRONESIAN

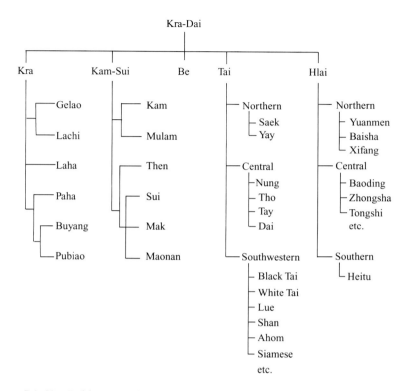

Figure 7.1 Kra-Dai language family.

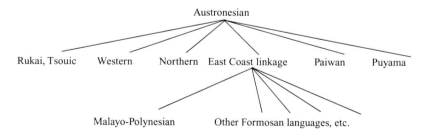

Figure 7.2 AN language family.

35 basic word list (indicated by bold glosses) and 42 items from Swadesh's 100 basic word list (words that do not belong to either list are italicised).

In Table 7.1, Siamese, Sui (Li-Ngam), Heitu and Gelao (Anshun) languages represent respectively Tai, Kam-Sui, Hlai and Kra branches. When reflexes from the representative dialects are lacking, forms from other varieties will be cited

Table 7.1 A core list of Kd vocabulary

	Tai	Kam-Sui	Hlai	Gelao	Kd tones
1 Blood	l at	phjaat	da:t	pl	D
2 Bone	duuk	laak	r ːɤ	ta	D
3 Ear	huu	qhaa	(zai)	zau	A
4 Eye	taa	daa	tsha	tau	A
5 Excrement	khii	qee	hai	q	C
6 Fart	tot	ti t	thu:t	tæ (Lz)	D
7 Fingernail	lep	ljap	li:p	kle	D
8 Grease	man	man	man (B)	mal (Lh)	A
9 Hand	m	mjaa	me	mpau	A
10 Head	klau	ku	rau	(kl B)	C
11 Knee	khau	quu	(rou)	qo (Lz)	B
12 Leg, thigh	khaa	qaa	ha	qau	A
13 Liver	tap	tap	(a:n)	tæ (Lz)	D
14 Navel	d ɤ	dwaa	re	zo (Qs)	A
15 Nose	da	ɤna	do	da (Lh)	A
16 Shoulder	baa	wie (Lk)	va	baa (Lh)	B
17 Tooth	fan	wjan	phen	pan	A
18 Bear, n.	mii	ɤmii	mui	mi (Lz)	A
19 Bird	nok	nok	(taʈ)	ntau	D
20 Dog	maa	Úaa	ma	mpau	A
21 Fish	plaa	paa (K)	da	lau	A
22 Horn	khau	qaau	hau (Bd)	qa	A
23 Louse (head)	hau	tuu	tshou	ta	A
24 Tail	(haa)	hi t	tshut	tshan	D
25 Leaf	bai	waa (Lk)	be	(vu)	A
26 Seed	fan (Wt)	wan	phen	pa (Qs)	A
27 Sesame	aa	ɤ aa	ke (Bd)	klau	A
28 Cloud	faa	faa	fa (Bd)	phaa (Lh)	C
29 Fire	fai	wii	pei	pai	A
30 Moon	d an	njaan	a:n	daan (Lh)	A
31 Path	hon	khun	ku:n	qan	A
32 Rain	fon	fi n	pun	(jal) (Lh)	A
33 Stone	hin	tin	tshi:n	(pˑ aa)	A
34 Smoke	khwan	kwan	hwo:n	q	A
35 Water	naam	nam	nom	(i C)	C
36 Black	dam	ɤnam	dom C	ɤdam (By)	A
37 Dry	kha (L)	khu C	khe	xau	B
38 Full	(tem)	tik	thi:ɤ	tei	D
39 Green	khiau	Mɨ	khi:u	(ten)	A
40 Long	rii	ɤˑ aai	loi (B)	&i C (By)	A
41 Live, raw	dip	djup	ri:p	te	D
42 Come	maa	Úaa	pe (Bd)	mu	A
43 Eat	kin	tsjaan	khan (Bc)	kaan (By)	A
44 Kill	khaa	haa	hau	(ven)	C
45 Walk, go	pai	paai	pei	pai	A
46 Child, person	luuk	laak	d ːɤ	lei	D
47 Grandmother	jaa B	jaa C	tsa C (Bd)	® C	B/C
48 This	nii	naai	nei	ni	B/C
49 I	kuu	(ju)	hou (Bd)	kuu (By)	A
50 You	m	maa (Lk)	me	maa (By)	A

Table 7.2 Kd-related AN etyma

	PAN		PAN
4 Eye	maCa	5 Excrement	Caqi
6 Fart	qe(n)tut	8 Grease	SimaR
9 Hand	(qa)lima	10 Head	qulu
12 Leg	paqa	15 Nose	iju [1]
16 Shoulder	qabaRa	17 Tooth	nipen
18 Bear (n.)	Cumay	19 Bird	manuk PMP[2]
23 Louse (head)	kuCu	25 Leaf	(ɒabag)[3]
27 Sesame	le a	29 Fire	Sapuy
30 Moon	bulaN	35 Water	daNum
36 Black	tidem[4]	41 Live, raw	qudip
43 Eat	kaen	46 Child	aNak
47 Grandmother	aya	48 This	i-ni
49 I	aku	50 You	kamu

Notes
1 This is a PMP form according to Blust, who reconstructs PAN *muji for this root. Zorc reconstructs *i jú for PAN. (Zorc's reconstructed forms are cited from the Glossary that appears in Tryon 1995 (Part 1, Fascicle 2).)
2 The typical PAN root for 'bird' is *qayam. The cited form *manuk is reconstructed for PMP, with semantic shift from 'chicken' to 'bird' (Blust 2002). Kd shows independent semantic shift, and the reflexes point to PKd *maNuk (see evidence for Kd *-N- in the following section on phonological development). PMP does not distinguish *n and *N, thus the Kd form provides external evidence for PAN *-N- in this root.
3 The cited form is from Atayal (Mayrinax dialect, Li 1981). Blust reconstructs PAN *biRaq and PMP *dahun 'leaf'.
4 This is a PMP form according to Zorc (*ti dem). Blust reconstructs PAN *Ce en, PMP *ma-qitem 'black'.

and are marked with dialect abbreviations in parentheses. All Kd syllables may belong to one of the three tonal categories, labelled as *A, *B and *C. An additional category, *D, indicates syllables ending with a stop. These proto-tonal categories have usually developed into more complex tonal systems in modern languages. A detailed discussion and summary of tonal splits and mergers in various Kd languages may be found in Ostapirat (2000).

Over half of these basic Kd etyma appear to be relatable to AN. Among these are 11 words from Yakhontov's and 19 words from Swadesh's basic lists. AN forms are according to Blust's reconstructions, unless otherwise indicated (Table 7.2).

To these we may add PAN *pudeR 'kidney', which may be linked with item 14 'navel', if the semantic shift is acceptable (the phonological correspondences between AN and Kd are regular, as shown in the next section). AN *quzaN 'rain' may also be related to Kra *jal (item 32), though the word has not been found in other Kd branches. It does not seem likely that the very high number of roots between Kd and AN that emerge from the core list could be accidental or simply result from borrowings. I will discuss the phonological correspondences of AN–Kd roots in the following section.

Phonological development

Discussion of sound changes

In this section I will discuss in detail the phonological development of some selected AN–Kd roots. These examples are chosen partly to demonstrate some important phonological features such as the distinction between AN *t and *C in Kd, and how we may reconstruct disyllabic Kd forms in spite of the fact that modern Kd languages have mainly become monosyllabic. I will also refer to Thurgood's comments on some of these roots (Thurgood 1994); he is of the opinion that sound correspondences among Kd languages are often irregular and thus the AN-related etyma in Kd may not be cognates but borrowings. I hope to point out that, in many cases, the irregularities claimed by Thurgood result from his over-looking crucial material and from inadequacy of his reconstructed proto-forms.

In the following discussions, I will give relevant reflexes from representative Kd branches and from different subgroups of each branch. For instance, Siamese (Si), Lungming (Lm) and Wuming (Wm) dialects represent the three main branches of Tai (Southwestern, Central and Northern branches respectively). Likewise, Baoding (Bd), Heitu (Ht) and Yuanmen (Ym) represent respectively Central, Southern, and Northern branches of Hlai (Ostapirat 1993).

Fart

The Kd reflexes for 'to fart', AN *qe(n)tut, are tabulated in Table 7.3.

Thurgood (1994: 358) cites Li's PT *tlot$_7$ and states that this medial -l- presents a problem since the other Kd and PAN forms show no evidence of such a medial. He presents PAN and Kd reconstructed forms as follows:

AN	PT	PKS	PH
*qe(n)tut	*tlot$_7$	*tut$_7$	*thu:t

The PKS form reconstructed by Thurgood is inadequate; he failed to take into account such reflexes as Mulam /khꞌi t/ (*k-t- k-V khꞌ -). In the Tai branch, the Northern-Tai spirant reflexes (e.g. Sk and Wm r-) similarly result from the

Table 7.3 Kd reflexes for 'to fart', AN *qe(n)tut

Tai		Kam-Sui		Hlai		Kra	
Si	tot	K	ti t	Bd	thu:t	Gl	tæ
Lm	ti t	S	ti t	Ht	thu:t	Ph	&at
Wm	rot	M	tut	Ym	thut	By	tut
Sk	r‡t	T	tet				
		Ml	khꞌi t				
		Lk	kjot				

Table 7.4 Kd reflexes for 'head louse', AN *kuCu

Tai		Kam-Sui		Hlai		Kra	
Si	hau	K	ta:u	Bd	fou	Gl	ta
Lm	thau	S	tu	Ht	tshou	Lh	tou
Wm	rau	M	ti u	Ym	fhou	Ph	ɬ uu
Sk	rau	T	tiu			By	tuu
		Ml	khʼ i u				
		Lk	kjou				

lenition of the medial *-t-. The cited PT medial *-l- is thus in fact spurious and cannot be taken as evidence against regular correspondences. See also the similar development in the next root.

Head louse

The Kd reflexes for 'head louse', AN *kuCu, are tabulated in Table 7.4.
For this root, Thurgood lists the following reconstructed forms:

AN	PT	PKS	PH
kutu	*thri u$_1$	—	*srou$_1$

Thurgood does not give the PKS reconstruction of this root, claiming that the reflexes are irregular in all respects (i.e. in initial, vowel and tonal reflexes). The examples he cites, however, all show tone 1 (*A1) and it is unclear on what basis he claims that the tonal reflexes are irregular. Kam-Sui initial reflexes are exactly the same as those in the previous root ('fart'), and we do not have any difficulty in reconstructing PKS *k-tu. Northern Tai dialects also show similar spirantised reflexes as those of 'fart' above.

The medial *-C- in this root, however, has to be distinguished from *-t- in 'fart'. Hlai varieties usually have /th/ as the reflex of *t, but /tsh/ for *C (cf. Ht dialect). For instance, in 'eye', all Hlai varieties have /tsh/: Bd /tsha/, Ht /tsha/, and Ym /tsha/, PAN *maCa. The initial reflex /f-/ for 'head louse' in Bd and Ym arose from the influence of the preceding rounded vowel *-u-. If the root 'eye' is to be reconstructed with PH initial *tsh-, the initial of 'head louse' should be *tshw-, not *sr-. We have more examples of a similar influence of Kd *-u- on Hlai initial reflexes, as in #3 'live, raw' and #4 'head' below.

Live, raw

The Kd reflexes for 'live, raw', AN *qudip, are tabulated in Table 7.5.
Parallel to the development from *-uC- ('head louse' *kuCu) to Ht /tsh-/ and Bd and Ym /f-/, Kd *-ud- has become Ht /r-/ but Bd and Ym /v-/ through the rounding influence of the preceding vowel. In the Kra branch, the Laha (Tamit)

Table 7.5 Kd reflexes for 'live, raw', AN *qudip

Tai		Kam-Sui		Hlai		Kra	
Si	dip	S	ɔdjup	Bd	vi:p	Gl	te
Lm	nip	M	ɔdip	Ht	ri:p	Lh	kthop
Wm	ɔdip	T	lip	Ym	fip	By	ɔdip
Sk	rip						

Table 7.6 Kd reflexes for 'head', AN *qulu

Tai		Kam-Sui		Hlai	
Si	klau	K	kaau	Bd	gwou
Wm	rau	S	ku	Ht	rau
Sk	thrau	M	tMu	Ym	vo
		T	ki u		
		Ml	kɔ o		
		Lk	kj‡u (A1)		

reflex shows a retention of the first syllable initial (*k- in /kthop/). The devoicing of early Laha voiced stop into a voiceless aspirated stop in Tamit dialect is a regular development. For instance, Laha (Nong Lay) /dak/, Laha (Tamit) /thak/, from Early Laha *dak 'bone' (see also Ostapirat 2000: 36).

Head

The Kd reflexes for 'head', AN *qulu, are tabulated in Table 7.6.
Thurgood provides the following forms for this root:

AN	PT	PKS	PH
qulu	*thrue$_1$	*kru$_3$	*ɣwɔo$_3$

Like Benedict, Thurgood links a PT word which appears to be unrelated with those in other Kd languages. The cited PT etymon is limited to the non-Northern-Tai languages, and its tone (*A) is not matched with that of the others (tone *C). The Tai forms in Table 7.6 reflect the correct tonal category *C (the word is listed under Li's PT *kl-). Though the root now means 'hair-knot' in Siamese and some other Tai dialects, it usually means 'head' in Northern Tai and in most other Tai dialects (Li 1977). Evidence from Kam-Sui and Hlai confirms that the meaning 'head' is original.

The Kd medial of this root is best reconstructed as *-!-, which has become *-r- in Kam-Sui (PKS *kr-) and PH *!-. Again, we see that the preceding *-u- has influenced initial reflexes of Bd and Ym dialects of Hlai (gw- and v- respectively). At this point, we may summarise the development of Kd syllables with initial vowel *-u- in the Hlai languages (Table 7.7.)

KRA-DAI AND AUSTRONESIAN

Table 7.7 Development of Kd syllables with initial vowel *-u- in the Hlai languages

	Bd	Ht	Ym	Examples
*-uC-	f-	tsh-	f-	Head louse
*-ud-	v-	r-	v-	Live, raw
*-u!-	gw-	r-	v-	Head

Table 7.8 Kd reflexes for 'fire', AN *Sapuy

Tai		Kam-Sui		Hlai		Kra	
Si	fai	K	pui	Bd	fei	Gl	pai
Lm	fai	S	wi	Ht	pei	Lh	pi i
Wm	foi	M	vi i	Ym	fhei	Ph	pui
Sk	vii	T	wii			By	fii
		Ml	fii				
		Lk	pui				

Fire

The Kd reflexes for 'fire', AN *Sapuy, are tabulated in Table 7.8.

Thurgood provides the following comparisons:

| AN | PT | PKS | PH |
| Sapuy | *v‡i_2 | *pwai$_1$ | *pei$_1$ |

Thurgood reconstructs PKS *pwai and mentions that the final -ai has an unexpected correspondence within Kam-Sui. In fact, the rime is better reconstructed as *-ui. The rounded main vowel *-u- after *-p- suffices to cause various kinds of labial reflexes such as w-, v-, f-, and thus the reconstructed medial *-w- also becomes unnecessary. After a non-labial consonant the vowel is preserved in most Kam-Sui languages; for instance, 'snow', Kam /nui/, Sui /ɒnui/, Then /nuei/, Mulam /nui/, from PKS *k-nui A (cf. Lakkja /kjãi/ for the *k- presyllable. See also Ostapirat 1994a). PT *v- is clearly a result of spirantisation of the medial *-p-. See also the next root for a similar development.

Tooth

The Kd reflexes for 'tooth', AN *nipen, are tabulated in Table 7.9.

For this root, Thurgood notes that his reconstructed PKS *pjw- is a rare cluster (thus doubtful). The reflexes are similar to those of 'fire', with an extra medial -j- in some languages (Kam and Sui). This -j- came from Kd preceding *-i-, and we may reconstruct PKS *ipi n for this root (cf. 'hand' for a similar development). Some Gelao dialects have *pl- as a reflex (e.g. Niupo /pl $_1$/), and we have

Table 7.9 Kd reflexes for 'tooth', AN *nipen

Tai		Kam-Sui		Hlai		Kra	
Si	fan	K	pjan	Bd	fan 1	Gl	pan 1
Lc	fan	S	wjan	Ht	phen 1		
Wm	fan	T	wen	Ym	fhan 1		
		Ml	fan				
		Lk	wan				

Table 7.10 Kd reflexes for 'hand', AN *(qa)lima

Tai		Kam-Sui		Hlai		Kra	
Si	m	K	mjaa	Bd	me	Gl	mpau
Lm	mi	S	mjaa	Ht	me	Lh	maa
Wm	fa	M	mii	Ym	me		
Sk	m	T	mjaa				
		Ml	njaa				
		Lk	mie				

reconstructed PK *l-pin for this etymon, assuming the metathesis *l-p- pl- (Ostapirat 2000). PAN variants *lipen/Nipen are sometimes given for this item (Tryon 1995).

Hand

The Kd reflexes for 'hand', AN *(qa)lima, are tabulated in Table 7.10.

This root shows another example of preceding *-i- developing into medial -j- in some Kam-Sui languages (cf. 'tooth' above). Also, it is relevant here to contrast the Hlai reflexes of this root with those of 'five':

	Bd	Ht	Ym	PKd	PAN
hand	me	me	me	*(l)íma	*(qa)lima
five	pa	ma	pa	*l(i)má	*lima

Note that, for 'hand', all Hlai dialects show a straightforward nasal reflex of *-m-. For 'five', however, *-m- has changed to an obstruent in some varieties. These variant reflexes result from an early accentual distinction. 'Hand' had penultimate stress, while 'five' had final stress. When the preceding syllable was unstressed ('five'), its vowel became short and the following medial consonant became long or geminate. Thus *limá 'five' became Hlai *mma, which then developed to *mpa   pa in some dialects. When the preceding syllable was stressed ('hand'), the medial *-m- was relatively short and the final unstressed vowel reduced to *-i . Thus *líma 'hand' became Hlai *mi   mi   (secondary diphthongisation).

Table 7.11 Kd reflexes for 'water', AN *daNum

Tai		Kam-Sui		Hlai	
Si	naam	K	nam	Bd	nom
Lm	nam	S	nam	Ht	nom
Wm	ram	M	nam	Ym	nam
		T	nam		
		Ml	ni m		
		Lk	num		

For the first syllable initial, Kd *l- can be reconstructed for 'five' as evidenced by such reflexes as Gelao (Lz) /ml¥/ *mlã *l-ma (parallel to *l-p- pl- in 'tooth' above). For 'hand', however, no evidence of *l- has been found so far, and the Kd form may be simply reconstructed as *íma.

Water

The Kd reflexes for 'water', AN *daNum, are tabulated in Table 7.11.

For this root, Thurgood notes that the Kam-Sui reflexes are irregular because the particular mix of odd- and even-numbered tones is not otherwise attested (1994: 352). The odd- and even-numbered tones indicate early voiceless and voiced initials respectively. For this root, the Kam-Sui tonal reflexes are as follows: K /nam$_2$/, S /nam$_1$/, M /nam$_1$/, T /nam$_2$/, Ml /ni m$_2$/. However, contrary to what Thurgood states, such Kam-Sui tonal correspondences can be found with other roots, including 'hand' above.

Based on the fact that the reflexes in daughter languages may be either voiced or voiceless nasals at the time of tonal split (cf. also Shangnan /n̥am/ where a voiceless nasal initial is attested), I have proposed elsewhere that the initial must have been breathy at an early Kam-Sui stage (Ostapirat 1994b). This breathiness occurred when the medial nasal was preceded by a stressed syllable with voiced onset. Thus *(d)áNum became Kam-Sui *| nam 'water' and *(l)íma became Kam-Sui *| mjaa 'hand'.

Kd medial *-N- is kept apart from *-n- in several Northern Tai dialects which show various kinds of spirant reflexes (e.g. r-, &, z-, › -). Such Northern Tai spirant initials cannot be explained as having resulted from lenition of *-n- in medial position. For example, the medial *-n- in Kd *t-na 'thick' has typically remained n- in all Tai dialects. The distinction between *-N- and *-n- possibly reflects a difference in points of articulation, namely, between dental or retroflex versus alveolar.

Bird

The Kd reflexes for 'bird', AN *manuk, are tabulated in Table 7.12.

This root provides another example of Kd medial *-N-, which is similarly reflected in Northern Tai dialects as a spirant initial. The initial syllable nasal

Table 7.12 Kd reflexes for 'bird', AN *manuk

Tai		Kam-Sui		Be		Kra	
Si	nok	K	mok	Lg	nok	Gl	ntau
Lm	nok	S	nok			Lh	nok
Wm	rok	M	nok			Ph	n|ook
		T	n~k			Pb	nok
		Ml	n~k				
		Lk	mlok				

Table 7.13 Kd reflexes for 'eye', AN *maCa

Tai		Kam-Sui		Hlai		Kra	
Si	taa	K	taa	Bd	tsha	Gl	tau
Lm	thaa	S	daa	Ht	tsha	Lh	taa
Wm	raa	M	daa	Ym	tsha	Ph	daa
Sk	praa	T	ɴdaa			By	ma taa
		Ml	laa				
		Mn	ndaa				

*m- is still evidenced in such languages as Lakkja (mlok *m-Nuk). In AN, the word has not been found in critical Formosan languages, thus evidence for reconstructing PAN *-N- (as opposed to *-n-) for this root has been lacking.

Eye

The Kd reflexes for 'eye', AN *maCa, are tabulated in Table 7.13.

As in root #2 'head louse', Kd *-C- is reflected as Hlai tsh-. The *m- initial is still in evidence in some Kd languages. In Kra, the Buyang language has the form /ma taa/, and in Paha d- instead of t- is a result of prenasalisation (*m-ta da). Kam-Sui reflexes also indicate a prenasalised feature and point to PKS *N-ta. In several Northern-Tai dialects, the medial *-C- was spirantised (Wm and Sk -r-). Saek further occluded the initial *m- p-, thus *m-Ca p-ta praa. The change *m- p- in Saek is also found in another root of similar phonological shape: 'die', Saek /praai/, AN *m-aCay.

Correspondences

The AN–Kd sound correspondences will be summarised in this section. I shall start with final consonants. The main correspondences are exemplified in Table 7.14. AN and Kd final nasals *-m, *-n, *- , stops *-p, *-t, *-k and approximants *-w, *-y usually correspond one-to-one and need no clarification. A discussion of the other endings will follow.

Table 7.14 Main AN–Kd correspondences of final consonants

	PAN	Tai	Kam-Sui	Hlai	Kra (Lh)	Kd
Water	daNum	nam	nam	nom	—	*-m
Tooth	nipen	fan	wjan	phen	pan (G)	*-n
Nose	iju PMP	da	ɒna	do	da	*-
Live, raw	qudip	dip	ɒdjup	ri:p	kthop (Tm)	*-p
Fart	qe(n)tut	tot	ti t	thu:t	tut (By)	*-t
Pungent[1]	paqiC	phet	—	geṭ	pat	*-C
Fowl, bird	manuk PMP	nok	nok	no:k (Bd)	nok	*-k
Taro	biRaq	ph ak	ɒ› aak	ge:k (Bd)	haak	*-k
Weep	Ca is	hai	ɒ e	ei	it	*-c
Star[1]	qalejaw	daaw	ɒdaau (M)	ra:u	—	*-w
Fire	Sapuy	fai	wi	pei	pi i	*-y
Navel[1]	pudeR	d ɒ	daa	re	dau	*-›

Note
1 Glosses are given according to Kd. The typical meanings of these words in AN are as follows: *paqiC 'bitter', *qalejaw 'sun', *pudeR 'kidney'.

Table 7.15 Contrast between *-C and *-t in Kd and AN

	Siamese	Saek	Be	Hlai (Bd)	Kd	AN
Fart	tot	rʑt	dut	thu:t	*-t	*-t
Bitter, spicy	phet	—	—	geṭ	*-C	*-C
Skin, scale	klet	trʑk	liɒ	—	*-C	*-C
Ant	mot	mʑk	muɒ	puṭ	*-C	—

Table 7.16 Kd correspondences for AN final *-q

	PAN	Tai	Kam-Sui	Hlai (Bd)	Kra (Lh)	Kd
Taro	biRaq	ph ak	ɒ› aak	ge:k	haak	*-k
Otter	Sanaq	naak	—	te:k	—	*-k
Ten	puluq	—	—	phu:t	put (By)	*-C

PAN final *-C is distinguished from *-t at PKd level as shown by several varieties. PKd final *-C is usually reflected as -k in Saek (Tai branch), as -ɒ in Be, and as -ṭ in the Baoding dialect of Hlai. The phonetic realisation of this Kd *-C was probably a (pre)palatal stop or affricate. Note also that the last etymon 'ant' has related AA forms reconstructible with a palatal final *-c (cf. Khmer /sramaoc/, etc.). Note the contrastive reflexes of PKd *-t and *-C in key varieties (Table 7.15).

PAN final *-q usually merged with *-k in Kd (Table 7.16). When preceded by *-u-, however, final *-q appears to have become *-C (*-uq *-uiq *-uC, cf. 'ten'). For evidence of Kd medial *-l- in this root, cf. Gelao (Qs) /vlo/.

Table 7.17 Kd correspondences for AN final *-s

	PAN	Tai	Kam-Sui	Hlai	Kra	Kd
Weep	Ca is	hai	ʔ e	ei	it	*-c
Stream	qaRus	huai	kui	—	—	*-c

Table 7.18 Kd correspondences for AN final -R and -N

	PAN	Tai	Kam-Sui	Hlai	Kra (Lh)	Kd
Navel	pudeR	d ʔ	daa	re	dau	*-ʔ
Fat, n.	SimaR	man	man	—	mal	*-l
Moon	bulaN	d an	njaan	aːn	daan	*-n
Rain	quzaN	—	—	—	jal	*-l

Table 7.19 A special Kd development corresponding to AN -R

	PAN	Tai	Kam-Sui	Be	Kra (Lh)	Kd
Flow	qaluR	lai	lui	li i	kli i	*-y

PAN final *-s appears to have become (*-c) *-yʔ in most Kd varieties, but (*-c)*-t in Kra (cf. 'weep'). This glottal constriction *-ʔ developed into Kd tone *C, which is the case for the two roots in Table 7.17.

Final *-R and *-N seem to each have two reflexes: either -ʔ or -l for *-R, and either -n or -l for *-N (Table 7.18).

These variations probably result from accentual distinctions. Note that the two examples which result in *-l ('fat, n.' and 'rain') have short vowel reflexes, while those that result in -n have long vowels. Thus, we may hypothesise that *-R and *-N in unstressed syllables have become *-l; in stressed syllables the two endings are distinct, *-R has become *-ʔ and *-N has become -n.

There is also a case where *-uR developed to (* uiR) *-uy (Table 7.19). This is parallel to the development of *-uq (-uiq) *-uC.

AN-Kd etyma with voiced stop endings are very rare. The tentative examples in Table 7.20, however, may suggest that AN voiced stop codas have become Kd approximants.

In Table 7.20, 'yawn' is typically reconstructed as PAN *Suab. Atayal medial -r- has been noted as peculiar to this group of languages (Li 1981: 276, referring to an observation of Blust's). For evidence of Kd medial *-r- of this root, see for example, Buyi /zvaau/ (PT *hr-), Mulam /khˀ ø/ (PKS *khr-). The second root is reconstructed as PK *hlay, but other Kd branches usually have different forms which point to Kd *k-niw 'mouse' (e.g., Siamese /nuu/, Sui /ṇoo/, Hlai (Ht) /niu/, Lakkja /kjiu/). Li did not give a Proto-Atayalic form for 'leaf', but the Mayrinax reflex points to Atayal final *-g.

Table 7.20 Kd correspondences for AN voiced stop endings

	P-Atayal	Tai	Kam-Sui	Hlai	Kra	Kd
Yawn	surab	haau	kho	kaːu	—	*-w
Mouse	qawlid	—	—	—	lai	*-y
Leaf	ʢabag	bai	—	be	—	*-ʔ

Note
Proto-Atayal forms are from Li (1981).

Table 7.21 A possible correspondence for AN final *-l

	PAN	Tai	Kam-Sui	Hlai	Kra	Kd
Clam, snail	ku(S)ul[1]	h~~i	khuy	tshei	ci	*-y

Note
1 For this root, Blust reconstructs PWMP *kuhul 'land snail', implying that the root may not be reconstructed at higher levels. If the relation with Kd forms is acceptable, Kd reflexes point to early medial *-S- (which usually became PWMP *-h-).

Table 7.22 Summary of PAN and PKd final correspondences

PAN	PKd	PAN	PKd
-p	-p	-m	-m
-t	-t	-n	-n
-k	-k	-ng	-
-q	-k		
-C	-C	-N	-N (-n, -l)
-s	-c	-R	-R (-ʔ, -l)
-b	-w	-w	-w
-d	-y	-y	-y
-g (?)	-ʔ	-l	-y

The only example of a possible AN–Kd root with final *-l has *-y in Kd (Table 7.21).

Table 7.22 presents a summary of PAN and PKd final correspondences.

The developments of Kd medial consonants are more complex than those of Kd finals, and I will not be able to discuss them in great detail. However, I hope that the discussion in the preceding section gives some idea of how these Kd medials may be reconstructed. In general, I hope I have explained crucial distinctions that may not be apparent from the reflexes of representative dialects. For instance, the reflexes of medial *-n- and *-N- are the same in representative dialects below, but some dialects have kept the distinction.

Examples of AN–Kd medial correspondences are listed in Table 7.23.

Table 7.23 Examples of AN–Kd medial correspondences

	PAN	Tai	Kam-Sui	Hlai	Kra (Lh)	PKd
Tooth	nipen	fan	wjan	phen	pan (G)	-p-
Fire	Sapuy	fai	wi	pei	pi i	-p-
Fart	qe(n)tut	tot	ti t	thu:t	tut (By)	-t-
Head louse	kuCu	hau	tu	tshou	tou	-C-
Eye	maCa	taa	daa	tsha	taa	-C-
I	aku	kuu	—	hou (Bd)	kuu (By)	-k-
Leg	paqa	khaa	qaa	ha (Ts)	kaa	-q-
Excrement	Caqi	khii	qe	hai	kai	-q-
Hand	(qa)lima	m	mjaa	me	maa	-m-
Bear, n.	Cumay	mii	ꞌmi	mui	me	-m-
Otter	Sanaq	naak	—	na:ꞌ	—	-n-
This	i-ni	nii	naai	nei	ni i	-n-
Bird	manuk PM	nok	nok	no:k (Bd)	nok	-N-
Water	daNum	naam	nam	nom	—	-N-
Weep	Ca is	hai	ꞌ e	ei	it	- -
Sesame	le a	aa	ꞌ aa	ke (Bd)	aa (By)	- -
Shoulder	qabaRa	baa	wie(Lk)	va	baa	-b-
Navel	pudeR	d ꞌ	daa	re	dau	-d-
Live, raw	qudip	dip	ꞌdjup	ri:p	kthop (Tm)	-d-
Black	tidem	dam	ꞌnam	dom	ꞌdam (By)	-d-
Nose	iju PMP	da	ꞌna	do	da	-d-
Grand-mother	aya	jaa	jaa	tsa	jaa	-j-
Rain	quZaN	—	—	—	jal	-j-(?)
Taro	biRaq	ph ak	ꞌ aak	ge:k (Bd)	pꞌ aak	-R-
Net	aray	h‡‡	re (T)	ra:i	—	-R-
Saliva	alay	laai	wee (K)	la:i	laai (By)	-l-
Head	qulu	klau	kꞌ o (Ml)	rau	—	-!-
Sour	qa(l)sem	som	fum	—	—	-s-
Centipede[1]	qalu-Sipan	khep	khup	ri:p	—	-S-
Clam, snail	ku(S)ul	h~i	khuy	tshei	ci	-S-

Note
1 I assume the syllable reduction *qalu-Sipan *qaSipan Kd *qaSip. A number of AN languages also have reduced forms of this root (Tsuchida simply reconstructs PAN *(qa)lipan). Hlai *r- of this root, contrasting with *tsh- of the following root 'clam, snail', resulted from lenition after unaccented syllable. That is, Kd *qaSip ri:p, but Kd *kúSuy tshei. See also AN *qudip, Kd *kudip Hlai ri:p 'live, raw'.

Kra-Dai tones in Austronesian –Kra-Dai roots

Kra-Dai syllables are usually divided into two types: syllables ending with a vowel or a sonorant (called 'live syllables') and syllables ending with a stop (called 'dead syllables'). The former type may further belong to one of three proto-tonal categories, labelled *A, *B and *C. The latter type is assigned to the

*D class. A very similar system is found in other mainland languages, such as Chinese and Miao-Yao.

AN–Kd etyma are often found with Kd forms in tones *A and *D. In other words, AN syllables ending with a vowel or a sonorant often correspond to Kd syllables with tone *A, and AN syllables ending with a voiceless stop correspond to Kd syllables with tone *D. The correspondences of these two Kd tonal categories are usually straightforward and need no further explanation. However, there are some AN etyma that correspond to Kd forms in tonal categories *B or *C, though statistically fewer.

Austronesian–Kra-Dai roots in Kra-Dai tonal category *B

Tai syllables in tone *B might have earlier ended with a glottal spirant or slack voice *-h. Indic loans in Tai such as /loha/ 'shield', which has become monosyllabicised into /lo:h/ (Written Siamese) and is pronounced /lo:/, belong to the tone *B class (see Gedney 1986). Also, words in tone *B sometimes have corresponding MK forms ending with -h, for example, 'bark (v.)' Wa (a MK language) /rauh/, Siamese /hau/, Kam /khi u/, Mulam /khꞌ au/, all tone *B. A majority of words in this tonal category have corresponding Chinese forms in departing tone (qù sheng), which is hypothesised to have developed from *-s *-h (cf. Haudricourt 1954; Pulleyblank 1962).

Examples of AN–Kd etyma in this category are rare and include such roots as 'chaff' and 'shoulder' (Table 7.24).

For the first root, if we write *-h for Kd tone *B, the Kd form will be *qi(m)pah 'chaff, bran'. For evidence of Kd *q- initial, cf. Mulam /kwaa/, Then /xwaa/, Lakkja /kuo/ (*q-w- *q-p-). The tentative medial *-(m)- is suggested by Paha /bwaa/ PK *m-pa. Interestingly, the PAN form is reconstructed by Zorc as *qepah, which suggests there might be some connection between Kd *-h (tone *B) and Zorc's hypothesised PAN *-h. On the other hand, there are also counter-examples. For instance, 'sesame' is reconstructed by Zorc as AN *lĕ ah, but corresponding Kd forms point to *li a with tone *A. In any case, it seems possible that a laryngeal ending may be needed to be reconstructed for AN, though this may not be the same as PAN *-h as reconstructed by Zorc. For 'shoulder', it is possible to assume that PAN *-R- became Kd *-h (*qabaRa *qabaR *qabah), cf. PAN *taRa 'wait', Siamese thaa (*taRa *taRa). In AN–Kd perspective, Kd *-h in this root is thus secondary.

Table 7.24 AN comparanda for Kd words in tone B

	AN	Tai	Kam-Sui	Hlai	Kra (Lh)	Kd
Chaff, bran	qepa	(ram)	paa	vo (B)	paa	*B
Shoulder	qabaRa	baa	wie (Lk)	va	baa	*B

Table 7.25 AN–Kd kinship terms showing tone B in Tai

	Tai	Kam-Sui	Hlai	Kra (By)	Tones
Grandfather	puu B	—	phau C	puu B	*B
Grandmother	jaa B	jaa C	tsa C	jaa C	*C

Table 7.26 AN–Kd roots in Kd tonal category *C

	PAN	Tai	Kam-Sui	Hlai	Kra	Kd
Excrement	Caqi	khii	qe	hai	kai	*C
Head	qulu	klau	ku	rau	(kl)	*C
Water	daNum	nam	nam	nom	—	*C
Sour	qa(l)sem	som	fum	—	—	*C

The other AN–Kd roots that show tone *B in Tai are kinship terms: AN *e(m)pu 'grandparent' and AN *aya 'grandmother' (Table 7.25).

However, we may see that Hlai usually has tone *C for these words and Kra has tone *B for the former and tone *C for the latter. We may thus hypothesise that Tai and Hlai have levelled out an early tonal distinction by analogy, and that Kra has preserved the originals. In other words, for the first root the original tone is *B; for the latter root the original tone is *C. If this is the case, we may reconstruct Kd *(m)puh for 'grandfather'. For evidence of the tentative medial *-(m)-, cf. Paha /baau/   PK *m-pu.

Good examples of AN–Kd words in Kd tone *B appear to be found only with open syllables. It is interesting to see whether any new AN–Kd cognates will turn up with closed syllables. If the rarity and limited distribution of this category are confirmed, it seems likely that Kd tone *B in AN–Kd roots indeed developed from an early ending rather than from an original pitch or tone, which should occur with any kind of syllable.

Austronesian–Kra-Dai roots in Kra-Dai tonal category *C

There is evidence that early Kd syllables in tone *C could have been constricted. Stiff voice or its variants (such as creakiness or vowel constriction) are found in the reflexes of tone *C in several Tai and Kra dialects (Gedney 1986 for Tai; Ostapirat 2000 for Kra). We may represent this feature in Kd with *-ʔ.

Examples of AN–Kd etyma in Kd tone *C include the roots in Table 7.26.

For 'head', note Zorc's PAN *qúluH. This laryngeal *-H looks as if it might have some connection with Kd *-ʔ (tone C). However, as in the previous case of Zorc's PAN *-h and Kd tone B, counter-examples abound. For instance, Zorc's PAN *kúCuH 'head louse' correspond to PKd tone A (*kuCu).

Finally, there are a couple of examples where tone *C in some Kd groups has developed secondarily from Kd ending *-c (*-yʔ). These have been noted in

Table 7.27 Tone C from *-c in some Kd groups

	PAN	Tai	Kam-Sui	Hlai	Kra	Kd
Weep	Ca is	hai C	ɑ e C	ei C	it	*-c
Stream	qaRus	huai C	kui C	—	—	*-c

earlier discussions on final consonants; we present them again in Table 7.27 for easy reference.

Discussion

Are Kra-Dai and Austronesian genetically related?

We hope to have shown that phonological correspondences and vocabulary distribution support the relation of Kd to AN. The high numbers of shared AN–Kd basic words in Yakhontov's and Swadesh's lists seem unlikely to result from chance or from simple borrowings. Most of these AN–Kd roots are distributed widely across Kd languages and their sound correspondences can be systematically worked out. Other language families that may have a claim to be genetically related to Kd, such as Chinese, do not seem to compete as well in most respects. Those etyma that are shared between Tai and Chinese are seldom found in all Kd branches and almost none of them belong to the core vocabulary.

If the relation between Kd and AN indeed is a genetic one, when, may we ask, did they split from each other? Was Kd a language group, or a branch of an extinct language group, co-ordinate with PAN within a larger Austro-Tai phylum, or was it a daughter language group within AN (see also Sagart, who in Chapter 10 of this book proposes that Kd is closely related to Malayo-Polynesian)?

The answer to these questions seems to depend partly on whether PKd has any features that cannot be accounted for by the reconstructed PAN system. Benedict (1975) has tried just this by positing a number of initial clusters, among others, that he claimed to be evidenced in Kd but not in PAN. For instance, he reconstructed Austro-Tai *mapḷa 'eye' (AN *maCa) and *qatḷu 'head louse' (AN *kuCu), assuming that such Austro-Tai *-pḷ- and *-tḷ- have become PAN *-C-. According to the present correspondence system, this kind of hypothetical clusters appears extravagant ('proto-form stuffing') and spurious. Modern Kd clusters mainly result from syllable reduction of disyllabic roots such as *k-t-   khr-, etc.

As far as our AN–Kd correspondences are concerned, there is yet no clear evidence that PKd consonants and vowel reflexes require us to posit any sounds that are lacking in PAN. However, the origins of Kd tones cannot yet be fully explained from what we currently know about the PAN system. Such Kd prosodies could be a retention of early features that are lacking in PAN and thus set PKd apart from PAN. On the other hand, there seems to be evidence within AN (e.g. from some Formosan and Philippine languages) which suggests that laryngeal, stress and other prosodic features may finally need to be reconstructed for PAN. These features might turn out to be systematically relatable to Kd tones. Future studies in this area of prosodic correspondences will be crucial to clarify this issue.

If Kd was a daughter language group within AN, however, it would seem likely that they must have belonged to one of the primary branches. Blust (1999) has set up useful phonological criteria that distinguish PMP from PAN. These include the following sound changes and mergers in PMP:

PAN	PMP
*t and *C	*t
*n and *N	*n
*S	*h

PKd has preserved all these PAN features that are lacking in PMP. Thus, Kd is unlikely to be part of or closely related to Malayo-Polynesian or the other lower-order AN groups. The merger of *t/*C is also characteristic of the eastern Formosan group as a whole (PMP is a daughter language which split from this group). Thus, if Kd were an AN language, it would possibly be outside of the eastern Formosan primary branch.

There are also AN–Kd roots that have not been found in PMP such as some faunal terms recently explored by Blust (2002). These include PAN *Cumay 'bear, n.', Tai /mii/, Kam /mee/, Hlai /mui/, Laha /mee/; the root has not been found in AN languages outside Taiwan where another form is attested (PWMP *biRua). We may note, however, that the Kd root *maNuk 'bird' is related to PMP *manuk 'bird' (semantic shift from 'chicken, fowl') rather than to PAN *qayam 'bird'. This is taken by Sagart (Chapter 10, this volume) as indicating a close relation between PMP and Kd. However, the semantic shift from 'chicken' to 'bird' in Kd could have occurred independently after the other mainland root for 'chicken' was integrated into the language (Kd *ki, Si /kai/, Sui /qaai/, Ht /khai/, Lh /ki i/, etc). This mainland 'chicken' root is widespread in South China and is found across language families, such as Chinese (OC *kej) and Miao-Yao (Miao /qai/, etc). Also, Kd reflexes point to medial *N which is lacking in PMP, and possibly suggests an original AN root *maNuk 'chicken, fowl'.

Kra-Dai and Austronesian in pre-historical perspective

Archaeologists and linguists working on AN have recently elaborated an impressive account of the AN homeland and migrations (Chang 1995; Tsang 1995; Bellwood 1997; Blust 1988, among others). According to their hypothesis, PAN was spoken in Taiwan or the adjacent coastal areas of South China around 6,000 BP. In view of this proposal, the likely homeland of the Kd ancestor language must have been in the coastal areas of Fujian or Guangdong, and the PKd people are likely to have been part of the Neolithic Lungshanoid cultures that flourished in the area during the fifth to fourth millennia BP.

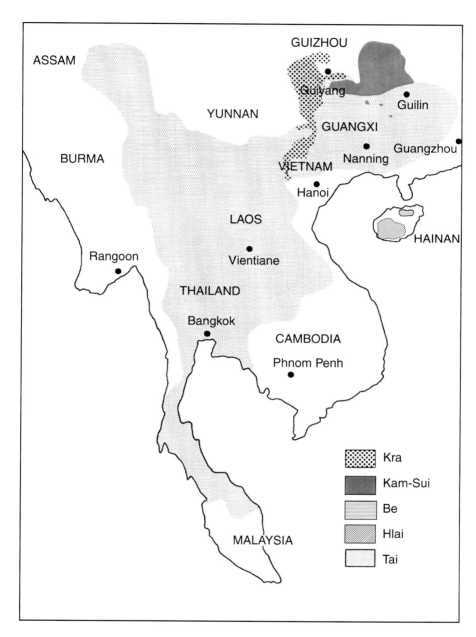

Map 7.1 Current geographical distribution of Kd languages.

It is difficult to know when the ancestral Kd language started to split up. By the fourth millennium, its speakers might have already split into coastal (southern) and inland (northern) groups in the central plain and southern coastal areas of Guangdong. The southern groups may have included Tai and Hlai, which separated during the following millennium in south-western Guangdong, where the Hlai would cross to Hainan island. The Tai would further expand west and settle in most of Guangxi and northern Vietnam. The northern groups include Kra and Kam-Sui that would later settle mainly in Guizhou. The Kra lived roughly to the west while the Kam-Sui lived in the eastern areas bordering Hunan and Guangxi. Towards the end of the third millennium BP, the ethnic Chinese would have expanded considerably south of the Yangzi. It was probably about this time that heavy contact between Chinese and Tai and Kam-Sui occurred (contact between them is possible at an earlier period, but not on such a large scale). At that time, Hlai was already established on Hainan, and Kra was further to the west in western Guizhou; these areas have remained immune to heavy Chinese settlement until the present millennium. This would explain the high number of Chinese elements (especially cultural terms) that are found in the Tai and Kam-Sui groups.

During the 2–3,000 years of migration and expansion from eastern Guangdong coast to Guangxi/Guizhou areas, the Kd people must have come into contact with several other ethnic groups, including the Miao-Yao and AA speakers. Such contact would both enrich and complicate the Kd lexicon. The Kd-related language groups who remained along the Fujian-Guangdong coastal areas, if there were any, must have subsequently become extinct or so heavily Sinicised that they became just varieties of Chinese. Kd thus seems to be the only AN-related group whose survival in southern China over the millennia was probably due to their expansion into the Guangdong plain. This (agricultural?) expansion would enormously increase their population and territory, as well as strengthen their socio-economic and political power, to such a degree that they were able to resist, though heavily influenced by, the great waves of Chinese domination of the last few millennia (Map 7.1).

Acknowledgements

The early draft of this paper benefited from my research visit at the National Museum of Ethnology, Osaka, in the years 2000 and 2001. I would like to thank Yasuhiko Nagano for his unfailing support and ensuring the best environment for my research. This revised version was written under partial support from the National Sciences Council, Taiwan. I also thank Panarai Ostapirat for producing the figures and map for this article.

Abbreviations

Abbreviations of language names in Kra-Dai reflex charts are tabulated in Table 7.28.

Table 7.28 Abbreviations of language names in Kd reflex charts

Tai		Kam-Sui		Hlai		Kra	
Si	Siamese	K	Kam	Bd	Baoding	Gl	Gelao
Lm	Lungming	S	Sui	Ht	Heitu	Lh	Laha
Wm	Wuming	M	Mak	Ym	Yuanmen	Ph	Paha
Sk	Saek	T	Then			By	Buyang
		Ml	Mulam			Pb	Pubiao
		Lk	Lakkja				

Other abbreviations:
AA	Austro-Asiatic
AN	Austronesian
B	Be
Kd	Kra-Dai
Lg	Lingao (a Be dialect)
Lz	Laozhai (a Gelao dialect)
MK	Mon-Khmer
PAN	Proto-Austronesian
PH	Proto-Hlai
PK	Proto-Kra
PKd	Proto-Kra-Dai
PKS	Proto-Kam-Sui
PMP	Proto-Malayo-Polynesian
PT	Proto-Tai
PWMP	Proto-Western Malayo-Polynesian
Qs	Qiaoshang (a Gelao dialect)
Wt	White Tai

Note

1 See also Gedney (1976) for an elaborate critical review on these issues.

Bibliography

Bellwood, P. (1997) Prehistory of the Indo-Malaysian Archipelago, Honolulu: University of Hawaii Press.

Benedict, P.K. (1942) 'Thai, Kadai, and Indonesian: A new alignment in Southeastern Asia', American Anthropologist n.s. 44: 576–601.

—— (1975) Austro-Thai: Language and Culture, With a Glossary of Roots, New Haven: HRAF Press.

—— (1990) Japanese-Austro-Tai, Ann Arbor: Karoma.

Blust, R. (1980) 'Austronesian etymologies', Oceanic Linguistics 19: 1–181.

Blust, R. (1983–84) 'Austronesian etymologies II', Oceanic Linguistics 22–23: 29–49.
—— (1985) 'Austronesian etymologies III', Oceanic Linguistics 25: 1–123.
—— (1988) 'The Austronesian homeland: a linguistic perspective', Asian Perspectives 26.1: 45–67.
—— (1989) 'Austronesian etymologies IV', Oceanic Linguistics 28.2: 111–80.
—— (1999) 'Subgrouping, circularity and extinction: some issues in Austronesian comparative linguistics', in E. Zeitoun and J.K. Li (eds) Selected Papers from the Eighth International Conference on Austronesian linguistics, 31–94, Taipei: Institute of Linguistics (preparatory office), Academia Sinica.
—— (2002) 'The history of faunal terms in Austronesian languages', Oceanic Linguistics 41.1: 89–139.
Chang, K.C. (1995) 'Taiwan Strait archeology and Proto-Austronesian', in J.K. Li, C.H. Tseng, Y.K. Huang, D.A. Ho, C.Y. Tseng (eds) Austronesian Studies Relating to Taiwan, 161–83, Taipei: Institute of History and Philology, Academia Sinica.
Dempwolff, O. (1934–38) Vergleichende Lautlehre des austronesische Wortschatzes, 3 vols, Berlin: Dietrich Reimer.
Diller, A. (1998) 'The Tai language family and the comparative method', Proceedings of the International Conference on Tai Studies, 1–32, Bangkok: Mahidol Universiy.
Gedney, W.J. (1976) 'On the Thai evidence for Austro-Tai', Computational Analyses of Asian and African Languages 6: 65–82.
—— (1986) 'Speculations on early Tai tones', in J. McCoy and T. Light (eds) Contributions to Sino-Tibetan Studies, 144–56, Leiden: E.J. Brill.
—— (1991) The Tai Dialect of Lungming (Michigan papers on South and Southeast Asia no. 38, edited by Thomas J. Hudak), Ann Arbor: Center for South and Southeast Asia Studies, University of Michigan.
Hashimoto, M. (1980) The Be Language: A Classified Lexicon of Its Limkow Dialect Tokyo: Institute for the Studies of Languages and Cultures of Africa and Asia.
Haudricourt, A.G. (1954) 'Comment reconstruire le chinois archaique', Word 10.2–3: 351–64.
Ho, D.A. (1998) 'Taiwan Nandaoyu de Yuyan Guanxi', Chinese Studies 16.2: 141–71.
Li, F.K. (1965) 'The Tai and Kam-Sui languages', in G.B. Milner and E. Henderson (eds) Indo-Pacific Linguistic Studies, Vol. 1: 148–79, Amsterdam: North Holland Publishing Co.
—— (1968) 'Notes on the T'en or Yanghuang language: Glossary', Bulletin of the Institute of History and Philology, Academia Sinica 40.1: 397–504.
—— (1977) A Handbook of Comparative Tai, Honolulu: University of Hawaii Press.
Li, J.K. (1981) 'Reconstruction of Proto-Atayalic phonology', Bulletin of the Institute of History and Philology, Academia Sinica 52.2: 235–301.
Ostapirat, W. (1993) Proto-Hlai vowel system, M.A. thesis, Mahidol University.
—— (1994a) 'Two series of Proto Kam-Sui preglottalized nasals', Kadai 4: 73–8.
—— (1994b) 'Speculations on Proto Kam-Sui breathy sounds', Kadai 4: 79–87.
—— (2000) 'Proto-Kra', Linguistics of the Tibeto-Burman Area, 23.1 (Monograph).
Ouyang, J.Y. and Zheng, Y.Q. (1983) Liyu Diaocha Yanjiu, Beijing: Zhongguo Shehui Kexue Chubanshe.
Pulleyblank, E.G. (1962) 'The consonantal system of Old Chinese', Asia Major n.s. 9.1: 58–144, 200–21.
Reid, L. (1984–85) 'Benedict's Austro-Tai hypothesis – An evaluation', Asian Perspectives 26: 19–34.

Schlegel, G. (1901) 'Review of Frankfurter's Siamese grammar', T'oung Pao 2: 76–87.

Thurgood, G. (1994) 'Tai-Kadai and Austronesian: the nature of the historical relationship', Oceanic Linguistics 33.2: 345–68.

Tryon, D. (ed.) (1995) Comparative Austronesian Dictionary, 5 vols, Berlin, New York: Mouton de Gruyter.

Tsang, C.H. (1995) 'New archeological data from both sides of the Taiwan Straits and their implications for the controversy about Austronesian origins and expansion', in J.K. Li, C.H. Tseng, Y.K. Huang, D.A. Ho, C.Y. Tseng (eds) Austronesian Studies Relating to Taiwan, 185–225, Taipei: Institute of History and Philology, Academia Sinica.

Tsuchida, S. (1976) Reconstruction of Proto-Tsouic Phonology, Study of Languages and Cultures of Asia and Africa, monograph series, no. 5, Tokyo: Institute for the Study of Languages and Cultures of Asia and Africa.

Wang, J. (1984) Zhuang-Dong Yuzu Yuyan Jianzhi Beijing: Minzu Chubanshe.

Wulff, K. (1942) Über das verhältnis des malayo-polynesischen zum indochinesischen', Det Künglige Danske Videnskabernes Selskab, Historisk-filologiske Meddelser 27.2.

Zhang, Y.S., Ma, J.L., Wen, M.Y. and Wei, X.L. (1985) Hainan Lingaohua, Nanning: Guangxi Minzu Chubanshe.

8

THE CURRENT STATUS OF AUSTRIC

A review and evaluation of the lexical and morphosyntactic evidence

Lawrence A. Reid

Introduction

The purpose of this chapter is to review and evaluate the set of evidence that has so far appeared in support of a genetic relationship for the Austric family of languages, here defined as constituting the AN family as its eastern branch and the AA languages as its western branch. It thereby excludes consideration of evidence which suggests that the Tai-Kadai family of languages might be included as part of the family and avoids the obfuscation that discussion of the Austro-Tai hypothesis has had on the basic question of the genetic relationship of AA and AN.

There have been a number of articles, beginning with Schmidt (1906) that have presented sets of corresponding lexical items purporting to establish a genetic relationship between AA and AN. Much of this work has been shown to be spurious, but Diffloth (1994) presents a number of what he terms 'lexical agreements' between the two families which he considers to be probable. Subsequent work by Hayes (1997, 1999) has introduced a considerable number of new equations into the arena especially in the area of so-called 'basic vocabulary' that need to be evaluated. Some of these have already appeared in earlier work, but are reintroduced to us by Hayes in his attempt to show that, although, as Diffloth (1994: 312) says, 'the lexical evidence is not impressive, it is undoubtedly there', especially in that area of the lexicon that counts most strongly towards the establishment of a genetic relationship.

Schmidt (1906) was also the first to draw attention to the striking morphological comparisons that exist between the two families. Reid (1994, 1999) expanded on this work and noted also certain syntactic characteristics, which along with the reconstructed morphology suggested an ergative structure for the parent of the two families.

The first part of the chapter will be a detailed evaluation of the basic vocabulary comparisons between PAA and PAN proposed by Hayes (1999), to determine to what degree they may be said to constitute a body of cognates, supported by the usual requirements of recurrent sound correspondences and reasonable semantic equivalence. Hayes does not specifically claim that the pairs of forms he cites are cognates (this term does not appear in his paper), he refers to them by the less strict label of 'lexical comparison', a term which allows for forms which may be similar, not only because they are cognate, but also because they may be borrowings from one group into the other, or they may be the result of universal phonological developments, or they may simply be similar by chance. In order for the comparanda to constitute true cognates, it is imperative that a clear set of recurrent sound correspondences be established between the two proto-languages, and that the forms being compared have reasonably similar semantics.

The second part of the chapter will summarise the morphological evidence that has been proposed as evidence for a genetic relationship between AA and AN, and will discuss some of the alternative hypotheses that have been proposed to account for this evidence.

The lexical evidence for Austric

An adequate evaluation of Hayes' comparisons should consist of at least three parts: (1) an evaluation of the status of his PAA reconstructions and the methodology that he used to establish them, (2) an evaluation of the PAN reconstructions used in the comparisons and (3) an evaluation of the phonological correspondences and semantic features that supposedly relate the forms.

Hayes' PAA reconstructions

It is unclear from Hayes' paper whether the forms that he cites as evidence for each of his reconstructions constitute the total sum of his available evidence. I suspect that they probably do not, and that the few forms that he cites are representative of a (much?) larger body of evidence for which there was no room in the publication. However, I must assume that the forms that he cites constitute the best evidence available for his reconstructions.

For his PAA reconstructions, Hayes claims that most phonemic correspondences between the lexical items cited 'are in fact regular, at least where the consonants are concerned' (1999: 7), although in few cases does he attempt to make explicit what those regular correspondences are. As a non-specialist in AA languages, I have had to take this statement at face value in order to make my evaluation of his comparisons with PAN, although I suspect that a good deal of ingenuity was required in some cases to actually make the correspondences work. Hayes is, however, careful to indicate the relative time-depth of his own reconstructions.

The best claim to PAA status are those forms that he claims have reflexes in both the eastern and the western branches of the family. Of the approximately

150 forms that he reconstructs, 76 have proposed reflexes from both major branches of the family. Of the remaining reconstructions, 70 have proposed reflexes in more than one language in one or more of the EAA subfamilies. The remaining forms have reflexes in only one language, but Hayes claims that in these cases the comparisons are, in effect, too good to be ignored. I have relabeled his reconstructions that do not have a western AA reflex as PEAA, and consider that these have lower probative value than those that can justly be claimed to be PAA.

The Austronesian reconstructions

On the AN side, all of Hayes' comparisons are with reasonably well-established reconstructions. Hayes used the list of 200 basic vocabulary reconstructions for PMP, provided in Blust (1993), rather than with the smaller set that have been reconstructed for PAN. However, in evaluating the comparisons, I have chosen to compare Hayes' AA reconstructions with PAN rather than with the historically subsequent PMP, whenever an appropriate PAN form exists. The PAN reconstructions with which I made my comparison are those which are also summarised alongside the PMP reconstructions in Blust (1999). Of the 150 or so comparisons for which Hayes cites a PMP reconstruction, there are some 79 for which the PMP form is a continuation of a reconstructed PAN reconstruction. This set potentially has high probative value when compared with an AA reconstruction. The 52 forms which compare with a PAA reconstruction (marked with a single asterisk in Table 8.1) have the highest value, while the remaining 27 that compare with only a PEAA reconstruction (marked with a double asterisk in Table 8.1) are of lower value. However, given the possibility that the Munda languages may have split off prior to the split of the eastern branch from pre-AN, this set of lexical comparisons may take on greater significance. The full set of potentially comparable PAA (and PEAA) forms with presently reconstructed PAN forms is shown in Table 8.1.

It is apparent that in making his comparisons, Hayes has operated on the assumption that PA must have been a highly affixing language, with PAN inheriting many of the forms in their affixed state, while their corresponding PAA forms were inherited either as roots, or with different affixes. Table 8.2 gives a list of some of the PAN forms that have been reanalysed by Hayes as originally consisting of a root plus one or more affixes.

Table 8.3 shows many of the proposed PA affixes that Hayes implies are present in his AN reconstructions. Although some of these forms may indeed have been affixes in the putative parent of PAN (as they are in PAN and some of its daughter languages) and some of the PAN reconstructions may have been morphologically complex (e.g. *Si-kan 'fish', *ma-ka-Sepal 'thick', *C in aqi 'guts', even *q al ejaw 'day', on the basis of comparisons such as Bontok ʔalgew 'sun, day', reflecting the full, infixed form, with reflexes of apparently unaffixed maʔégew 'to be fine, after rain', ʔagʔagew 'morning', maggew 'handsome [bright appearance?]', etc.), it is methodologically unwise to equate any

Table 8.1 Proposed lexical correspondences between PAA (and PEAA) and PAN (79)

	PAA and PEAA	PAN	Gloss
1.0	Nature		
1.1	*qabuh	*qabu	ashes
1.2	**[j](a)raw	*qalejaw	day
1.3	*[s]uy,*[sa](m)puy(s)	*Sapuy	fire
1.4	**li w	*danaw	lake
1.5	**b(i,a)lal	*bulaN	moon
1.6	**ka[ñj]al	*quzaN	rain
1.7	*qa(m)puc(i)	*timus	salt
1.8	**si[ʔ]aq,**su[ʔ]ak	*qasiRa	salt
1.9	**lay	*qenay	sand
1.10	*(m)pi l̥	*qebel	smoke
1.11	*t[o]q(i)	*bituqen	star
1.12	**tamuq	*batu	stone
1.13	*[⌐]om	*daNum	water
2.0	Flora		
2.1	**(m)b[o⌐a]q	*buaq	fruit
2.2	**k(i,a)hi(uq)	*kaSiw	wood
3.0	Fauna		
3.1	*cu(q)	*asu	dog
3.2	*teloR	*qiCeluR	egg
3.3	*(n)qa(q)	*Sikan	fish
3.4	**k[o]t(i)	*kuCu	head louse
3.5	*b[i w]	*labaw	rat
3.6	*[su][!]aR	*SulaR	snake
4.0	Anatomy		
4.1	**ko[d(i)]	*likud	back
4.2	*ta⌐al, *ti⌐al	*tiaN	belly
4.3	*cinqaˇ, *canqaˇ	*CuqelaN	bone
4.4	*n[s]uq	*susu	breast
4.5	**(n)[q!]eˇ	*Caliˇa	ear
4.6	*mi(n)ta(q)	*maCa	eye
4.7	*saʔ, *suʔ	*SimaR	fat/oil
4.8	*[⌐]aqi, *laqi	*Cinaqi	guts
4.9	*(n)lem[a]	*(qa)lima	hand
4.10	**(n)qolu(q)	*qulu	head
4.11	**p[a]le(q)	*qaCay	liver
4.12	*c(i,i)ci	*Sesi/isi	meat/flesh
4.13	*(n)qe[R]	*liqeR	neck
4.14	*(ba)Ra(q)	*qabaRa	shoulder
4.15	**[taN]Gep	*nipen	tooth
5.0	Kinship		
5.1	*(qa)ma(ma)	*t-ama	father
5.2	*a[x]i, *bu[x]i, *mpa[x]i	*bahi	female/woman
5.3	*(n)qalay	*ma-RuqaNay	male/man
5.4	*(na)na	*t-ina	mother
5.5	*(kal)i wu(q)	*Cau	person

(Table 8.1 continued)

Table 8.1 Continued

	PAA and PEAA	PAN	Gloss
6.0	Cultural artifacts		
6.1	**[u]› aq, *(sun)› um[aq]	*Rumaq	house
6.2	*(n)jam[u]s	*˘ajan	name
6.3	{**Rom}	*zaRum	needle
6.4	*k(a,u)la̦	*zalan	road
6.5	*tal̦	*CaliS	rope
7.0	Descriptives		
7.1	*(can)› aya(q)	*ma-Raya	big
7.2	**qi[R]u(q)	*ma-baqeRu	new
7.3	**ti(n)qas(i)	*ma-tuqaS	old (people)
7.4	*›ok	*ma-buRuk	rotten
7.5	* (i,a)haq(i)	*ma-Siaq	shy/ashamed
7.6	*(n)qa[l], *qampa[l]	*ma-kaSepal	thick
8.0	Verbs		
8.1	**(n)k[o]t	*ma-takut	afraid
8.2	*(n)› at(i)	*kaRat	bite
8.3	*[q]uyu	*Siup	blow
8.4	**[ɒ]us(i), **t[u]nus	*CuNuh	burn
8.5	*pi [l]i	*beli	buy
8.6	**(u)laqi̦	*piliq	choose
8.7	**ta› aq, **ta› ak	*taRaq	cut (wood)
8.8	**tak, **tek	*tektek	cut (wood)
8.9	*(n)ka[l]	*kalih	dig up
8.10	*(m)pe(qi)	*Sepi	dream
8.11	*(in)ka(q)	*kaen	eat
8.12	**qo›,**[qa]lo›	*qaluR (?)	flow
8.13	*(n)ki m	*gemgem	hold (in fist)
8.14	*(n)[r]op, *(c,s)[r]op	*qaNup	hunt
8.15	*ntaw	*Cawa	laugh
8.16	**(s)[R]ai	*kita	see
8.17	**(n)qiq	*taSiq	sew
8.18	*[ɒ]aq	*panaq	shoot
8.19	*(n)zo›	*tuduR	sleep
8.20	*(z)ye›	*diRi	stand
8.21	*kalaw, *kumlaw̦	*Cakaw	steal
8.22	*s[e]p, *(n)c[e]p	*sepsep	suck
8.23	*[ɒ]i q(i),*bur[i q]	*baReq	swell
8.24	*la(n)[ɒ]oy	*Na˘uy	swim
8.25	*taq	*utaq	vomit
8.26	{**ma[q]}	*qumah	work in fields
8.27	*(can)qap	*ma-Suab	yawn

non-corresponding set of phonemes with an affix, unless justification can be found for it in the daughter languages. Such forms have therefore been eliminated from the set of potential cognates. This is not a trivial concern. Ignoring non-agreeing segments by calling them affixes without justification, allows for the inclusion of almost any non-cognate form into the comparative set.

Table 8.2 Morphological reanalysis of PAN reconstructions (implied in Hayes 2000) (26)

PAN (Blust 1999)	Gloss	Hayes' Reanalysis
*qalejaw	day	*q al ejaw
*Sapuy	fire	*S ap uy, *Sa-puy
*qasiRa	salt	*qa-siRa
*bituqen	star	*bituq-en
*daNum	water	*d aN um
*Sikan	fish	*Si-ka-n
*CuqelaN	bone	*Cu-q el aN
*Cali˜a	ear	*Cali˜-a
*SimaR	fat/oil	*S im aR
*Cinaqi	guts	*C in aqi(?)
*(qa)lima	hand	*(qa)lim-a
*nipen	tooth	*nip-en
*Cau	person	*Ca-u
*Rumaq	house	*R um aq, *Rum-aq
*˜ajan	name	*˜aja-n
*zalan	road	*zala-n
*CaliS	rope	*Cal-iS
*ma-kaSepal	thick	*ka-Se-pal
*Siup	blow	*Siu-p
*kalih	dig up	*kal-ih
*kaen	eat	*ka-en
*qaluR (?)	flow	*q al uR, *qa-luR
*Cawa	laugh	*Caw-a
*panaq	shoot	*p an aq
*diRi	stand	*diR-i
*baReq	swell	*b aR eq, *baR-eq

Table 8.3 Hayes' proposed PA affixes in PAN reconstructions

Infixes	-al-, -an-, -aN-, -ap-, -aR-, -um-, -im-, -in-, -el-
Prefixes	qa-, Si-, Cu-, ka-, Se-
Suffixes	-en, -n, -u, -iS, -a, -aq, -i

The remaining set of PAN comparable forms are given in Table 8.4.

After eliminating the proposed sets that contain a PAN form that Hayes implies is morphologically complex, there remain some 19 sets, shown in Table 8.5.

The remaining AN reconstructions that Hayes cites are PMP forms that can be grouped into three types: (1) those which continue a PAN form but which have undergone an irregular phonological change, such as metathesis (M); (2) those which constitute a lexical replacement of an earlier PAN form (L) or are an innovation alongside a PAN form than has undergone a semantic shift in PMP (I); and (3) those for which no PAN form has as yet been reconstructed (?). These forms are shown in Table 8.6.

Table 8.4 Potential PAA–PAN comparisons (31)

	PAA	PAN	Gloss
1.1	*qabuh	*qabu	ashes
1.7	*qa(m)puc(i)	*timus	salt
1.10	*(m)pi cl	*qebel	smoke
3.1	*cu(q)	*asu	dog
3.2	*teloR	*qiCeluR	egg
3.5	*b[i w]	*labaw	rat
3.6	*[su][!]aR	*SulaR	snake
4.2	*ta al, *ti al	*tiaN	belly
4.4	*n[s]uq	*susu	breast
4.6	*mi (n)ta(q)	*maCa	eye
4.12	*c(i,i)ci	*Sesi/isi	meat/flesh
4.13	*(n)qe[R]	*liqeR	neck
4.14	*(ba)Ra(q)	*qabaRa	shoulder
5.1	*(qa)ma(ma)	*t-ama	father
5.2	*a[x]i, *bu[x]i,*mpa[x]i	*bahi	female/woman
5.3	*(n)qalay	*ma-RuqaNay	male/man
5.4	*(na)na	*t-ina	mother
7.1	*(can)› aya(q)	*ma-Raya	big
7.4	*› ok	*ma-buRuk	rotten
7.5	*g(i,a)haq(i)	*ma-Siaq	shy/ashamed
8.2	*(n)› at(i)	*kaRat	bite
8.5	*pi [!]i	*beli	buy
8.10	*(m)pe(qi)	*Sepi	dream
8.13	*(n)ki m	*gemgem	hold (in fist)
8.14	*(n)[r]op,*(c,s)[r]op,	*qaNup	hunt
8.19	*(n)zo›	*tuduR	sleep
8.21	*kalaw, *kumlaw	*Cakaw	steal
8.22	*s[e]p, *(n)c[e]p	*sepsep	suck
8.24	*la(n)[ ]oy	*Na˘ uy	swim
8.25	*taq	*utaq	vomit
8.27	*(can)qap	*ma-huab	yawn

Of these groups, I have only included those marked with (?) in Table 8.6 as possible PMP comparisons, in that they may constitute a continuation of a PAN form which no longer exists in Formosan languages. These forms are considered to have lower probative value than true PAN reconstructions, and are labeled as PMP. From this set I have likewise eliminated those that Hayes implies were retentions of morphologically complex PA forms. The remaining set is provided in Table 8.7.

The final group of potentially comparable sets, and those that are of least value to supporting an Austric hypothesis are those that compare a PEAA form with a PMP form. This set (minus those that Hayes implies were retentions of morphologically complex PA forms) is provided in Table 8.8.

Sagart (email comm. 2001) has suggested 'some of the evidence for Austric is also extra-Formosan rather than PAN, suggesting again an early contact relationship rather than a genetic one'. If in fact there was a post-PAN return to the

Table 8.5 Potential PEAA–PAN comparisons (19)

	PEAA	PAN	Gloss
1.5	**b(i,a)lal	*bulaN	moon
1.6	**ka[ñj]al	*quzaN	rain
1.9	**lay	*qenay	sand
1.12	**tamuq	*batu	stone
2.1	**k(m)b[o a]q	*buaq	fruit
2.2	**k(i,a)hi(up)	*kaSiw	wood
3.4	**k[o]t(i)	*kuC	head louse
4.1	**ko[d(i)]	*likud	back
4.10	**(n)qolu(q)	*qulu	head
4.11	**p[a]le(q)	*qaCay	liver
7.2	**qi[R]u(q)	*ma-baqeRu	new
7.3	**ti(n)qas(i)	*ma-tuqaS	old (people)
8.1	**(n)k[o]t	*ma-takut	afraid
8.4	**[ ]us(i), **t[u]nus	*CuNuh	burn
8.6	**(u)laqi	*piliq	choose
8.7	**ta›aq, **ta›ak	*taRaq	cut (wood)
8.8	**tak, **tek	*tektek	cut (wood)
8.2	**(s)[R]ai	*kita	see
8.2	**(n)qiq	*taSiq	sew

mainland, it is possible that some of the lexical sets proposed by Hayes which do not have a PAN reconstruction may be evidence for that. However, even these sets need to be critically evaluated, and are beyond the scope of this chapter.

The sound correspondences

My procedure was to begin with the reconstructed consonant system of PAN and PMP (Blust 1999: 34) shown in Table 8.9, and to compare, in order, each phoneme with the apparently corresponding phoneme in each of Hayes' comparisons.

It should be noted that I made no attempt to compare the vocalic systems. Although Hayes has made a provisional reconstruction of a 6-vowel system for PAA, he notes that 'additional vowel phonemes and diphthongs will probably have to be reconstructed eventually'. Comparison was based on the distributional features of the PAN phonemes in each of the (usually) disyllabic AN reconstructions. In many cases (100/154) the comparable form in Hayes was also disyllabic, and the determination of the appropriately corresponding phoneme was not difficult. The remaining forms, however, needed to be compared with what Hayes has reconstructed on the AA side with a monosyllabic form. For some 100 forms, the correspondence is between the final syllable of a PAN form (or the putative monosyllabic root of those forms that Hayes believes are continuations of affixed PA forms) and a PAA monosyllable. The full set of correspondences are shown in Table 8.10. Shading indicates distinctly different AA correspondences for the same PAN proto-phoneme.

Table 8.6 Hayes' PAA–PMP comparisons (36)

	PAA	PMP	Gloss
1.0	Nature		
1.1	*›[a]mb[o]l	*Rabun (L)	cloud
1.2	*buk	*qabuk (?)	dust
1.3	*teq	*taneq (I)	earth, soil
1.4	*(m)put	*kabut (?)	fog, mist
1.7	*(bi)lat(i)	*kilat (M)	lightning
1.9	*gi r	*gurgur (L)	thunder
2.0	Flora		
2.2	*(m)pu˘	*bu˘ a (?)	flower
2.3	*(n)je	*baliji (L)	grass
2.5	*(s)u›(at)	*uRat (L)	root
2.6	*(n)qa›	*wakaR (L)	root
4.0	Anatomy		
4.2	*(n)suk	*buhek (M)	head hair
4.4	*(di)laq(i)	*dilaq (I)	tongue
5.0	Kinship		
5.1	*(n)qu an[ak]	*anak (?)	child
5.2	*saw[a]	*qasawa (?)	spouse
5.4	*(lan)qe(q)	*laki(I)	male/man
6.0	Cultural artifacts		
6.1	*(n)ti p	*qatep (?)	roof/thatch
7.0	Descriptives		
7.2	*(i)ti m	*ma-qitem (L)	black
7.3	*(z)le˘	*ma-di˘ di˘ (?)	cold
7.6	*p(a,u)›a˘	*ma-Ra˘ aw (L)	dry
7.8	*jar[ ]uq	*ma-zauq (L)	far
7.11	*(n)kit	*kepit (?)	narrow
7.12	*›a(k,q)	*ma-iRaq (L)	red
7.13	*su(q)	*ma-busuk (I)	rotten
7.14	*(n)zekiq	*dikiq (I)	small
8.1	*r(a,u)wa(i)	*mañawa (?)	breathe
8.0	Verbs		
8.2	*maq(i)	*mamaq (L)	chew
8.4	*[ ]a›	*maRi (?)	come
8.5	*[ ]om	*inum (?)	drink
8.6	*t(a,u)(m)puq	*nabuq (?)	fall
8.7	*m[b]uk	*tu(m)buq (?)	grow
8.8	*zi˘ [i› (i)]	*de˘ eR (L)	hear
8.15	*(n)qa›(i)	*kaRi (?)	say
8.21	*›i t(s)	*peRes (I)	squeeze
8.20	*(ba)laq(i)	*belaq (?)	split
8.22	*(n)cuk(i)	*suksuk (?)	stab
8.23	*da(q)	*tudaq(?)	throw

Table 8.7 Potential PAA–PMP comparisons (13)

	PAA	PMP	Gloss
1.2	*buk	*qabuk	dust
1.4	*(m)put	*kabut	fog, mist
5.1	*(n)qu an[ak]	*anak	child
5.2	*saw[a]	*qasawa	spouse
6.1	*(n)ti p	*qatep	roof/thatch
7.3	*(z)le˜	*ma-di˜ di˜	cold
7.7	*tu[!]	*pundul	dull/blunt
8.1	*r(a,u)wa(i)	*mañawa	breathe
8.6	*t(a,u)(m)puq	*nabuq	fall
8.7	*m[b]uk	*tu(m)buq	grow
8.20	*(ba)laq(i)	*belaq	split
8.22	*(n)cuk(i)	*suksuk	stab
8.23	*da(q)	*tudaq	throw

Table 8.8 Potential PEAA–PMP comparisons (13)

	PEAA	PMP	Gloss
4.3	**(m)paq	*baqbaq	mouth
5.3	**na(q)	*bana	husband
7.4	**bi r, **bi ni r	*ma-bener	correct, true
7.5	**mi z	*cemeD (?)	dirty
7.7	**tu[!]	*pundul (?)	dull/blunt
7.9	**i[ ]ak, **u[ ]aq	*ma-pia	good
7.10	**baRe(n)qi t	*ma-beReqat	heavy
7.15	**[b]acaq	*ma-baseq (?)	wet
8.11	**(i)li p	*qinep	lie down
8.14	**ntuk	*tuktuk	pound
8.18	**zaq(i), **ñjaqi	*luzaq	spit
8.19	**ta[q]	*sitaq	split
8.24	**(n)ki t	*hiket	tie

Table 8.9 PAN and PMP phonemic systems

PAN						PMP				
p	t			k	q	p	t		k	q
	C	c						c		
b	d		j	g		b	d	j	g	
		z						z		
m	n	ñ		˜		m	n	ñ	˜	
	N									
	S	s			h		s			h
	l						l			
	r			R			r		R	
w			y			w			y	

Table 8.10 AN–AA phonological correspondences (based on Hayes' complete set of proposed lexical correspondences)

PAN	PMP	PAA	Reconstruction #	
			PAN	PMP
pV.CV	pV.CV	Ø.	8.6, 8.18	7.7, 7.9, 8.21
-p-		-(m)p-	1.3	
		-mp-	(7.6)	
	-p-	(m)p-	8.10	3.4
		-p	4.15	
		(n)q-	(7.6)	
-p	-p	-p	8.14	6.1, 8.11
		Ø	8.3	
CVp.CVp		CVp	8.16	
tV.CV	tV.CV	Ø.	8.1, 8.17, 4.2	8.7, 8.13, 8.17, 8.23
		tV.CV	7.3, 8.7, 8.10	
		t-VC		1.3
		sV.CV	1.7	
tVC.tVC	tVC.tVC	tVC	8.8	8.14
-t-	-t-	t-	1.10, 1.11, 8.25	7.2, 8.19
		-nt-		
		-[R]-	8.17	
				1.4, 1.7, 2.5, 7.10, 7.11, 8.16, 8.24
-t	-t	-t(i)	8.2	
kV.CV	kV.CV	Ø.	8.2	1.4
		kV.CV	2.2	3.4
		k-	3.4, 4.1, 8.21	
		(n)k-	8.9, 8.11	
		qV.CV	7.6	
		(n)q-		7.11, 8.15
		bV.CV		1.7
-k-	-k-	-k-		7.14, 8.3, 8.26
		-k		8.12
		(n)k-	8.1	8.24
		(n)q-	3.3	1.6, 5.4
				1.2, 3.1, 3.4, 4.1, 4.2, 7.16, 8.7
-k	-k	-k	7.4	
		-ki		3.2
		-(q)		7.13
CVk.CVk	CVk.CVk	CVk	8.8	8.14, 8.22
			1.9, 1.10, 3.2, (8.12), 8.14	1.2, 1.8, 5.2, 6.1, 7.2, 8.11
qV.CV	qV.CV	Ø.		
		qV.CV	1.1, 1.7, (8.12), 4.10	
		[j]a.	1.2	
-q-	-q-	-q-	1.11, 4.3, 4.8	2.1, 8.10, 8.16, 7.10
		(n)q-	4.13	
		-q		7.1
			2.1, 7.5, 8.6,	1.3, 1.6, 4.4, 7.8, 7.14,

(Table 8.10 continued)

Table 8.10 Continued

PAN	PMP	PAA	Reconstruction # PAN	Reconstruction # PMP
-q	-q	-q	(8.7), 8.17, 8.18	7.15, 8.2, 8.6, 8.18, 8.20
		-(q)		7.12, 8.23
CVq.CVq	CVq.CVq	-k	(8.8)	
		CVq		4.3
CV.CV		Ø.	4.5, 5.5, (8.4), 8.21	
		tV.CV	(8.4)	
		tVC	6.5	
		ntVC	8.15	
		CV.CV	3.2	
		cV.CV	4.3	
-C-		-t-	4.6	
		-C-	3.4	
		-l-	4.11	
cV.CV		Ø.		7.5
bV.CV	bV.CV	Ø.	1.11, 1.12, 7.2, 7.4	2.3, 4.2, 5.3, 7.13, (7.15), 8.9, 8.25
		bV.CV	1.5, (5.2), 8.23	(7.4), 7.10, (7.15), (7.16)
		(bV)-	4.15	8.20
		b-	2.1	(7.4), (7.16)
		p-	8.5	8.12
		(m)p-		2.2
bVC.bVC		(m)p-	4.13, (5.2)	4.3
-b-		-b-	1.1	
		(m)b-	2.1	
	-b-	-mb-		1.1
		m[b]-		8.7
		b-	3.5	1.2
		p-		1.4
		-mp-		8.6
-b		-p		8.27
dV.CV	dV.CV	Ø.	1.4, 1.13	
		dV.CV		2.4
		(d)-		4.4
		zV.CV		2.1, 7.14, 8.8
		(z)-	8.20	
	dVC.dVC	(z)VC		7.3
-d-		d-		8.17, 8.23
		(n)z-	8.19	
-nd-		t-		7.7
-d		-d	4.1 (?)	
-j-		(n)j-	6.2	2.3
		-r-	1.2	
g				

(Table 8.10 continued)

Table 8.10 Continued

PAN	PMP	PAA	Reconstruction #	
			PAN	PMP
zV.CV		Ø.	6.3	
	zV.CV	jV.CV		7.8, 8.16
		ñj-		7.1
		kV.CV	6.4	
-z-	-z-	ñj-		(8.18)
		-[ñj]-	1.6	
		z-		(8.18)
	mV.CV	Ø.		3.1, 8.4
mV.CV		mV.CV	4.16	4.1
-m-	-m-	m-	3.2	7.5, 8.2
			8.26, 4.9, 5.1,	
		-m-	6.1	
		-(m)p-	1.7	
-m		-m	1.13, 6.3, 8.13	7.2, 8.5, 8.13
	ñV.CV	rC.CV		8.1
	nV.CV	tV.CV		7.6
-n-	-n-	n-	5.4	5.3
		-n-		5.1, 7.4
		-n		8.9
		l-	1.4, 1.9	3.1, 8.11
-n	-n	-l	1.1	2.4, 8.17
		-m[u]s	6.2	
l V.CV		Ø.	6.1	
	-l-	-l-		8.8
-l-		-l	4.5	2.2, 7.6
-l	-l	-l	4.3	7.3, 8.25
NV.CV		lV.CV	8.24	
-N-		-l-	5.3	
		-n-	8.4	
		(c,s)[r]-	(8.14)	
		(n)[r]-	(8.14)	
-N		-l	4.2	
SV.CV		Ø.	3.3, 8.3, 8.10	
		sV.CV	3.6	
		[s]V.CV	(1.3)	
		sVC	4.7	
		[s]VC	(1.3)	
		cV.CV	4.12	
		gV.CV	7.5	
-S-		-h-	2.2	
		q-	8.17	
-S		-s(i)	7.3	
	sV.CV	Ø.		8.19
sV.CV		sV.CV	1.8	5.2
		[n]sV		

(Table 8.10 continued)

Table 8.10 Continued

PAN	PMP	PAA	Reconstruction #	
			PAN	PMP
		cV.CV		8.3
sVC.sVC		sVC	(4.22)	
	sVC.sVC	cVC	(4.22)	8.22
	-s-	s-		7.13
-s-		c-	3.1	1.10
		-c-	4.12	7.15
-s		-c(i)	1.7	1.5
	hV.CV	Ø.		8.24, 8.27
-h-		(n)s-		4.2
	-h-	-[q]-		
		-[x]-	5.2	
-h		-s	8.4	
		-[q]	8.26	
lV.CV	lV.CV	Ø.	3.5, 4.1, 4.13	2.3, (3.3), 8.18
		lCV.CV	4.9, 8.6	
-l-	-l-	-l-	1.5, 3.2, 3.6, 4.10, 6.4	1.7, (3.3)
		-[l]-	8.5	1.6, 8.25
		-l	6.5	
		l-	4.5	1.5, 4.4, 8.20
		[ ]l-	8.12	
-l		-l	1.10	
		-[l]	7.6, 8.9	7.7
	rV.VC	Ø.		(7.16)
		-r-		(7.16)
	CVr.CVr	CVr		1.9
	-r	-r		7.4
RV.CV	RV.CV	›V.CV	7.1	1.1
		›VC	6.1	7.6
-R-	-R-	-›-	8.7	2.5
		-[›]-	1.8	
		›-	7.4, 8.2	7.12, 8.21
		-›	8.20	8.4, 8.15
		-R-	4.14	7.10
		R-	6.3	
		-r[]	8.23	
-R	-R	-›	4.7, 8.12, 8.19	8.8
		-R	3.2, 3.6	
		-[R]	4.13	
		-[R]-	7.2	
		-y		2.6

Table 8.11 Results of the evaluation of Hayes' basic vocabulary comparisons

	Probable	Possible	Weak	Rejected
A. PAA-PAN	9	9	2	12
B. PAA-PMP	3	5	9	8
C. PEAA-PAN	3	5	0	5
D. PEAA-PMP	2	3	1	7
Totals	17	22	12	24

The Appendix to this chapter provides my evaluation of what I consider to be the potentially corresponding forms among the Hayes' list of basic vocabulary. Table 8.11 summarises the results.

The morphosyntactic evidence for Austric

Ross (2000: 447), in his careful review of my most recent paper on the subject (Reid 1999), wondered whether I was no longer satisfied that the morphosyntactic evidence I had cited in my earlier paper was still viable as evidence. In that I was presenting 'new evidence for the hypothesis' I did not think it was necessary to restate the old evidence.[1] However, for those who may not be familiar with the earlier work in this area, I will restate it here.

Evidence given in my 1994 paper includes:

1 The AA causatives *pa-/ ap and *ka- are considered to correspond to AN causatives *pa-, *ka- and *paka-.
2 The AA agentives * um and *ma-/ am are considered to correspond to AN agentives *mu-/ um and *maRa-.
3 The AA instrumentals * an , in are considered to correspond to EF instrumental *paN-, and AN nominalising affix *ni-/ in , respectively.
4 The AA objective *-a is considered to correspond to AN objective *-a.
5 Evidence from Sora, Khasi, Nancowry and Car Nicobarese suggest a PAA attributive linker *(n)a corresponding to the AN 'ligature' *(n)a
6 The Nicobarese determiners marking case of NPs ʔin, ʔan, nun, etc., appear to have developed by the same well-known grammatical processes that have brought about the nasal final determiners in many AN languages, that is, by the fusion of a reduced form of the ligature *na. What is important here is that the Malayic languages reflect a PMP (my use of the term, not Blust's) innovation *na *˜ a, hence Tag. ang, nang Kawi ang, Malay yang, etc., so that the Nicobarese forms could not have been borrowed from sailors speaking a Malayic language.
7 Evidence from Nicobarese, Old Khmer, Khmu and Mal suggest a PAA *ta 'locative' preposition corresponding to PAN 'locative preposition, demonstrative' *ta.
8 Car Nicobarese ʔi 'locative preposition' corresponds to PAN *i 'locative preposition'. Note that although reflexes of this preposition are found all the way to Proto-Polynesian, the Proto-Malayic locative preposition is

reconstructed as *di (Adelaar 1992), and is a reflex of PAN *di 'locative preposition, demonstrative', so if borrowed, the Nicobarese locative preposition could not have come from sailors speaking a Malayic language.

Ross (2000: 446–7) neatly summarises the morphosyntactic evidence that I had presented in my 8ICAL paper as follows:

9   The Nicobarese causative verbal infix   um   is taken to be cognate with PAN infix *   um   that marked a verb as an unergative intransitive and formed deverbal nouns expressing non-agentive causers (e.g. Bontok s   um   akít 'that which makes [someone] sick'). (Refer also Schmidt 1916.)
10 PAN and PAA are both taken to have been ergative with a contrast between nominative and genitive pronouns, the genitive denoting both possessor and transitive agent.
11 The PAN and PAA first-person singular pronouns appear to be cognate.
12 Nominative pronouns in both PAN and PAA are taken to have been prefixed with *a-.
13 Ruc, a conservative language of the Vietic branch of AA, has a dative prefix pa- that appears to be cognate with PAN *pa 'go'.
14 A non-proximal demonstrative *en is reflected in both AA and AN languages.

Several arguments have been raised in recent years in an attempt to find alternatives to the morphological comparisons cited earlier.

Borrowing is the primary explanation that has been proposed. Sagart (email comm. 2001) states, 'I have come to the conclusion that the "accidental/involuntary action" prefix ta- in AA languages of Vietnam: Pacoh, Chrau, Katu and Bahnar, is borrowed from Chamic. So this argues that transmission of morphology from AN to AA is possible'.

There is little question that morphological processes can be borrowed between languages of different families. Whether or not it is possible for 'morphemes', that is, meaningful phonological units which constitute part of a word, to be borrowed without their host words also being borrowed is a matter still open for discussion. But whatever the answer to that question, the morpheme ta- itself has not been proposed as evidence for Austric, and what is more important, the morphemes that have been proposed have such an extensive distribution, within the AA family, that no reasonable explanation can be given for either the time of borrowing or the possible source language.

The possibility of borrowing seems likely in the case of the strong Nicobarese morphosyntactic similarities with AN, where it is assumed early AN sailors may have made frequent landfall, perhaps in some cases staying, intermarrying and influencing the local language. But there remain two strong barriers to the acceptance of this position. One is that several of the proposed comparisons between Nicobarese languages and AN are not limited to Nicobarese, but are found across wide areas of the AA family. Comparisons in some cases (especially   um   and   in , however, are clearest with Nicobarese because other EAA languages have either lost the form (in the case of verbal suffixes) or modified them as the result of the strong areal influence of Chinese. Moreover it is clear that if Nicobarese borrowed the suspect forms, it could not have been from a language of the Malayic family, because by Proto-Malayic times the forms had been either lost or changed from the earlier forms that I claim are reflected in Nicobarese (as noted earlier (6) and (8)).

The claim has also been made (Sagart email comm. 2001) that the vowels of the *mu-/ um and *ni-/ in affixes

> are more or less colored by the main consonant, they could be secondary. The vowel is essentially an epenthetic schwa which serves to break the consonant cluster formed by prefixed m- or n- and the root initial, or the root initial plus infixed -m- and -n-. In both cases the prefix or infix tends to color the schwa: you get rounding with m, and a high-and-somewhat fronted vowel with n. It is possible that in each particular word the root initial also plays a role coloring schwa.

Whether or not this may ultimately be the source of the vowels in these affixes, the evidence that we have from Nicobarese, and from AN languages suggests that in these languages at least, the vowels of the affixes were full vowels, and not epenthetic. PAN alone has a number of reconstructions which show m followed and/or preceded by vowels other than u (e.g. *mimah 'drink', *SimaR 'fat, oil', *maCa 'eye', *gemgem 'hold (in fist)', etc.), and n followed and/or preceded by vowels other than i (e.g. *tanek 'cook', *tenem 'sea, saltwater', etc.). Similar data could be drawn from Nicobarese as well as from Munda languages, and these are the only places that one could look in AA for evidence to support the thesis.

With respect to my claim that the AA instrumentals * an , in are considered to correspond to the EF instrumental *paN-, and the AN nominalising affix *ni-/ in , respectively, the argument has been made that the functions of the AA and AN affixes are not close enough, the former being 'instrumental' or 'agentive' (Thurgood 1999) while the latter was an 'objective' nominalisation specifying the result of the action of the verb. However, AA data not only shows 'instrumental' nominalisations, but nominalisations of the AN type. Thurgood (1999: 245) quotes Banker as claiming that the Bahnar infix ən sometimes means 'the result of a verbal action', so that bât 'to make a dam', becomes b ən ât 'a dam'. It is probable that the agentive function of the affix was also present in PAN, given the form *C in aqi 'guts', which can only be interpreted as meaning 'that which produces *Caqi "faeces" '. That the same affix can be reconstructed with these two apparently quite different functions should not be surprising, given the fact that forms such as b ən ât 'a dam' are potentially ambiguous between 'the object that is the result of damming', and 'the object that dams'.

One of the facts which is of high value in supporting the morphological comparisons between AA and AN languages, is not simply the forms and their functions, but also the apparently unique phonological process (not, as far as I know, reported anywhere else in the world), whereby the consonant of the affix and the initial consonant of the root metathesise, producing alternation historically not only between the *mu-/ um and *ni-/ in affixes, but also between the *ma-/ am and *pa-/ ap affixes, with varying distributions in both families, and clearly with the original metathesis (producing infixes) reversible, so that in some daughter languages the prefixal forms reappear either alone, or in alternation with the infix, depending (usually) upon the manner of articulation of the root-initial consonant.

Ross (2000) has questioned the identification of *mu-/ um as a causative nominaliser in PAN, suggesting that it is by no means certain that it was a nominaliser at all, thereby questioning its functional association with the corresponding PAA forms. If PAN was anything like most present-day AN languages, whether or not it functioned primarily as a nominaliser or not, verbs that were formed with it, would also have been zero-derived as nouns, when appearing as the heads of noun phrases, just as the Bontok form s um akit can mean either 'to make one sick' when occurring as a verb, or 'the thing that makes one sick', when occurring as a noun.

He further questions my identification of *a- as a nominative marker in PAA and PAN with the observation that in Taoih, this prefix is found not only on subject pronouns, but on dative pronouns as well. Of course, if PAA was ergative, as I claim, what is today a dative pronoun in an accusative language (as Taoih probably is) would have been the grammatical subject of a transitive sentence at an earlier stage and would have been marked as nominative, as it is in AN languages that are ergative, for example, Bontok,

Agtam	sak-en	si	ítab
give.Gen.2s	Nom.1s	of	beans

Give me some beans.

To me this is further evidence in support of the ergative nature of PAA. Compare also the ʔan subject marking of some NPs in Nicobarese. Ross questions my claim that the initial *a- of the PAN nominative pronouns *aku, *aken, *aten and *amen was the original nominative marking component of these forms, by claiming that genitive forms such as Seediq n-aku, Pazeh n-aki, Thao n-ak, n-am, Amis n-ako, etc., showed that even in PAN the *a- was part of the pronominal root and could occur as a genitive. The hyphens in these forms represent Ross' analysis of the forms, as having an intial n- genitive marker. I claim however that such forms are better analysed as: Seediq na-ku, Pazeh na-ki, Thao na-k, na-m, Amis na-ko, etc., an analysis which is more consistent with general patterns of genitive noun formation in a wide range of AN languages, including Talubin Bontok in which nak 'my', nam 'your' have independently developed from a combination of na 'the, non-referential noun' plus genitive pronominal endings.

Conclusion

Ross claims that in order to be convinced of the validity of Austric, he would need either a substantial quantity of regularly corresponding cognates, or a seemingly cognate paradigm of grammatical morphemes. It would be great if we were able to provide either one or the other, but at the time-depths we are looking at, and the imperfect state of our knowledge of AA languages, and the extremely limited amount of reconstruction that has been done in the family (compared at least to the AN side), what I have presented in this chapter is at present the best we can do. I believe that the number of apparent cognates cited here between PAA (and PEAA) and PAN (and PMP) from the area of basic vocabulary, come close to providing such a convincing body. The hope of providing seeming cognate paradigms of grammatical morphemes comes closest with the sets of what were probably originally demonstrative nouns, but which in both families have grammaticised into a wide range of determiners, ligatures, prepositions and the like. There is no question that the range of forms is there, including *a, *ta and *na, with corresponding functions on both sides of the family. It is unlikely, however, that it will be possible to find any paradigm of verbal morphology (which I suspect is what Ross is looking for), because I don't think there was much of this in early AN. The paradigm of so-called 'focus' morphology, even if it was present in PAN (which I think is doubtful), is clearly a catch-bag of prefixes, infixes and suffixes which must have existed in pre-AN times as probably nominalising affixes, but never in any sense constituting a paradigm.

The evidence then is not as convincing as one would like, but as Diffloth said in 1994, the evidence 'is undoubtedly there', and I believe it is considerably stronger now, than it was then. The evidence is for a genetic relationship, but is it evident that the families in question descended from a common immediate ancestor, Proto-Austric? With the accumulation of evidence presented by Sagart in this volume and elsewhere, that AN can also be shown to be genetically related to the Sino-Tibetan family of languages, and his claim (Sagart p.c.) that some of the lexical items and affixes claimed to be shared by AN and AA are found also in Sino-Tibetan languages, the possibility exists that the relationship between AA and AN is more remote than earlier considered. The concept of 'Austric' as a language family may eventually need to be abandoned in favour of a wider language family which can be shown to include both AN and AA language families, but not necessarily as sisters of a common ancestor.

Appendix

Evaluation of potentially corresponding forms among the Hayes list of basic vocabulary

A. PAA–PAN
1. Probable

ashes
PAA *qabuh
PAN *qabu
Pacoh *abóh*, Chrau *vuh* 'ashes',
Bonda *bu?* 'to smoke'
Comments: Accepted by Diffloth as possible (1994: 313). Restricted to Katuic (Pacoh) and Bahnaric (Stieng and Sre), and a Munda cognate with questionable semantics. Probably not borrowed.

dog
PAA *cu(q)
PAN *asu
Bonda gusɔʔ, PW *s~ɳ, VN chó 'dog'
Comments: Accepted by Diffloth as probable (1994: 313).

snake
PAA *[su](l)aR
PAN *SulaR
Kharia lur, Sora loʔor, (CF lor) 'a kind of snake', Bahnar 'bih tep-lar 'a very small snake that is extremely poisonous'
Comments: Possible final syllable reflexes in Munda and Bahnar.

belly
PAA *taɢal, *tiɢal
PAN *tiaN
Sora taʔal 'spleen', Thavung khaʔal 'belly, stomach, abdomen', Pacoh acheal 'heart'
Comments: Final syllables match from Munda through the Muong and Katuic comparisons. Semantics are acceptable, and PAA *l corresponds to PAN *N in several cases.

eye
PAA *mi(n)ta(q)
PAN *maCa
Kharia (V250) mɔ'ḍ, PVM *mat 'eye', Proto-Plang *hak¹-kitaɢ¹ 'eyebrow'
Comments: Accepted by Diffloth as probable (1994: 317). Note Proto-Plang (Waic) *hak¹-kitaɢ¹ 'eyebrow' Lit. hair-eye, which supports the final PAA syllable.

father
PAA *(qa)ma(ma)
PAN *t-ama
Santali mama 'maternal uncle', Katu ama, Pacoh a-ám 'father', Bahnar ma 'younger brother of father or mother'
Comments: Widely distributed with appropriate phonology and semantics, but suspect as a possible nursery word.

mother
PAA *(na)na
PAN *t-ina
Kharia nana 'elder sister', Bonda tuna 'younger sister (addressed by a brother), wife's younger brother's wife', Sedang na 'older sister, cousin'
Comments: Widely distributed with appropriate phonology and semantics, but suspect as a possible nursery word.

rotten
PAA *ˀok
PAN *ma-buRuk
Kharia lorog 'to rot, decay', VN rục 'be rotten', NK phròok 'spoiled'
Comments: Phonologically plausible with possible reflexes in Munda, Monic and Viet–Muong groups.

buy
PAA *pi[l]i
PAN *beli
Khasi pli 'change', MUK pál, pánh 'sell', Kharia paṭay 'fix price, bargain'
Comments: The Khasi, Muong and Katuic forms appear to be cognate, and probably correspond to the PAN form.

2. Possible

salt
PAA *qa(m)puc(i)
PAN *timus
Pareng b.sut, Kuy pos, Jehai mpɔj 'salt'
Comments: Possible cognates in Munda, Pearic, and Aslian.

smoke
PAA *(m)pi l̩
PAN *qebel

Sora poro 'become smoky', mor 'spread as smoke', Stieng pôr 'smoke out of a hollow tree'
Comments: Possible cognates in Munda and Bahnaric.

egg
PAA *teḷoR
PAN *qiCeluR
Juang susuter(ɔ), Pacoh tireal, tiro᷇l, PVM *t(i)lur¤ 'egg'
Comments: The Munda comparison is doubtful. The Katuic and Viet–Muong comparisons seem more secure.

male/man
PAA *(n)qalay
PAN *ma-RuqaNay
Bonda laĩbuʔ 'male pig', Pacoh alay, Stieng clay 'brother-in-law'
Comments: The Munda, Katuic and Bahnaric forms possibly correspond. If they do, they probably correspond to the PAN form.

rat
PAA *b[i w]
PAN *labaw
Bonda gubu 'a kind of rat', Riang (Black) kə̃bu¹ 'rat, mouse', Mah Meri (Bes. K.L., R33) kanē' rẽbu 'mouse'
Comments: The Munda, Bahnaric and Aslian forms seem to be cognate. The final syllable is a possible comparison with the PAN form. None of the AA initial syllables correspond with the PAN initial syllable.

head
PAA *(n)qoḷu(q)
PAN *qulu
Bahnar (PB) kŏl, Jeh kāl, Mal klɨq 'head'
Comments: Reasonable phonological correspondences between Bahnaric and Aslian, possibly corresponding with the PAN form.

shoulder
PAA *(ba)Ra(q)
PAN *qabaRa
Kharia taran, Theng blah 'shoulder', Khasi ta-bla 'shoulder piece of animal'
Comments: The Khmuic and Khasi comparisons appear good, and probably correspond with the PAN form, but the Munda term is questionable.

hold (in fist)
PAA *(n)ki m
PAN *gemgem
Kensiu cəkam, VN (*gi m) câm 'hold', Sora kum-siː 'hold in one's fist, hold a handful'
Comments: The Aslian, Vietic and Sora are possible cognates, and if so, probably correspond well with the PAN form.

yawn
PAA *(can)qap
PAN *ma-Suab
Santali (V68) aŋgɔ'b, PM *s˘¤aap, VN ngáp 'yawn'
Comments: The Munda, Vietic and Mon forms are possible cognates. They possibly correspond to the PAN form.

3. Weak

meat/flesh
PAA *c(i, i)ci
PAN *Sesi/isi
Sora sissid, VN (*ñfic) thịt 'flesh, meat', PM *sac 'fruit, nut, berry, acorn, pod'
Comments: Insecure phonological correspondences.

swim
PAA *la(n)[¤]oy
PAN *Na˘uy

Mundari (K519) *oiyar*, Ruc, *lɔy*, Riang Lang *_ŋɔy* 'swim'
Comments: The Munda form is probably not cognate with the eastern forms. The Palaungic and Ruc forms are likewise doubtful comparisons.

4. Rejected

breast
PAA *n[s]uq
PAN *susu
Bonda *daʔtu kŭi*, PW *tis 'breast', Semai *ntoh* 'chest'
Comments: Phonological correspondences don't work.

neck
PAA *(n)qe[R]
PAN *liqeR
MUK *kel* 'neck', Pacoh *cŏl* 'wear around neck', Sengoi *kelkeil* 'ankle, wrist'
Comments: The Muong form possibly corresponds with the PAN form, but the Katuic and Aslian forms are semantically doubtful.

female/woman
PAA *a[x]i, *bu[x]i, *mpa[x]i,
PAN *bahi
Pacoh *a–i* 'mother', Kharia (K349) *bui* 'girl', Mon *imbay* 'elder brother's wife, husband's elder sister'
Comments: Unconvincing phonological and semantic correspondence.

big
PAA *(can)ɣaya(q)
PAN *ma-Raya
PW *ra 'big', Theng *yaʔ* 'far', Sora (V40) *saŋa: j-ən* 'be at a distance'
Comments: The Proto-Wa form is possibly cognate, but the semantics and phonology of the Khmuic and Munda forms are unconvincing.

shy/ashamed
PAA *g(i,a)haq(i)
PAN *ma-Siaq
Bonda *gĭak'* 'shame', PW *[gac] 'ashamed, shy', Stieng *haas* 'feel ashamed, bashful'
Comments: Phonological correspondence with the PAN form is unlikely.

bite
PAA *(n)ɣat(i)
PAN *kaRat
Sora (V334) *gad* 'cut', *raj* 'cut into small pieces as wood', PM *rac* 'cut with a sickle, reap', Katu *karóóch* 'cut kernels off'
Comments: Phonology may be possible, but semantics unlikely.

dream
PAA *(m)pe(qi)
PAN *Sepi
Chrau *vĭq*, Katu *bâch* 'lie down, sleep', Sora *mimid̪* 'sleepy'
Comments: Phonological correspondences don't work.

hunt
PAA *(n)[r]op, *(c,s)[r]op
PAN *qaNup
Jeh *rŭp* 'catch, seize', Khasi *kynrup* 'pounce upon, seize', Bonda *sɔp* 'hold, catch', Stieng *choop* 'hunt'
Comments: Only the rhyme works.

sleep
PAA *(n)zoɣ
PAN *tuduR
Pacoh *chur* 'sleepy or sad eyes', Birhor (V111) *durum* 'to sleep', Khmu' *hmdir* 'to snore'
Comments: Unlikely semantics and phonology.

steal
PAA *kaḷaw *kumḷaw
PAN *Cakaw
Nicobar kǝlɔ:-hǝŋǝ 'steal', Mundari (V242) kumɓu, Santali kombŕo 'thief, theft, steal'
Comments: Phonological correspondences unlikely.

suck
PAA *s[e]p, *(n)c[e]p
PAN *sepsep
VN tọp 'sip', Mundari (V354) si'b 'to smoke', Pacoh dyép 'suck'
Comments: Phonological correspondences unlikely.

vomit
PAA *taq
PAN *utaq
PM *taa¤ 'vomit', Bonda taʔmi 'sneeze', Semelai tahtɔh 'to spit'
Comments: Unlikely semantics.

B. PEAA–PAN
1. Probable

lake
PEAA {**li w} (Hayes)
PAN *danaw
Chrau tanlô 'lake, pond'
Comments: Hayes notes that the lateral in the Chrau reflex he cites (tanlô 'lake') suggests that the form could not be a borrowing from Chamic.

head louse
PEAA **k[o]t(i)
PAN *kuCu
Katu kóót 'lice, fleas, bugs', Khmer sarikœc 'bedbug, flea', Chrau sicăch 'tick'
Comments: With apparent cognates in Katuic, Bahnaric and Khmer, this is an attractive set to correspond with the PAN form.

afraid
PEAA **(n)k[o]t
PAN *ma-takut
Jeh kokùat 'detest, hate', Khmer kot 'hold in awe', Mon takuit 'take fright'
Comments: With apparent cognates in Aslian, and both Mon and Khmer, the phonology looks reasonable and the semantics plausible.

2. Possible

wood
PEAA **k(i,a)hi(uq)
PAN *kaSiw
PW *kho¤'tree', PM *chuu¤ 'tree, wood', Semai jǝhuʔ 'tree'
Comments: An interesting set of forms which look as though they may well be cognate but the phonological correspondences are uncertain.

fruit
PEAA **(m)b[o¤a]q
PAN *buaq
Kensiu kǝbǝʔ, Sabum kǝmɔʔ 'fruit', Stieng moq 'type of small fruit'
Comments: The Aslian and Bahnaric appear to be cognate, and there is the possibility that they correspond also with the PAN form.

new
PEAA **qi[R]u(q)
PAN *ma-baqeRu
PW *cro¤ 'new', Bahnar chrêu 'strange'
Comments: The Waic and Bahnaric forms seem to be cognate. At least their final syllable may correspond to the PAN form.

burn
PEAA **[¤]us(i), **t[u]nus
PAN *CuNuh
Katu pa–óh 'cook', Khmer 'us 'firewood', Bahnar tonuh 'hearth'

Comments: The Bahnar form is suspiciously similar to the PAN form. But the form is not reconstructed for Proto-Chamic and is probably not a borrowing. Other AA languages show a lateral corresponding to PAN *N.

cut (wood)
PEAA **ta›aq, **ta›ak
PAN *taRaq
Rengao chră 'split, divide, crack open', Sre trac 'shave', Pacoh trěq 'chop'
Comments: The Bahnaric forms may well be cognate with Pacoh. They may correspond to the PAN form.

3. Weak

rain
PEAA **ka[ñj]al
PAN *quzaN
Brou cuyal, Old Mon kyāl, Khmer khya'l 'wind'
Comments: Although the AA forms are probably cognate, only the rhyme appears to correspond with the PAN form.

stone
PEAA **tamuq (Hayes); PMK *ti m(o:)¤ (Diffloth)
PAN *batu
Khasi *máw, PW *smo¤, PM *tm~~¤ 'stone'
Comments: Diffloth (318) notes this as a possible correspondence. The evidence is weak.

burn
PEAA **[¤]us(i), **t[u]nus
PAN *CuNuh
Katu pa–óh 'cook', Khmer 'us 'firewood', Bahnar tonuh 'hearth'
Comments: The Bahnar form is suspiciously similar to the PAN form. But the form is not reconstructed for Proto-Chamic and is probably not a borrowing. Other AA languages show a lateral corresponding to PAN *N.

cut (wood)
PEAA **tak, **tek
PAN *tektek
Katu ntaak 'chop', Pacoh tích 'chop firewood', Rengao kotěk 'snap, break, cut skin'
Comments: The consonants appear to correspond, but the forms are probably onomatopoetic.

4. Rejected

moon
PEAA **b(i,a)lal
PAN *bulaN
Katu baraal 'pale', Bateg Deg bəyɛl (*r y) 'white', Bahnar monhal 'very bright light or sunshine'
Comments: Unlikely semantics.

sand
PEAA **lay
PAN *qenay
VN lây 'miry, swampy, marshy', Bahnar lai 'mound of dirt', Nyah Kur lɛɛ, rèɛ 'ore, mineral'
Comments: The may phonology be possible, but the semantics are unlikely (none means 'sand').

back
PEAA **ko[d(i)]
PAN *likud
Boriwen kúat 'back', Halang kuyq 'small of the back of the head', Jeh kung kuyq 'back of head'
Comments: The Bahnaric are probably not cognate with Boriwen, nor with the PAN form.

liver
PEAA **p[a]le(q)
PAN *qaCay

Mon *pli* 'spleen', PVM *pleʔ,
Sengoi *pele* 'fruit'
Comments: The AA forms may be cognate, but they certainly don't seem to relate to the PAN form, either in phonology or semantics.

old (people)
PEAA **ti(n)qas(i)
PAN *ma-tuqaS
Khmer *cā's*, Pearic *čhu:s* 'old', Katu *takóh* 'grown'
Comments: The phonological correspondences between AA and the PAN form don't work.

choose
PEAA **(u)laqi
PAN *piliq
PW *ras, Pacoh *rôih*, Semai (Serau, C120A) *chenlas* 'choose'
Comments: Impossible phonology.

see
PEAA (**)(s)[R]ai
PAN *kita
Pacoh *lây*, Chrau *sây*, VN *thây* 'see'
Comments: Impossible phonology.

sew
PEAA **(n)qiq
PAN *taSiq
Pacoh *ĕh*, Katu *jih*, Sengoi *ceik* 'sew'
Comments: Impossible phonology.

C. PAA-PMP
1. Probable

dust
PAA *buk
PMP *qabuk
Bonda *tubɔk'/tubuk'* 'earth', Chrau *vŏq* 'mud', Mon *khabuik* 'fine powder or dust'

Comments: Reasonable semantics, and good (final syllable) correspondences from Munda through Bahnaric and Mon.

roof/thatch
PAA *(n)təp
PMP *qatep
Khasi *tap* 'to cover', Mundari (V3) *da'b* 'cover a roof, thatch', Palaung *dăp* 'to cover, thatch'
Comments: Good phonological and semantic correspondence across AA, with regular correspondences to the PMP form.

split
PAA *(ba)laq(i)
PMP *belaq
Katu *blah* 'split', Kharia (V304) *la'j* 'slice', Khmer *-la's* 'separate, detach'
Comments: The Katuic form is cognate with reconstructed forms in PMong *blah, as well as in three branches of Bahnaric (Thurgood 1999: 284) so is probably not a Chamic borrowing.

2. Possible

fog/mist
PAA *(m)put
PMP *kabut
Sora (V384) *umod-ən* 'fog, mist', Khmu' *(hm)puut* 'clouds, fog'
Comments: Restricted distribution to Munda and Khmuic, but semantics are reasonable, and phonological correspondences possible.

spouse
PAA *saw[a]
PMP *qasawa
Kharia (K535) *sou* 'husband', Katu *sasaau* 'father's cousins, sister's husband, father's sister's children', Proto-Semai *bnsaaw* 'wife's elder brother'

Comments: The phonological comparison is attractive, and the semantics possible.

fall
PAA *t(a,u)(m)puq
PMP *nabuq (?)
Mundari (K149b) tɔmbɔʔ 'fall forwards', Katu tampoh 'drop', Bahnar puh 'slip, fall into a hole'
Comments: The AA forms appear to be cognate, and possibly relate to the PMP form.

stab
PAA *(n)cuk(i)
PMP *suksuk
Sora suj, VN chọc 'pierce', Sengoi cok 'stab, pierce'
Comments: Possibly cognate.

throw
PAA *da(q)
PMP *tudaq
Santali (V173) lebda 'throw', Khasi pda 'throw to the farthest distance possible', Chrau randắh 'throw down'
Comments: The final syllable of the AA forms could correspond to the PMP form.

4. Rejected

child
PAA *(n)quɒan[ak]
PMP *anak
Santali (V205) hɔn 'son, child', PM *k~ŋn 'child, offspring, young (animals)', Mintil ʔawaʔ 'child'
Comments: The Aslian form would be good were it not for the medial consonant that doesn't correspond. The other forms don't correspond at all to the PMP form.

cold
PAA *(z)le˘
PMP *ma-di˘ di˘
Kharia (K208) raŋga, VN lạnh 'cold', Khmer sreñ 'to cool'
Comments: Phonological correspondence lacking.

breathe
PAA *r(a, u)wa(i)
PMP *mañawa
Mundari (K537) rowa, Sengoi ruai 'soul, spirit', Pocoh rvai 'soul'
Comments: Phonological correspondence uncertain.

grow
PAA *m[b]uk
PMP *tu(m)buk
Kharia (V286) muʔ 'come out', Muk moc 'grow, come up', OM mok 'appear'
Comments: The Kharia and Old Mon forms appear to be cognate, but the semantics of the Muk form is only questionably related. Insufficient evidence to establish a correspondence with the PMP form.

split
PAA *(ba)laq(i)
PMP *belaq
Katu blah 'split', Kharia (V304) la'j 'slice', Khmer -la's 'separate, detach'
Comments: The Katuic form is cognate with reconstructed forms in PMong *blah, as well as in three branches of Bahnaric (Thurgood 1999: 284) so is probably not a Chamic borrowing.

D. PEAA-PMP
1. Probable

mouth
PEAA **(m)paq

PMP *baqbaq
Pacoh piaq 'mouth, opening, end of river', Mah Meri pak, Sengoi mpak 'mouth'
Comments: Although corresponding forms are limited to Aslian and Pacoh, it is unlikely because of their shape that they were borrowed from either Malay (in the case of Aslian) or Chamic (in the case of Pacoh). Note PChamic *babah 'mouth' (Thurgood 1999: 283). Probably cognate with the PMP form.

dull/blunt
PEAA **tu[l]
PMP *pundul
Pacoh túl múl '(expressive) of blunt end', Bahnar tŭl 'dull, not pointed', NK th*uu*l 'blunt, not pointed'
Comments: Possibly cognate forms with distribution in Katuic, Bahnaric and Monic branches, appear to correspond well with the PMP form.

2. Possible

husband
PEAA **na(q)
PMP *bana
Thavung nAA² 'mother's younger brothers', Sengoi menah 'parent's younger brother', Bahnar nă 'parent's elder sibling'
Comments: Possible phonology, semantics questionable.

pound
PEAA **ntuk
PMP *tuktuk
Khmer ṭuk 'beat, pound', PM *knd~k 'pound (earth)', MUK (*duk) tục 'to chisel'
Comments: Plausible phonological and semantic correspondence but possibly onomatopoetic.

tie
PEAA **(n)ki t
PMP *hiket
Cua takoot 'tie a knot', VN cột 'tie up, chain', Pearic khɔ:t 'tie'
Comments: The AA forms are probably cognate, and possibly correspond to the PMP form. The vowel however may be problematic.

3. Weak

split
PEAA **ta[q]
PMP *sitaq
Chrau tăh 'slit open, cut up', Stieng tah 'disembowel'
Comments: The AA forms clearly cognate, but semantics don't match well with the PMP form.

4. Rejected

correct, true
PEAA **bi r, **bi ni r
PMP *ma-bener
Sengoi bor 'good, fine, beautiful', bernor 'goodness, righteousness, true', Pacoh nnôr 'happy'
Comments: Too restricted distribution in AA, questionable semantics.

dirty
PEAA **mi z
PMP *cemeD (?)
Mon mih 'body dirt', Mintil kamah 'dirty'
Comments: Too restricted distribution in AA, questionable phonology.

good
PEAA **i[¤]ak, **u[¤]aq
PMP *ma-pia
VN uóc 'to desire, wish for, hope for', Khasi kwah [kaw¤] 'wish for', Jeh wă [wa¤], 'want, like, be fond of, desire'

Comments: Insufficient phonological correspondence.

heavy
PEAA **baRe(n)qi t
PMP *ma-beReqat
Cua parêq, Chrau gât, Mendriq (Pang. Gal., H68) hĕnjut 'heavy'
Comments: Insufficient phonological correspondence.

wet
PEAA **[b]acaq
PMP *ma-baseq
Pearic pəča'k, Chrau suh, Tampuan tšətšuih 'wet'
Comments: Insufficient phonological correspondence.

lie down
PEAA **(i)li p
PMP *qinep
Nha Heun plîp, Thavung kñiip, Bahnar 'nhĭp 'close eyes'
Comments: Semantics not close enough.

spit
PEAA **zaq(i), **ñjaqi
PMP *luzaq
Bahnar kosoh, OM ksas 'spit', Khmer khjā'k 'spit out'
Comments: Insufficient phonological correspondence.

Abbreviations

AA	Austro-Asiatic
AN	Austronesian
EAA	Eastern Austro-Asiatic
PA	Proto-Austric
PAA	Proto-Austro-Asiatic
PAN	Proto-Austronesian
PEAA	Proto-Eastern Austro-Asiatic
PMP	Proto-Malayo-polynesian

Note

1 Ross also faulted me for including a reference to Hayes' basic vocabulary reconstructions, but not providing any examples. At the time when my paper was presented (at 8ICAL), Hayes' paper was not yet published, and I had been given a pre-publication version of it, with the promise that I could refer to it but not cite any of his data. In addition, I had not at that time had the opportunity of evaluating the quality of his reconstructions.

Bibliography

Adelaar, K.A. (1992) Proto-Malayic: The Reconstruction of its Phonology and Parts of its Morphology and Lexicon, Canberra: Pacific Linguistics C-119.

Blust, R.A. (1993) 'Central and Central-Eastern Malayo-Polynesian', Oceanic Linguistics 32, 2: 241–94.

—— (1999) 'Subgrouping, circularity and extinction: some issues in Austronesian comparative linguistics', in E. Zeitoun and P.J.-K. Li (eds) Selected Papers from the Eighth International Conference on Austronesian Linguistics, Taipei: Academia Sinica.

Diffloth, G. (1994) 'The lexical evidence for Austric, so far', Oceanic Linguistics 33: 309–22.
Hayes, L.H. (1997) 'On the track of Austric: Part II. Consonant mutation in early Austroasiatic', Mon-Khmer Studies 27: 13–44.
—— (1999) 'On the track of Austric: Part III. Basic vocabulary comparison', Mon-Khmer Studies 29: 1–34.
Parkin, R. (1991) A Guide to Austroasiatic Speakers and Their Languages, Oceanic Linguistics Special Publication, no. 23, Honolulu: University of Hawai'i Press.
Reid, L.A. (1994) 'Morphological evidence for Austric', Oceanic Linguistics 33, 2: 323–44.
—— (1999) 'New linguistic evidence for the Austric hypothesis', in E. Zeitoun and P.J.-K. Li (eds) Selected Papers from the Eighth International Conference on Austronesian Linguistics, Taipei: Academia Sinica.
Ross, M.D. (2000) 'Review of E. Zeitoun and P.J.-K. Li (eds) Selected Papers from the Eighth International Conference on Austronesian Linguistics', Oceanic Linguistics 39, 2: 445–56.
Schmidt, W. (1906) 'Die Mon-Khmer-Völker, ein Bindeglied zwischen Völkern Zentralasiens und Austronesiens', Archiv der Anthropologie, n.s. 5: 59–109.
—— (1916) 'Eineges über das Infix mn und dessen stellvertreter p in den austroasiatischen Sprachen', Aufsätze zur Kultur- und Sprachgeschichte, vornehmlich des Orients, Ernst Kuhn zum 70, Breslau: Marcus.
Thurgood, G. (1999) From Ancient Cham to Modern Dialects: Two Thousand Years of Language Contact and Change, Oceanic Linguistics Special Publication No. 28, Honolulu: University of Hawai'i Press.

9

SINO-TIBETAN–AUSTRONESIAN
An updated and improved argument

Laurent Sagart

In several articles (Sagart 1990, 1993, 1994) I have argued from sound correspondences, shared vocabulary and shared morphology that Chinese and AN are genetically related within a macrophylum which I called 'Sino-Austronesian'. The accuracy of the Chinese and AN material used in the comparisons has not been faulted, and neither have the sound correspondences underlying the comparisons. Criticism has concentrated on three points: first, paucity of comparisons involving basic vocabulary; second, the position of TB outside Sino-Austronesian; third, sound correspondences that leave out non-final syllables of AN words. I present here an updated and improved argument which answers these issues.

In this chapter, Old Chinese (OC, c.2,500 BP) is reconstructed according to the system presented in Sagart (1999), a modification of Baxter (1992). PAN reconstructions are drawn from the literature, a few are mine. I adhere to the view that PAN was spoken in Taiwan from around 5,500 BP on, on archaeological grounds. The first diversification of PAN took place on the West coast of Taiwan. Soon one group of West coast speakers moved to the East coast where a second diversification occurred, resulting in a dialect linkage (ECL). Later on, perhaps around 4,500 BP, a group of ECL speakers left Taiwan to settle the northern Philippines. Their language, PMP, is ancestral to all conventionally recognised AN languages outside of Taiwan. Another group of early AN speakers left Taiwan to settle coastal areas in Guangdong or Guangxi, where their language, which I call AAK was to a great extent relexified by a local language, later to become Proto-Kadai (more on this in Chapter 10, this volume). The subgrouping of AN is therefore as in Figure 9.1 (based on Ho 1998 with modifications).

For PMP innovations, see Blust (1977). The following innovations are shared uniquely by PMP and ECL languages:

- PAN *C *t (Siraya, Bunun, Amis, Kavalan, Basay-Trobiawan, PMP: Ferrell 1969)
- PAN *N *n (Bunun, Kavalan, Basay-Trobiawan, Kanakanabu,[1] PMP: Ho 1998)

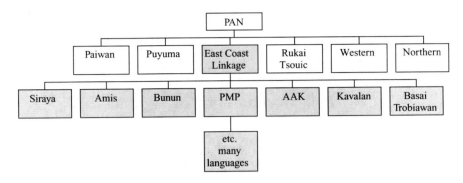

Figure 9.1 Higher AN subgrouping.

- PAN *qayam replaced by *manuk in the meaning 'bird' (Basay-Trobiawan, PMP)
- pang-V instrumental construction (Amis, PMP: Starosta 2001)

From Figure 9.1 one can see that MP material is not essential in reconstructing PAN forms; these can be based on Formosan exclusively. In my earlier work, all AN reconstructions were drawn from the works of Blust or Dempwolff and necessarily included MP material. The practice of reconstructing PAN forms based on evidence from Formosa only was initiated by Blust himself (1999). Reconstructing PAN in this way adds a significant number of basic vocabulary comparisons between PAN and Chinese. Most of these have TB comparanda, as shown in Table 9.1. Remarkably, TB and PAN agree against Chinese in certain matters of phonology (Table 9.5). TB morphology, better preserved than Chinese morphology, also has many points of agreement with PAN. Since TB and Chinese do have more basic vocabulary in common than either does with PAN and since some features shared by TB and Chinese against PAN appear to be innovations (Sagart forthcoming), I recognise here (contra Sagart 1990) that ST is a valid construct and claim that it, as a whole, is genetically related to PAN. I refer to the resulting macrophylum as STAN. Available reconstructions of TB (Benedict 1972) and ST (Coblin 1986; Gong 1995; Peiros and Starostin 1995) differ widely, due to continuing uncertainty on subgrouping, sound correspondences and the amount of contact between Chinese and the rest of ST. For this reason, Old Chinese will serve here as the main representative of ST.

Linguistic evidence

In the following three sections I present evidence of basic and cultural vocabulary shared with sound correspondences, and of shared morphological processes.

Table 9.1 Sixty-one basic vocabulary comparisons between AN, Chinese and TB

	PAN or PECL	OC	TB
1 Body hair	gumuN	眉 ^{b}mu[r] (eyebrow)	B. mul (Moshang kemul)
2 Bone	kukut	骨 ^{a}kut	
3 Brain	punuq	腦 ^{a}nu	B. (s-)nuk
4 Elbow	siku(H_2)	肘 ^{b}t-r-ku	Gyarong tkru
5 Female breast	nunuH_1	乳 ^{b}no	B. nuw
6 Foot	kakay		B. kriy
7 Head	quluH_1	首 ^{b}hlu	Lushai lu
8 Palm of hand	dapa	扶 ^{b}pa	B. pa
9 Pus	nanaq		Tib. rnag
10 Mother	ina(-q)	女 ^{b}nra (woman)	B. m-na
11 Egg	qiCeluR	卵 ^{a}Ci -lo[r]	B. twiy t-l-?
12 Horn, antler	(q)uRung	角 ^{a}k-rok	B. rung rwang
13 Leech	Limatek	蛭 ^{b}tik	
14 Snake	bulay	蛇 ^{b}m-la[r]	P-Loloish lay$_{1/2}$ 'python'
15 Worm	[ ]ulej	蚓 ^{b}lin F?	
16 Cloud, cloudy	-qem	陰 ^{b}ïm	Bur. um'
17 Earth	-taq	土 ^{a}tha	Tib. ^{n}dag pa 'mud'
18 Moon	qiNaS		B. s-la
19 Salt	siRaH_1	鹵 ^{a}ra S!	B. la I!
20 Sunlight	siNa	陽 ^{b}lang	Bur. lang 'to be light'
21 Water	daNum	瀋 ^{b}t-hlïm (liquid, juice)	
22 Wind	bali		B. g-liy
23 Cave, hole	b[e]lung	洞 ^{a}long S!	Kachin kin$_{31}$ lu $_{33}$
24 Year	kawaS	歲 ^{b}s-hwat-s S!	
25 Carry	baba		B. ba
26 Chew	paqpaq	哺 ^{a}m-pa -s	
27 Close, shut	kupit	閉 ^{a}pit	
28 Come, go	duwa	于 ^{b}wa	B. s-wa
29 Cut off, short	[p,b]utul	斷 ^{a}to[r,n] ; ^{a}to [r,n]	Lepcha tultul
30 Dig	-kut	堀 ^{b}khut, 掘 ^{b}m-kut	Kachin kot
31 Drown, disappear	Nemes	滅 ^{b}met	B. mit 'extinguish' (fire)
32 Fall	-luR	墮 ^{a}lo[r]	
33 Flow water, river	qaluR 'to flow'	水 ^{b}hlu[r] (water, river) 沭 ^{b}t-lu[r] (water)	B. twiy t-l-, lwiy 'to flow'
34 Follow	duNuR	隨 ^{b}s-lo[r]	
35 Grasp, embrace	-kep	夾 ^{a}m-kep, ^{a}s-kep, ^{a}k-r-ep	
36 Hold sth in fist/mouth	gemgem (in fist)	含 ^{a}gïm (in mouth)	B. gam 'put into mouth'
37 Lick	dilaq	舐 ^{b}m-le	B. m-lyak
38 Meet	Cebung	逢 ^{b}bung S!	PS pung 'assemble'?

(Table 9.1 continued)

Table 9.1 Continued

	PAN or PECL	OC	TB
39 Open	-kaq	啟 ᵃkhe	Kachin kha -k 'parted, open'
40 Put together	pulung	同 ᵃlong	
41 Ruin, damage	r[i]bas	敝 ᵇbet-s	
42 Scrape I	kuSkuS	括 ᵃk-r-ot	Tib. r-ko, Gyarong ka rkos Kuki-Naga d-kew
43 Scrape II	ku[Ct]ku[Ct]	括 ᵃk-r-ot	B. kut
44 Sink	-neb		B. nup
45 Sleep	-zem	寢 ᵇtshim	Tib. gzim, Dhimal d im
46 Speak, say	kawaS	話 ᵃm-kw-r-at-s; 曰 ᵇwat S!	Tib. s-go
47 Think	nemnem	念 ᵃnim-s	Tib. s-nyam-pa 'to think'
48 Vomit, spit	utaq	吐 ᵃtha	B. (m-)tuk V!
49 Wash	basuq	溲 ᵇs(r)u	Lushai shuk, Luoba uk
50 Wrap around (belt)	-kes	繫 ᵃket	
51 Bent, crooked	-kuk	局 ᵇN-k(r)ok	B. kuk
52 Broad	-bang	旁 ᵃbang	Boro go2 bang1 'wide, many'
53 Curled, bent	-kul	卷 ᵇN-k(h)ro[r,n]	PS kuar
54 Dark	-lem	黭 ᵃlïm , ᵃhlïm	
55 Far	ma-dawiN	遠 ᵇwa[r,n] V!	B. wiy
56 High, tall	-kaw	高 ᵃkaw	Bur. kaw: (heavy tone) 'rise up, swell, bulge'
57 Hot	qa(i)nget	熱 ᵇnget	
58 Old, grownup	-da	丈 ᵇdrang	
59 Sharp	Cazem	[GSR 660a] ᵇtsïm	
60 Thick	-tul	敦 ᵃtu[r,n]	PS tu:r
61 This	di	時 ᵇdï I	Tib. ⁿdi 'this'

Note

I! V! F! T! S! irregular Initial, Vowel, Final, Tone, Syllable type.

Shared vocabulary

I present 61 lexical comparisons involving basic vocabulary items (Table 9.1), and 14 comparisons involving cultural items (Table 9.2). The Chinese and AN members of these comparisons conform to the sound correspondences presented in the next section.

Basic vocabulary comparisons

Ten among these comparisons between Chinese and AN: bone, breast, head, egg, horn, earth, salt, speak, hot, this, are on Swadesh's 100-word list, and six: bone, egg, horn, salt, year, this, on Yakhontov's highly basic 35-word list. It is significant that

SINO-TIBETAN–AUSTRONESIAN

Table 9.2 Fourteen cultural vocabulary comparisons between AN, Chinese and TB

1 Setaria	beCeng	稷 ^{b}tsïk	
2 Panicum sp.	Numay	麻 黍 ^{a}maj	
3 Husked rice	beRas	糲 ^{b}mi-rat-s	Tib. ^{m}bras 'rice' m-ras
4 Paddy	Sumay 'rice as food'	米 ^{a}mij 'grain of cereal'	B-G may 'rice; paddy'
5 Chicken	kuka	雞 ^{a}ke	B. ka 'kind of fowl'
6 Cage, enclosure	kurung	籠 ^{a}ki-rong	B. kru:
7 Net	aray	羅 ^{a}raj	
8 Broom	CapuH$_1$	帚 ^{b}t-pu	
9 Stopper, plug	se se	塞 ^{a}sïk	
10 To bury, tomb	-buN 'to bury'	墳 ^{a}bu[r] 'tomb, tumulus'	
11 Loincloth, robe	sabuk	服 ^{b}buk	Tib. ^{m} bog 'k. o. garment'
12 To plait, braid	-pid	編 ^{a}pin( ) F?	B. byar~pyar
13 To shoot	panaq	弩 ^{a}na (crossbow)	
14 To hunt	qaNup	獵 ^{b}Ci-lap	Chepang krup

the percentage of hits on the more basic list (Yakhontov's) is higher than on the less basic list (Swadesh's): 17 per cent against 10 per cent. I do not consider these figures to be final. Missing are the personal pronouns and numerals, which have undergone far-reaching paradigmatic changes (analogy, politeness shifts involving deictics). They will be discussed elsewhere.

Cultural vocabulary comparisons

One notes the presence of terms for agriculture, animal husbandry, hunting, house utensils and the absence of terms for metal. This points to a Neolithic, pre-metal, ancestral culture.

Sound correspondences

Due to canonical reduction of the initial syllable(s) of ancestral polysyllables, sound correspondences relate the last syllable of PAN words with Chinese and TB monosyllabic word stems. In addition, Old Chinese syllable type (A or B) correlates with the nature of the initial of AN penultimate syllables, as detailed in Table 9.7. Tables 9.3 and 9.4 present the correspondences of syllable-initial and final consonants, and Table 9.6 presents the vowel correspondences.

One can see from Table 9.4 that OC - has two corresponding sounds among the final consonants of PAN: -q and -H. This distinction, lost by Chinese, is actually maintained by TB, which has -k and zero corresponding to PAN -q and -H respectively, as shown in Table 9.5.

Table 9.3 Correspondences of syllable-initial consonants (PAN final syllable initial: Chinese root initial: TB)

PAN	OC	TB	Examples
p-	p(h)-	p-	Palm of hand, chew, plait, close, broom
t-	t(h)-	t-	Leech, earth, vomit, thick, short
k-	k(h)-	k-	Elbow, bone, chicken, dog, high, curled, crooked, dig, grasp, wrap around, scrape I, scrape II, open
q-	-	0-	Cloud(y)
b-	b-	(p-)	Carry, broad, loincloth, meet, tomb, ruin
d-	d-	d-	Old, this
g-	g-	g-	Hold in fist or mouth
m-	(h)m-	m-	Body hair, drown
n-	n-	n-	Brain, breast, pus, mother, think, shoot, sink
-	-	-	Hot
N-	(h)l-	l-	Hunt, water, follow, sunlight, moon
l-	(h)l-	l-	Head, snake, head, flow, lick, put together, fall, wind, cave, worm
R-	r-	r-	Horn, salt, husked rice
w-	(h)w-	w- (Tib. g-)	Year, far, say, come/go
s-	s-	?	Wash, stopper
z-	ts-	?	Sharp, sleep, wink

Table 9.4 Correspondences of syllable-final consonants

PAN	OC	TB	Examples
-0	-0	-0	Palm of hand, chicken, carry, this, come/go
-k	-k	-k	Leech, crooked, loincloth
-t	-t	-t	Bone, hot, dig, close
-p	-p	?	Hunt, grasp
-ng	-ng	-ng	Put together, broad, cage, meet, sunlight, cave, old
-ng	-k	-ng	Horn, stopper, Setaria
-m	-m	-m/-p	Water, think, hold in fist or mouth, dark, cloud
$-H_{1,2}$	-	-0	Head, female breast, elbow, salt, broom
-q	-	-k	Brain, pus, earth, lick, vomit, chew, shoot, wash, open
-l	[-r]	-r	Curled, thick
-R	[-r]	-y	Dog, egg, flame, flow, fall, follow
-y	-j	-y	Snake, net, Panicum sp.
-S	-t	-0	Say, year, scrape I, moon
-s	-t	-s (/a_) -t (else)	Husked rice, drown, wrap around, ruin
-N	[-r]	-y~-l	Body hair, far, tomb

SINO-TIBETAN–AUSTRONESIAN

Table 9.5 Preservation by PAN and TB of a contrast in consonant endings lost by Chinese

	PAN	OC	TB
Brain	punuq	腦 ᵃnu	(s-)nuk
Pus	nanaq		Tib. rnag
Lick	dilaq	舐 ᵇm-le	m-lyak
Open	-kaq	啟 ᵃkhe	Jingpo kha -k 'parted, open'
Wash	basuq	溲 ᵇs(r)u	Lushai shuk, Luoba uk
Female breast	nunuH₁	乳 ᵇno	nuw
Head	quluH₁	首 ᵇhlu	Lushai lu
Salt	siRaH₁	鹵 ᵃra S!	la I!

Table 9.6 Vowel correspondences (PAN last vowel : Chinese root vowel)

STAN	PAN : Chinese	Examples
u (before labials)	-u- : -ï-	Water
u (elsewhere)	-u- : -u-	Head, brain, elbow, bone, body hair, dog, flow, thick, dig, meet, tomb
o (before labials)	-u- : -a-	Hunt
o (elsewhere)	-u- : -o-	Breast, egg, horn, fall, put together, curl, crooked, cut off, cage, cave
a (before y)	-a- : -i-	Grain
a (elsewhere)	-a- : -a-	Palm, mother, snake, year, salt, earth, vomit, shoot, speak, broad
æ	-a- : -e-	Chicken, lick, ruin, open
e (after grave cons.)	-e- : -e-	Grasp, wrap around, drown, hot
e (elsewhere)	-e- : -i-	Think, leech, worm, sleep
i (open syll.)	-i- : -ï-	This
i (closed syll.)	-i- : -i-	Plait, close
i	-e- : -ï-	Dark, sink, hold in fist, stopper, sharp

Table 9.7 Correspondences of Chinese syllable type and manner of articulation in PAN penultimate syllable initial consonant

PAN penultimate syllable initial	Chinese syllable type	Examples
Voiceless stop (except q), or zero	ᵃ(non-division 3)	Bone, brain, horn, close, put together, spit
Other initials (including q)	ᵇ(division 3)	Elbow, head, palm, leech, snake, water, drown

Old Chinese had two contrastive syllable types: A and B, of uncertain phonetic interpretation. In my notation these are marked by superscript 'a' and 'b' preceding the reconstruction. These syllable types exhibit a statistical correlation with the nature of the penultimate syllable initial of PAN words: if the penultimate syllable of a PAN word begins with a voiceless stop (excluding q) or zero, then type A is predicted in Chinese. If the penultimate syllable began in another sound (including q), type B is predicted. With PAN monosyllables and roots (always monosyllabic), including reduplicated monosyllables/roots, no prediction can be made. With PAN penultimate initial *C, no prediction can be made either (perhaps PAN *C results from the merger of two PSTAN sounds, a voiceless stop/affricate, and another kind of sound).

Shared morphology

Several morphological processes are shared by AN and ST, including three of the main verbal 'focus' constructions which form the backbone of AN verbal morphology:

The Proto-Austronesian nominaliser and Goal Focus marker - ən and the TB nominalising suffix -n

A process deriving nouns from verbs by means of a suffix -n or -in exists in AN and in ST:

AN	Atayal	niq 'to eat' : niq-un 'eaten thing'
	Paiwan	alap 'to take' : alap-en 'object being taken'
	Amis	aIik 'to sweep' : aaIik-en 'place to sweep'
ST	Tibetan	za-ba 'to eat' : za-n 'food, fodder, pap, porridge'
		skyi-ba 'to borrow' : skyi-n-pa 'borrowed thing, loan'
		rdzu-ba 'to delude, to falsify' : rdzu-n-pa 'falsehood, fiction, lie'
	Lepcha	hru 'to be hot' : ÷-hru-n 'heat'
		bu 'to carry' : ÷-bu-n 'vehicle'

In AN, according to the theory known as SPQR, this nominalising process is the source of the GF construction, where -in is the GF marker. Consider the following verb-initial Atayal sentence in GF (from Egerod 1980), where -un is the GF marker:

baq-un   maku   tuqii
know-GF   my$_{GEN}$ way
I know the way

Under SPQR, the verb-initial, GF parsing of this sentence is a reinterpretation of an earlier cleft sentence meaning 'my known thing (baq-un maku) [is] the way (tuqii)'. Comparison with TB provides the STAN source of this AN nominalising suffix: that is precisely the -n nominaliser found in TB languages. The reinterpretation of the NP 'my known thing' as a GF verb meaning 'I know' occurred after verb-initial word order became generalised in pre-PAN.

The Proto-Austronesian Actor Focus prefix and infix m-/-m- and the ST intransitive prefix m-

The AN AF marker is a nasal affix m- (prefix) or -m- (infix) depending on language and root shape. In Starosta's ergative interpretation of AN grammar (Starosta 1991, 1994), assumed here, all verbs in AF are intransitive, with m-/-m- deriving intransitive verbs from transitive ones. Contrast the following Tagalog sentences:

s-in-agot	ng-istudyante	ang-propesor
OF-answer	GEN-student	NOM-professor
s-um-agot	sa-propesor	ang-istudyante
AF-answer	LOC-professor	NOM-student

Both sentences mean 'The student answered the professor'. The first sentence is in OF, marked on the verb with infixed -in-. It is a typical ergative construction, with the patient marked as nominative, and the agent marked as genitive. Starosta regards verbs in OF as transitive. The second sentence is in AF, marked with infixed -um-. In Starosta's analysis this is really an antipassive construction, with the patient marked in an oblique case form (locative). Infixed -um- marks the verb as intransitive, even though it occurs with two arguments.

PST had a prefix m- which turned transitive verbs into intransitives. Wolfenden (1929: 25–26, 76) characterised it as 'inactive' and 'intransitive'. Examples (Wolfenden 1929: 30 for Tibetan and Kachin; Bhattacharya 1977: 184, 328–330 for Boro):

Tibetan	m-nam-ba	'to smell (intr.), stink'
Kachin	ma-nam	'to smell' (intr.)
	ma-ni	'to laugh'
Boro	mo$_2$-nam$_1$	'to spread smell'
	mi$_2$-ni$_2$ 'to laugh'	

This prefix, illustrated before nasals in the preceding examples, reduced to prenasalisation preceding voiceless stops. In Gyarong, a TB language from Sichuan, prenasalisation has secondarily voiced the following stop. Examples (Lin Xiangrong 1993: 193):

Gyarong ka-tIop 'to set fire to' : ki -nd op 'to catch fire'[2]
 k -p' k 'to split open' : ki -mb k 'to be rent'
 k -t 'op 'to break' : ki -nd®p 'broken'
 k -kl k 'to wipe off' : ki - –l k 'to fall'

In Tibetan, Kiranti, Bahing, Vayu, Bodo-Garo, prenasalisation has further been lost and only secondary voicing of the root initial marks the intransitive member (Benedict 1972: 124 for examples and discussion[3]). MC (mid-first millennium CE) likewise had contrasting pairs of transitive verbs with voiceless stop initials vs intransitive verbs with voiced stop initials:

別 pjet (III) 'to separate, distinguish' : 別 bjet (III) 'to take leave'
箸 trjak 'to put something in a certain place' : 箸 drjak 'to occupy a fixed position'
斷 twanH 'to cut, sever' : 斷 dwanH 'broken off, cut off from; to cease'
折 tsyet 'to break, to bend' (trans.) : 折 dzyet 'to bend' (intrans.)

I have shown (Sagart 1994, 1999, 2003) that intransitive voicing in MC verbs reflects OC prenasalisation, as shown in particular by early loans to Miao-Yao.

The Proto-Austronesian Instrumental/Beneficiary Focus prefix Si- and the valency-increasing s- in Sino-Tibetan

A prefix PAN Si-: OC s-: TB s- allows a verb to take a NP with real-world roles such as causer, beneficiary, instrument, etc. and treat it formally as its patient (that is, as its grammatical object in Chinese, an accusative language, and as its subject in ergative AN). The AN Si-V construction is known as 'Instrument focus' (also 'Beneficiary Focus') but its semantics are complex. Huang (1991: 45) characterises the Si-construction in Atayal as 'circumstantial voice' and states that one characteristic of circumstantial voice is 'increased transitivity'. As an illustration, I cite here examples with a transitive/causative character, because the semantic difference between prefixed and non-prefixed forms can be apprehended directly through simple lexical glosses, even though this is an oversimplification of the functions of this prefix.

Atayal	m- u u 'to be afraid' : s- u u 'to frighten'
Paiwan	k/m/avuL 'to beg' : si-kavuL 'cause someone to beg'
Bunun	da adx 'to stop' (intr.) : is-da adx 'to stop' (trans.)
Old Chinese	順 *^{b}m-lun-s 'to be pliant, obedient' : 馴 *^{b}s-lun 'to tame'
Tibetan	Nbar 'to burn, catch fire, be ignited' : s-bar-pa 'to light, to kindle, to inflame'
	m-nam-pa 'to smell, stink' (intransitive) : s-nam-pa 'to smell' (transitive)
Gyarong	rong 'to see' : s-rong 'to show'
Boro	gi 'to be afraid of, fear' : si-gi 'to frighten'
Proto-Loloish[4]	(C)-no$_2$ 'to awake' : si -no$_2$ 'to awaken' (tr.)

-ar- distributed action; distributed object

This infix was inserted between the root initial and the first vowel of a stem. Attached to verbs of action it indicated that the action was distributed in time (occurring over several discrete occasions), or in space (involving several agents/patients/locations); attached to nouns it indicated a referent distributed in space, that is having double or multiple structure. The reflex of this infix in the AN languages is -ar-, marking verbs of distributed action and nouns of distributed object, including names of paired or multiple body parts. Infixation is often, but not always, in the first of two reduplicated syllables:

Paiwan	k-ar-akim 'to search everywhere' (kim 'search')
	k-ar-apkap-an 'sole of foot'
Puyuma	D-ar-ukap 'palm of hand'
Bunun	d-al-apa 'sole of foot' (PAN *dapa 'palm of hand')
Amis	p-ar-okpok 'to gallop'
	t-ar-odo 'fingers, toes'
	k-ar-ot 'harrow'
Tagalog	d-al-akdak 'sowing of rice seeds or seedlings for transplanting' (dakdak 'driving in of sharp end of stakes into soil')
	k-al-aykay 'rake'
Malay	ketap 'to bite teeth' : k-er-etap 'to bite teeth repeatedly'

Other AN languages show an infix -aR- with similar functions (not illustrated here). According to the sound correspondences presented above, both -r- and -R- correspond to OC -r-. Although no living TB language has -r- infixation as a living process, paired nouns and verbs with what appears to be an infix -r- show up here and there, with similar semantics as in Chinese:

Burm.	pok 'a drop (of liquid)' : prok 'speckled, spotted'
	pwak 'to boil up and break, as boiling liquid' : prwak 'ibid.'
	khwe$_2$ 'curve, coil' : khrwe$_2$- 'to surround, attend'
Kachin	hpun 'of pimples, to appear on the body' : hprun 'pimples, on the body; to appear on the body, of pimples'
Chepang -r-	pop, prop 'the lungs'
	brok 'be partly white, grey, streaked' (of hair); compare TB bok 'white'.

I first identified the Chinese -r- distributed action/object infix from minimal pairs in Old Chinese (Sagart 1993). Later on, I described some infixed pairs in modern dialects where the infix showed up as the regular modern reflex -l-, preceded either with a schwa or with a full or partial copy of the syllable's rime (Sagart 1994, 2001). Here are some examples of infixed nouns and verbs from Yimeng, a Jin dialect of Inner Mongolia, where the infixed string is -i 1-^{5} (Li 1991):

p-i 1-ai$_3$ 'to swing, oscillate'
p-i 1-i n$_1$ 'to run on all sides'
xu-i 1-a$_4$ 'to scribble'
t-i 1-i u$_1$ 'cluster(s) of fruit hanging from branches'
khu-i 1-u$_3$ 'wheel(s) of a car'

Reduction to monosyllables and maintenance of prefixation and infixation

How did PSTAN prefixes and infixes survive the loss of non-final syllables, to which they were attached, in the evolution to Chinese? The answer was provided by Starosta (1995). Starosta argued that PSTAN had both monosyllables and polysyllables: only polysyllabic words were affected by the loss of initial syllables and attached affixes: monosyllables could then act as a refuge for prefixes and infixes. PSTAN monosyllables survive in PAN as roots and reduplicative disyllables. Judging from the high number of verbs among PAN roots, and from the high number of PAN roots in the lexical comparisons for verbs presented above (Table 9.1), it appears likely that many PSTAN verbs were monosyllabic. PSTAN verbal morphology, then, could easily continue in ST languages after canonical reduction had started operating.

Archaeology and agricultural origins

What historical reality lies behind the proposed linguistic relationship? Both in the modern cultures and archaeologically, evidence of a substantial cultural unity between the AN peoples of Taiwan and the ST peoples can be discerned. The principal is an agriculture based on two millets: Setaria italica and Panicum miliaceum, with rice as a third cereal. In northern China, the millets appear archaeologically in different sites of the Cishan-Peiligang culture between 8,500 and 7,500 BP (Lu, Chapter 3, this volume), and continue to be present down to historical times. The earliest Chinese inscriptions and texts (late second to first millennium BCE) show millets to be the main crops of the Shang and Zhou states. The Zhou rulers thought themselves descended from a mythical ancestor, Hou Ji 侯稷 ('Lord Setaria'). Millets played a major role in religious rituals. Domesticated Setaria also occurs in the Karuo culture of Eastern Tibet, c.5,555–4,750 BP (Fu Daxiong 2001: 66) and in Changguogou in the mid-Yalu Tsangpo River Valley, c.3,370 BP (Fu Daxiong 2001). Many TB peoples cultivate millets to this day. In the lower Huang He Valley, downriver from the Peiligang culture, the Beixin and Dawenkou cultures of Henan, south Shandong and northern Jiangsu (from c.7,000 BP) were also millet-based (Chang 1986). Chang regards them as a probable eastward expansion from the mid-Huang He Valley communities of millet farmers. Millets, regarded by the AN peoples of Taiwan as sacred, had long been missing from the archaeological record in Taiwan, generating speculations that these cereals could have been acquired at a relatively recent date, even though one millet-related term: *beCeng 'Setaria' can be securely reconstructed to PAN. The recent discovery in southwestern Taiwan of thousands of carbonised grains of millet (Tsang, Chapter 4, this volume), in conjunction with rice grains, in a TPK cultural context dated to 4,500 BP, has laid these speculations to rest. TPK, the oldest ceramic culture in Taiwan, is generally identified with the PAN speech community. The antiquity of millets in AN culture cannot now be doubted. The PAN speakers were farmers, and their main crops were rice and millet. In contrast, the scarcity of the millets, not just archaeologically, but ethnologically, in South China, is striking. It is not clear how the early Austronesians could have possessed millet if their immediate ancestors were a southern Chinese people.

Not only were rice and millets grown by the early TBs, Chinese and Austronesians, the very names of these cereals are shared, with the same sound correspondences as the rest of the shared vocabulary (Table 9.2). My current interpretation of the facts is as follows. Between 8,500 and 7,500 BP, farming communities with domesticated Setaria, Panicum and rice began to appear in the mid-Huang He Valley, whether as a northern extension of the Yangzi rice Neolithic (Bellwood, Chapter 1, this volume), or as an independent transition to the Neolithic (Lu, Chapter 3, this volume) is still uncertain. I call PSTAN the language spoken by these early farmers. Subsequent population growth resulted in geographical expansion, both up- and down-river, of PSTAN speakers. A western and an eastern dialect individualised. The western dialect, in the mid- and upper Huang He Valley, later evolved into PST, whose speakers eventually expanded southward and westward. The eastern dialect was spoken in the lower Huang He and Huai He Valleys. There its speakers adapted to a wetter environment (marine, riverine, lacustrine). The site of Longqiuzhuang, dated to c.7,000–5,500 BP in the lower Huai Valley, has both rice and millet (Lu, Chapter 3, this volume, Figure 3.1). A migration brought some of the speakers of this eastern dialect speakers to Taiwan,[6] reached by 5,500 BP. There their language began to diversify into the modern AN languages. Southern elements (cord-marked pottery, bark beaters, etc.) probably entered early AN culture through contact with peoples of southern China. These southern elements do not, however, indicate a south mainland origin of the Austronesians. As to the Tai-Kadai languages, which show strong evidence of relatedness with the AN languages, I have hypothesised that they are not a sister group of AN having remained on the mainland when the pre-Austronesian migrated to Taiwan, but a daughter group of AN, sharing some innovations with the MP languages (see my other Chapter, this volume).

Conclusion

In this chapter I have answered criticisms levelled at earlier versions of my theory. I have significantly increased the number of basic-vocabulary comparisons with sound correspondences between OC and PAN. I have shown that these comparisons, for the most part, have comparanda among the TB languages, and that in some cases TB preserves phonological distinctions reflected in AN but lost in Chinese. I have shown that the OC syllable-type distinction correlates with the nature of the penultimate syllable's initial consonant in AN and that important sections of AN and ST morphology are shared, as well as how PSTAN prefixes and infixes survived the loss of initial syllables. Finally, I have argued that, better than any other theory, a STAN unity explains the spread of a millet-based agriculture to Taiwan. I therefore maintain, with increasing confidence, my original verdict, voiced in 1990: Chinese and AN are genetically related. Contra my original assessment, however, I am claiming here that the relationship with AN includes not just Chinese but the whole of ST.

Acknowledgement

This work was supported in part by a grant from the Origine de l'homme, origine du langage, origine des langues programme of the Centre National de la Recherche Scientifique, France.

Abbreviations

AAK	Austronesian Ancestor of Kadai
AF	Actor Focus
AN	Austronesian
B.	Benedict (1972)
Bur.	Written Burmese
ECL	(Formosan) East Coast Linkage
GEN	Genitive
GF	Goal Focus
LOC	Locative
MC	Middle Chinese
MP	Malayo-Polynesian
OC	Old Chinese
OF	Object Focus
PAN	Proto-Austronesian
PECL	Proto-East Coast Linkage
PMP	Proto-Malayo-Polynesian
PS	Peiros and Starostin (1995)
PST	Proto-Sino-Tibetan
PSTAN	Proto-Sino-Tibetan-Austronesian
SPQR	Starosta, Pawley and Reid (1982)
ST	Sino-Tibetan
STAN	Sino-Tibetan-Austronesian
TB	Tibeto-Burman
Tib.	Written Tibetan
TPK	Tapenkeng

Notes

1 It is assumed that this change spread secondarily to Kanakanabu.
2 Gyarong ka-, k - and ki - are verb prefixes for controllable (ka-, k -) and non-controllable (ki -) actions.

3 Facts from Gyarong were not available to Benedict: he did not realise that voiceless-transitive vs voiced-intransitive alternations in TB verb roots have their origin in intransitive prenasalisation. Neither did he realise that TB intransitive prenasalisation/voicing and Wolfenden's intransitive m- prefix are in complementary distribution with respect to initials: he therefore treated them as two distinct processes.
4 Bradley (1979).
5 The glottal stop was probably artefactually introduced by the transcriber, who assigned the first syllables to the 'entering tone', a glottal-stop-carrying tone, on account of their shortness.
6 A cultural trait found in essentially identical form in the Dawenkou culture of coastal north Jiangsu and south Shandong (in the region of the mouths of the Huang He and Huai River Valleys) and among the modern Formosans, is ritual extraction of upper lateral incisors in both boys and girls, in puberty. Although this feature is widespread among modern southern Chinese populations, it first appears archaeologically in south Shandong c.6,500 BP, and is found nowhere else in China at that date (Han and Nakahashi 1996).

Bibliography

Baxter, W.H.III (1992) A Handbook of Old Chinese Phonology, Berlin: Mouton de Gruyter.
Benedict, P.K. (1972) Sino-Tibetan: A Conspectus, Cambridge: University Printing House.
Bhattacharya, P.C. (1977) A Descriptive Analysis of the Boro Language, Gauhati: Gauhati University Department of publications.
Blust, R.A. (1977) 'The Proto-Austronesian pronouns and Austronesian subgrouping: a preliminary report', University of Hawaii Working Papers in Linguistics 9, 2: 1–15.
—— (1999) 'Subgrouping, circularity and extinction: some issues in Austronesian comparative linguistics', in E. Zeitoun and P.J.-K. Li (eds) Selected Papers from the Eighth International Conference on Austronesian Linguistics, Taipei: Institute of Linguistics (preparatory office).
Bradley, D. (1979) Proto-Loloish, London and Malmø: Curzon.
Chang K.C. (1986) The Archaeology of Ancient China, 4th edn, New Haven and London: Yale University Press.
Coblin, S. (1986) A Sinologist's Handlist of Sino-Tibetan Lexical Comparisons, Nettetal: Steyler Verlag.
van Driem, G. (1997) 'Sino-Bodic', Bulletin of the School of Oriental and African Studies 60, 3: 455–88.
Egerod, S. (1980) Atayal-English Dictionary, London and Malmø: Curzon Press.
Feng, A.-Z. (1998) Fuzhou fangyan cidian, Nanjing: Jiangsu Jiaoyu.
Ferrell, R. (1969) Taiwan Aboriginal Groups: Problems in Cultural and Linguistic Classification, Nankang: Academia Sinica.
Fu, D.-X. (2001) Xizang Changguogou yizhi xin shiqi shidai nongzuowu yicun de faxian, jianding he yanjiu, Kaogu 3: 66–74.
Gong, H.-C. (1995) 'The system of finals in Sino-Tibetan', in W.S.-Y. Wang (ed.) The Ancestry of the Chinese Language, Journal of Chinese Linguistics monograph series no. 8.
Han, K.-X. and Nakahashi, T. (1996) 'A comparative study of ritual tooth ablation in ancient China and Japan' Anthropol. Sci. 104, 1: 43–64.
Ho, D.-A. (1998) 'Taiwan Nandaoyu de Yuyan Guanxi', Chinese Studies 16, 2: 141–71.

Huang, L.M.-J. (1991) 'The semantics of s- in Atayal', Studies in English Literature and Linguistics 17: 37–50, Taipei: Department of English, National Taiwan Normal University.

Li, Z.-G. (1991) 'Yi Meng fangyan de "fenyinci"', Fangyan 3: 206–10.

Lin, X.-R. (1993) Jiarong yu yanjiu, Chengdu: Sichuan Minzu.

Peiros, I. and Starostin, S. (1995) A Comparative Vocabulary of Five Sino-Tibetan Languages, Melbourne: Department of Linguistics and applied Linguistics, University of Melbourne.

Sagart, L. (1990) 'Chinese and Austronesian are genetically related', Paper presented at the 23rd International Conference on Sino-Tibetan Languages and Linguistics, Arlington, October 1990.

—— (1993) 'Chinese and Austronesian: evidence for a genetic relationship', Journal of Chinese Linguistics 21, 1: 1–62.

—— (1994) 'Old Chinese and Proto-Austronesian evidence for Sino-Austronesian', Oceanic Linguistics 33, 2: 271–308.

—— (1999) The Roots of Old Chinese, Amsterdam: John Benjamins.

—— (2001) 'Vestiges of Archaic Chinese Derivational Affixes in Modern Chinese Dialects', in H. Chappell (ed.) Sinitic Grammar – Synchronic and Diachronic Perspectives, Oxford: University Press.

—— (2003) 'Sources of Middle Chinese manner types: Old Chinese prenasalized initials in Hmong-Mien and Sino-Tibetan perspective', Language and Linguistics, 4.4: 757–68.

Starosta, S. (1991) 'Ergativity, transitivity, and clitic coreference in four Western Austronesian languages', Paper presented at 6th International Conference on Austronesian Linguistics, Honolulu, May 1991.

—— (1994) 'Formosan clause structure: transitivity, ergativity, and case marking', revised version (18 October 1994) of a paper presented at the 4th International Symposium on Chinese languages and Linguistics, Nankang, July 1994.

—— (1995) 'The Chinese-Austronesian connection: a view from the Austronesian morphology side', in W.S.-Y. Wang (ed.) The Ancestry of the Chinese Language, Journal of Chinese Linguistics monograph series no. 8.

—— 'Reduplication and the subgrouping of Formosan languages', Paper presented at International Symposium on Austronesian cultures: Issues relating to Taiwan, Taipei, December 2001.

Starosta, S., Pawley, A. and Reid, L. (1982) 'The evolution of Focus in Austronesian', in A. Halim, L. Carrington and S. Wurm (eds) Papers from the Third International Conference on Austronesian Linguistics, vol. 2, Canberra: Pacific Linguistics.

Wang, F.-S. and Mao, Z.-W. (1995) Miao-yao yu guyin gouni, Beijing: Zhongguo Shehui Kexue.

Wolfenden, S. (1929) Outlines of Tibeto-Burman Linguistic Morphology, London: Royal Asiatic Society.

10
TAI-KADAI AS A SUBGROUP OF AUSTRONESIAN[1]

Laurent Sagart

Is the Austronesian-related vocabulary in Tai-Kadai due to chance resemblances?

Benedict (1942, 1975) argued from similarities in basic vocabulary, including personal pronouns and numerals, that Tai-Kadai and AN are two distinct phyla going back to a common ancestor – PAT. Benedict's lists of cognates contain many look-alikes and undetected Chinese loans to Tai,[2] but one set of words suffices to show that at least some vocabulary is genuinely shared by Tai-Kadai and AN, not as a result of chance (Table 10.1).

Is the Austronesian-related vocabulary in Tai-Kadai due to borrowings?

Thurgood (1994) claimed that within Tai-Kadai, the AN-related vocabulary obeys different correspondences from the rest.[3] He concluded that the AN-related vocabulary is borrowed from an early pre-AN source. However the vocabulary shared by Tai-Kadai and AN is very basic: it includes the 1sg, 2sg and 2pl personal pronouns; all the numerals above 'one'; bodypart terms like 'eye', 'tongue', 'hand'; terms for natural objects like 'moon', 'water'; verbs like 'die', etc. Borrowing such a set of vocabulary is probably not impossible, given sufficient pressure, but if so, one should also expect to find many, many loanwords in the cultural vocabulary. This is precisely where the difficulty arises: items of cultural vocabulary shared by Tai-Kadai and AN are quite scarce (terms for rice cultivation, for instance, are all but missing; see Blench, Chapter 2, this volume). It appears, then, that neither chance nor borrowing are likely explanations for the lexical comparisons between Tai-Kadai and AN. The only remaining explanation is genetic, as Benedict argued. For a realistic list of likely cognates between AN and Tai-Kadai, see Ostapirat, Chapter 7, this volume.

Table 10.1 A sound correspondence between AN and Tai-Kadai

	PAN	PMP	Tai	Lakkia
Die	maCay	matay	ta:i_1	plei$_1$
Eye	maCa	mata	ta$_1$	pla$_1$
Bird		manuk	nok$_8$	mlok$_7$

The Austronesian-related vocabulary in Tai-Kadai lacks features older than Proto-Austronesian

If Benedict is right that Tai-Kadai and AN are coordinate taxa under Austro-Tai, then we should find in Tai-Kadai some features which are more conservative than, and throw light on, reconstructed PAN. Benedict thought that the comparisons in Table 10.1 provided just that kind of evidence. He reconstructed the PAT words for 'die', 'eye' and 'bird' as *mapla, *maplay, *mamluk, with medial clusters[4] preserved in Lakkia and Saek but simplified to -t-, -t- and -n- in Tai; the first syllable (ma- in all three cases ! a meaningless fact in his interpretation) being lost. He thought that the medial clusters -pl- and -ml- of PAT evolved to PAN -C- and -N- respectively. However, another account of the genesis of the Tai and Lakkia forms is possible. The following is based on Haudricourt (1956; here slightly modified):

> 'eye'   mata   mta   pta   Tai ta, Lakkia pla
> 'die'   matay   mtay   ptay   Tai tai, Lakkia plei
> 'bird' manuk   mnuk   Tai nok, Lakkia mlok

Haudricourt's explanation is preferable to Benedict's because it accounts for the Tai-Kadai facts without requiring any consonant clusters in the ancestral language; because it does not treat as coincidence the fact that the first syllable of the three words is ma-; and because it does not require the rather unusual sound change pl- t- to occur independently in AN and in Tai-Kadai. Haudricourt's explanation also makes stronger predictions for the Tai-Kadai data: it predicts that if an AN-related Tai-Kadai form for 'eye' or 'die' shows a cluster such as pl- or pr-, the first syllable ma- in the corresponding AN form will not be separately reflected (for instance as pre-nasalisation), since m- in the first syllable is already reflected as Tai-Kadai p-; while in the case of a Tai-Kadai form for 'eye' or 'die' with a non-cluster alveolar stop initial, prenasalisation is possible. This prediction is verified: for example, Shui nda$_1$ 'eye' (from *nta mta mata), but no Tai-Kadai language ever shows mpl- or mpr- in either 'eye' or 'die'.

The Austronesian-related vocabulary in Tai-Kadai has Malayo-Polynesian features

According to many Austronesianists, PAN, the ancestor of all living AN languages, was spoken in Taiwan around 5,500 BP. It is also widely recognised that one migration out of Taiwan around 4,500 BP resulted in a language ancestral to all living AN languages outside of Taiwan – PMP. MP languages share characteristics which are regarded as innovations defining PMP. The most important of these relate to the second-person pronouns (Blust 1977). According to Blust, there were two sets of personal pronouns in PAN – nominative and genitive. These two sets had the same endings for each person – thus all PAN 2sg pronouns ended in -Su, and all 2pl pronouns ended in -mu. Neither -Su nor -mu occurred at any other position in either paradigm. Evolution to PMP was complex and asymmetrical. -Su forms were maintained as 2sg pronouns but one of them – *(n)i-Su, in an unexplained change, was transferred to a plural function, becoming 2pl in both sets, where it competed with original -mu forms. Conversely, the PAN 2pl form in the genitive set *(n)i-mu became a 2sg polite form. These innovations – transfer of the 2sg (n)i-Su to 2pl and politeness shift of genitive 2pl *(n)i-mu to polite 2sg – occur in AN languages outside of Taiwan, but not within it.

The corresponding Tai-Kadai forms (or rather PKT, as reconstructed by Liang and Zhang 1996) are shown in Table 10.2. Table 10.2 shows that the Tai-Kadai second-person pronouns share with PMP the transfer of a -Su form to a plural function, and the politeness shift resulting in a -mu form being used as a singular pronoun. This mismatch between PAN and Tai-Kadai second-person pronouns was known to Benedict: he spoke (1975: 208) of a 'flip-flop' but did not explain it. While the politeness shift affecting PAN *(n)i-mu 'you pl.' could well have taken place independently in Tai-Kadai and in PMP, the transfer of a -Su form to a plural function is highly idiosyncratic and can hardly have occurred twice.

Another MP feature in Tai-Kadai concerns the word for 'bird': this word, PAN *qayam, changed its meaning to 'domesticated animal' in a language ancestral to PMP and Ketagalan, a northeastern Formosan language, and was subsequently replaced by a new form – PMP *manuk 'bird', Ketagalan manuk(i), manukka 'bird' (Tsuchida, Yamada and Moriguchi 1991). Tai-Kadai, again, aligns with PMP (and Ketagalan), not PAN (see Table 10.1).

It cannot be the case, however, that the AN-related forms in Tai-Kadai originate in a MP language, because the AN vocabulary in Tai-Kadai also has some features older than PMP (though none is older than PAN): for instance, retention of a sibilant articulation for PAN *S in some words (such as the 2pl pronoun in

Table 10.2 PAN second-person pronoun (endings) compared with PKT

	PAN	PKT
2sg	-Su	*mi
2pl	-mu	*sou

Source: Liang and Zhang (1996).

Table 10.2), while PMP changes *S to *h. Ostapirat (Chapter 7, this volume) finds evidence for Tai-Kadai preservation of the PAN contrast between *C and *t; while PAN *N, which merges with *n in PMP, has some l- reflexes in Tai-Kadai (Proto-Kra *lak 'child'   PAN *aNak[5]).

A new hypothesis

Both Benedict and Thurgood regard Tai-Kadai as a very old phylum, with considerable diversification among daughter languages. Ostapirat (2000; Chapter 7, this volume) depicts a more compact and relatively recent taxon, with the first split taking place no more than 4,000 BP. This makes Tai-Kadai young enough to be a subgroup, rather than a sister phylum, of AN. That would help explain why Tai-Kadai shares some post-PAN innovations with certain AN languages. I will therefore hypothesise that Tai-Kadai has its origin in an early AN language called here 'AAK'. AAK was a daughter language of PAN, and a close relative of PMP: it shared some innovations with PMP, but was more conservative in other respects. I tentatively place it within the ECL, a primary branch of AN (see Chapter 9, Figure 1). AAK left no descendants in the AN world proper. In historical terms, one may suppose that AAK speakers, perhaps from eastern Taiwan, settled the Guangdong coast. There they sustained intimate contact with a local population. As a result of this interaction, AAK was to a large extent relexified, with only the most basic elements of its vocabulary resisting. The linguistic identity of the relexifier remains an open question: that much of the Kadai vocabulary of rice cultivation is apparently of AA origin (Ferlus, p.c.; Blench, Chapter 2, this volume) is weakly suggestive of an early AA-related language,[6] but the fact that much of the non-AN and non-Chinese vocabulary in Tai-Kadai is without clear connections points in the direction of a language belonging to an extinct phylum, though conceivably one with macrophylic connections to AA or Hmong-Mien.

Abbreviations

AA	Austro-Asiatic
AAK	Austronesian Ancestor of Tai-Kadai
AN	Austronesian
ECL	East Coast Linkage
MP	Malayo-Polynesian
PAN	Proto-Austronesian
PAT	Proto-Austro-Tai
PKT	Proto-Kam-Tai
PMP	Proto-Malayo-Polynesian

Notes

1 This work was supported in part by a grant from the Origine de l'homme, origine du langage, origine des langues programme of the Centre National de la recherche scientifique, France.
2 See for instance the discussion of metal names in Sagart (1999: 199–200).
3 See Ostapirat, Chapter 7, this volume, for a different view.
4 He sometimes wrote these clusters as -pr-, -pr-, -mr-.
5 Some Tai-Kadai forms reflect PAN *N as n, however: Siamese naam$_C$ 'water', PAN *daNum 'id.': but see Ostapirat (Chapter 7, this volume).
6 Peiros (1998: 229–45) draws attention to Tai-Kadai words shared with AA (mostly with Vietnamese), which are possibly loans from AA: 'big', 'come', 'drink', 'dry', 'ear', 'full', 'green', 'long', 'moon', 'many', 'mountain', 'neck', 'new', 'one', 'speak', 'tooth', 'this', 'tongue', 'yellow', 'you' (sg).

Bibliography

Bellwood, P. (1997) Prehistory of the Indo-Malaysian Archipelago, Honolulu: University of Hawai'i Press.
Benedict, P.K. (1942) 'Thai, Kadai and Indonesian: a new alignment in Southeastern Asia', American Anthropologist 44: 576–601.
—— (1975) Austro-Thai: Language and Culture, New Haven: HRAF Press.
Blust, R.A. (1977) 'The Proto-Austronesian pronouns and Austronesian subgrouping: a preliminary report', University of Hawai'i Working Papers in Linguistics 9, 2: 1–15.
Haudricourt, A.-G. (1956) 'De la restitution des initiales dans les langues monosyllabiques: le problème du thai commun', Bulletin de la Société de Linguistique de Paris 52: 307–22.
Liang, M. and Zhang, J.-R. (1996) Dong-Tai Yuzu Gailun, Beijing: Zhongguo Shehui Kexue Chubanshe.
Ostapirat, W. (2000) 'Proto-Kra', Linguistics of the Tibeto-Burman Area 23, 1.
Peiros, I. (1998) Comparative Linguistics in Southeast Asia, Canberra: Pacific Linguistics.
Sagart, L. (1999) The Roots of Old Chinese, Amsterdam: John Benjamins.
Thurgood, G. (1994) 'Tai-Kadai and Austronesian: the nature of the relationship', Oceanic Linguistics 33, 2: 345–68.
Tsuchida, S. Yamada, Y. and Moriguchi, T (1991) Linguistic Materials of the Formosan Sinicized populations I: Siraya and Basai, Tokyo: The University of Tokyo, Linguistics Department.

11

PROTO-EAST ASIAN AND THE ORIGIN AND DISPERSAL OF THE LANGUAGES OF EAST AND SOUTHEAST ASIA AND THE PACIFIC

Stanley Starosta[1]

Introduction

Over the past century, but especially during the last 15 years, linguistic, archaeological, and genetic evidence has been accumulating which indicate that at least some of the major language phyla of South Asia, East Asia, Southeast Asia and the Pacific Ocean (AA, AN, HM, ST and Tai-Kadai) are genetically related to each other. At the conference on Asian Mainland and Austronesian Connections held at the University of Hawaii in 1993, it was suggested by Peter Bellwood and Laurent Sagart that in fact all of these language phyla might descend from a single common ancestor, tentatively named PEA (allegedly by me). See Figure 11.1. In this chapter I would like to make this proposal a bit more concrete and therefore easier to support, correct and/or refute.

The major influences on the scenario I will present are Peter Bellwood, Robert Blust, Gérard Diffloth, George van Driem, Charles Higham, Laurent Sagart and Hongkai Sun. The original version of the chapter included extensive footnotes containing supporting material and documentation especially from the works of these authors. This had to be omitted in the present version because of considerations of space. Let me emphasise at this point though that only part of this chapter represents original ideas; much of it is just a rearrangement of the ideas of various colleagues, especially those mentioned above. In its present stage, it is a set of conjectures somewhat enlightened by facts and reconstructions. I have adjusted the conjectures as necessary to make them more consistent with each other. As parts of the overall scenario are rejected and replaced by better founded replacements, I hope it may evolve into a serious hypothesis about EA prehistory. Chinese provinces and South and Southeast Asian countries are used to locate peoples and migrations, though of course such political divisions did not yet exist at this period.

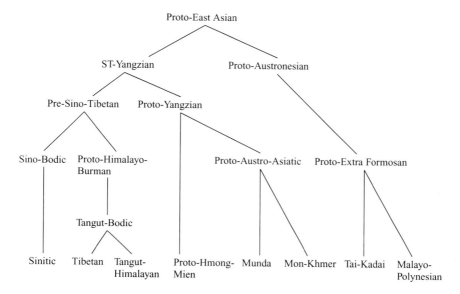

Figure 11.1 PEA and the origin and dispersal of the languages of East and Southeast Asia and the Pacific.

East Asian

Date, culture: 6,500 to 6,000 BCE; Peiligang and Cishan cultures on the North China Plain
Agriculture: millet
Linguistic characteristics:
Word canon: disyllabic; CVCVC
Proposed nominalisation processes in PEA

    [m../[..mV: agent of V-ing
    ..Vn]:   patient of V-ing
    [sV..:   instrument of V-ing

In addition, there was a [n../[..nV.. 'perfective', which could be zero-nominalised as 'thing already V-ed' (Laurent Sagart, email, 31/Jan/2001).[2]

L. Sagart has found 23 basic vocabulary items, cognate sets from PAN, OC and Himalayo-Burman (Sagart 2001).[3] Other linguists have identified common vocabulary and morphology shared between AN and AA, and Sagart has found some of the same morphology in ST.

Based on preliminary linguistic and archaeological evidence and suggestions of colleagues working in this area, I propose that there was a single language or linkage, which I will refer to as EA, which was spoken in the Han River, Wei River and central Yellow River (Huang He) areas of Central China, between the

Huang He and the Yangzi, and that it and its descendants expanded south and west with the development of more productive agricultural economies (see Bellwood, Chapter 1, this volume), resulting in the modern distribution of their descendants. South of the PEA area and extending down to Việtnam were the cord-marking people, conceivably Negritos, who made cord-marked pottery and spoke a monosyllabic tone language.

Pre-Austronesian

Date, culture: 5,000 BCE; Dawenkou, Hemudu
Agriculture: millet, rice

The Pre-Austronesians, forming the Longshan Culture, spread east down the Huang He to the Bo Hai (Gulf of Chihli). Those who remained in this area were later known to the Chinese as the Yi (Sagart, p.c.). Riverine navigation techniques developed into more sophisticated littoral seafaring technology, and some began moving south down the east coast of China, alternating periods of fishing, trading and raiding with periods of farming in river deltas between flood stages. During the Zhou dynasty, easterly expansion of the Chinese assimilated the Yi. Their main settlement south of Shandong was the area on the south side of Hangzhou Bay, including Hemudu. Knowledge of rice agriculture and some other cultural characteristics now thought of as AN were acquired in this region from the HM Majiabang culture on the north side of the bay.

With the beginning of millet agriculture, EA spread out through the Huang He and Wei river basins, and subsequently spread out into the Yangzi valley to the south with the beginning of rice cultivation. The language remaining in the Huang He region evolved into a dialect chain that subsequently split into two languages, the progenitors of Sino-Tibetan-Yangzian (west and central end of the Huang He population, the Wei and Han valleys, and the central Yangzi region) and Pre-Austronesian (east end of the Huang He region).

Proto-Austronesian

Date, culture: 3,500 BCE; Yuanshan
Agriculture: millet, rice
Linguistic characteristics:
Nominalisation processes in PAN: no change from PEA

[m../[..mV: agent of V-ing
..Vn]: patient of V-ing
[sV..: instrument of V-ing
[n../[..nV.. perfective; thing already V-ed

According to Sagart (Laurent Sagart, email, 31/Jan/2001), these processes subsequently entered the AN verbal focus system by means of the abductive mechanism proposed in SPQR. By Starosta's morphological reconstruction, however, only the [n../[..nV.. perfective member of this set can be reconstructed at the PAN level based on AN-internal evidence, although all four certainly appear at later stages of the language. Sagart has not accepted this limit on the PAN reconstruction, but has also so far failed to provide an alternate scenario that accounts for the same facts and diachronic generalisations.

Eventually one group of pre-Austronesians crossed the Straits of Taiwan, possibly via the Pescadores Islands, and landed on the southwest coast (Starosta 1995). Those who remained were eventually absorbed by the successive waves of HM, Sinitic and Kadai peoples who occupied the southeast China mainland (the 'Bai Yue'). In Taiwan, the newly arrived Longshanoid pre-Austronesians encountered and eventually overwhelmed the aboriginal population of the DPK cord-marked pottery culture (hereafter CM). It should be noted that both the DPK and pre-Austronesian cultures were 'Neolithic', but in different senses. As Charles Higham has pointed out, 'Neolithic' in archaeology in general refers to the presence of agriculture, pottery and polished stone implements. However, terminological uncertainty is introduced by the fact that pottery doesn't always imply agriculture, and because the term 'Neolithic' is sometimes used by Chinese and Vietnamese archaeologists to refer to the presence of pottery and polished stone implements alone, with or without settled agriculture. The DPK culture was apparently 'Neolithic' only in the pottery sense,[4] while the later Pre-Austronesian incursion was Neolithic in the standard agricultural sense.

There are three questions that need to be considered here: (1) Is the DPK culture distinct from a later cultural level in Taiwan, (2) did DPK have agriculture and (3) is DPK the culture that was brought to Taiwan by the Pre-Austronesians? On the first question, it is agreed that DPK is the earliest post-Paleolithic culture on the island, and it has been assumed without comment that the DPK tradition is the one that continues up until the ethnographic present in Taiwan. This second assumption is however not supported. In fact, several archaeologists have distinguished the DPK culture from the later Lungshanoid culture, which in my scenario was carried from the lower Huang He to Taiwan by the pre-Austronesians.

On question (2), some scholars have claimed that DPK had no agriculture, but others, and sometimes the same ones, have claimed that it did, but without presenting evidence in support of this claim. Gina Barnes is an exception here: she presents evidence for the association of DPK with agriculture, but the dates are far too early for association with the Austronesians. Otherwise, what I find is circular reasoning:

1 DPK was Neolithic, so DPK must have had agriculture;
2 the Austronesians brought agriculture, and so DPK must have been AN-speaking;
3 archaeologically related areas on the China mainland must be the AN homeland.

This is questionable because of the ambiguous definition of 'Neolithic'. The DPK cord-markers may or may not have been agriculturalists.

The Austronesians could not have brought agriculture to Taiwan, because the Austronesians never came to Taiwan; the Pre-Austronesians did. Pre-Austronesian became PAN at the ethnographic instant when the Proto-Rukai group separated off from the first Pre-Austronesian community and moved inland up the Lower Tamshui river valley, and the spot where that happened was the homeland of PAN. Failure to make this distinction has resulted in endless vacuous arguments about the homeland of PAN. Pace Blust (1999: 31), no language that existed before the moment that Rukai split off was 'Austronesian',[5] and pace Bellwood (1995: 106), no language that existed after that moment was 'Proto-Austronesian'.

The remaining group of Austronesians spread up and down the west coast in a dialect chain and differentiated into successive chunks, with the first several Tsouic groups separating from the chain and moving east and northeast up river valleys. Some languages crossed to eastern Taiwan by going around the north and south ends of the island, and one group crossed the central mountain range into the same area. More sophisticated seafaring techniques were developed on the east coast, and one group, Extra-Formosan, began exploring their neighbourhood by sea. The first successful sea-born colonists from this area, the Siraya, landed in the southwest Taiwan heartland. The second, the AAK expedition,[6] migrated back to the Hainan, Guangdong and the adjacent North Vietnam areas on the mainland. The third, the Malayo-Polynesians, landed in the northern Philippines and began subdividing and working south and east or west, eventually populating most of the Pacific land areas except for mainland Papua-New Guinea and Australia.

Austro-Thai

My subgrouping scenario assumes no Austro-Thai node. Graham Thurgood has shown why Paul Benedict's original hypothesis does not work, and Laurent Sagart has proposed an alternative account of the origin of the Kadai languages (see the following text; see Sagart's paper in Chapter 10, this volume) which deals better with the facts and with the paradoxes uncovered by Thurgood.

Sino-Tibetan-Yangzian

Date, culture: 5,500 BCE; Yangshao
Agriculture: millet
Linguistic characteristics:
Word canon: disyllabic; C' $_1$C Ø$_2$C
Nominalisation processes in PSTY

[m.. / [..mV..:	agent of V-ing
[sV..:	instrument of V-ing
Vn]:	'patient of Ving'
[n.. / [..nV:	perfective; thing already V-ed (adapted from Laurent Sagart, email, 31/Jan/2001)

After the split-off of PAN and its migration down the Huang He toward the Yellow Sea, an 'iambic' word form canon spread through the 'stay-at-home' Sino-Tibetan-Yangzian subgroup. I have no indication as to whether the innovation began internally or whether it had an external non-EA source. The effect of the change was to de-stress the first syllable of original PEA disyllables $[CV_1CV_2C]$ $[C'_1CØ_2C]$ and reduce the inventory of vowels which could occur in the unstressed syllable. A further reduction of the first vowel diffused through the lexicon a word at a time, eliminating the first vowel altogether in some words to produce initial [CC.. clusters.

Sino-Tibetan

Date, culture: 5,000/5,500 BCE; Yangshao
Agriculture: millet
Linguistic characteristics:
Nominalisation processes in PST

    [m-V: agent of V-ing
    [s-V   instrument of V-ing
    Vn]   patient of Ving
    [n.. / [..nV disappears (Laurent Sagart, email, 31/Jan/2001)

SINO-BODIC

Date, culture: 5,800 BCE; Yangshao
Agriculture: millet
Linguistic characteristics:
At the west end of the earlier STAN chain, ST split into Himalayo-Burman, at the far western end, and Sino-Bodic (see van Driem, this volume). Sino-Bodic divided into Sinitic, which initially occupied the centre of the Huang He area and then spread east and south, and the Tangut-Bodish subgroup.

Sinitic

Date, culture: 1,500 BCE
Agriculture: millet
Linguistic characteristics:
Nominalisation processes in OC (Sagart email 29/Jan/2001)

    ..s] suffixing   -s gives a kind of verbal noun, a gerund 'the V-ing'
    [s.. prefixing   s- gives a noun which is either an instrument, or a place, in short a circumstance of the action (Sagart 1999: 73)
    [m.. prefixing   m- gives an agentive noun 'V-er' (Sagart 1999: 84–5)
    ..n] suffixing   -n gives a name of patient 'thing V-ed'

From a typological point of view, OC was more similar to modern East Asian languages like Gyarong, Khmer or Atayal than to its daughter language MC: its morphemes were nontonal and not strictly monosyllabic; its morphology was essentially derivational, and largely prefixing; but it also made use of infixes and suffixes.

(Sagart 1999: 13)

The [CV_1CV_2C] [C' $_1C\emptyset_2C$] iambicisation that took place in Sino-Tibetan-Yangzian continued sporadically in Sinitic, in the middle of the Huang He speech community. The first unstressed vowel often disappears altogether: [C' $_1C\emptyset_2C$] [$CC\emptyset_2C$].. When a [$CC\emptyset_2$.. form coexisted with its [C' $_1C\emptyset_2$.. etymological source in the same dialect or in adjacent dialects, the result was doublets. Sagart hypothesises that all OC word-initial consonant clusters are morphologically complex (Sagart 1999: 21), and describes such doublets in terms of a difference in OC between 'fused' and 'loosely attached' prefixes (Sagart 1999: 15, 17–18). However, the idea of the morphological complexity of all [CC.. words is inconsistent with my scenario in which at least some [CC.. forms evolved from earlier monomorphemic [CVCVC] forms by vowel loss.

Proto-Sinitic was the source of the first three dynasties of Chinese legend and history: the Xia, Shang and Western and Eastern Zhou cultures. The earliest identifiable Chinese writing is found on oracle bones from the Shang dynasty, and the OC language reconstructed by linguists was the language of the Western Zhou dynasty. The Qiang nation at the western end of the Sinitic chain allied with the Zhou in overthrowing the earlier Shang dynasty. It acted as a buffer between Sinitic and the hostile peoples to the west, and after the chaotic Warring States period of the Eastern Zhou dynasty, the king of Qin, also a western state, conquered the entire Sinitic region and the Chu domains to the south and unified something like the modern China for the first time. The subsequent Han dynasty continued the expansion and unification. The subjugated HM peoples, who were by then speaking monosyllabic tone languages, acquired Chinese from the conquerors and adapted the iambic language to their own speech patterns. They reduced CvCVC and CCVC patterns to CVC and added lexical tone, with the choice of tone and syllable type ultimately determined by the (descendents of) initial and final consonants in PEA (Sagart 2001). The result of these drastic typological changes was MC, the language of the Nan-bei-chao period (c.500 CE), and one that finally 'looks Chinese'.

Tangut-Bodish   Tangut-Bodish moved further west up the Huang He river and divided into two subgroups. Bodish continued moving up the Huang He, while Tangut-Himalayan moved farther northwest and eventually established the Tangut (Xixia) kingdom. This kingdom developed its own writing system and lasted until the Mongol conquest. This same migration continued on through the Gansu Corridor along the future route of the Silk Road, turned south, and crossed the Karakoram Range into Kashmir, where it begat the Himalayan subgroup (cf. van Driem 1998). This Sino-Bodish subgroup occupied part of the southern region of the Himalayas between the previously occupied North Indian plain and Tibet. Bodish, the other branch of Tangut-Bodish, had in the meantime moved farther up the Huang He and into the Tibetan plateau, giving rise to Tibetan.

HIMALAYO-BURMAN

Date, culture: 6,500 BCE; Dadiwan
Agriculture: millet

Qiangic The other branch of ST, Himalayo-Burman, moved a bit farther up the Huang He to the Gansu area and gave rise to the Qiangic state, which was more or less contemporaneous with the Chinese Shang dynasty.[7] Qiang groups expanded into Sichuan, and Sanxingdui, which may have been the capital of the Shu state, had a bronze industry which greatly exceeded its Shang counterpart in technical sophistication and artistic creativity. The Qiang state later allied with the Zhou dynasty in overthrowing the Shang dynasty (Pulleyblank 1983: 422), and served as a buffer between the Zhou and hostile tribes farther west. It was eliminated from its northern domains by the westward expansion of the Western Zhou and finally defeated by the Chinese kingdom of Qin in 330 BCE. The Qiang language was the ancestor of the Qiangic branch of Himalayo-Burman, a group which differentiated and eventually spread southward through Sichuan and into Yunnan. Qiangic has been in intimate contact with Tibetan along its western flank from the beginning of the southward migration, and some Qiangic languages are spoken by ethnic Tibetans.

Kamarupan The Qiangic groups in Sichuan soon came under pressure from the Tibetans in the west and the expanding Han Chinese in the east. This gave rise to two further migrations, the southward movements of Kamarupans and Southern Himalayo-Burmans. The Kamarupan migration followed the 'Khasi Corridor' (Gérard Diffloth's term) into Assam and spread west along the Himalayas. They remained in the lower southern part of the Himalayas as they continued westward toward Nepal, possibly for their health and at least partly because the plains to the south and the Tibetan plateau to the north were already occupied by agriculturalists. They eventually met their long-lost Himalayan subgroup cousins moving across from the west through the same mountainous zone.

Southern Himalayo-Burman A second major southward migration moved into Yunnan and eventually into Southeast Asia. They brought the bronze expertise of Sanxingdui with them as far as Lake Dian in Yunnan. They were the technologically advanced helmeted drum-making horse-riding headhunting culture who erased all linguistic traces of the AA speakers who had arrived earlier via the Yangzi and settled in the Kunming area. The Himalayo-Burmans continued south, eliminating all the AA languages in China on their expansion into Southeast Asia, and in the process isolating Khasi in Assam, which thus became the only survivor of the previous MK languages in this region.

Part of the southern Himalayo-Burman group moved south as far as the Andaman Sea. The Karen spread into the Thai-Burmese border area and Lolo-Burmese-Naxi migrated down the Irrawaddy into Burma around 1,000 BC (van Driem 1998). The 'stay-at-homes' in the Yunnan–Northern Burma area evolved into the modern Kachinic group (Jingpho-Nungish-Luish).

Yangzian

At about the same time the Huang He languages were forming, the language chain along the Yangzi River, which I will refer to as Proto-Yangzian, took rice rather than millet as its agricultural staple. It differentiated into the ancestors of the upriver AA and downriver HM languages.

HMONG-MIEN

HM languages are now found scattered in mountainous pockets all across China from Yunnan and Guizhou in the southwest to north Guangdong in the east to Hainan Island in the southeast, and in northern Vietnam, Laos and Thailand. This remarkably broad and fragmented distribution is the result of a successful agriculture-powered expansion followed by being in the path of other people's successful expansions. The initial expansion occurred at the expense of the cord-markers and carried them through most of China south of the Yangzi. It culminated politically in the emergence of the powerful state of Chu (770–223 BC; cf. Pulleyblank 1983) during the Eastern Zhou dynasty. Chu expanded and rivaled its Sinitic northern neighbours in cultural development and political power and organisation.

> The extent of the ancient state of Chu should not be underestimated, nor should aspects of its culture. By the time of the Warring States period of the Eastern Zhou, from the fifth to the third century BC, the state of Chu occupied almost the entire southern half of the Chinese landmass.
>
> The Chu state then gradually expanded until it covered an area whose boundaries would today pass through the western province of Sichuan, the southern provinces of Yunnan, Guangxi and Guangdong, and as far north as Henan.
>
> (Yu 1996: 266)

This state may have had a primarily HM population with a Han (Zhou) governing class (Sagart 1999: 8), rather like the Norman-Saxon situation in Britain after the Norman conquest. After it came under the influence of the Zhou dynasty, it was subjected to the influence of the Chinese language via a Chinese-speaking political elite, and used the Chinese writing system.

Partly due to its advanced technology and political organisation, Chu overrode and absorbed the previous non-agricultural cord-marking groups in the areas into which it moved. Expansion of technologically less advanced HM groups beyond the Chu borders continued southward, westward and eastward, reaching the East China Sea in the east and the edge of the Tibetan Highlands in the west. On the east coast, the rise of the states of Wu and Yue followed the evolution of Chu. The Majiabang sites north of Hangzhou Bay were early HM sites. The Bai Yue, the 'hundred Yue' (Meacham 1996) of Chinese history, were primarily HM speakers the Han Chinese encountered and overwhelmed during their southward expansion. The populations overrun by the advancing HM may have been the pre-agricultural people (Negritos?) who were the makers of the earlier cord-marked pottery found in South China and Southeast Asia. They included the DPK culture, which reached Taiwan about 1500 years before the pre-Austronesians arrived.

When the HM started expanding in a westward direction, they put pressure on the other first-order subgroup of the Yangzian branch, the AA, who had been stay-at-home rice agriculturalists and herdsmen, and started them on their migration up the Yangzi. The advancing Qin armies subsequently destroyed the state of Chu (223 BC), and the other HMs farther south eventually succumbed to the advancing Han Chinese as well (though one group, called the Mountain Yao, continued to resist until well into the Tang dynasty). Eventually only scattered groups in remote areas across the old HM domain have continued to maintain their languages and separate identity up until the present.

Intimate contact with the cord-marking groups made a strong typological impression on the advancing HMs. As the HM language(s) expanded throughout southern China, they underwent a major typological shift, evolving a comparatively monosyllabic word form canon (morphologically simple single-syllable words, no consonant clusters, and lexical tones). At the beginning of the HM southward expansion, OC was still a morphologically complex AA-type language. Then HM became monosyllabic and tonal. After China was unified under the Qin dynasty in 221 BC, large linguistically diverse areas of southern China were absorbed, including almost all of the former HM areas. Many HM groups scattered southwest and southeast out of the path of the expanding Qin and Han, but the Chu state and other materially advanced HM areas were absorbed into the Sinosphere. The strong HM substratum underlying a relatively thin Chinese layer influenced Chinese to change into a similar monosyllabic tonal form, MC.

AUSTRO-ASIATIC

Date, culture: 4,000 BCE; Yangzi, Kunming
Agriculture: rice

Subsequent to the HM expansion and possibly as a partial result of it, the AA language, the other first-order branch of Yangzian, moved west up the Yangzi River toward the Yunnan Plateau, bringing rice agriculture to this area.

Here it initially prospered and spread southward along the Mekong and other rivers southeast and south, occupying most of Laos. Other groups crossed several major watersheds into northern Burma and Assam via the 'Khasi Corridor' (G. Diffloth, course notes 1996[8]) or the Cachar Hills Zone (van Driem 1998) or the 'Burma Road' of Second World War fame. From Assam, the pre-Mundas followed the Brahmaputra River into the northeast Indian plain, leaving behind the Khasis in Assam and acquiring many of the characteristic South Asian phonological and grammatical features from the previous Dravidian residents. All the remaining AA speakers other than the Munda are the ancestors of the modern MK languages.

A southeastern MK group, Pre-Proto-eastern MK, moved further down the Mekong River to the Vietnam-Cambodia-Laos border area and split into five subgroups to occupy Cambodia and Vietnam. The Vietic subgroup crossed the Truong Mountains eastward to the South China Sea and then northward, displacing the coastal Tai (AAK) languages which had moved down the eastern seaboard from the north, as well as some of the inland Tai languages. A third group, Pre-Proto-southern MK, moved down the Salween River to the Andaman Sea, central Thailand, and the Malay Peninsula. An earlier cord-marking population in the peninsula adopted a southern MK language, and their descendants constitute the Senoi Negrito group. Two subgroups of southern MK, the Mons in Thailand and the Aslians in the Malay Peninsula, developed seafaring abilities and colonised the Nicobar Islands, northeastern Sumatra and the inland western part of Borneo, where they later formed substrata for the AN migrations through Indonesia. The remaining AA 'stay-at-home' languages form the Northern MK group, which by my scenario should not constitute a subgroup in the comparative linguistic sense.

Austro-Asiatic speakers no longer exist in the original Yunnan heartland. They obstructed the later Himalayo-Burman southward movement from Sichuan. In Yunnan, they engaged in prolonged warfare with the technologically more advanced TB Dian culture and were defeated and eliminated. This was also the fate of the other AA languages that intervened between the southward-moving TBs and the Andaman Sea, and any that may have been left would have been mopped up by the subsequent Han Chinese advances. Only the Khasis in Assam were far enough west to be spared.

Austric

In my scenario, there was no Austric family composed solely of AN and AA. There is some agreement that the two languages are quite distantly related (cf. Shorto 1976 and Diffloth 1994), but there is a growing consensus in that any real shared lexical and morphological elements between these families must go all the way back to their closest common ancestor, PEA ('Macro-Austric': Schiller 1987; Diffloth 1996: 3), and are frequently shared with TB as well. My PEA is essentially a kind of 'macro-Austric', so the additional Austric node is unnecessary. An Austric node has also not been properly supported in modern work by Hayes and Reid.

Hayes' lexical reconstruction work (Hayes 1992, 1997, 1999) uses a new method of his own devising which is almost a parody of Paul Benedict's almost-paradox of the comparative method. It is arbitrary and unconstrained and thus has no empirical content, and so will not be further considered here. Reid's approach to Austric suffers from similar failings. I will not detail all of them, but just raise basic questions connected with subgrouping and reconstruction methodology and practice.

A lexical item or grammatical feature is reconstructible at the proto-level only if it has reflexes in two of the first-order subgroups of a given proto-language. According to this principle, a morphological reconstruction of Proto-Austric requires that the form in question be present in both of the first-order subgroups of Proto-Austric, that is, PAA and PAN. This in turn requires that the form be present in two or more first-order subgroups of PAA and in two or more first-order subgroups of PAN respectively. A justification of Austric should thus minimally tell us what first-order subgroups are being assumed, and then demonstrate that the forms being used as evidence have reflexes in all four relevant first-order subgroups. Reid doesn't do this. As far as I can determine, the question of subgrouping is not directly addressed at all in any of the three recent articles or papers (Reid 1994, 1999, 2001) he has presented on the subject. What can we say about the AN-looking PAA reconstructions that are listed bravely in the same format as the reconstructed AN morphemes, but without any indication of where they come from? I think it is fair to say that they are not reconstructions but rather fabrications. In accordance with the comparative method, each of them should have a reflex in Proto-Munda and a reflex in Proto-Mon-Khmer, but none of them satisfies this requirement, if for no other reason than the fact that no morphological reconstruction has yet been done on MK (Diffloth, p.c.). It seems that both Hayes and Reid start off with Austric as a given, and then create the reconstructions and methodology it will take to produce that desired result.

On the AN side, the subgrouping question is different but equally serious. As with Austric, the question of what first-order subgroups in PAN were being assumed was not answered directly. What we do know is that (1) Reid is using Blust's PMP and PAN reconstructions, (2) that these reconstructions were based on Blust's claim that PMP is a first-order subgroup of PAN and (3) that Reid himself does not accept the claim that PMP is a first-order subgroup of PAN (Reid 1982: 213). Thus the PAN reconstructions he uses are, by his own criteria, incoherent.

Austronesian Ancestor of Kadai, Kadai

Date, culture: 2,500 BCE? 800–400 BCE (Weera Ostapirat, p.c. 2001)
Agriculture: rice
Linguistic characteristics:
AN disyllabic words (reduce or) lose initial syllables and acquire tone under influence of the HM language with which they are in intimate contact.

AAK was the first AN language to leave Taiwan. It moved to the EA mainland, first to Hainan, then to the coastal areas of north Vietnam north to Guangdong.

It spread into areas occupied previously by CMs, and expanded inland along the Xi ('West'; 'Pearl') River. The resulting language, Proto-Kadai, formed a dialect chain through Lingnan, from Hainan to the Guangxi-Guizhou-Hunan triangle, the area of greatest diversity (Edmondson and Solnit 1988: 15), before breaking up into the modern Tai-Kadai languages. The Tai subgroup eventually expanded as far as Assam in the west and the Malay Peninsula in the south.

During its initial Hainan phase and inland expansion, the Kadai language and its descendants absorbed and merged with the CM languages already present, forming a creole that at one point occupied most of southeast China. The creole was radically relexified from CM sources, and adapted phonologically to their canonical 'monosyllabic' form. Proto-Kadai and its descendants were thus Malayo-Polynesian languages with a major CM substratum and extensive relexification. Original AN disyllabic words were replaced with CM words or forced into the CM pattern, with the first syllables reduced and either lost or fusing into consonant clusters with the initial consonant of the second syllable. All the original AN words were assigned tones in accordance with the canonical patterns of the new HM substratum.

Austronesian and Nicobarese

I will not go through the post-MP AN migrations in detail, but two are relevant to the overall language picture on the Asian mainland. As the Austronesians moved south from the Philippines, one tendency was a migration west along the north coasts of Borneo and Sumatra. These islands were at that time already at least partly inhabited by southern MK migrants from the Mon and Aslian areas. The two families interacted fairly closely in Borneo (Adelaar 1995)[9] and in Sumatra, where the AN speakers settled the northwest end and acquired a substantial phonological substratum in the process.

From Sumatra, one branch of the migration moved up the Indo-China Peninsula, moving inland in Vietnam and eventually establishing the Cham kingdom (Thurgood 1999). This became a further source (in addition to AAK) of lexical and grammatical loans into MK languages on the peninsula as far west as Cambodia and as far north as the Chinese border. The second migration went around to the other side of the Malay peninsula. It was a coastal trading-raiding-farming-fishing shuttle which interacted with MK speakers on the Malay Peninsula and the Nicobar Islands, leaving lasting linguistic traces in both areas. A subsequent migration route from Borneo went beyond this one, continuing on around the coast of the Indian Ocean to Africa to settle Madagascar and give rise to Malagasy.

Conclusion

The scenario I propose here is almost certainly wrong in a number of points. Its potential utility is in helping to focus scholars' efforts on particular specific questions, resulting in the replacement of parts of this hypothesis with better supported arguments.

Abbreviations

AAK   Austronesian Ancestor of Kadai
CM   Cord-Marker
DPK   Dapenkeng
EA   East Asian
HM   Hmong-Mien
MC   Middle Chinese
MK   Mon-Khmer
OC   Old Chinese
PAA   Proto-Austro-Asiatic
PAN   Proto-Austronesian
PEA   Proto-East Asian
PMP   Proto-Malayo-Polynesian
PST   Proto-Sino-Tibetan
PSTY Proto-Sino-Tibetan-Yangzian
SPQR Starosta, Pawley and Reid (1981)
ST   Sino-Tibetan
STAN Sino-Tibetan-Austronesian

Notes

1 Stanley Starosta passed away on 18 July 2002. This version of his paper was received on 6 July only twelve days before his death. Since unfortunately Starosta could not interact with the editor of his paper, L. Sagart, during the editing process, Starosta's paper is presented here accompanied with a number of editor's notes; endnotes not marked as '[editor's note]' are Starosta's own.
2 Passages cited from Sagart's emails contain ideas and conjectures put to Starosta for discussion. They do not always represent Sagart's current understanding of the grammatical evolution of EA languages [editor's note].
3 The modified version of Sagart's Périgueux paper published as Chapter 9 of this volume lists 61 such comparisons [editor's note].
4 When he wrote this passage, Starosta could not have known that carbonised millet grains in large quantities, along with shell reaping knives and stone adzes, would soon be discovered at Nan-kuan-li East, a DPK site in Taiwan, in the course of excavations conducted September 2002–March 2003 (Tsang Cheng-hwa, Chapter 4, this volume; see Plates II, III and V). This discovery virtually leaves no doubt that the DPK people were Neolithic in the agricultural sense of the term [editor's note].
5 Starosta is referring here to statements such as 'It is likely that the Austronesian homeland included portions of southern China' in the abstract of Blust's 1999 paper [editor's note].
6 This name has been proposed by Laurent Sagart. The idea that there was such a back-migration was to my knowledge first advanced by Sagart in 1997 or before. See Sagart's paper 'Tai-Kadai as a subgroup of Austronesian' (Chapter 10, this volume).
7 Information on Qiangic is based primarily on Sun Hongkai (2001).
8 Notes of a course given by G. Diffloth at Academia Sinica in 1995–96, Taiwan, which Stanley Starosta attended [editor's note].
9 In this article, Adelaar points out a small number of striking lexical similarities between Land Dayak and the Aslian languages, proposing that they are the result of language

shift: either Aslian speakers shifting to Land Dayak in Borneo, or speakers of an unidentified language shifting to Aslian in Malaysia and to Land Dayak in Borneo [editor's note].

Bibliography

Adelaar, K.A. (1995) 'Borneo as a Cross-roads for Comparative Austronesian Linguistics', in P. Bellwood, J.J. Fox and D. Tryon (eds) The Austronesians: Historical and Comparative Perspectives, Canberra: Department of Anthropology, Research School of Pacific and Asian Studies, Australian National University.

Bellwood, P. (1995) 'Austronesian prehistory in Southeast Asia: homeland, exodus and transformation', in P. Bellwood, J.J. Fox and D. Tryon (eds) The Austronesians: Historical and Comparative Perspectives, Canberra: Department of Anthropology, Research School of Pacific and Asian Studies, Australian National University.

Blust, R.A. (1999) 'Subgrouping, circularity and extinction: some issues in Austronesian comparative linguistics', in E. Zeitoun and P.J.-K. Li (eds) Selected papers from the Eighth International Conference on Austronesian Linguistics, Taipei: Institute of Linguistics, Academia Sinica.

Diffloth, G. (1994) 'The lexical evidence for Austric, so far', Oceanic Linguistics 33.2: 309–2.

—— (1996) An Introduction to Comparative Mon-Khmer, notes of a course given by G. Diffloth at Academia Sinica, recorded by Stanley Starosta.

van Driem, G. (1998) 'Neolithic correlates of ancient Tibeto-Burman migrations', in R.M. Blench and M. Spriggs (eds) Archaeology and Language II, London: Routledge.

Edmondson, J. and Solnit, D.B. (1988) Comparative Kadai: Linguistic Studies Beyond Tai, Arlington: Summer Institute of Linguistics and the University of Texas at Arlington.

Hayes, L.V. (1992) 'On the track of Austric: Part I. Introduction', Mon-Khmer Studies 21: 143–177.

—— (1997) 'On the Track of Austric, Part II. Consonant mutation in early Austroasiatic', Mon-Khmer Studies 27: 13–44.

—— (1999) 'On the track of Austric: Part III. Basic vocabulary comparison', Mon-Khmer Studies 29: 1–34.

Meacham, W. (1996) 'Defining the hundred Yue', Bulletin of the Indo-Pacific Prehistory Association 15: 93–100.

Pulleyblank, E.G. (1983) 'The Chinese and Their Neighbors in Prehistoric and Early Historic Times', in D.N. Keightley (ed.) The Origins of Chinese Civilization, Berkeley, Los Angeles, London: University of California Press.

Reid, L.A. (1982) 'The Demise of Proto-Philippines', in A. Halim, L. Carrington and S.A. Wurm (eds) Papers from the Third International Conference on Austronesian Linguistics, vol. 2: Tracking the Travelers; Pacific Linguistics C-75, Canberra: Research School of Pacific Studies, The Australian National University.

—— (1985) 'Some Proto-Austro-Tai morphology', Paper presented to the 18th Sino-Tibetan Conference, Bangkok, August 1985.

—— (1988) 'Benedict's Austro-Tai Hypothesis–An Evaluation', Asian Perspectives 26.1: 19–34.

—— (1994) 'Morphological evidence for Austric', Oceanic Linguistics 33, 2: 323–44.

—— (1996) 'The current state of linguistic research on the relatedness of the language families of East and Southeast Asia', Bulletin of the Indo-Pacific Prehistory Association 15: 87–91.

—— (1999) 'New linguistic evidence for the Austric hypothesis', in E. Zeitoun and P.J.-K. Li (eds) Selected Papers from the Eighth International Conference on Austronesian Linguistics, Taipei: Institute of Linguistics (Preparatory Office), Academia Sinica.

Sagart, L. (1999) The Roots of Old Chinese, Amsterdam/Philadelphia: John Benjamins.

—— (2001) 'Connections across the south Pacific: a personal synthesis', Paper presented at Pacific Neighborhood Consortium Conference, Hong Kong, January 2001.

Schiller, E. (1987) 'Which way did they grow? (Morphology and the Austro-Tai/(Macro)-Austric debate)', Proceedings of the 13th Annual Meeting of the Berkeley Linguistic Society, 235–46.

Shorto, H.L. (1976) 'In Defense of Austric', Computational Analyses of Asian and African languages 6: 95–104.

Starosta, S. (1995) 'A grammatical subgrouping of Formosan languages', in P.J.-K. Li, D.-A. Ho, Y.-K. Huang, C.-H. Tsang and C.-Y. Tseng (eds) Austronesian Studies Relating to Taiwan, Symposium series of the Institute of History and Philology, Academia Sinica, no. 3, Taipei: Academia Sinica.

Starosta, S., Pawley, A. and Reid, L. (1981) The Evolution of Focus in Austronesian, unpublished manuscript. [A reduced version of this paper was published as 'The evolution of Focus in Austronesian', in A. Halim, L. Carrington and S.A. Wurm (eds) Papers from the Third International Conference on Austronesian Linguistics, vol. 2, 145–70. Pacific Linguistics, C-75 (1982).]

Sun, H.-K. (2001) 'Lun Zang-Mian yuzu zhong de Qiang yuzhi yuyan', Language and Linguistics 2, 1: 157–80.

Thurgood, G. (1999) From Ancient Cham to Modern Dialects: Two Thousand Years of Language Contact and Change, Oceanic Linguistics Special Publication, No. 28, Honolulu: University of Hawai'i Press.

Yu, W. (1996) 'The State of Chu', in J. Rawson (ed.) Mysteries of Ancient China, New Discoveries from the Early Dynasties, 266–68, London: British Museum, and New York: George Braziller.

Part III

GENETICS AND PHYSICAL ANTHROPOLOGY

12

THE PHYSICAL ANTHROPOLOGY OF THE PACIFIC, EAST ASIA AND SOUTHEAST ASIA

A multivariate craniometric analysis

Michael Pietrusewsky

Introduction

Physical anthropology has made substantial contributions to understanding the biological relationships and origins of the people who occupy Oceania (including Australasia), and the neighbouring continental landmass of East Asia and Southeast Asia. This corpus of biological data, too numerous to review in a single chapter, includes measurements and somatological studies of living people, genetic studies beginning with traditional blood group antigen marker data, and more recently, molecular genetic evidence such as mtDNA and Y-chromosome data. Another source of biological data is that provided by the human skeletal record, both ancient and modern. It is this latter evidence, specifically measurements recorded in the skulls of modern and near-modern indigenous inhabitants of Oceania, East Asia and Southeast Asia, that is the focus of this chapter.

Although an overstatement and recently criticised by Terrell et al. (2001), two great human colonisations of the Pacific continue to provide a baseline for expectations regarding the biology and prehistory (including historical reconstructions of language) of the inhabitants of this vast geographical expanse. The first major colonisation event coincides with the human crossing of Wallacea during late Pleistocene times (c.45,000 BP), an event which ultimately led to the peopling of the Sahul and surrounding islands extending as far as the Bismarck Archipelago and Solomon Islands, an area popularly referred to as Near Oceania (Green 1991). A second, much later colonisation event, beginning approximately 3,500 BP has been linked with the dispersal of people speaking AN languages, people whose descendants now inhabit a region that extends from Madagascar to Easter Island. The evidence for this second major colonisation event has been linked with the Lapita cultural complex, which is associated with the presumed immediate ancestors of the Polynesians and other inhabitants of Remote Oceania (see e.g. Green 1979; Kirch 1997).

While biological, historical linguistic and archaeological evidence suggests that the ancestors of both great epochs of colonisation are primarily of Asiatic origin, the timing and sequence of events associated with these human dispersals, especially the peopling of Remote Oceania and Polynesia, have been controversial topics for much of the past century. While somewhat simplified, two polar views [recently summarised by Merriwether et al. (1999)] continue to guide current research into the origins of the Polynesian and related descendants of AN-speaking peoples. The first of these, the 'Out of Asia' hypothesis (Bellwood 1985: 250–3; Bellwood 1997), proposes a relatively rapid expansion of the ancestors of Polynesians out of Southeast Asia beginning approximately 3,500 BP. Evidence from archaeology (Bellwood et al. 1995; Green 1997; Kirch 1997; Spriggs 1997), historical linguistics (e.g. Pawley and Green 1973; Pawley and Ross 1993, 1995) and biological anthropology (Brace and Hunt 1990; Brace et al. 1990; Howells 1990; Pietrusewsky 1990a,b, 1994, 1996a,b, 1997a,b, 1999, 2000; Turner 1990) have been used to support this scenario. An alternative view, the so-called 'Indigenous Melanesian Origin', argues for an in situ derivation of the ancestors of the Polynesians from people living in island Melanesia during a comparable time period (Allen 1984; White et al. 1988). The 'Voyaging Corridor' model, drawn primarily through a different interpretation of the archaeological record, proposes essentially the same in situ derivation within Melanesia (Terrell 1986, 1989; Terrell and Welsch 1997).

Merriwether et al. (1999), using the mtDNA 9-bp deletion variant, found no support for an indigenous Melanesian origin for the ancestors of the Polynesians. Their study also focussed attention on the vastly heterogenous populations of island Melanesia. Similar analyses using mtDNA, HLA, human Y chromosome and other molecular genetic variants have reached similar conclusions (e.g. Hagelberg 1998; Hagelberg et al. 1999; Lin et al. 1999; Lum and Cann 1998; Lum et al. 1998; Melton et al. 1995; Redd et al. 1995; Richards et al. 1998; Su et al. 2000).

Recent advances in our knowledge of East and Southeast Asian prehistory and the expansion of language families for the region, centred on rice domestication and the development of agriculture, have provided new archaeological and linguistic perspectives on evolution of human society in Southeast Asia and East Asia. Many archaeologists (e.g. Bellwood 1996; Glover and Higham 1996; Higham 1996, 2001) now argue against both the in situ agricultural development and diffusion of agricultural technology to the indigenous hunter-gathering populations in late Pleistocene Southeast Asia in favour of an agricultural colonisation model. This view has also received support, as well as added insights from linguistics (e.g. Bayard 1996; Bellwood 1993; Blust 1996). Physical anthropologists have advanced similar, although opposing, scenarios. For example, Turner (1987, 1989, 1990) using dental non-metric traits, has proposed that Southeast Asia was the ultimate source, rather than the recipient, of a 'southern Mongoloid' (Sundadont) population that ultimately spread northward to give rise to a 'northern Mongoloid' (Sinodont) dental complex.

Physical anthropology, especially studies of human skeletal remains that span the transition from hunting and gathering to agriculture in Southeast Asia, as well as studies of living people and modern and near-modern skeletal assemblages, should help demonstrate whether the indigenous peoples of Southeast Asia were displaced by later colonists or if population continuity, characterised by a common genetic heritage of people, bridged the technological and social transition in this region. Alternatively, the evidence from physical anthropology may require a more complex scenario.

Previous multivariate craniometric studies by Pietrusewsky (1990a,b, 1994, 1996a,b, 1997a,b, 1999, 2000), which have examined variation in East and Southeast Asian cranial series, have demonstrated internal differentiation as well as broad external patterning reflecting historical–biological relationships and past migrations. For example, while cranial series from Southeast Asia, East Asia and North Asia ultimately group into a single major constellation, there are also provocative connections between island Southeast Asia and Remote Oceania. Likewise, connections between mainland and island Southeast Asia, between Bronze-age Chinese and Hainan Island and Taiwan (including Taiwan Aboriginal series) were found. These connections may reflect earlier exchanges between peoples, cultures and languages of these regions.

The primary focus of this study is to investigate, using craniometric data, the historical–biological relationships of Asian and Pacific peoples. Comparisons of these results with those based on genetic, archaeological and historical linguistic data will be used to evaluate some of the competing hypotheses that relate to the settlement and colonisation of the Pacific and the biological connections within the Asian continent that may inform on population movements in this region of world. This new craniometric analysis, which focuses on more near-contemporaneous cranial samples, expands on earlier recent work (e.g. Pietrusewsky, 1990a,b, 1994, 1995, 1996a, 1997a,b, 1999, 2000) by including new or seldom used cranial series (e.g. Burma, Gambier Islands, Loyalty Islands, New Caledonia, Santa Cruz Islands, Solomon Islands, Dawson Strait Islands, etc.). Not included in this new study are prehistoric cranial series (e.g. Jomon, Yayoi, Kofun, Anyang, etc.) used in earlier analyses.

Crania and biodistance studies

The use of craniometric data for understanding biological relatedness and evolution of human populations has a long history in physical anthropology. The earliest studies, modelled primarily on racial typological classifications, failed to achieve their predicted goal primarily because of flawed theory and unrefined methodology. Improvements in statistical method, especially the development of multivariate statistical procedures (Mahalanobis 1936; Mahalanobis et al. 1949; Rao 1948), provided a much more objective means for comparing human groups and for classifying individual specimens (Howells 1973, 1989, 1995). Likewise, breakthroughs in evolutionary and population biology theory provided a much sounder basis for understanding human population structure and past biological relationships.

Measurements, especially cranial measurements, continue to be an important and valuable source of information for examining relatedness between and within populations, past and present (e.g. Howells 1973, 1989, 1995; Pietrusewsky 2000; van Vark and Howells 1984). The continued interest in metric variation is the result of the precision and repeatability of measurement techniques, the conservative nature of continuous variation, the direct link with the past, the demonstration that craniometric traits have a genetic component (e.g. Droessler 1981; Kohn 1991; Sjøvold 1984), and the amenability of measurements to multivariate statistical procedures.

While morphological variation, including craniometric variation, is subject to non-genetic, or environmental influences, this category of variation is generally viewed as reflecting genetic similarity and provides the basis for biodistance studies (Buikstra et al. 1990; Larsen 1997: 302–32). Concordance in results based on anthropometric and quantitative genetic analyses strengthens this assertion (Konigsberg and Ousley 1995), which allows distances based on metric data to be interpreted within a population genetic framework.

Material and methods

Cranial series

A total of 2,805 male crania representing 63 cranial series are included in this study (Appendix, Map 12.1). The cranial series represent modern and near-modern indigenous inhabitants of Remote Oceania (Polynesia, Micronesia, island eastern Melanesia), Near Oceania (New Guinea, Bismarck Archipelago, Solomon Islands), Australia, island Southeast Asia, mainland Southeast Asia, East Asia and North Asia. The samples, including their sizes and other details, are given in the Appendix to this chapter. Although the language spoken by the once living individuals represented in these cranial series cannot be determined, the cranial series do coincide with groups of people whose ethnographic and linguistic affiliations are well-known.

Cranial measurements

Twenty-seven standard measurements (see note 3 in the Appendix) of the cranial vault and face, the largest number of measurements comparable to all the series, are used in the present study. The methods used to record these cranial measurements primarily follow those of Martin and Saller (1957) and Howells (1973).

Multivariate statistical procedures

Two multivariate statistical procedures, step-wise discriminant function analysis and Mahalanobis' generalised distance statistic (Mahalanobis D^2), are applied to the cranial measurements. These methods and the clustering algorithm used to

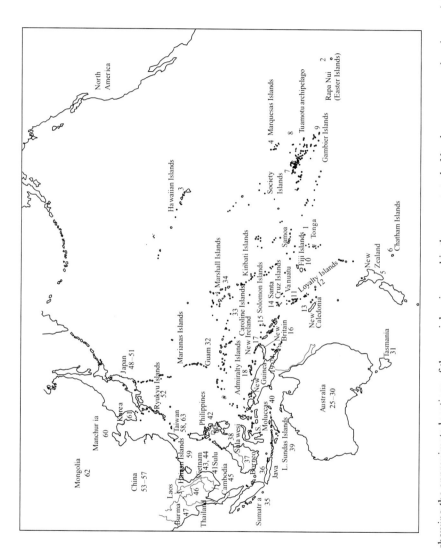

Map 12.1 Map showing the approximate locations of the cranial series used in the present study. Numbers correspond to the cranial series listed in the Appendix to this chapter.

construct the diagram of relationships (dendrograms) are explained in Pietrusewsky (1994, 1997b, 1999, 2000).

Results

Stepwise discriminant function analysis

Stepwise discriminant function analysis was applied to 27 cranial measurements recorded in 63 male cranial series using the computer programme, BMDP-7M (Dixon 1992), written for the mainframe computer. Because of space limitation, tables ordinarily used to summarise these results are not presented.

A summary of the measurements, ranked according to the F-values (tests of equality of group means using classical one-way ANOVA) received in the final step of discriminant function analysis provides an indication of the discriminatory power of the original variables. Among the variables that are ranked the highest (i.e. they contribute the most to the discrimination produced) in this analysis are three breadth measurements (maximum cranial breadth, biorbital breadth and minimum cranial breadth), and basion-nasion length and nasion-alveolare length.

Eigenvalues, which represent the amount of variance accounted for by each function or canonical variate, expressed as the percentage of total dispersion, and level of significance (Rao 1952: 323) for the 29 canonical variates (table not shown) indicate that the first three canonical variates account for 63.7 per cent of the total variation. All eigenvalues are significant at the 1 per cent level, indicating significant heterogeneity for these functions.

Canonical coefficients, those values by which an individual's measurements may be multiplied to obtain its score, for 27 measurements, for the first three canonical variates (table not shown) indicate that biorbital breadth, nasion-alveolare height, nasal height and basion-prosthion length (those variables with the highest coefficients regardless of sign) are the most important variables in producing group separation in the first canonical variate. This first variate may, therefore, be defined as a biorbital breadth, facial and nasal height, and cranial basal length discriminator. Minimum cranial breadth, orbital height, alveolar breadth, nasal height and nasal breadth are most responsible for group separation produced in the second canonical variate. Maximum cranial length, orbital breadth, nasal height and bijugal breadth are primarily responsible for the discrimination produced in the third canonical variate.

A summary of the group classification results (table is not shown), regular and jackknifed, indicate that Mongolia, Swanport (Australia), Chatham Island, Rapa Nui (Easter Island), Guam, Dawson Strait, Ainu, Tasmania and Western Australia are among the series having the best classification results (i.e. more than 57 per cent of the cases are correctly assigned to their original group). The poorest jackknifed classification results (less than 20 per cent of the cases correctly classified to their original group) are found for the Solomon Island, Lesser Sunda Island, New Ireland, Hangzhou, Sulawesi, Hainan Island, Nanjing, Borneo, Sumatra,

Shanghai and Fiji Islands series. Four of the latter series represent Chinese samples and four more represent island Southeast Asian series.

Closer inspection of some of the jackknifed classification results (table not shown) for 63 groups reveals where the most frequent misclassifications occur for each group. For example, only three of the 49 crania originally assigned to the Solomon Islands are reassigned to this series, the remaining 'misclassifications' for this series are to cranial series from island Melanesia. Four of the island Southeast Asian series, Lesser Sunda Islands, Sulawesi, Borneo and Sumatra, also have high misclassifications, most of these being to other cranial series from Southeast Asia. The Lesser Sunda Islands crania are misclassified to the greatest number (32) of groups. Six of the crania originally assigned to the Lesser Sunda Islands series are reclassified to New Zealand and Tonga-Samoa and four are reclassified as Solomon Islands and New Britain. New Ireland, Solomon Islands, Sumatra and southern Moluccas each have reclassifications to 25 or more groups in this analysis. Misclassifications for the southern Molucca Islands' crania are further noteworthy since at least 14 of these cases are reclassified to Polynesian series (e.g. Marquesas, New Zealand and Hawaii) and at least 17 more are reassigned to Melanesian and New Guinea series.

Turning to other groups, six of original 29 crania originally assigned to Vietnam are reclassified as Philippines, four as Atayal, and four more as Ryukyu Islands. A quarter (4/16) of the crania from Burma are reclassified to that same group, three to Cambodia-Laos, and four more to one of the island Southeast Asian cranial series. Likewise, 4/64 of the Ryukyu Island crania are reclassified as Vietnam, five as Ainu, three as Taiwan Chinese, and two as Atayal. Almost half of the Taiwan Chinese specimens are misclassified, including three each to Hainan Island and Korea and seven to Southeast Asian series. Only six of the Hainan Island crania are reclassified to their original group. Six more Hainan specimens are misclassified as Korea, four each are misclassified as Burma, Ryukyu Islands and Taiwan, and three are classified as Thailand. Five of the specimens assigned to Korea are reclassified as Hainan Island and six more as modern Japanese. Unexpectedly, four of the 36 Atayal specimens are reclassified as Dawson Strait, a group of islands located between Normanby and Fergusson Islands of the D'Entrecasteaux group of islands off the southeastern tip of New Guinea, and at least ten more are reassigned to modern Japanese, Korean, or Ainu series. Two of the Dawson Straits crania are reclassified as Atayal and two more as southern Moluccas.

These classification results serve to highlight those regions (e.g. Solomon Islands, Lesser Sundas Island, southern Moluccas, Vietnam, Taiwan and Hainan Islands) exhibiting the greatest heterogeneity and possibly where contact with outsiders was the most intense or long-term.

When the 63 group means are plotted on the first two canonical variates (Figure 12.1), three separate clusters are apparent. Cranial series from Australia, New Guinea and geographical Melanesia form one of these general clusters. There is little overlap between the Australian and Melanesian series within this

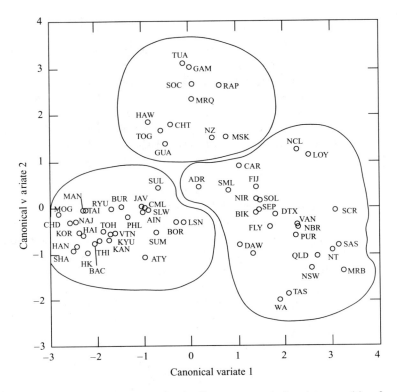

Figure 12.1 Plot of 63 group means on the first two canonical variates resulting from the application of stepwise discriminant function analysis.

cluster. The Polynesian cranial series and those from Guam and the Marshall-Kiribati Islands form a second isolated constellation. The remaining groups, representing cranial series from eastern and northern Asia, and mainland and island Southeast Asia form a relatively dense third grouping. The cranial series representing the southern Moluccas and Caroline Islands are peripheral members of the greater Melanesian–Australian grouping.

To facilitate the viewing of the group means on the first three canonical variates, the groups have been divided, more or less evenly, into two diagrams (Figures 12.2 and 12.3). Atayal is included in both plots for continuity. The Polynesian and two Micronesian cranial series are well separated from the Australian and Melanesian samples in Figure 12.2. The Admiralty Island, Marshall-Kiribati and Caroline cranial series occupy intermediate positions between these two major groupings. Island and mainland Southeast Asian cranial series form a relatively distinct grouping in Figure 12.3. Chinese, Japanese, Manchuria and Korea cranial series, including the Ainu, form another. The cranial series from Mongolia is the most isolated series.

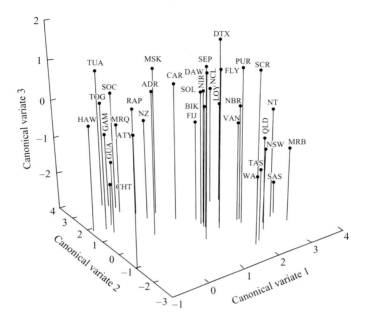

Figure 12.2 Plot of the first 35 groups on the first three canonical variates resulting from the application of stepwise discriminant function analysis.

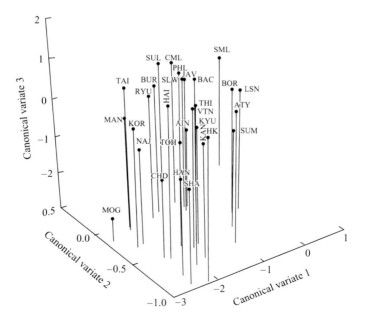

Figure 12.3 Plot of the last 28 groups on the first three canonical variates resulting from the application of stepwise discriminant function analysis.

Mahalanobis' generalised distance – D^2

Mahalanobis' generalised distance statistic was applied to the same measurements used in stepwise discriminant function analysis. Applying the UPGMA clustering algorithm to these distances results in the dendrogram shown in Figure 12.4. Two major divisions are evident in this diagram of relationship, the first includes

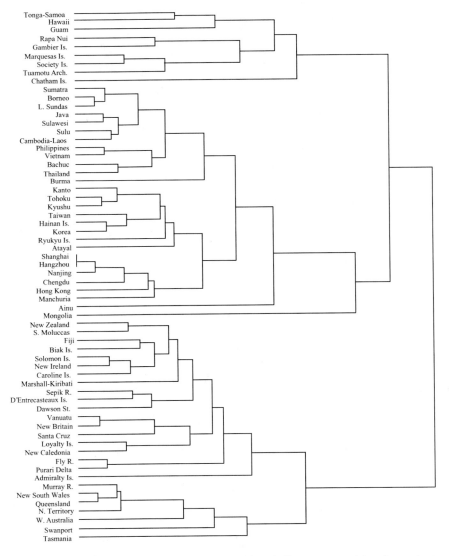

Figure 12.4 Dendrogram showing the relationship of 63 groups resulting from cluster analysis (UPGMA) of Mahalanobis' D^2.

all Asian (North, East and Southeast Asia) and Polynesian cranial series and the second includes all Australian, Tasmanian, New Guinea and Melanesian cranial series.

The majority of the Polynesian cranial series and Guam form a distinct cluster which ultimately connects to one containing East Asian, North Asian and Southeast Asian cranial series. Rather unexpectedly, the New Zealand Maori and southern Moluccas cranial series are grouped together outside the Asian branch forming a loose association with three Melanesian (Fiji, Solomon Islands, and New Ireland) series, a single north coastal New Guinea series (Biak Islands) and two Micronesian cranial series (Caroline Islands and Marshall-Kiribati Islands).

The cranial samples representing Southeast Asia occupy two separate clusters, representing primarily mainland and island Southeast Asian series. The cranial series representing modern Japanese align with Taiwan and Hainan Island Chinese, Korea, and more remotely with the Ryukyu Islands and Atayal (Taiwan Aboriginal) series. The remaining series representing China and Manchuria occupy a separate branch. The Ainu and Mongolian series are the last two series to connect with this exclusively Asian complex which comprises the cranial series from northern, eastern, and Southeast Asia.

The groups having the smallest distances when compared to Polynesian cranial series include a number of island Southeast Asian series (e.g. Lesser Sunda Islands, Sulawesi, Sulu Archipelago and Borneo).The Caroline Islands and Marshall-Kiribati Islands series show affinities with one another and to New Zealand, Marquesas, several Melanesian series and the southern Moluccas. The cranial series from the southern Moluccas, followed by Marquesas, Marshall-Kiribati, Solomon Islands, Caroline Islands, New Ireland and Biak Island are among the groups closest to the New Zealand Maori series.

Inspection of the smallest distances for the island Melanesia and New Guinea series reveals that the majority of these are cranial series from the same geographic region. The cranial series from neighbouring regions of island Melanesia and Australia are generally closest to those from island Melanesia. The distances closest to the Australian series include other Australian/Tasmanian series followed by the Bismarck Archipelago series (e.g. New Britain) and those from island Melanesia (e.g. Vanuatu, Santa Cruz). One series from geographical Melanesia, Admiralty Island, is closest to the southern Moluccas series and several other island Southeast Asian series including Borneo, Sulu and Lesser Sunda Islands.

With the exception of the southern Moluccas series, the cranial series closest to the island and mainland Southeast Asian series are generally from Southeast Asia. Korea is generally among the top ten closest groups to the Japanese and Chinese series. Although not significant, Korea is closest to the Hainan Island series. Other groups closest to Hainan Island include Taiwan Chinese, two Vietnamese series, Thailand and the Ryukyu Islands.

The groups found to be closest to the Ainu cranial series include several modern Japanese followed by the Ryukyu Islanders and several island Southeast Asian series. Distances closest to the Ryukyu Islands include Vietnam, Kyushu,

Korea, Hainan Island, Taiwan, Lesser Sunda Islands and Sumatra. The series closest to the Atayal (Taiwan Aborigines) series include three Japanese series: Korea, Hainan Island and Vietnam.

Discussion

The results of this new multivariate craniometric analysis agree with the results of previous craniometric analyses (Pietrusewsky 1990b,c, 1994, 1996a, 1999, 2000) in demonstrating the presence of two major divisions representing the inhabitants of eastern Asia and the Pacific. All cranial series from Australia, Tasmania, New Guinea and geographical (western and eastern island) Melanesia, represent one of these divisions. The second major division includes all the cranial series from East/North Asia, Southeast Asia (including island Southeast Asia), Polynesia and other parts of Remote Oceania. The sharpness of this division suggests separate origins for these two major groups.

The results presented in this craniometric analysis further suggest that the indigenous inhabitants of Australia, Tasmania and geographical Melanesia, because of their close biological relationships, share a common origin, one which sharply contrasts to that shared by Southeast Asians and East Asians. Similar conclusions have been reached by Howells using anthropometric (Howells 1970) and craniometric evidence (e.g. Howells 1973, 1989, 1995). Taken as a whole, these results support an earlier colonisation of Australia and Near Oceania by a group of people morphologically distinct from those who now occupy Remote Oceania, Southeast Asia and East Asia.

The present results also support the existence of a much later migration of people who ultimately occupied Remote Oceania. In the present results, Polynesian cranial series occupy a separate branch of the greater East/Southeast Asian division, one well removed from all the cranial series that derive from the Melanesian–Australian division. This relationship is most consistent with an ancestral Polynesian homeland in East/Southeast Asia and not one within geographically-adjacent Melanesia. Further, the groups that are closest (i.e. have the smallest distances) are Polynesians and island Southeast Asians (e.g. Lesser Sunda Islands, Sulawesi, southern Moluccas).

While the Polynesian series form a discrete and isolated cluster in the present study, one unexpected association found in the present results is the connection between New Zealand Maori (a Polynesian series) and the southern Moluccas, a cranial series from eastern Indonesia, seen in the dendrogram of Mahalanobis D^2 in Figure 12.4. In turn, these two groups are connected to a branch containing Fiji, Solomon Islands, New Ireland, Biak Island and two Micronesian series, Caroline Islands and Marshall-Kiribati Islands. These affinities are confirmed by the distance and classification results. In the latter, 16 of the 65 southern Moluccas specimens are reclassified as Polynesians (six each as Marquesas and New Zealand). Likewise, eight of the Lesser Sunda Islands specimens reclassify as Polynesians.

These results also demonstrate connections between some eastern Indonesian cranial series and coastal New Guinea (e.g. Biak Islands, Admiralty Islands) and other cranial series from western island Melanesia (e.g. New Ireland, Solomon Islands). These biological relationships suggest a shared ancestry as well as possible admixture as people moved eastward through Near Oceania as well as westward movement of Melanesians. Guam and Marshall-Kiribati, two cranial series from opposite ends of Micronesia, show affinities with Polynesians while the Caroline Islands series reveals influence from geographically adjacent Melanesia.

Studies of archaeology, historical linguistics and comparative ethnography (e.g. Kirch 2000; Kirch and Green 1987) as well as other biological evidence [see Howells and Schwidetzky (1981) and Kirch (1997: 100–13) for summaries of some of this evidence from human biology] are unanimous in acknowledging the primary unity of Polynesian cultures and language, a homogeneity which implies a singleness of origin. The present craniometric results support a similar hypothesis, which are more consistent with archaeological and linguistic models which favour a relatively rapid eastward migration and colonisation by prehistoric peoples and cultures (the so-called Lapita expansion) that would eventually result in the appearance of Polynesians (see, for example, Bellwood 1997; Blust 1995; Kirch 1997). However, the present results do not support an eastern Asian (i.e. Taiwan) ancestral homeland for the Polynesians suggested by these same researchers. In this analysis, only one Taiwan Aboriginal cranial series (Atayal) is represented. Both the distance results and those from stepwise discriminant function analysis reveal no Atayal-Polynesian affinities. Closer inspection of the distances, jackknifed classification results, and Figures 12.2 and 12.3, suggest some affinities between Atayal and Southeast Asia, however.

Recently, Merriwether et al. (1999) have demonstrated that all Oceanic-speaking, and especially AN-speaking, groups possess the mtDNA 9-bp deletion variant while NAN speakers, especially those NAN speakers inhabiting remote or inland regions, have low frequencies, or the complete absence of the same genetic variant. This genetic patterning has been interpreted by the same authors as support for the hypothesis that the deletion was introduced to the region with the arrival of AN-speaking peoples from the West approximately 3,500 BP (Merriwether et al. 1999). Similar conclusions have been reached in earlier (e.g. Friedlander 1987; Giles et al. 1965; Schanfield 1977) and more recent genetic work, including the human Y chromosome (Su et al. 2000) and mtDNA (Hagelberg 1998; Lum et al. 1998; Melton et al. 1995; Redd et al. 1995; Richards et al. 1998), supporting an East Asian or Southeast Asian origin of the Polynesians. A recent genetic study that utilises genetic evidence (Oppenheimer and Richards 2001) suggests that the Polynesians originated not in China/Taiwan as popularised in the 'express train to Polynesia' model (Diamond 1988), but in eastern island Southeast Asia, a view which is more consistent with the results presented in this chapter.

Overall, there is broad similarity in the patterns of relationship among Pacific peoples based on genetic and craniometric evidence. The biological evidence, both genetic and non-genetic, supports two distinctive groups of Pacific people, one more ancient, and presumably the ancestors of NAN speakers, while the other represents the more recent arrivals who speak AN languages.

The genetic evidence, especially the mtDNA evidence, has also demonstrated admixture between AN and NAN-speaking groups and extreme variability in the Solomon Islands and Vanuatu Islands group. The present craniometric results, while demonstrating marked differentiation between Polynesian and island Melanesia, also reveal that there is heterogeneity among island Melanesian series (e.g. Solomon Islands, New Ireland, Vanuatu, Loyalty Islands, New Britain etc.), but the closest affinities are with neighbouring Melanesian groups and not those from Polynesia.

Turning to Southeast Asia and East Asia, the present craniometric results also allow an examination of some of the current models that attempt to explain major peopling events which account for the present distribution of people in Southeast Asia and East Asia. Bellwood (1997), perhaps more than any one else, has argued strongly for a population displacement to account for the people who now inhabit the Indo-Malaysian Archipelago. Specifically, Bellwood has maintained that the indigenous inhabitants of Southeast Asia were replaced by an immigrant group of people of a more northern origin, or, to use his terminology, 'Australoids' were displaced by 'Mongoloids'. The entry route suggested by Bellwood is the Philippines and possibly also via the Malay Peninsula (Bellwood 1997: 87). Such a scenario should, at least in theory, result in the presence of a somewhat hybridised population living in this region. An alternative model (population or continuity model) argues that the present day inhabitants of Southeast Asia evolved within this region from the late Pleistocene onward. The work of Turner (1987, 1989, 1990, 1992), focusing on dental non-metric traits, and the recognition of two polar dental complexes, Sundadonty for Southeast Asia and Polynesia, and Sinodonty for the inhabitants of East Asia, represents a new and recent variant of this viewpoint. Others who have championed the continuity model include Bulbeck (1982) for Southeast Asian and Pope (1992) for East Asian populations.

The dendrogram of Mahalanobis D^2 (Figure 12.4) shows a clear separation between East/North Asian and Southeast Asian cranial series. Closer inspection of the distances further reveals that the groups closest to the East Asian series are generally from East Asia and North Asia (e.g. Manchuria, Korea, Mongolia). The only exceptions are two, more southern, Chinese cranial series, Hainan and Taiwan Islands, which reveal distances that imply connections with some Southeast Asian series, (e.g. Vietnam and Thailand), as well as Korea. Overall, both Hainan and Taiwan unite with Korea to form a loose connection with modern Japanese, Ryukyu Islanders and the Atayal from Taiwan.

Closer inspection of the jackknifed classification results further reveals that only a few of the East Asian specimens reclassify as Southeast Asians. The misclassifications for Hainan Island, however, reveal 14 being misclassified into one of the Southeast Asian series and eight of the original 47 Taiwan specimens reclassify as Southeast Asians.

Within Southeast Asia, the strongest connections are between mainland and island Southeast Asian series. This association is most clearly seen in the dendrogram in Figure 12.4 where the majority of the island and mainland Southeast Asian series fall into two separate branches. The exceptions are Cambodia-Laos and the Philippines. Inspection of the smallest distances confirms, with the possible exception of the Southern Moluccas series, that the island Southeast Asian series share the greatest similarities. The island Southeast Asian series showing the greatest similarities to mainland Southeast Asian are the Philippines (with Vietnam) and Sulu (with Cambodia-Laos). Inspecting the smallest distances for the five mainland Southeast Asian groups demonstrates that, the greatest similarities are to other mainland and island Southeast Asian groups and not to the East Asian series. An exception to the latter is the connection between Hainan Island and Bachuc Village (Vietnam). With the exception of Southern Moluccas, the majority of the misclassifications for the island and mainland Southeast Asian series are to other Southeast Asian series.

In summary, the present craniometric results indicate a clear distinction between the inhabitants of East/North Asia and Southeast Asia (mainland and insular), a distinction that implies long-term in situ evolution in both these regions and argues against displacement to account for the present-day inhabitants of Southeast Asia. Similar conclusions have been reached by Turner (1987, 1989, 1990, 1992) using dental morphology and Hanihara (1993) using craniometric data.

Finally, contrary to the view expressed by Brace and colleagues (Brace and Tracer 1992; Brace et al. 1990) a close biological connection between the Ainu and Polynesians is not supported by the present multivariate craniometric results. Rather, the Ainu are members (albeit marginal) of a greater East/North Asian division and do not connect directly with any of the Polynesian series. Similar conclusions has been reached by several different researchers using skeletal evidence (see for example, Hanihara 1993).

Conclusion

The results of this new multivariate craniometric study allow an independent means of assessing the biological relationships of the inhabitants of East Asia Southeast Asia and the Pacific, an assessment which invites comparisons with linguistic, archaeological and molecular genetic reconstructions for this region of the Old World. The main points of the present craniometric study are outlined as follows:

1. Two sharply contrasting divisions, an Australo-Melanesian and an Asian complex, strongly suggest separate origins for the indigenous inhabitants of these two regions.
2. Australian and Tasmanian Aborigines and the majority of the inhabitants of geographical Melanesia form one of these major divisions which implies a separate and common origin for these people.

3 The inhabitants of East and North Asia, Southeast Asia and Remote Oceania unite to form the second major division.
4 The Polynesians form a discrete branch of the larger Asian complex which is closest to cranial series from island Southeast Asia, their presumed homeland.
5 Micronesian series are variable, some (e.g. Guam) show Polynesian affinities while others (e.g. Caroline Islands) reveal connections with Melanesia.
6 Island and mainland Southeast Asian cranial series form two separate branches well separated from the East and North Asian series, a distinction which implies long-term separation and continuity for the inhabitants of these two regions.
7 There is no support for an Ainu-Pacific connection in these results.

Appendix

Sixty-three male cranial series used in the present study

Series name (abbrev.)[1]	No. of crania	Location[2] and number of crania	Remarks
Polynesia			
1 Tonga-Samoa (TOG)	19	BER – 3; AMS – 2; DRE – 1; PAR – 1; BPB – 4; AIM – 2; AUK – 5; SIM – 1	Fourteen specimens are from Tonga and five are from Samoa. Included in the Tongan series are three skulls from Pongaimotu excavated by McKern in 1920; two from To-At-1, 2 excavated by Janet Davidson in 1965; and five from To-At-36 excavated by Dirk Spennemann in 1985/6. The remaining specimens are from museums in Berlin, Paris and Sydney. Although the exact dates for a few specimens are not known, the majority are believed to be prehistoric.
2 Rapa Nui (RAP)	50	BER – 5; DRE – 9; PAR – 36	Most of the crania in Paris were collected by Pinart in 1887 at Vaihu and La Perouse Bay, Rapa Nui (Easter Island). The exact dates of these specimens are not known.
3 Hawaii (HAW)	60	BPB – 20; HON – 20; SIM – 20	An equal number of specimens have been randomly chosen from three different skeletal series: Mokapu (Oahu), Honokahua (Maui) and Kauai. All specimens are presumed to be prehistoric (pre-1778).
4 Marquesas (MRQ)	63	PAR – 49; LEP – 1; BLU – 1; BPB – 12	Crania are from four islands, Fatu Hiva, Tahuata, Nuku Hiva and Hiva Oa. The exact dates of these specimens are not known.

(Appendix continued)

Appendix Continued

Series name (abbrev.)[1]	No. of crania	Location[2] and number of crania	Remarks
5 New Zealand (NZ)	50	BRE – 3; PAR – 21; SAM – 1; AIM – 13; GOT – 1; ZUR – 5; DRE – 6	A representative sample of New Zealand Maori crania from the North and South Islands of New Zealand. The exact dates of these specimens are not known.
6 Chatham Island (CHT)	45	DUN – 8; OTM – 2; WEL – 4; CAN – 10; AIM – 3; DRE – 5; AMS – 2; DAS – 3; GOT – 4; PAR – 4	Moriori crania from the Chatham Island, New Zealand. The exact dates of these specimens are not known.
7 Society Islands (SOC)	44	PAR – 33; BPB – 11	Crania are from the island of Tahiti, Society Islands. The exact dates of these specimens are not known.
8 Tuamotu Archipelago (TUA)	18	PAR – 18	The majority of the specimens are from Makatea in the Tuamotu Archipelago. The exact dates of these specimens are not known.
9 Gambier Islands (GAM)	7	PAR – 7	The majority of these crania were collected by Dumoutier from an abandoned cemetery on Magareva Island, Gambier Islands, French Polynesia, c.1874.

Island Melanesia

10 Fiji (FIJ)	42	BER – 1; SAM – 3; QMB – 1; DRE – 4; FRE – 3; CHA – 1; BPB – 11; PAR – 7; AMS – 3; DUN – 6; SIM – 2	Crania are from all major islands including the Lau Group in the Fiji Islands. The exact dates of these specimens are not known.
11 Vanuatu (VAN)	47	BAS – 47	Most of the specimens were collected by Felix Speiser in 1912 from Malo, Pentecost and Espiritu Santo Islands, Vanuatu. The exact dates of these specimens are not known.
12 Loyalty Islands (LOY)	50	BAS – 43; PAR – 7	Crania are from Mare, Lifou and Ouvea Island Groups, Loyalty Islands. The exact dates of these specimens are not known.
13 New Caledonia (NCL)	50	BAS – 34; PAR – 16	Crania are from several coastal and inland locations on New Caledonia. The majority of these specimens were collected in the late nineteenth century. The exact dates of these specimens are not known.

(Appendix continued)

Appendix Continued

Series name (abbrev.)[1]	No. of crania	Location[2] and number of crania	Remarks
14 Santa Cruz Islands (SCR)	46	SAM – 4; AMS – 2; BAS – 40	The crania in Basel were collected by Felix Speiser in 1912 (Speiser 1928). The exact dates of these specimens are not known.
15 Solomon Islands (SOL)	49	DRE – 3; BER – 1; NMV – 1; QMB – 3; AMS – 16; DAS – 10; BAS – 14; GOT – 1	Crania are from New Georgia (5), Guadalcanal (9), San Cristobal Island (7) and other locations in the Solomon Islands. The exact dates of these specimens are not known.
16 New Britain (NBR)	50	CHA – 20; DRE – 30	The specimens from New Britain in Dresden were collected by A. Baessler in 1900 and those in Berlin were collected by R. Parkinson in 1911. These specimens were collected from trading posts near Rabul in the Gazelle Peninsula and most likely represent Tolai crania (see Pietrusewsky 1990a: 236–7; Howells 1973: 24–5). The exact dates of these specimens are not known.
17 New Ireland (NIR)	53	AMS – 4; BER – 2; BLU – 6; DRE – 18; GOT – 15; QMB – 1; SAM – 6; TUB – 1	Most of the crania in Dresden were collected by Pöhl in 1887–88 from the northern end of the island; the specimens in Göttingen were collected during the Südsee Expedition in 1908. The exact dates of these specimens are not known.
18 Admiralty Islands (ADR)	50	DRE – 20; GOT – 9; CHA – 6; TUB – 15;	Specimens from Hermit, Kaniet and Manus Islands of the Admiralty Islands. The exact dates of these specimens are not known.
New Guinea			
19 Sepik R. (SEP)	50	DRE – 33; GOT – 10; TUB – 7	The specimens in Dresden were collected by Otto Schlaginhaufen in 1909 from various locations along the Sepik River, Papua New Guinea. The exact dates of these specimens are not known.
20 Biak Island (BIK)	48	DRE – 48	Most (45) of the specimens were collected by A.B. Meyer in 1873 on Biak Island (Mysore), Geelvink Bay, Irian Jaya. The exact dates of these specimens are not known.
21 Fly River (FLY)	42	DRE – 35; QMB – 7	Most of the skulls in Dresden were collected by Webster in 1902 along

(Appendix continued)

Appendix Continued

Series name (abbrev.)[1]	No. of Crania	Location[2] and number of crania	Remarks
22 Purari Delta (PUR)	50	DRE – 50	the Fly River of Papua New Guinea. Many of the crania are decorated and have engraved frontal bones (see Pietrusewsky, 1990a: 235–6 for further details). The exact dates of these specimens are not known. Decorated (engraved) skulls obtained by Gerrard and Webster between 1900 and 1902 are from along the Purari River and Purari Delta regions, Papua New Guinea. The exact dates of these specimens are not known.
23 D'Entrecasteaux Islands (DTX)	26	FRE – 21; DRE – 4; QMB – 1	Crania are from Fergusson (16) and Normanby (10) Islands of the D'Entrecasteaux Island group. The exact dates of these specimens are not known.
24 Dawson Strait Islands (DAW)	48	ROM – 48	Crania are from the islands of the Dawson Straits (between Normanby and Fergusson Islands of the D'Entrecasteaux Islands) which were collected by L. Loria on a voyage to Papua New Guinea between 1889–90. The exact dates of these specimens are not known.
Australia/Tasmania			
25 Murray R. (MRB)	50	AIA – 39; DAM –11	Australian Aboriginal crania were collected by G.M. Black along the Murray River (Chowilla to Coobool) in New South Wales between 1929–50. The exact dates of these specimens are not known.
26 New South Wales (NSW)	62	AMS – 21; DAS – 41	Australian Aboriginal crania from the coastal locations in New South Wales. The exact dates of these specimens are not known.
27 Queensland (QLD)	54	AMS – 21; DAS – 3; QMB – 30	Australian Aboriginal crania from the southeastern and middle-eastern regions of Queensland. The exact dates of these specimens are not known.
28 Northern Territory (NT)	50	AIA – 4; AMS – 3; MMS – 1; NMV – 38; QMB – 1; SAM – 3	Australian Aboriginal crania from Port Darwin (39) and Arnhem Land (36) in the Northern Territory, Australia. The exact dates of these specimens are not known.

(Appendix continued)

Appendix Continued

Series name (abbrev.)[1]	No. of crania	Location[2] and number of crania	Remarks
29 Swanport, SA (SAS)	36	SAM – 36	Australian Aboriginal crania representing the Tarildekald and Warki-Korowalde tribes in the lower Murray River basin. The specimens were collected by F.R. Zeitz in 1911 from an aboriginal cemetery located approximately 10 km southeast of the Murray Bridge in South Australia (Howells 1973: 21). The exact dates of these specimens are not known.
30 Western Australia (WA)	47	WAM – 47	Australian Aboriginal crania from central (20), eastern (4), northern (14), and southern (9) regions of western Australia. The exact dates of these specimens are not known.
31 Tasmania (TAS)	26	THM – 22; CHA – 1; SAM – 2; NMV – 1	The crania represent Tasmanian Aborigines. The exact dates of these specimens are not known.
Micronesia			
32 Guam (GUA)	46	BPB – 42; PAR – 4	Pre-Spanish Chamorro crania associated with latte structures collected in the 1920s by Hans Hornbostel along Tumon Beach, Tumon Bay, Guam. The majority of these specimens represent prehistoric (pre-1521) Chamorro.
33 Caroline Islands (CAR)	24	TRO – 7; DRE – 9; PAR – 4; GOT – 3; AMS – 1	The crania are from Kosrae Island (1), Pohnpei (16) and Chuuk (7) Islands of the central and eastern Caroline Islands, Federated States of Micronesia. The exact dates of these specimens are not known.
34 Marshall/ Kiribati Islands (MSK)	13	PAR – 6; GOT – 3; FRE – 3; BER – 1	Crania are from the Marshall (7) and Kiribati (6) Islands of eastern Micronesia. The exact dates of these specimens are not known.
Island, Southeast, Asia			
35 Sumatra (SUM)	39	BER – 1; BRE – 1; DRE – 5; LEP – 4; PAR – 3; ZUR – 25	The specimens in Zurich are designated 'Battak', specific locations within the island of Sumatra are not known. The exact dates of these specimens are not known.
36 Java (JAV)	50	BER – 1; BLU – 8; CHA – 9; DRE – 1; LEP – 24; PAR – 7	Crania were collected from several different localities in Java. The exact dates of these specimens are not known.

(Appendix continued)

Appendix Continued

Series name (abbrev.)[1]	No. of crania	Location[2] and number of crania	Remarks
37 Borneo (BOR)	34	BER – 2; BRE – 2; DRE – 6; FRE – 4; LEP – 8; PAR – 12	A great many of the specimens are indicated as representing Dayak tribes, some have elaborate decorations. The exact dates of these specimens are not known.
38 Sulawesi (SLW)	41	BAS – 7; BER – 10; DRE – 4; FRE – 7; LEP – 5; PAR – 8	An exact location is known for many of these specimens. The exact dates of these specimens are not known.
39 Lesser Sundas Islands (LSN)	61	BAS – 5; BER – 15; BLU – 2; CHA – 1; DRE – 24; LEP – 1; PAR – 6; ZUR – 7	Crania from Bali (13), Flores (9), Sumba (1), Lomblem (2), Alor (2), Timor (11), Wetar (2), Leti (4), Barbar (1), Tanimbar (13), Kai (2) and Aru (1) islands of the Lesser Sunda Islands. The exact dates of these specimens are not known.
40 Southern Moluccas Islands (SML)	65	FRE – 48; DRE – 17	Crania are from Seram (48) and Buru (17) Islands of the Southern Molucca Islands. The exact dates of these specimens are not known.
41 Sulu (SUL)	38	LEP – 1; PAR – 37	The specimens in Paris were collected by Montano-Rey c.1900. The exact dates of these specimens are not known.
42 Philippines (PHL)	28	BER – 9; DRE – 19	Most specimens are from Luzon Island. The exact dates of these specimens are not known.
Mainland, Southeast, Asia			
43 Vietnam (VTN)	49	HCM – 49	Near-modern crania from Hanoi (Van Dien Cemetery) and Ho Chi Minh City.
44 Bachuc Village, (BAC)	51	BAC – 51	Victims of the 1978 Khmer Rouge massacre in Bachuc Village in western Angiang Province, Vietnam.
45 Cambodia and Laos (CML)	40	PAR – 40	A combined sample of crania from various locations in Cambodia and Laos collected between 1877 and 1920. The exact dates of these specimens are not known.
46 Thailand (THI)	50	SIR – 50	Most of the specimens represent dissecting room cases from Bangkok.
47 Burma (BUR)	16	ZUR – 16	The crania in Zurich are from a series (Cat. Nos. 93–125) of skulls collected in Mandalay, Myanmar (Burma), described in a catalogue dated c.1900. The exact dates of these specimens are not known.

(Appendix continued)

Appendix Continued

Series name (abbrev.)[1]	No. of crania	Location[2] and number of crania	Remarks
East Asia			
48 Kanto (KAN)	50	CHB – 50	A dissecting room population of modern Japanese from the Kanto District of eastern Honshu. The majority of the individuals were born during the Meiji period (1868–1911) and died well before 1940.
49 Tohoku (TOH)	53	SEN – 53	Dissecting room specimens of modern Japanese from the Tohoku District in northern Honshu Island.
50 Kyushu (KYU)	51	KYU – 51	Modern Japanese which derive mostly from Fukuoka Prefecture in Kyushu Island. Other specimens are from Yamaguchi, Saga, Nagasaki and adjoining prefectures.
51 Ainu (AIN)	50	SAP – 18; TKM – 5; TKO – 27	Modern to near-modern skeletons collected by Koganei in 1888–89 from abandoned Ainu cemeteries in Hokkaido (Koganei 1893–94).
52 Ryukyu Islands (RYU)	60	KYO – 18; KAN – 21; RYU – 8; KYU – 5; TKO – 8	Eighteen near modern crania are from Tokunoshima Island of the Amami Islands located north of the Okinawa Group in the central Ryukyu Islands; 21 specimens are from two different locations on Kume Island, an island located west of Okinawa Island: Yattchi (17) and Hiyajo (4); 21 specimens are from five separate islands in the Sakishima Group of the southern Ryukyu Islands: Hateruma Island (2); Miyako (4); Iriomote Island (2); Ishigaki Island (1) and Yonaguni Island (12).
China/East and Northeast Asia			
53 Shanghai (SHA)	50	SHA – 50	The specimens are mostly from post-Qing (pre-1911) cemeteries in Shanghai.
54 Hangzhou (HAN)	50	SHA – 50	The series represents near-modern crania exhumed in the modern city of Hangzhou, Zhejiang Province, eastern China.
55 Nanjing (NAJ)	49	SHA – 49	The series represents near-modern crania exhumed from the modern city of Nanjing, Jiangsu Province, eastern China.

(Appendix continued)

Appendix Continued

Series name (abbrev.)[1]	No. of crania	Location[2] and number of crania	Remarks
56 Chengdu (CHD)	53	SHA – 10; CHE – 43	A majority of these specimens date to the Ch'en dynasty (AD 1644–1911) and are from Chengdu, Sichuan Province in western China. Ten crania are from Leshan, Lizhong County, Sichuan Province.
57 Hong Kong (HK)	50	HKU – 50	Specimens represent individuals who died in Hong Kong between 1978–79.
58 Taiwan (TAI)	47	TPE – 47	Modern Chinese living in Taiwan who trace their immediate origins to Fujian and Guangdong Provinces on the mainland of China.
59 Hainan Island (HAI)	47	TPE – 47	Near-modern Chinese whose ancestors began migrating from the Canton region of China to Hainan Island around 200 BC (Howells 1989: 108). This material was excavated by Takeo Kanaseki in Haikou City on Hainan Island.
60 Manchuria (MAN)	50	TKO – 50	Many of the specimens are from northeastern China or the region formerly referred to as 'Manchuria', which today includes Heilongjiang and Jilin Provinces and adjacent northern Korea. A great many of these specimens are identified as soldiers, or cavalrymen, who died in battle in the late nineteenth century AD.
61 Korea (KOR)	32	KYO – 7; SEN – 3; TKM – 2; TKO – 20	Specific locations in Korea are known for most of these near-modern specimens.
62 Mongolia (MOG)	50	SIM – 50	The skulls are identified as coming from Ulaanbaatar (Urga), Mongolia and were purchased by A. Hrdlička in 1912.
63 Atayal (ATY)	36	TPE – 28; TKM – 7; TKO – 1	The Atayal are the second largest surviving Aboriginal tribe in Taiwan. The specimens are Atayal slain in the Wushe incident in 1930. The specimens were collected by Takeo Kanaseki in 1932 (Howells 1989: 109).

Notes
1 The numbers assigned to each cranial series correspond to the numbers given in Map 12.1. Permission to examine the cranial series used in the present study has been previously acknowledged. My thanks to Billie Ikeda of the University of Hawaii's Instructional Support Center for

Appendix Continued

assistance with producing the figures that accompany this chapter. Mr Scott Reinke assisted with many aspects of data analysis and preparation of the manuscript. Rona Ikehara-Quebral assisted with computer programming associated with data analysis and Michele Toomay Douglas read and provided helpful comments on previous drafts of this chapter. Finally, I am grateful to Laurent Sagart and the late Stanley Starosta for inviting me to participate and present this chapter as a paper at the workshop on 'Perspectives on the Phylogeny of East Asian Languages' held in Périgueux, France, August 28–31, 2001.

2 AIM, Auckland Institute and Museum, Auckland, New Zealand; AIA, Australian Institute of Anatomy, Canberra, Australia; AMS, The Australian Museum, Sydney, Australia; AUK, University of Auckland, Auckland, New Zealand; BAC, Bachuc Village, Angiang Province, Vietnam; BAS, Naturhistorisches Museum, Basel, Switzerland; BER, Museum für Naturkunde, Berlin, Germany; BLU, Anatomisches Institut, Universität Göttingen, Göttingen, Germany; BPB, B. P. Bishop Museum, Honolulu, USA; BRE, Über-see Museum, Bremen, Germany; CAN, Canterbury Museum, Christchurch, New Zealand; CHA, Anatomisches Institut der Charité, Humboldt Universität, Berlin, Germany; CHB, Chiba University School of Medicine, Chiba, Japan; CHE, Department of Anatomy, Chengdu College of Traditional Chinese Medicine, Chengdu, China; DAM, Department of Anatomy, University of Melbourne, Melbourne, Australia; DAS, Department of Anatomy, University of Sydney, Sydney, Australia; DUN, Department of Anatomy, University of Otago, Dunedin, New Zealand; DRE, Museum für Völkerkunde, Dresden, Germany; FMN, Field Museum of Natural History, Chicago, USA; FRE, Institut für Humangenetik und Anthropologie, Universität Freiburg, Freiburg im Breisgau, Germany; GOT, Institut für Anthropologie, Universität Göttingen, Göttingen, Germany; HCM, Faculty of Medicine, Ho Chi Minh City, Vietnam; HON, Honokahua, Maui, Hawaii, USA; HKU, University of Hong Kong, Hong Kong; KAN, Kanegusuku Storage Room, Board of Education Cultural Division, Kanegusuku, Okinawa, Japan; KYO, Physical Anthropology Laboratory, Faculty of Science, Kyoto University, Kyoto, Japan; KYU, Department of Anatomy, Faculty of Medicine, Kyushu University, Fukuoka, Japan; LEP, Anatomisches Institut, Karl Marx Universität, Leipzig, Germany; MMS, Macleay Museum, University of Sydney, Sydney, Australia; NMV, National Museum of Victoria, Melbourne, Australia; NTU, Department of Anatomy, National Taiwan University, Taipei, Taiwan; OTM, Otago Museum and Art Gallery, Otago, New Zealand; PAR, Musée de l'Homme, Paris, France; QMB, Queensland Museum, Brisbane, Australia; ROM, Instituto di Antropologia, University of Rome, Rome, Italy; RYU, University of the Ryukyus, Naha, Okinawa Island, Japan; SAM, South Australian Museum, Adelaide, Australia; SAP, Department of Anatomy, Sapporo Medical College, Sapporo, Japan; SEN, Department of Anatomy, School of Medicine, Tohoku University, Sendai, Japan; SHA, Institute of Anthropology, College of Life Sciences, Fudan University, Shanghai, China; SIM, National Museum of Natural History, Smithsonian Institution, Washington DC, USA; SIR, Department of Anatomy, Siriraj Hospital, Bangkok, Thailand; THM, Tasmanian Museum and Art Gallery, Hobart, Australia; TKM, Medical Museum, University Museum, University of Tokyo, Tokyo, Japan; TKO, University Museum, University of Tokyo, Tokyo, Japan; TPE, Academia Sinica, Nankang, Taipei, Taiwan; TUB, Institut für Anthropologie u. Humangenetik, Universität Tübingen, Tübingen, Germany; WAM, Western Australian Museum, Perth, Australia; WEL, National Museum of New Zealand, Wellington, New Zealand; ZUR, Anthropologisches Institut, Universität Zürich, Zürich, Germany.

3 The 27 measurements used in the present study are described in Martin and Saller (1957) and Howells (1973); Maximum cranial breadth (M-8); Biorbital breadth (H-EKB); Minimum cranial breadth (M-14); Basion-nasion length (M-5); Nasion-alveolare (M-48); Maximum cranial length (M-1); Basion-bregma height (M-17); Biauricular breadth (M-11b); Basion-prosthion (M-40); Nasal height (M-55); Nasio-occipital length (M-1d); Bijugal breadth (M-45(1)); Nasal breadth (M-54); Bifrontal breadth (M-43); Alveolar breadth (M-61); Mastoid height (H-MDL); Cheek height (H-WMH); Nasion-bregma chord (M-29); Orbital height, left (M-52); Bimaxillary breadth (M-46); Orbital breadth, left (M-51a); Bistephanic breadth (H-STB); Maximum frontal breadth (M-10); Minimum frontal breadth (M-9); Mastoid width (H-MDB); Bregma-lambda chord (M-30); Biasterionic breadth (M-12); M   Martin and Saller; H   Howells (1973).

Abbreviations

AN　　　Austronesian
ANOVA　Analysis of variance
mtDNA　mitochondrial DNA
NAN　　non-Austronesian

Bibliography

Allen, J. (1984) 'In search of the Lapita homeland', Journal of Pacific History 19: 186–201.
Bayard, T.D. (1996) 'Linguistics, archaeologists, and Austronesian origins: comparative and sociolinguistic aspects of the Meacham-Bellwood debate', Bulletin of the Indo-Pacific Prehistory Association 15: 71–85.
Bellwood, P. (1985) Prehistory of the Indo-Malaysian Archipelago, New York: Academic Press.
—— (1993) 'Cultural and biological differentiation in Peninsular Malaysia: the last 10,000 years', Asian Perspectives 32: 37–60.
—— (1996) 'Early agriculture and the dispersal of the Southern Mongoloids', in T. Akazawa and E.J.E. Szathmáry (eds) Prehistoric Mongoloid Dispersals, Oxford: Oxford University Press.
—— (1997) Prehistory of the Indo-Malaysian Archipelago: Revised Edition, Honolulu: University of Hawaii Press.
Bellwood, P., Fox, J.J. and Tryon, D. (1995) 'The Austronesians in history: common origins and diverse transformations', in P. Bellwood, J.J. Fox and D. Tryon (eds) The Austronesians: Historical and Comparative Perspectives, Canberra: Department of Anthropology, Australian National University.
Blust, R. (1995) 'The prehistory of the Austronesian-speaking peoples: a view from language', Journal of World Prehistory 9: 453–510.
—— (1996) 'Beyond the Austronesian homeland: the Austric hypothesis and its implications for archaeology', in W. Goodenough (ed.) Prehistoric Settlement of the Pacific, Philadelphia: Transactions of the American Philosophical Society.
Brace, C.L. and Hunt, K.D. (1990) 'A nonracial craniofacial perspective on human variation: (A)ustralia to (Z)uni', American Journal of Physical Anthropology 82: 341–60.
Brace, C.L. and Tracer, D.P. (1992) 'Craniofacial continuity and change: a comparison of late Pleistocene and recent Europe and Asia', in T. Akazawa, K. Aoki and T. Kimura (eds) The Evolution and Dispersal of Modern Humans in Asia, Tokyo: Hokusen-sha.
Brace, C.L., Brace, M.L., Dodo, Y., Leonard, W.R., Li, Y., Shao, X., Sood, S. and Zhang, Z. (1990) 'Micronesians, Asians, Thais and relations: a craniofacial and odontometric perspective', Micronesica Supplement 2: 323–48.
Buikstra, J.E., Frankenberg, S.R. and Konigsberg, L.W. (1990) 'Skeletal biological distance studies in American physical anthropology: recent trends', American Journal of Physical Anthropology 82: 1–7.
Bulbeck, D. (1982) 'A re-evaluation of possible evolutionary processes in Southeast Asia since the late Pleistocene', Bulletin of the Indo-Pacific Prehistory Association 3: 1–21.
Diamond, J.M. (1988) 'Express train to Polynesia', Nature 326: 307–8.
Dixon, W.J. (ed.) (1992) BMDP. Statistical Software Manual, Vol. 1, Berkeley: University of California Press.

Droessler, J.B. (1981) 'Craniometry and Biological Distance: Biocultural Continuity and Change at the Late-Woodland–Mississippian Interface', Center for American Archeology Research Series, Vol. 1, Evanston: Center for American Archeology.

Friedlaender, J.S. (1987) 'Conclusion', in J.S. Friedlaender (ed.) The Solomon Islands Project: A Long-term Study of Human Biology and Culture Change, Oxford: Oxford Scientific Publications.

Giles, E., Ogan E. and Steinberg, A.G., (1965) 'Gamma-globulin factors (Gm and Inv) in New Guinea: anthropological significance', Science 150: 1158–60.

Glover, I.C. and Higham, C.F.W. (1996) 'New evidence for early rice cultivation in South, Southeast, and East Asia', in D.R. Harris (ed.) The Origins and Spread of Agriculture and Pastoralism in Eurasia, Washington, D.C.: Smithsonian Institution Press.

Green, R.C. (1979) 'Lapita', in J.D. Jennings (ed.) The Prehistory of Polynesia, Cambridge: Harvard University Press.

—— (1991) 'Near and Remote Oceania – disestablishing "Melanesia" in culture history', in A.K. Pawley (ed.) Man and a Half: Essays in Pacific Anthropology and Ethnobiology in Honour of Ralph Bulmer, Auckland: The Polynesian Society.

—— (1997) 'Linguistic, biological, and cultural origins of the initial inhabitants of Remote Oceania', New Zealand Journal of Archaeology 17: 5–27.

Hagelberg, E. (1998) 'Genetic perspectives on the settlement of the Pacific', in C.M. Steveson, G. Lee and F.J. Morin (eds) Easter Island in Pacific Context: South Seas Symposium Proceedings of the Fourth International Conference on Easter Island and East Polynesia, Los Osos: The Easter Island Foundation Occasional Paper 4.

Hagelberg, E.M., Kayser, M., Nagy, I., Roewer, H Z., Krawczak, M., Lió, P. and Schiefenhövel, W. (1999) 'Molecular genetic evidence for the human settlement of the Pacific: analysis of mitochondrial DNA, Y chromosome, and HLA markers.' Philosophical Transactions of the Royal Society of London B354: 141–52.

Hanihara, T. (1993) 'Dental affinities among Polynesian and circum-Polynesian populations', Nichibunken Japan Review 4: 59–82.

Higham, C.F.W. (1996) The Bronze Age of Southeast Asia Cambridge: Cambridge University Press.

—— (2001) 'Prehistory, language, and human biology: is there a consensus in East and Southeast Asia?', in L. Jin, M. Seielstad and C. Xiao (eds) Genetic, Linguistics and Archaeological Perspectives on Human Diversity in Southeast Asia, New Jersey: World Scientific.

Howells, W.W. (1970) 'Anthropometric grouping analysis of Pacific peoples', Archaeology and Physical Anthropology in Oceania 5: 192–217.

—— (1973) 'Cranial variation in man', Papers of the Peabody Museum of Archaeology and Ethnology, Vol. 67, Cambridge: Peabody Museum of Archaeology and Ethnology.

—— (1989) 'Skull shapes and the map: craniometric analyses in the dispersion of modern Homo', Papers of the Peabody Museum of Archaeology and Ethnology, Vol. 79, Cambridge: Peabody Museum of Archaeology and Ethnology.

—— (1990) 'Micronesia to Macromongolia. Micro-Polynesian populations with special reference to the Pacific peoples', Micronesica Supplement 2: 363–72.

—— (1995) 'Who's who in skulls: ethnic identification of crania from measurements, Papers of the Peabody Museum of Archaeology and Ethnology, Vol. 82, Cambridge: Harvard University Press.

Howells, W.W. and Schwidetzky, I. (1981) 'Oceania', in I. Schwidetzky (ed.) Rassengeschichte der Menschheit. Asien I: Japan, Indonesien, Ozeanien, Munich: Oldenbourg.

Kirch, P.V. (1997) The Lapita Peoples: Ancestors of the Oceanic World, Oxford: Blackwell.

—— (2000) On the Road of the Winds: An Archaeological History of the Pacific Islands Before European Contact, Berkeley: University of California Press.

Kirch, P.V. and Green, R.C. (1987) 'History, phylogeny and evolution in Polynesia', Current Anthropology 28: 431–56.

Koganei, Y. (1893–94) 'Beiträge zur physischen Anthropologie der Aino', Mittheilungen aus der Medicinischen Facultät der Kaiserlich-Japanischen Universität zu Tokyo 2: 1–249, 251–404.

Kohn, L.A. (1991) 'The role of genetics in craniofacial morphology and growth', Annual Review of Anthropology 20: 261–78.

Konigsberg, L.W. and Ousley, S.D. (1995) 'Multivariate quantitative genetics of anthropometric traits from the Boas data', Human Biology 67: 481–98.

Larsen, C.S. (1997) Bioarchaeology: Interpreting Behavior for the Human Skeleton, Cambridge: Cambridge University Press.

Lin, M., Chu, C.C., Lee, H.L., Chang, S.L., Ohashi, J. and Tokunaga, K. (1999) 'Heterogeneity of Taiwan's indigenous population: possible relation to prehistoric Mongoloid dispersals', Tissue Antigens 55: 1–9.

Lum, J.K. and Cann, R.L. (1998) 'mtDNA and languages support a common origin of Micronesians and Polynesians in Island Southeast Asia', American Journal of Physical Anthropology 105: 109–19.

Lum, J.K., Cann, R.L., Martinson, J.J. and Jorde, L.B. (1998) 'Mitochondrial and nuclear genetic relationships among Pacific Island and Asian populations', American Journal of Human Genetics 63: 613–24.

Mahalanobis, P.C. (1936) 'On the generalized distance in statistics', Proceedings of the National Institute of Sciences of India 2, 1: 49–55, Calcutta.

Mahalanobis, P.C., Majumdar, D.N. and Rao, C.R. (1949) 'Anthropometric survey of the United Provinces, 1941: a statistical study', Sankhya 9: 89–324.

Martin, R. and Saller, K. (1957) Lehrbuch der Anthropologie, Stuttgart: Gustav Fischer Verlag.

Melton, T., Peterson, R., Redd, A.J., Saha, N., Sofro, A.S.M., Martinson, J. and Stoneking, M. (1995) 'Polynesian genetic affinities with Southeast Asian populations as identified by mtDNA analysis', American Journal of Human Genetics 57: 403–14.

Merriwether, D.A., Friedlaender, J.S., Mediavilla, J, Mgone, C., Gentz, F. and Ferrell, R.E. (1999) 'Mitochondrial DNA variation is an indicator of Austronesian influence in Island Melanesia', American Journal of Physical Anthropology 110, 3: 243–70.

Oppenheimer, S.J. and Richards, M. (2001) 'Polynesian origins: slow boat to Melanesia?', Nature 410: 166–7.

Pawley, A.K. and Green, R.C. (1973) 'Dating the dispersal of Oceanic languages', Oceanic Linguistics 12: 1–67.

Pawley, A.K. and Ross, M. (1993) 'Austronesian historical linguistics and culture history', Annual Review of Anthropology 22: 425–59.

—— (1995) 'The prehistory of the Oceanic languages: a current view' in P. Bellwood, J.J. Fox, and D. Tryon (eds) The Austronesians: Historical and Comparative Perspectives, Canberra: Department of Anthropology, Australian National University.

Pietrusewsky, M. (1990a) 'Cranial variation in New Guinea and neighboring populations of the Pacific: A multivariate study of specimens in the Museum für Völkerkunde

Dresden and the German Democratic Republic', Abhandlungen und Berichte des Staatlichen Museums für Völkerkunde 45: 233–57.

—— (1990b) 'Craniofacial variation in Australasian and Pacific populations', American Journal of Physical Anthropology 82: 319–40.

—— (1990c) 'Craniometric variation in Micronesia and the Pacific: a multivariate study', Micronesica Supplement 2: 373–402.

—— (1994) 'Pacific-Asian relationships: a physical anthropological perspective', Oceanic Linguistics 33, 2: 407–30.

—— (1995) 'Taiwan Aboriginals, Asians, and Pacific Islanders: a multivariate investigation of skulls' in P.J. Li, C. Tsang, Y. Huang, D. Ho and C. Tseng (eds) Austronesian Studies Relating to Taiwan, Taipei: Symposium Series of the Institute of History and Philology.

—— (1996a) 'Multivariate craniometric investigations of Japanese, Asians, and Pacific Islanders', in K. Omoto (ed) Interdisciplinary Perspectives on the Origins of the Japanese: International Symposium No. 11-B, Kyoto: International Research Center for Japanese Studies.

—— (1996b) 'The physical anthropology of Polynesia: a review of some cranial and skeletal studies', in J. Davidson, G. Irwin, F. Leach, A. Pawley and D. Brown (eds) Oceanic Culture History: Essays in Honour of Roger Green, Wellington: New Zealand Journal of Archaeology Special Publication.

—— (1997a) 'Biological origins of Hawaiians: evidence from skulls', Man and Culture in Oceania 13: 1–37.

—— (1997b) 'The people of Ban Chiang: an early bronze-age site in northeast Thailand', Bulletin of the Indo-Pacific Prehistory Association 16: 119–48.

—— (1999) 'A multivariate craniometric investigation of the inhabitants of the Ryukyu Islands and comparisons with cranial series from Japan, Asia, and the Pacific', Anthropological Science 107: 255–81.

—— (2000) 'Metric analysis of skeletal remains: methods and applications', in M.A. Katzenberg and S.R. Saunders (eds) Biological Anthropology of the Human Skeleton, New York: Wiley-Liss.

Pope, G.G. (1992) 'Replacement versus regionally continuous models: the paleobehavioral and fossil evidence', in T. Akazawa, K. Aoki and T. Kimura (eds) The Evolution and Dispersal of Modern Humans in Asia, Tokyo: Hokusen-sha.

Rao, C.R. (1948) 'The utilization of multiple measurements in problems of biological classification', Journal of the Royal Statistical Society B 10: 159–93.

—— (1952) Advanced Statistical Methods in Biomedical Research, New York: John Wiley.

Redd, A.J., Takezaki, N., Sherry, S.T., McGarvey, S.T., Sofro, A.S.M. and Stoneking, M. (1995) 'Evolutionary history of the COII/tRNA^{Lys} intergenic 9 base pair deletion in human mitochondrial DNA from the Pacific', Molecular Biological Evolution 12: 604–15.

Richards, M., Oppenheimer, S.J. and Sykes, B. (1998) 'Mt-DNA suggests Polynesian origins in eastern Indonesia', American Journal of Human Genetics 63:1234–6.

Schanfield, M.S. (1977) 'Population affinities of the Australian Aborigines as reflected by the genetic markers of immunoglobulins', Journal of Human Evolution 6: 341–52.

Sjøvold, T. (1984) 'A report on the heritability of some cranial measurements and non-metric traits', in G.N. Van Vark and W.W. Howells (eds) Multivariate Statistics in Physical Anthropology', Dordrecht: D. Reidel Publishing Co.

Speiser, F. (1928) 'Anthropologische messungen aus dem St. Cruz-Inseln', Archiv für Anthropologie 19: 89–146.

Spriggs, M.J.T. (1997) The Island Melanesians, Cambridge: Blackwell Publishers.
Su, B., Jin, L., Underhill, P., Martinson, J., Saha, N. McGarvey, S.T., Shriver, M.D., Chui, J., Oefner, P., Chakraborty, R. and Deka, R. (2000) 'Polynesian origins: insights from the Y chromosome', Proceedings of the National Academy of Sciences (U.S.A.) 96, 15: 8225–8.
Terrell, J.E. (1986) Prehistory in the Pacific Islands, Cambridge: University of Cambridge Press.
—— (1989) 'What Lapita is and what Lapita isn't', Antiquity 63: 623–6.
Terrell, J.E. and Welsh, R.L. (1997) 'Lapita and the temporal geography of prehistory', Antiquity 71: 548–72.
Terrell, J.E., Kelly, K.M. and Rainbird, P. (2001) 'Foregone conclusions? In search of "Papuans" and "Austronesians" ', Current Anthropology 42: 97–124.
Turner, C.G. II. (1987) 'Late Pleistocene and Holocene population history of East Asia based on dental variation', American Journal of Physical Anthropology 73: 305–21.
—— (1989) 'Teeth and prehistory in Asia', Scientific American 260: 88–96.
—— (1990) 'Major features of Sundadonty and Sinodonty, including suggestions about East Asian microevolution, population history and late Pleistocene relationships with Australian Aborigines', American Journal of Physical Anthropology 82: 295–317.
—— (1992) 'The dental bridge between Australia and Asia', Archaeology in Oceania 27: 143–52.
van Vark, G.N. and Howells, W.W. (eds) (1984) Multivariate Statistics in Physical Anthropology, Dordrecht: D. Reidel Publishing Co.
White, J.P., Allen, J. and Specht, J. (1988) 'Peopling the Pacific: the Lapita homelands project', Australian Natural History 22: 410–16.

13

GENETIC DIVERSITY OF TAIWAN'S INDIGENOUS PEOPLES

Possible relationship with insular Southeast Asia

Marie Lin, Chen-Chung Chu, Richard E. Broadberry,
Lung-Chih Yu, Jun-Hun Loo and Jean A. Trejaut

Introduction

The diversity of language, culture and physical appearance of tribal peoples in the island of Taiwan has attracted the interest and attention of anthropologists, archaeologists and linguistic scientists since the nineteenth century. Since the Japanese occupation in 1895, there have been extensive anthropological studies and archaeological excavations. The origin of Taiwan's indigenous peoples was initially sought in the south (i.e. the Malay) (Mabuchi 1974; Mackay 1895). After the Second World War, it was proposed that this first settlement consisted of ethnic minorities from China (Sung 1980). A more recent theory, based on linguistic and archaeological evidence, placed the homeland of the AN-speakers in Taiwan (Bellwood 1991). This involved an early Neolithic migration from southeast China, an independent development in Taiwan, and a further expansion towards the south.

Physical anthropological studies on Taiwan's indigenous peoples have been carried out since the late nineteenth century. An early genetic study was also done using ABO blood groups (Kutsuna and Matuyama 1939). Over the years, many genetic markers including blood groups (Lin and Broadberry 1998), serum proteins (Matsumoto et al. 1972; Schanfield et al. 2002), red cell enzymes (Jin 1992), HLA (Chu et al. 2001a; Lin et al. 2000), microsatellites (Lee et al. 2002), mtDNA (Melton et al. 1995; Richard et al. 1998; Sykes et al. 1995; Trejaut et al. 2004) and Y chromosome (Su et al. 2000) have been analysed. Human genetic studies on modern populations were carried out to help understanding prehistoric migrations of human populations. In this report, we review our previous works performed on RBC blood groups (Lin and Broadberry 1998), HLA (Chu et al. 2001a; Lin et al. 2000), platelet-specific alloantigens (HPA) and human neutrophil antigens (HNA-1) (Chu et al. 2001b), secretor genes (Yu et al. 2001) and microsatellites (Lee et al. 2002) of nine of Taiwan's indigenous peoples. Our aim is to better understand their origins.

Populations studied

Taiwan's indigenous peoples are traditionally represented by nine Mountain (or 'aboriginal') peoples and ten Plains (or 'Sinicised') peoples. The Mountain group is further subclassified into central (the Atayal and the Saisiat in the north, the Bunun and the Tsou in the centre, and the Rukai and the Paiwan in the south), and east coast (the Ami and the Puyuma in the east coast of Taiwan, and the Yami or Tao on Orchid island) (Map 13.1). These peoples are all AN-speaking. The Plains peoples originally lived in the west of Taiwan, but most have been gradually displaced during the last 400 years through war, intermarriage and integration into the Minnan and Hakka ethnic groups, which are the descendants of early Chinese settlers from the southeast coast of China. As a consequence, only Chinese-speaking groups (the 'Taiwanese') now occupy the western plains, and constitute most of the population in Taiwan (91 per cent).

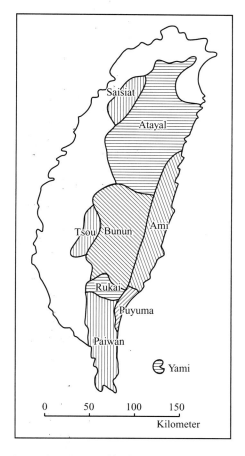

Map 13.1 Geographical distribution of Taiwan's indigenous peoples (Lin et al. 2000).

Linguistic and archaeological studies have suggested that mountain peoples from Taiwan were the ancestors of other AN populations through Oceania (Bellwood 1991). The present study is entirely based on samples from the mountain tribes. The locations where blood samples were collected are shown in Table 13.1. All samples were from healthy unrelated individuals whose parents were also from the same tribe.

Results

HLA polymorphism

A summary of the most frequent alleles observed is given in Table 13.2 (top). Except at locus A where A*2402 has a remarkably high frequency in most peoples, each tribe shows very distinct allele distributions. The most unusual allelic profiles

Table 13.1 Samples and sampling locations

Tribe	No. tested	Sampled site
HLA, Secretor genes, HPA, HNA, Microsatellites		
Atayal	50–52	Wu-Lai Sian, Taipei County
Saisiat	50–62	Wu-Fong Sian, Sin-Chu County
		Nan-Chuan Sian, Miao-Li County
Bunun	52–99	Sing-I Sian, Nan-Tou County
		Su-Lin, Taipei County (moved from Nan-Tou County)
Tsou	51–57	Tofuya and Ta-Pan Villages, A-Li-San Sian
Rukai	49–50	Wu-Tai Sian, Pin-Tong County
Paiwan	51–54	Chun-Ju Sian, Pin-Tong County
Ami	50–98	Sih-Chu, Taipei County (moved from east coast villages)
		Tai-Pa-lan, Hwa-Lien County
Puyuma	50–52	Shia-Pinlang Village, Nan-Wan Village, Tai-Tong County
Yami	50–63	Hong-To Village, Lang-Tau Village, Yu-Jen Village,
		Ye-Yu Village, Tong-Chin Village, Orchid Island
RBC blood groups		
Atayal	219	Jen-Ai Sian, Nan-Tou County;
		Shiou-Ling Sian, Hwa-Lien County
Saisiat	120	Nan-Chuan Sian, Miao-Li County
Bunun	192	Sing-I Sian, Nan-Tou County
		Shuan-Long Sian, Nan-Tou County
Tsou	205	Ta-Pan Village, A-Li-San Sian
Rukai	95	Wu-Tai Sian, Pin-Tong County
Paiwan	165	Vakava, Ma-Chia Sian, Pin-Tong County
		Chin-Lung Village, Tai-Ma-Li, Tai-Tong County
Ami	162	Sou-Fong Sian, Hua-Lien County
		Kuan-Fu Sian, Hua-Lien County
Puyuma	52	Shia-Pinlang Village, Tai-Tong County
		Tai-Ma-Li, Tai-Tong County
Yami	67	Orchid Island

Table 13.2 Summary of alleles with extremely high frequencies (in %, in parentheses) found in Taiwan indigenous tribes

	Central mountain tribes						East coast tribes		
	Atayal	Saisiat	Bunun	Tsou	Rukai	Paiwan	Ami	Puyuma	Yami
HLA-A	A*2402 (68)	A*1102 (12.3)	A*2601 (18.2)	A*2402 (78.4)	A*2402 (75.6) A*2601 (13.9)	A*2402 (86.3)	A*2402 (63) A*3401 (20)	A*2402 (64)	A*2402 (52.1) A*1101 (37.5) A*2407 (4.7)
HLA-B	B55 (18) B39 (19) B60 (33) B48 (21)	B39 (53.5) B60 (33.3)	B13 (24.4)	B13 (16.4) B39 (24.3)	B13 (27.9)	B13 (25.5) B60 (32.4)	B56 (18) B48 (24)	B13 (17) B75 (18)	B62 (37.4) B75 (14.8) B61 (21.8)
HLA-C	Cw7 (30.1)	Cw7 (66)			Cw10 (36.8)	Cw9 (32.6)		Cw8 (32.1)	
HLA-DRB1							*0404 (35) *0405 (21)		*1401 (35.8)
ABO				O (79.7)	B (36.9)				A (31.8)
RH	r' (6.8)			R⁰ (8.8)	R² (32.1)		R¹ (90.7)		R¹ (94)
MNS			Ms (74)		Ms (78.7)		Ms (83)	Ms (73)	
JK						Jk (0.6)			
FY							Fyᵃ (97.5)		
MiIII							MiIII (88.4)#	MiIII (21.2)#	MiIII (34.3)#
Se gene			se⁸⁴⁹ (17.3) se⁵⁷¹ (15.4)	se⁸⁴⁹ (27.5) se⁵⁷¹ (13.7)	se⁸⁴⁹ (22)	se⁸⁴⁹ (11.1) se⁶⁸⁵ (4.6)	se⁵⁷¹ (14.7) se⁶⁸⁵ (2.9)	se⁸⁴⁹ (9.8) se⁶⁸⁵ (1)	se⁵⁷¹ (15)
HNA							HNA -1 null (19.8)		

Note
These are phenotype frequencies.

are found in the Ami (e.g. high frequency of A*3401 and DRB1*0404, rarely seen elsewhere) and Yami (e.g. high frequency of A*1101 and DRB1*1401). In addition, some differences are observed between southern (mostly Paiwan, Rukai, Bunun and Tsou) and northern (Atayal, Saisiat) peoples of the central mountain ranges, for example, contrasting frequencies of B13 (frequent in the former) and Cw7 (frequent in the latter). Also, DRB1*1502 is only observed in the east-coast peoples (10.6–21 per cent), while DRB1*08032 is restricted to the central mountain peoples (14–27.6 per cent).

A common feature of all indigenous peoples of Taiwan is a low number of HLA class I and class II alleles often reaching high frequencies (Chu et al. 2001a; Lin et al. 2000). Actually, many alleles reported here have the highest frequencies reported so far in the literature. These peoples are thus unique, with remarkable inter-tribal diversity and a high intra-tribal genetic homogeneity.

As natural selection is commonly believed to influence the evolution of HLA allelic frequencies (Meyer and Thomson 2001), we checked a possible deviation from neutrality in our data. Figure 13.1 plots normalised deviates of homozygosity, or Fnds, (Salamon et al. 1999) on the HLA-A, B, C and DR allele frequencies in the different indigenous peoples. A positive Fnd indicates a low level of internal genetic diversity, whereas a negative value indicates a high level in a given population.[1] We note that HLA-A allele distributions exhibit very high values (positive Fnds), while negative Fnds are mostly obtained for the other loci. However, significant excess of heterozygotes is only seen in the Bunun, the Tsou and the Ami for the HLA-C locus and the Puyuma for the HLA-B locus. Also, only

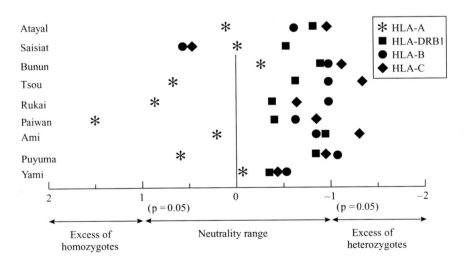

Figure 13.1 Normalised deviates of the homozygosity statistic (Fnds) for HLA-A, B, C, and DR loci in Taiwan (see text for explanations).

one tribe (Paiwan) presents a significant excess of homozygotes (HLA-A) relative to the neutral expectation (p   0.05).

As these data do not show any strong evidence for natural selection acting on HLA, the marked differences in allele distributions observed among the peoples and the unexpected high frequencies for some alleles are most likely the result of founder effects with genetic drift, and are consistent with long isolation of small populations.

Part of the HLA data presented above was used by Chu et al. (2001a) to plot a neighbour-joining population dendrogram of nine indigenous peoples of Taiwan and 26 other ethnic groups including Oceanians, Asians, Amerindians, Europeans and Africans (not shown). Their study indicates that Taiwan's indigenous peoples are clearly separated from other populations of Asia, and are further subdivided into two clusters, representing the central mountain and east coast peoples respectively. In the central mountain peoples, the northern Atayal and Saisiat cluster together. Similarly, two other subclusters are obtained with the central mountain Tsou and Bunun and the southern Paiwan and Rukai. On the east coast, the Yami and the Puyuma cluster with the Ivatan of the Philippines, in agreement with previous linguistic and archaeological findings suggesting that the Yami and the Ivatan are related (Kano 1955). The tree also connects the Ami with non-Austronesian groups, Australian Aborigines and Highlanders from Papua New Guinea (PNG). This correlates with our previous finding that haplotype HLA A34-Cw1-B56 found in the Ami (18 per cent) is shared with the PNG Highlanders (8.1 per cent) and the Australian Aborigines (4.1 per cent) (Lin et al. 2000). HLA-DRB1*0405, seen at high frequency in the Ami (21 per cent), is also elevated in the PNG Highlanders (16 per cent) (Chu et al. 2001a; Zimdahl et al. 1999).

As the different HLA genes are closely linked on chromosome 6 (region 6p21.3), particular combinations of alleles on a chromosome (HLA haplotypes) are inherited from parents to children. Particular HLA haplotypes observed in different populations are sometimes proposed as sharing the common ancestry of these populations in the past. The analysis of HLA haplotypes is thus a powerful approach for studying migration and/or the historical relationship between human populations (Tokunaga et al. 1992, 1997). The HLA A-B-C haplotype distributions among the nine mountain peoples of Taiwan reveal that HLA A24-Cw8-B48, A24-Cw9-B61 and A24-Cw10-B61 are present in most peoples, and are also found in northeast Asian populations (Inuit, Oroqen, Mongolians, Japanese, Manchurians, Buryat and Sakha [Yakut] and, surprisingly, the Tlingit from North America). Both A24-Cw7-B39 (found in most peoples) and A24-Cw1-B55 (found in the Atayal and the Tsou) are also observed in the Maori. HLA A34-Cw1-B56 found in the Ami and Puyuma is shared with PNG Highlanders and Australian Aborigines (Lin et al. 2000). Similar findings are also reported with HLA A-B-DRB1 haplotypes, where several haplotypes are shared with both northern and southern Asians (Chu et al. 2001a).

In this report, the HLA B-DRB1 haplotype frequencies of the nine peoples were newly estimated by a maximum likelihood method (Imanishi et al. 1992a) and the results are shown in Table 13.3. As for HLA A-B-C and HLA A-B-DRB1 haplotypes

Table 13.3 HLA B-DRB1 haplotype frequencies (in %) among Taiwan's indigenous tribes and other populations

Haplotype B-DRB1	Central mountain tribes						East coast tribes			Others[a,b]
	Atayal	Saisiat	Bunun	Tsou	Rukai	Paiwan	Ami	Puyuma	Yami	
N	50	57	88	51	50		50	50	64	
B13-*12021			14.6[c]	15.4	21.8	24.5		4.0	3.3	187 Man: 3.4
B48-*11011			10.0	4.9	7.0	4.9		3.9	4.0	73 Sing. Chinese: 4.4; 50 Ivatans: 3.0
B48-*1401	19.0					3.9	5.8	3.0		56 Tlingit: 5.0
B55-*1201					3.0	3.9		5.5		53 Maori: 13.9
B60-*1401	7.0	14.8		7.3						53 Maori:16.4; 50 Ivatans: 4.7
B61-*11011					9.0	3.9	3.0	3.0		53 Maori: 5.0;
B61-*1401				4.9		7.8			19.5	56 Tlingit: 5.0; 156 Inuit: 5.8
B62-*16021			5.9	3.9	4.6		4.0	7.0	29.4	68 Javanese: 4.0; 77 N.Han: 5.3; 93 Indian: 3.7; Timor: 17.8
B13-*08032	3.7		3.6		3.5					
B39-*08032	11.0	17.5	8.5	21.5	6.5	4.9				
B39-*12021		23.6								
B55-*12021			3.2	3.5	3.0					
B60-*0403	7.0		11.6		8.4	8.8				53 Maori: 13.9
B60-*08032	5.0				3.0	6.9				d
B60-*09012	8.0									
B60-*1101		6.1		3.9	5.6	12.7				53 Czech: 3.8; 79 S. Han: 5.6

Haplotype					Other populations
B56-*15021			17.0		53 Maori: 3.0
B13-*11011				4.0	
B13-*1401				4.9	
B27-*08032	3.3			7.0	
B27-*11011				3.8	48 Uralic: 3.1
B27-*1405				4.0	
B38-*15021					56 Tlingit: 9.3
B39-*0404			5.6		9.0 53 Maori: 2.9; 65 S. Amerindian: 8.2
B39-*11011		3.4			
B39-*1401	8.7				
B48-*0404			15.9		104 Mongolians: 3.5; 156 Inuit: 9.0
B48-*15011				5.0	
B55-*08032		3.9			
B55-*11011	16.9				
B55-*1401		7.8			
B55-*15011			4.1		
B60-*0404			12.5		d
B60-*04051			17.3		d
B60-*15011				5.0	71 Thai Chinese: 3.6
B62-*08032		4.8			
B62-*1401					10.3
B75-*12021					9 50 Ivatans: 20.9; 140 Vietnamese: 3.8
B75-*15021			13.9		

Notes

a DRB1 alleles were defined by sequence-based typing in Ivatan (Chu et al. 2001a), and by serological method in other ethnic groups (Imanishi et al. 1992b).
b The column lists, for each population, the number of individuals tested, the population name, and the haplotype frequency, in % (Imanishi et al. 1992b).
c Bold-faced are frequencies higher than 10%.
d HLA B60-DR4 haplotype was found in 53 Maori: 6.8; 71 Thai Chinese: 5.0; 77 British: 3.2; 142 Canadian: 3.7.

described in our previous reports, many haplotypes found among Taiwan's indigenous peoples are shared with both northern and southern Asians (Imanishi et al. 1992b). This indicates either a common origin or gene flow between these populations. Nevertheless, several haplotypes are seen only in some of Taiwan's indigenous peoples. For example, haplotypes B13-DRB1*12021 and B48-DRB1*11011 are found in most peoples but not in the northern central mountain peoples (Atayal and Saisiat) and the Ami, while HLA B39-DRB1*12021 is only seen in the latter. Several haplotypes are observed in the central mountain peoples but not in the east coast (B39-DRB1*08032, B39-DRB1*12021, B13-DRB1*08032, B55-DRB1*12021, B60-DRB1*0403, B60-DRB1*08032, B60-DRB1*09012 and B60-DRB1*11011), while HLA B56-DRB1*15021 is only found in east-coast peoples. Many peoples also exhibit unusual haplotypes not observed elsewhere. This suggests a long period of settlement and/or rapid genetic drift. As with the allele distributions, each tribe exhibits a limited number of HLA haplotypes, a few of them at high frequencies, indicating again a low level of internal genetic diversity. We also note that in the Ami, HLA A34-Cw1-B56 has a similar frequency to HLA B56-DRB1*15021 and HLA A34-B56-DRB1*15021 (17–18 per cent), suggesting that the expected haplotype HLA A34-Cw1-B56-DRB1*15021 may be a well-conserved ancestral haplotype.

Red blood cell (RBC) polymorphisms

All RBC samples from the various population groups in Taiwan were tested for the following blood group markers: A, B, H, D, P1, M, N, Le^a, Le^b, D, C^w, C, c, E, e, K, k, Fy^a, Fy^b, Jk^a, Jk^b, S and s. In addition, a proportion was also tested for Mg, He, Kp^a, Kp^b, Js^b, Lu^a, Lu^b, Ge, Co^a, Co^b, Di^a, Di^b, St^a and Mur. All Mur positive samples were then tested with anti-Anek and anti-Hil to distinguish the MiIII phenotype from MiIV, MiVI, MiIX phenotypes that are all Mur positive (Broadberry et al. 1996a; Lin and Broadberry 1998). The most relevant allele and haplotype frequencies are summarised in Table 13.2 (bottom).

Classical blood groups

The frequencies of ABO alleles vary greatly among the different peoples, with the highest frequencies of A in the Yami, B in the Rukai, and O in the Tsou. High B gene frequencies are observed in most of Taiwan's indigenous peoples, especially among southern peoples of central mountain peoples, the Ami and the Puyuma. High B frequencies have also been reported in Southeast Asians. With Rhesus, except for 6.8 per cent of r in the Atayal, haplotypes r, r , r and r^y are virtually absent in all peoples. The Ami and the Yami have extremely high frequencies of R^1, the Rukai a high frequency of R^2, and the Tsou a relatively high frequency of R^0. The S antigen of the MNS system is rare or absent from the southern central mountain peoples and east coast peoples, which results in high Ms frequencies. One Jk(a b) phenotype is found in Paiwan, and a family study reveals another Jk(a b) phenotype in the siblings. The Jk gene in the Paiwan tribe is therefore

0.6 per cent. Jk is a rare silent allele of Jk^a and Jk^b, and has been found to have high incidence in the Indians of Mato Grosso, Brazil (5 out of 88 tested, Silver et al. 1960) and also in some Polynesian ethnic groups (Maori, Samoans, Cook Islanders, Tongans and Niueans, 0.07–1.45 per cent) (Henry and Woodfield 1995). Incidentally, one Jk(a b) phenotype was found in the Rukai while routinely phenotyping a Rukai family. This may indicate that Jk gene is not uncommon in the southern central mountain peoples. There are a few Fy^a negative individuals in the central mountain peoples, but east coast peoples are all Fy^a positive. Finally, only 5 Di(a b) individuals are found among 809 indigenous samples tested (0.6 per cent), while Di^a antigen is considered as a relevant marker in East Asian and Amerindian populations (Levine et al. 1956).

MiIII phenotype

The MiIII phenotype (GP Mur) is commonly seen among Asians, but is rare among Europeans. The highest frequencies of the MiIII phenotype are here found in the east coast peoples of Taiwan, among the Ami, Yami and Puyuma. These frequencies are the highest reported to date (Broadberry and Lin 1996a). MiIII was also reported among the Thai (9.6 per cent) and Hong Kong Chinese (6.28 per cent). On the other hand, it is uncommon among the Ivatan (2 per cent, unpublished data), suggesting that other factors may contribute to the difference in frequencies with the Yami, to whom they are related both linguistically and genetically. Actually, the MiIII phenotype is a glycophorin B (GPB) molecule with a glycophorin A (GPA) insert and is encoded by the GYP (B-A-B)hybrid gene. As glycophorin has been considered as a possible receptor for Plasmodium falciparum (Pasvol et al. 1982), it was suggested that the MiIII phenotype conferred resistance for malaria, and that its high frequencies in east coast peoples, especially the Ami, was the result of natural selection. Central mountain peoples have rarely or never been found positive for the MiIII phenotype, for example the Paiwan, a southern central mountain tribe living at less than 1000-meter altitude, which was severely attacked by malaria in the past. However, a parasite invasion assay with MiIII cells from 3 Ami individuals tested against 3 different parasite lines of Plasmodium falciparum[2] failed to demonstrate the resistance of MiIII cells to the invasion of Plasmodium falciparum. Although the process causing the high frequency of MiIII phenotype among the east coast peoples is unknown, the absence of MiIII phenotype from central mountain peoples appears to be associated with reduced demographic expansion at low altitudes. However, the differences between the central mountain and the east coast peoples may also be due to the complex history of these peoples rather than to a selective effect, as suggested by Sanchez-Mazas et al. (Chapter 16, this volume).

Secretor status

Lewis phenotypes exhibit marked differences among different populations in Taiwan (Broadberry and Lin 1996b). The Le(a b) phenotype, which is not seen in

Europeans, is found in all population groups of Taiwan (9.0–31.8 per cent). This phenotype is postulated to be due to a weak secretor allele, Se^w, and has recently been confirmed to be present in all populations of Asian descent. The Se^w gene has now been cloned and found to be due to a point mutation, Se^{385} (Yu et al. 1995). A recent PCR-RFLP analysis of the secretor gene in various Taiwan populations has revealed an important polymorphism (Yu et al. 2001). Se^{385} (above mentioned) and Se^{357} are the major alleles in all peoples (24–55 per cent and 20.6–46.2 per cent respectively), although the 'wild-type' allele, Se, is also present. Se and the Se^{357} are responsible for the formation of the Le(a-b) phenotype. The Le(a b-) phenotype, present in about 20 per cent of Europeans, is rare or absent in the Taiwanese Chinese, but is present in many of the Taiwan indigenous groups. Three se genes, se^{571}, se^{685} and se^{849}, are found to be responsible for that phenotype among Taiwan's indigenous peoples and show different distributions. Allele se^{571} is present in all Taiwan's indigenous peoples, se^{685} only in east coast peoples and the neighbouring Paiwan and se^{849} in most peoples except in the northern central mountain peoples. Therefore, the distribution of se alleles also indicates that indigenous peoples of Taiwan are highly differentiated among them. Interestingly, alleles se^{571}, se^{685} and se^{849} are also found in the Maori, Filipinos and Indonesians, but are rare or absent in the Thai, Japanese, Chinese and Europeans (Chang et al. 2001; Yu et al. 2001). This suggests that Taiwan's indigenous peoples are genetically related to insular Southeast Asia.

Human platelet antigen (HPA) and human neutrophil antigen (HNA-1)

Genotyping of the gene responsible for the expression of HPA-1 through HPA-5 and HNA-1 systems in Taiwan's indigenous peoples (n 558) and in the 'Taiwanese' population (n 326) was performed by PCR with sequence-specific primers (PCR-SSP) (Chu et al. 2001b). The analysis showed that HPA-1b and HPA-4b are virtually absent from Taiwan's indigenous populations, and suggests that these rare alleles were not present among the ancestors of indigenous peoples before migration to Taiwan. The frequency of HPA-1b in Europeans is much higher than in Asians. HPA-2b shows a high frequency in the Atayal, and is rare in east coast peoples.

In the HNA system, the frequencies of HNA-1a are much higher than those of HNA-1b in all peoples, except the Yami, where both alleles have the same frequency (50 per cent). No HNA-1c is found. The HNA-1 null is a rare allele according to the literature, but this allele seems to be widely distributed in the Ami tribe, as 3 homozygous for the HNA-1 null phenotype are found among 98 individuals, leading to an estimated allele frequency of 19.8 per cent. In conclusion, east coast peoples, and especially the Ami, are genetically different from the other Taiwanese peoples.

Genetic relationships of Taiwan's indigenous peoples

A neighbour-joining population dendrogram was constructed by using D_A genetic distances (Nei et al. 1983). Distances were obtained from allele frequencies of

GENETIC DIVERSITY OF TAIWAN

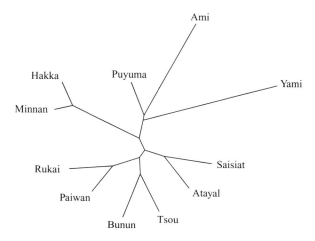

Figure 13.2 Neighbour-joining population dendrogram of Taiwan's indigenous peoples. The D_A genetic distances were calculated from allele or haplotype frequencies of HLA-A, B, C, DRB$_1$ loci, red cell blood groups, Se genes, human platelet antigen (HPA), human neutrophile antigen (HNA), and 13 STR loci (microsatellites).

HLA-A, B, C, DRB1 loci, 37 RBC blood groups (haplotype frequencies were used for Rh and MNS systems), Se gene polymorphism, human platelet antigens, human neutrophil antigens, as well as microsatellites of nine different Taiwan indigenous peoples. These microsatellites concern the D3S1358, VWA, FGA, D8S1179, D21S11, D18S51, D5S818, D13S317, D7S820, D16S539, TH01, TPOX and CSFIPO polymorphisms studied on 513 indigenous individuals (Lee et al. 2002).

The dendrogram in Figure 13.2 shows that Taiwan indigenous peoples cluster together and that this correlates well with their geographical distribution in Taiwan. For example, the Saisiat and the Atayal are patterned together, as are the Bunun and the Tsou (the central peoples) and the Rukai and the Paiwan (southern central mountain peoples). The east coast peoples, the Ami and the Puyuma, also cluster together and are differentiated from the Yami. The Taiwanese Chinese (Minnan and Hakka) form a cluster, well separated from the indigenous peoples. The clustering patterns of the Taiwan indigenous peoples seen in Figure 13.2 are in agreement with those based on HLA-A, B and DRB1 allele frequencies (Chu et al. 2001a), suggesting that the genetic relationships of Taiwan indigenous people are congruent when described by several independent systems.

Discussion

The genetic diversity of Taiwan's indigenous peoples is revealed through the use of HLA, RBC blood groups, Se genes, platelet alloantigens, HNA-1 system, and microsatellites. Overall, we observe a high level of genetic homogeneity within populations and a high level of heterogeneity between populations. These results are summarised in Table 13.2 where both unusual and high frequency alleles observed in Taiwan indigenous peoples are listed. Each tribe possesses specific genetic attributes that distinguish it from the others. On the other hand, several HLA haplotypes and Se genes are common among all groups, suggesting either that these populations share a common origin or have maintained gene flow. Nonetheless, the results in Figure 13.2 separate central mountain peoples from east coast peoples.

Similar results were found in a previous study of 13 RBC enzyme genetic markers in 654 individuals, showing that Taiwan's indigenous peoples probably came from five different origins. In particular the Ami, the Yami and the Tsou are distinct from all the others, the Rukai, the Paiwan and the Puyuma are possibly related, as are the Atayal, Saisiat and Bunun (Jin 1992). Among the nine peoples, only the Yami have a history of migration from the Batan Islands (northern Philippines), which may have happened in the last 1,000 years. The genetic affinity between the Yami and the Ivatan was described in our previous study (Chu et al. 2001c). Among the eight peoples on the island of Taiwan, the Ami are very unusual genetically for most markers. We also found that they cluster with the PNG Highlanders and the Australian Aborigines for HLA (Chu et al. 2001a), although this genetic link may also be due to chance. In general, all central mountain peoples belong to one cluster, and are separated from other populations of Asia. HLA A-B-C, A-B-DRB1 and B-DRB1 haplotypes are shared with haplotypes from both northern and southern Asian populations.

Taiwan's indigenous peoples show a closer relationship to southern Asia populations, especially from insular Southeast Asia (Indonesia, Philippines) where many high frequency HLA alleles specific for the Taiwan's indigenous peoples are also seen (Chu et al. 2001a). For example, HLA-DRB1*1502, frequent in the east coast peoples, and HLA-DRB1*1202, frequent in the central mountain peoples, are widely distributed in Southeast Asia and Oceania. HLA-A*3401, frequent in the Ami, is common in the Indonesians. Some relationships with New Guinea and Australia are indeed also apparent, although not exclusive: HLA-A*3401 (cited above) is also observed in the PNG Highlanders and Australian Aborigines, HLA-DRB1*0405 is seen both in the Philippines and PNG Highlanders, and DRB1*1101 in the Melanesians. HLA-DRB1*1401 has a high frequency in Australian Aborigines and the Melanesians, and finally DRB1*08032 is also seen in Australian Aborigines and Oceania. Except for HLA-DRB1*1101, the above-mentioned alleles are not commonly found in Europeans or Africans, but are seen in other Asian regions with lower frequencies. In our RBC blood groups studies, although only limited data was available, the MiIII phenotype is rarely found in north Asians (Japanese and northern Chinese) and Europeans, but is commonly observed in Southeast Asians (Hong Kong Chinese, Taiwanese, and Thai) (Broadberry and Lin 1996a). Three se genes (se^{571}, se^{685} and se^{849}) found in indigenous Taiwanese are also seen in Filipinos and Indonesians, but not in Japanese, Thai or Europeans. High frequencies of B and R^1 (DCe,) and the presence of Jk alleles are also common in some ethnic groups of Southeast Asia (Henry and Woodfield 1995; Mourant et al. 1976). Overall, these results suggest a strong relationship between Taiwan's indigenous peoples and populations of insular Southeast Asia.

Archaeological studies reveal intensive prehistoric human activities on Taiwan. More than 1,600 prehistoric sites have been found across a region of 54,600 km². The earliest prehistoric sites in Taiwan are the Changpin caves on the southeast coast of Taiwan (15,000–3,250 BC). They belong to the Changpin Culture of the post-Pleistocene Palaeolithic period (Sung 1978). The corresponding human remains (skull and teeth) found in southern Taiwan are fossils of Homo sapiens 'Tso-chen Man', estimated by fluorine and manganese dating to have lived some time between 30,000 and 20,000 BP (Lien 1981). The earliest Neolithic culture in Taiwan is the Tapengkeng culture, unrelated to the Changpin culture, and distributed on the west coast (4,000–2,500 BC; see Tsang, Chapter 4, this volume). Besides these sites, the records suggest more than 10 different prehistoric cultures (Sung 1980). These archaeological findings correlate well with the results of genetic studies, suggesting that the ancestors of Taiwan's indigenous peoples may have distinct origins. Before Taiwan became an island about 12,000 BP, it was geographically linked to Asia throughout the nearly 20,000 years of the glacial period (Map 13.2). At that time, the sea level was much lower than at present. The Taiwan Strait was a lowland in the glacial period: it

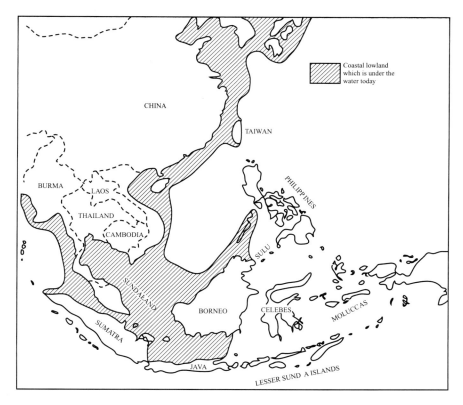

Map 13.2 Map of Southeast Asia and Oceania prior to 12,000 BP when Taiwan was connected to the continent.

connected to the coastal lowland along the Asian continental shelf from the gulf of Tonkin to Japan (Lin 1963) and to Sundaland in the south (Meacham 1985). We suggest there may have been migrations to Taiwan from the southern regions in this period. This may have taken place along the coastline, now under the sea. Long periods of settlement and isolation of the populations from each other would then explain the high levels of heterogeneity of Taiwan's indigenous peoples. On the other hand, the relationship between Taiwan's indigenous peoples and insular Southeast Asia would be the result of more recent southwards migrations out of Taiwan. In both cases, Taiwan might have been an impasse and/or a stopover on the route of ancient migrating populations of the prehistoric East Asian dispersal era.

Acknowledgements

We thank our friends and colleagues from the Presbyterian churches, from the health stations of indigenous peoples (the Lai-Yi Health Station of Ping Tong County and A-Li-San Health Station of Nan-Tou County), Pu-Li Christian Hospital, Tong Ho General Hospital of Tai-Tong City, Prof. Theodore Kay and the Institute of Ethnology, Academia Sinica, Taiwan, for helping us to collect blood samples. We are particularly grateful to the indigenous peoples of Taiwan who donated their blood for this work. We would also like to thank Prof. K. Tokunaga of the University of Tokyo, Prof. C.M. Lien of National Taiwan University for anthropological advice, Y.S. Chan, H.L. Lee, S.L. Chang for technical assistance, and Prof. T. Juji of the Japanese Red Cross Central Blood Centre for helping us in the HLA study. This work was supported by grants from the National Health Research Institute of Taiwan and the National Science Council of Taiwan.

Abbreviation

AN   Austronesian

Notes

1 The definition of Fnd described by Salamon et al. 1999 has been modified by one of us (JAT) so that all Fnd values higher than 1 or lower than 1 are out of the neutrality range at the 5 per cent significance level.
2 Kindly performed by Dr Alex Rowe from the Institute of Cell, Animal and Population Biology at the University of Edinburgh.

Bibliography

Bellwood, P. (1991) 'The Austronesian dispersal and the origin of language', Scientific American, July 70–3.
Broadberry, R.E. and Lin, M. (1996a) 'The distribution of the MiIII (Gp.Mur) phenotype among the population of Taiwan', Transfusion Medicine, 6: 145–8.

Broadberry, R.E. and Lin, M. (1996b) 'Comparison of the Lewis phenotypes among the different population groups of Taiwan', Transfusion Medicine 6: 255–60.

Chang, J.G., Ko, Y.C., Lee, J.C.I., Chang, S.J., Liu, T.C., Shih, M.C. and Pong, C.T (2001) 'Molecular analysis of mutations and polymorphism of Lewis secretor type alpha (1,2)-fucosyltransferase gene reveals that Taiwan aborigines are derived from Austronesian', Abstract in Transactions of Taiwan Society of Blood Transfusion, p. 24.

Chu, C.C., Lin, M., Nakajima, F., Lee, H.L., Chang, S.L., Tokunaga, K. and Juji, T. (2001a) 'Diversity of HLA among Taiwan's indigenous peoples and the Ivatans in the Philippines', Tissue Antigens 58: 9–18.

Chu, C.C., Lee, H.L., Chu, T.W. and Lin, M. (2001b) 'Genotyping of the human platelet antigen systems 1–5 and neutrophil antigens in Taiwan', Transfusion 41: 1553–8.

Chu, C.C., Trejaut, J., Lee, H.L. and Lin, M. (2001c) 'The genetic affinity between the Tao (Yami) and the Ivatans, a view from the human leucocyte antigen (HLA) system', in International Symposium on Austronesian Cultures: Issue relating to Taiwan. Taipei: Academia Sinica.

Henry, S. and Woodfield, G. (1995) 'Frequencies of the Jk(a-b-) phenotype in Polynesian ethnic groups', Transfusion 35: 277.

Imanishi, T., Akaza, T., Kumura, A., Tokunaga, K. and Gojobori, T. (1992a) 'Estimation of allele and haplotype frequencies for HLA and complement loci', in K. Tsuji, M. Aizawa, T. Sasazuki (eds) HLA 1991, Proceedings of the 11th International Histocompatibility Workshop and Conference, vol. 1, 76–9. Oxford: Oxford University Press.

Imanishi, T., Akaza, T., Kimura, A., Tokunaga, K. and Gojobori, T. (1992b) 'Allele and haplotype frequencies for HLA and complement loci in various ethnic groups', in K. Tsuji, M. Aizawa, T. Sasazuki (eds) HLA 1991, Proceedings of the 11th International Histocompatibility Workshop and Conference, vol. 1, 1064–74, 1127–41. Oxford: Oxford University Press.

Jin, F. (1992) 'Genetic study of native Taiwan populations based on the investigation of red cell enzyme genetic markers', unpublished thesis, University of Tokyo.

Kano, T. (1955) Outline review of the Taiwan archaeology and ethnology, Taipei: The Historical Research Commission of Taiwan.

Kutsuna, M. and Matsuyama, M. (1939) 'On the blood groups of the Taiwan aboriginal peoples', Journal of Taiwan Medical Association 38: 1153–78.

Lee, J.C., Lin, M., Tsai, L.C. et al. (2002) 'Population study of polymorphic microsatellite DNA in Taiwan', Forensic Science Journal 1: 31–7.

Levine, P., Robinson, E.A., Layrisse, M., Arends, T. and Domingues Sisico, R. (1956) 'The Diego blood factor', Nature 177: 40–1.

Lien, C.M. (1981) 'On the occurrence of fossil Homo sapiens in Taiwan', Bulletin of the Department of Archaeology and Anthropology, National Taiwan University 42: 53–74.

Lin, C.C. (1963) 'Geology and ecology of Taiwan prehistory', Asian Perspectives, 7: 203–13.

Lin, M. and Broadberry, R.E. (1998) 'Immunohematology in Taiwan', Transfusion Medicine Review 12: 56–72.

Lin, M., Chu, C.C., Lee, H.L., Chang, S.L., Ohashi, J., Tokunaga, K., Akaja, T. and Juji, T. (2000) 'Heterogeneity of Taiwan's indigenous population: possible relation to prehistoric Mongoloid dispersals', Tissue Antigens 55: 1–9.

Mabuchi, T. (1974) Ethnology of the Southwestern Pacific, Asian Folklore and Social Life Monographs, vol. 59, Taipei: The Orient Culture Service.

Mackay, G.L. (1895) From far Formosa , Toronto: Fleming H. Revell.

Matsumoto, H., Miyazaki, T., Fong, J.M. and Mabuchi, Y. (1972) 'GM and Inv allotypes of the Takasago Peoples in Taiwan', Japanese Journal of Human Genetics 17: 27–37.

Meacham, W. (1985) 'On the improbability of Austronesian origins in south China', Asian Perspectives 26: 89–105.

Melton, T., Peterson, R., Redd, A.J., Saha, N., Sofro, A.S.M., Martinson, J. and Stoneking, M. (1995) 'Polynesian genetic affinities with Southeast Asian populations as identified by mtDNA analysis', American Journal of Human Genetics 57: 403–14.

Meyer, D. and Thomson, G. (2001) 'How selection shapes variation of the human major histocompatibility complex: a review', Annals of Human Genetics 65: 1–26.

Mourant, A.E., Kopec, A. and Domaniewska-Sobczak, K. (1976) The Distribution of the Human Blood Groups and Other Polymorphisms, 2nd edn, London: Oxford University Press.

Nei, M., Tajima, F. and Tateno, Y. (1983) 'Accuracy of estimated phylogenetic trees from molecular data. II. Gene frequency data', Journal of Molecular Evolution 19: 153–70.

Pasvol, G., Jungery, M. and Meatherall, D.J. (1982) 'Glycophorin as a possible receptor for Plasmodium falciparum', Lancet ii: 947–50.

Richard, M., Oppenheimer, S. and Sykes, B. (1998) 'mtDNA suggests Polynesian origins in eastern Indonesia', American Journal of Human Genetics 63: 1234–6.

Salamon H., Klitz W., Easteal S., Gao X., Erlich H.A., Fernandez-Viña M. and Trachtenberg E.A. (1999) 'Evolution of HLA Class II Molecules: Allelic and Amino Acid Site Variability Across Populations', Genetics 152: 393–400.

Schanfield, M.S., Ohkura, K., Lin, M., Shyu, R. and Gershowitz, H. (2002) 'Immunoglobulin allotypes among Taiwan aborigines: evidence of malaria selection could affect studies of population affinity', Human Biology 74: 363–79.

Silver, R.T., Haber, J.M. and Kellner, A. (1960) 'Evidence for a new allele in the Kidd blood group system in Indians of Northern Mato Grosso, Brazil', Nature 186: 481.

Su, B., Jin, L., Underhill, P., Martinson, J., Saha, N., McGarvey, S.T., Shriver, M.D., Chu, J., Oefner, P. Chakraborty, R. and Deka, R. (2000) 'Polynesian origins: insights from the Y chromosome', Proceedings of the National Academy of Sciences USA 97: 8225–8.

Sung, W.H. (1978) 'Prehistoric Taiwan', Proceedings of Taiwan Historical Research Society Taipei, 10–24.

Sung, W.H. (1980) 'Archaeology in Taiwan', in Chuon Kuo te Taiwan. 93–220. Taipei: Chuon Yan Wen Wu Kong Ing Sho.

Sykes, B., Leiboff, A., Low-Beer, J., Tetzner, S. and Richards, M. (1995) 'The origins of the Polynesians: an interpretation from mitochondria lineage analysis', American Journal of Human Genetics 57: 1463–75.

Tokunaga, K., Ishikawa, Y., Ogawa, A., Wang, H. and Mitsunaga, S. (1997) 'Sequence-based association analysis of HLA class I and II alleles in Japanese supports conservation of common haplotypes', Immunogenetics 46: 199–205.

Tokunaga, K. and Juji, T. (1992) 'The migration and dispersal of east Asian population as viewed from HLA genes and haplotypes', in T. Akazawa, K. Aoki, T. Kimura (eds) The Evolution and Dispersal of Modern Humans in Asia, Tokyo: Hokusen-Sha, 599–611.

Trejaut, J.A., Kivisild, T., Loo, J.H., Li, Z.Y., Lee, H.L., Chang, H.L., Chu, C.C. and Lin, M. (2004) 'Traces of archaic mitochondrial lineages persist in Austronesian speaking Formosan populations', (in preparation).

Yu, L.C., Yang, Y.H., Broadberry, R.E., Chen, Y.H. and Lin, M. (1995) 'Correlation of a missense [???] mutation in the human secretor α (1,2) fucosyltransferase gene with the

Lewis(a b) phenotype: A potential molecular basis for the weak Secretor allele (Sew)', Biochemical Journal 312: 329–32.

Yu, L.C., Chu, C.C., Chan, Y.S., Chang, C.Y., Twu, Y.C., Lee, H.L. and Lin, M. (2001) 'Polymorphism and distribution of the Secretor α (1,2)–fucosyltransferase gene in various Taiwan populations', Transfusion 41: 1279–84.

Zimdahl, H., Schiefenhovel, W., Kayser, M., Roewer, L. and Nagy, M. (1999) 'Towards understanding the origin and dispersal of Austronesians in the Solomon Sea: HLA class II polymorphism in eight distinct populations of Asia-Oceania', European Journal of Immunogenetics 26: 405–16.

14

GENETIC ANALYSIS OF MINORITY POPULATIONS IN CHINA AND ITS IMPLICATIONS FOR MULTIREGIONAL EVOLUTION

Jiayou Chu

The Han nationality constitutes the majority of the population of China, but there are many minorities (about 6.7 per cent of the total population) predominantly found in peripheral regions (especially in the South) and generally speaking their own language. The total number of living languages listed for China is 205 (Grimes and Grimes 2000). Among these minorities, 25 have populations of more than 4,000 individuals at least in part in Yunnan Province, with 15 found only there[1]: Bai, Hani, Dai, Lisu, Lahu, Wa, Naxi, Jingpo, Bulang, Pumi, Nu, Achang, De'ang, Jinuo and Dulong (Table 14.1). This ethnolinguistic diversity may be the result of extensive migrations in historical times, but probably also reflects the mountainous terrain (You 1994). Between the fifth and the third centuries BC, a great change took place among populations in Northwest China. At that time, Xiongnu people on the Mongolian plain began to expand their territory to Qinghai and Gansu Province. As a result, two ancient populations recorded as Di and Qiang were pushed to Southwest China. In the meantime, as the Qin and Han dynasties developed in West China, part of the northern populations was forced to move to Southwest China. Wars also compelled some populations to migrate to the Heng Duan Mountain area. They sought asylum in Yunnan between the Chun Qiu, Zhan Guo and Qin-Han periods, and have been settled there since that period. Due to the diversified environment, the favourable climate and rich natural resources, the province became an ideal place for many different populations to settle. On the other hand, it remained isolated from the outside world because of persistent feudal patterns and inaccessibility. Therefore, many populations also remained isolated from one another. Yunnan is now regarded as a key region for the study of Chinese ethnolinguistic diversity.

The CHGDP has established cell and DNA banks for numerous Chinese nationalities, and informative DNA polymorphisms were analysed to investigate the origin of these peoples and their relationships to other East Asian populations

Table 14.1 Officially recognised populations in China and in Yunnan

No.	Nationalities	Population	No.	Nationalities	Population	No.	Nationalities	Population
1	Achang[b]	27,708	20	Jingpo[b]	119,209	39	Qiang[c]	198,252
2	Bai[b]	1,594,827	21	Jinuo[b]	18,000	40	Russian[c]	13,504
3	Baoan[c]	12,212	22	Kazak[c]	1,111,718	41	Sala[c]	87,697
4	Bulang[b]	82,280	23	Kirgiz[c]	141,549	42	She[c]	630,378
5	Bouyei[a]	2,545,059	24	Korean[c]	1,920,597	43	Shui[a]	345,993
6	Dai[b]	1,025,128	25	Lahu[b]	411,476	44	Tajik[c]	33,583
7	Daur[c]	121,357	26	Lhoba[c]	2,312	45	Tatar[c]	4,873
8	De'ang[b]	15,462	27	Li[c]	1,110,000	46	Tibetan[a]	4,593,330
9	Dong[c]	2,514,014	28	Lisu[b]	574,856	47	Tu[c]	191,624
10	Dongxiang[c]	373,872	29	Manchu[a]	9,821,180	48	Tujia[c]	5,704,223
11	Dulong[b]	5,816	30	Maonan[c]	71,968	49	Uygur[c]	7,214,431
12	Ewenki[c]	26,315	31	Miao[a]	7,398,035	50	Uzbek[c]	14,502
13	Gaoshan[c]	400,000	32	Moinba[c]	7,475	51	Wa[b]	351,974
14	Gelao[c]	437,997	33	Mongolian[a]	4,806,849	52	Xibe[c]	172,847
15	Han[a]	1.2 billion	34	Mulao[c]	159,328	53	Yao[a]	2,134,013
16	Hani[b]	1,253,952	35	Naxi[b]	278,009	54	Yi[a]	6,572,173
17	Hezhe[c]	4,245	36	Nu[b]	21,723	55	Yugur[c]	10,569
18	Hui[a]	8,602,978	37	Oroqen[c]	6,965	56	Zhuang[a]	15,489,630
19	Jing[c]	18,915	38	Pumi[b]	29,657			

Source: Fourth National General Survey of Chinese Populations, 1990.

Notes
a Distributed inside and outside of Yunnan Province;
b Distributed only in Yunnan Province;
c Distributed only outside of Yunnan Province.

(Chu et al. 1998; Ke et al. 2001; Qian et al. 2001; Su et al. 1999). The results obtained for microsatellite and Y chromosome markers were particularly relevant to the origin of East Asian populations as a whole. Chu et al. (1998) analysed microsatellite variation in a total of 28 populations sampled in China. These data were aggregated with populations from other continents to construct two phylogenies involving different loci. In both phylogenies, all populations from East Asia derive from a single lineage, suggesting a unique origin for these populations. The structure of the phylogeny did not support an independent origin of modern humans from earlier Homo in East Asia, as claimed by supporters of the multiregional model (Wolpoff 1989). Rather, the authors concurred with the more usual speciation–replacement model, concluding that 'modern humans originating in Africa constitute the majority of the current gene pool in East Asia' (Chu et al. 1998).

In a second paper, Ke et al. (2001) sampled 12,127 male individuals from 163 populations across Southeast Asia, Oceania, East Asia, Siberia and Central Asia, and typed three Y chromosome biallelic markers (YAP, M89 and M130) in these populations. In a previous Y chromosome study by Underhill et al. (2000), global populations were characterised by a marked geographic structure in which the oldest lineage represented Africans and the younger ones some African and all non-African populations. The M168 mutation (a C to T substitution) shared by all non-African populations was believed to derive from Africa some 44,000 BP (95 per cent confidence interval: 35,000–89,000 years), marking relatively recent migrations out of Africa. The M168T lineage further subdivided into three major sub-lineages defined by YAP(Alu insertion), M89 (C to T mutation), and M130 (C to T mutation) polymorphisms. Ke et al. (2001) found that each of the 12,127 individuals typed in their study carried one of the three polymorphisms YAP , M89T or M130T, and thus fell into the lineage of M168T that was said to derive from Africa. The authors concluded that 'modern humans of African origin completely replaced earlier populations in East Asia'.

The continuity of morphology of anatomically modern 'Homo sapiens' fossils found in China has repeatedly challenged the out-of-Africa hypothesis of the origin of modern humans, suggesting at least one independent evolution in Asia/Oceania. On the other hand, geneticists could not tackle that question for a long time due to the paucity of genetic data on Chinese populations. Recently, extensive studies of those populations, especially from the ethnically diverse Yunnan Province, using genetically informative markers were carried out. The results based on microsatellites and Y chromosome polymorphisms now provide compelling evidence that all East Asian populations, although genetically diverse, share a single origin that may be explained by the speciation–replacement model of modern human origins.

Acknowledgements

We thank our colleagues and collaborators: Jin Li, Li Pu, Xu Jiujin, Zhang Sizhong, Ke Yuehai, Qian Yaping, Yang Zhaoqing, Chu Zhengtao and Yu Jiankun. This project was completed under Z. Chen and B.Q. Qiang and funded by National Natural Sciences Foundation of China.

Abbreviation

CHGDP   Chinese Human Genome Diversity Project

Note

1 Although some do occur in neighbouring countries, such as Myanmar and Thailand.

Bibliography

Chu, J.Y., Huang, W., Kuang, S.Q., Wang, J.M., Xu, J.J., Chu, Z.T., Yang, Z.Q., Lin, K.Q., Li, P., Wu, M., Geng, Z.C., Tan, C.C., Du, R.F. and Jin, L. (1998) 'Genetic relationship of populations in China', Proceedings of the National Academy of Science USA 95: 11763–8.

Grimes, B.F. and Grimes, J.E. (eds) (2000) Ethnologue: Languages of the World, Dallas: SIL International.

Ke, Y., Su, B., Song, X., Lu, D., Chen, L., Li, H., Qi, C., Marzuki, S., Deka, R., Underhill, P., Xiao, C., Shriver, M., Lell, J., Wallace, D., Wells, R.S., Seielstad, M., Oefner, P., Zhu, D., Jin, J., Huang, W., Chakraborty, R., Chen, Z. and Jin, L. (2001) 'African origin of modern humans in East Asia: a tale of 12,000 Y chromosomes', Science 292: 1151–3.

Qian, Y.P., Chu, Z.-T., Dai, Q., Wei, C.-D., Chu, J.Y., Tajima, A. and Horai, S. (2001) 'Mitochondrial DNA polymorphisms in Yunnan nationalities in China', Human Genetics 46: 211–20.

Su, B., Xiao, J., Underhill, P., Deka, R., Zhang, W., Akey, J., Huang, W., Shen, D., Lu, D., Luo, J., Chu, J., Tan, J., Shen, P., Davis, R., Cavalli-Sforza, L., Chakraborty, R., Xiong, M., Du, R., Oefner, P., Chen, Z. and Jin, L. (1999) 'Y-Chromosome evidence for a northward migration of modern humans into eastern Asia during the last Ice Age', American Journal of Human Genetics 65: 1718–24.

Underhill, P.A., Shen, P., Lin, A.A., Jin, L., Passarino, G., Yang, W.H., Kauffman, E., Bonne-Tamir, B., Bertranpetit, J., Francalacci, P., Ibrahim, M., Jenkins, T., Kidd, J.R., Mehdi, S.Q., Seielstad, M.T., Wells, R.S., Piazza, A., Davis, R.W., Feldman, M.W., Cavalli-Sforza, L.L. and Oefner, P.J. (2000) 'Y chromosome sequence variation and the history of human populations', Nature Genetics 26: 358–61.

You, Z. (1994) History of Yunnan Nationalities, Kunming: Yunnan University Press.

15

COMPARING LINGUISTIC AND GENETIC RELATIONSHIPS AMONG EAST ASIAN POPULATIONS

A study of the RH and GM polymorphisms

Estella S. Poloni, Alicia Sanchez-Mazas,
Guillaume Jacques and Laurent Sagart

Introduction

According to palaeoanthropological and archaeological records, East Asia is probably one of the earliest regions settled by our species, Homo sapiens sapiens, after Africa and the Middle East (Lahr and Foley 1994, 1998). Research in this region of the world should thus provide important clues about the history of our species. Moreover, documenting the genetic diversity of East Asian populations is a crucial step in understanding the settlement history of such regions as Japan, insular Southeast Asia and Oceania, as well as the American continent. Continental East Asian populations have recently attracted the attention of molecular anthropologists, as attested by the numerous studies on variation of molecular markers in these populations published during the last four or five years (e.g. Chu et al. 1998; Ding et al. 2000; Karafet et al. 2001; Ke et al. 2001; Oota et al. 2002; Su et al. 1999; Yao et al. 2002a). These studies have provided contradictory results and lead to discrepancies in the interpretation of the genetic history of East Asian populations. There may be several reasons that explain this, including differential or restricted sampling of populations, but the most important is that each independent component of our genome has its own specific evolutionary history. For instance, gender-specific polymorphisms, such as those studied on the mitochondrial genome and the Y chromosome, have revealed the impact of differential migratory behaviour of men and women on the genetic structure of populations (Oota et al. 2001a; Poloni et al. 1997; Seielstadt et al. 1998). Thus, several polymorphic systems must be analysed if one aims at drawing more conclusive inferences about the genetic history of populations in East Asia.

Continental East Asia is also home to much cultural diversity, as attested among other traits by the number of distinct language families that coexist there.

However, the relationships between this linguistic diversity and the genetic variability of East Asian populations are only starting to be investigated (Su et al. 2000). This study analyses the genetic structure of East Asian populations with an emphasis on the linguistic classification of these populations, that is the classification of their languages into the great East Asian language families. It is part of an ongoing project to analyse multiple genetic systems. As a contribution to the investigation of the evolutionary information held by each specific component of the genome, we present here the results of the analysis of two serological markers, the Rhesus (RH) and GM polymorphisms, which have been extensively tested in East Asian populations. A companion chapter in this volume (Sanchez-Mazas et al.) investigates the genetic variation of HLA molecular alleles in East Asia.

The results based on the variability of the RH and GM systems indicate that both linguistic classification and geographic proximity explain a significant proportion of the genetic affinities observed among East Asian populations. At present, we interpret these results by suggesting the existence of a commonality in the history of genetic differentiation and linguistic diversification of East Asian populations and language families, with occurrences of strong genetic contacts across linguistic borders.

Materials

The choice of the RH and GM genetic systems, two classical markers,[1] is motivated by the fact that numerous samples drawn from populations of distinct geographic locations in East Asia have been tested over the years, providing a large body of data. The RH system consists of specific antigens expressed on the surface of the red cell and encoded in a set of genes on human chromosome 1. The GM system consists of antigens (allotypes) encoded in a set of genes on chromosome 14 and expressed on specific immunoglobulins (IgG class) circulating in the serum. The RH system comprises eight genetic variants (haplotypes), with variable frequencies among human populations; the GM system is more polymorphic in that it comprises more haplotypes, nine of which represent the vast majority of the human polymorphism (Dugoujon et al. 2004; Sanchez-Mazas 1990; Steinberg and Cook 1981).

The selection of samples was based on linguistic criteria (Table 15.1). We focused on populations whose languages belong to the ST family and its southern neighbours from mainland and insular Southeast Asia approximately down to Kalimantan: the AA, Tai-Kadai, HM (only for GM, not available for RH) and AN families (Figures 15.1a,b). Thus, we did not consider populations north of ST, for example, Altaic, Japanese and Korean. Overall, the analyses of the RH and GM genetic systems rely upon 10,972 and 15,437 individuals respectively (Table 15.1). All the genetic data used are included in the GeneVa databank (maintained by ASM in Geneva) and have been checked for reliability of gene frequencies.

Statistical analyses were performed using Arlequin ver. 2.0 (Schneider et al. 2000) and NTSYSpc ver. 2.1 (Rohlf 1998) software; great-circle distances

Table 15.1 Representation of the linguistic families by numbers of population samples (and numbers of individuals) in the analyses

	RH	GM
Austronesian	12 (2,222)	14 (3,515)
Austro-Asiatic	9 (1,165)	4 (944)
Tai-Kadai	6 (1,004)	11 (1,548)
Hmong-Mien	—	3 (345)
Sino-Tibetan	34 (6,581)	70 (9,555)
Total	61 (10,972)	102 (15,437)

between geographic localities were computed by means of a local program (N. Ray, p.c.). For the sake of clarity, the analyses are described in the relevant results sections.

Results

Genetic landscapes of the RH and GM polymorphisms in East Asia

In East Asia, the RH genetic landscape is mainly characterised by a high frequency (50 per cent) of haplotype R^1 in all populations, concomitant with substantial frequencies of haplotype R^2 and, to a lesser extent, of haplotype R^0 (Plate Va). Actually, the frequency of R^1 increases and that of R^2 decreases as one moves from the north to the south of the continent. The pattern of frequency distributions for the GM system is more diversified, in that more haplotypes are observed at polymorphic frequencies in the populations, especially in Northeast Asia (Plate Vb). In this region, four variants are present at substantial frequencies, that is GM*1,3;5*, GM*1,17;21, GM*1,2,17;21 and GM*1,17;10,11,13,15,16. When one moves from north to south, the populations become less diversified because of an increase in frequency of haplotype GM*1,3;5*, concomitant with a decrease in frequency of the other three common variants. Thus, both genetic systems display a pattern of continuity in variation of the frequency distributions along a north-to-south axis, with no abrupt changes.

Patterns of genetic affinities among populations

Genetic distances between population pairs were calculated as Reynolds et al. (1983) coancestry coefficients based on pairwise F_{ST} statistics estimated from the haplotype frequencies in the samples. The F_{ST} index expresses the proportion of the total genetic variability that is attributable to differences between two populations (the remainder being explained by differences among individuals within the populations). Multivariate analyses of these genetic distances were performed in order to study the patterns of genetic relationships among populations inferred

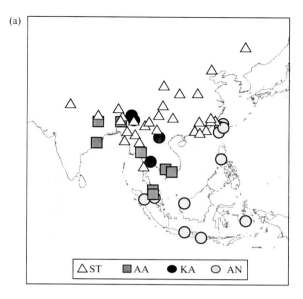

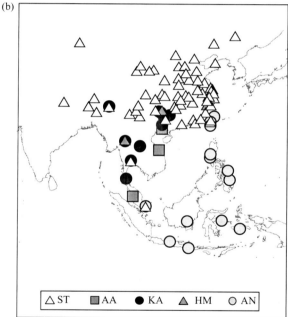

Figure 15.1 (a) Geographic location of 61 population samples tested for RH polymorphism. Samples symbols correspond to linguistic families (ST: Sino-Tibetan; AA: Austro-Asiatic; KA: Tai-Kadai; AN: Austronesian). (b) Geographic location of 102 population samples tested for GM polymorphism. Samples symbols correspond to linguistic families (ST: Sino-Tibetan; AA: Austro-Asiatic; KA: Tai-Kadai; HM: Hmong-Mien; AN: Austronesian).

from each genetic system. We used non-metric multidimensional-scaling (MDS) to obtain a graphic projection of the populations on a two-dimensional space in which the distances between the projected points bear a monotone relationship to the original genetic distances between the populations.

In the resulting MDS on RH data, no clear clustering of the samples is evidenced: the populations tend to group together according to their linguistic affiliation but without any discontinuity between groups (Figure 15.2). Indeed, substantial overlapping of these linguistically defined groups is readily observable, especially for AA and Tai-Kadai. A similar pattern of genetic affinities among populations is observed for the GM system (Figure 15.3), with even higher overlapping among the southern groups (i.e. AA, Tai-Kadai, HM and AN). The relationships among ST populations are further analysed below.

Levels of population genetic structure

The level of genetic differentiation in a set of populations, referred to as the level of population genetic structure, can also be estimated from an F_{ST} statistic. In this case, this statistic expresses the proportion of the total genetic variability attributable

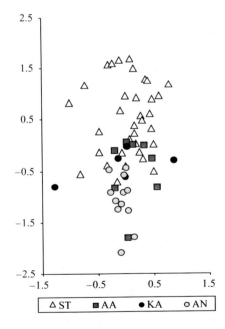

Figure 15.2 MDS of Reynolds et al. (1983) genetic distances among 61 population samples computed on RH frequency distributions. The goodness-of-fit of the 2-dimensional projection to the original configuration is fair (stress value 0.160). Samples symbols as in Figure 15.1a.

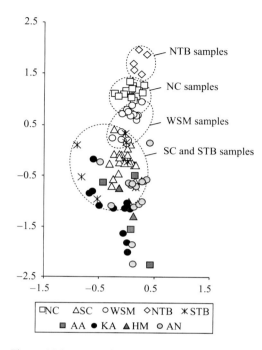

Figure 15.3 MDS of Reynolds et al. (1983) genetic distances among 102 population samples computed on GM frequency distributions. The goodness-of-fit of the 2-dimensional projection to the original configuration is good (stress value 0.085). Samples symbols as in Figure 15.1b, except that ST samples are further subdivided into: NC: Northern Chinese (all Mandarin but Southeastern); SC: Southern Chinese (Min, Xiang, Gan, Hakka, Min and Yue); WSM: Wu and Southeastern Mandarin; NTB: Northern Tibeto-Burman; STB: Southern Tibeto-Burman (see text).

to differences between all the populations (the remainder being explained by differences between individuals within these populations). The observed levels of genetic differentiation between populations are significant both for the RH and GM systems (Table 15.2). The structure is stronger for GM, with approximately 14 per cent of the total genetic variance being explained by differences between populations, versus approximately 4 per cent for the RH system.

The level of population structure within each of the linguistic groups represented in the data is also significant for both systems (Table 15.3). In all groups, these levels are always higher for GM than for RH, but for both systems the highest F_{ST} values are observed in the AA group, indicating a substantial level of genetic differentiation among AA populations.

In Table 15.3, these levels of genetic structure in the linguistically-defined groups are contrasted with a measure of the degree of genetic variability among

Table 15.2 Proportion of the total genetic variation that is due to differences between populations

	Percent of total genetic variance explained by differences	
	Between populations	Among individuals within populations
RH	3.9*	96.1*
GM	14.3*	85.7*

Note
Significance level: *p 0.005.

Table 15.3 Levels of genetic structure among populations within linguistic groups and mean expected heterozygosity in linguistic groups

	RH			GM		
	Group size[a]	F_{ST}[b]	h (s.d.)[c]	Group size[a]	F_{ST}[b]	h (s.d.)[c]
Austronesian	12	0.7*	0.26 (.07)	14	4.3*	0.37 (.15)
Austro-Asiatic	9	3.5*	0.36 (.10)	4	13.6*	0.26 (.23)
Tai-Kadai	6	1.7*	0.36 (.05)	11	4.9*	0.28 (.11)
Hmong-Mien				3	2.7*	0.43 (.21)
Sino-Tibetan	34	2.9*	0.47 (.09)	70	8.1*	0.63 (.10)

Notes
a Number of populations per linguistic group (see Table 15.1).
b Expressed as the per cent of total genetic variation due to differences among populations of the linguistic group.
c Gene diversity (standard deviation) averaged over populations in the linguistic group.
Significance level: *p 0.005.

individuals within the populations, that is gene diversity (h) averaged over the populations in each linguistic group. For both systems, we observe more intra-population variability in the ST group than in the other East Asian groups (although the large standard deviations associated with these measures indicate that the differences between the groups are not substantial).

In summary, ST populations display comparatively high levels of both genetic differentiation and internal diversity. At the opposite, AN and Tai-Kadai populations are both less differentiated and more homogeneous. AA populations also display a rather low level of internal diversity, but they are substantially differentiated. By contrast, HM populations are found to be quite heterogeneous and only slightly differentiated, but this group has to be regarded with caution as it is only represented by three samples, one of which (She) was drawn from an almost completely sinicised population (i.e. Hakka speakers).

Genetic and linguistic affinities among populations

A two-level hierarchical ANOVA was used to further investigate whether the genetic structure inferred from both polymorphisms can be related to linguistic classification (Table 15.4). The populations are first assigned to distinct groups, and the analysis performs a partition of the total genetic variability into three components, that is one due to differences between groups of populations, another due to differences between populations within groups, and a third due to differences among individuals within the populations. The groups are defined as AN, AA, Tai-Kadai and ST, plus HM for GM.

The results for the GM system do indeed suggest a correspondence between the genetic structure of the populations and linguistic groupings. We observe almost twice as much genetic variability between linguistic groups (approximately 12 per cent) as between populations within the linguistic groups (approximately 7 per cent). This correspondence does not apply to the RH system, as the observed level of genetic variability between linguistic groups is comparable to that within those groups (both 3 per cent).

A high level of genetic structure can arise from just a few diverging populations. To determine which linguistically-defined population groups are differentiated from others we performed two-level hierarchical ANOVAs on pairs of groups (Table 15.5). The analyses of RH data indicate that almost all groups are significantly differentiated, but levels of divergence are rather low. Indeed, in most cases, differentiation levels observed between the linguistically-defined groups are lower than those among populations within these groups, with the notable exception of the significant divergence between AN and ST.

In contrast, with the GM data, the ST group is highly and significantly differentiated from all other groups (with values of the 'between groups' component 9 per cent), whereas the latter are mostly undifferentiated between them. Among Southeast Asian groups, intra-group divergence levels are always higher than inter-group levels. Thus, by this analysis, the high level of genetic structure of the GM

Table 15.4 Proportion of the total genetic variation that is due to differences between linguistic groups, and between populations within linguistic groups

	N[a]	Per cent of total genetic variance explained by differences		
		Between groups	Among populations within groups	Among individuals within populations
RH	4[b]	2.2*	2.6*	95.2*
GM	5[c]	12.1*	6.8*	81.2*

Notes
a N: number of linguistic groups.
b The four groups are: AN, AA, Tai-Kadai and ST.
c The five groups are: AN, AA, Tai-Kadai, HM and ST.
Significance level: *p 0.005.

Table 15.5 Proportion of the total genetic variation[a] that is due to differences between linguistic groups compared two by two. Above diagonal: RH system, below diagonal: GM system

	Austronesian	Austro-Asiatic	Tai-Kadai	Hmong-Mien	Sino-Tibetan
Austronesian		0.9***	1.0***	—	4.0***
Austro-Asiatic	n.s.		n.s.	—	1.1**
Tai-Kadai	1.3***	n.s.		—	0.9*
Hmong-Mien	n.s.	n.s.	n.s.		—
Sino-Tibetan	11.5***	13.9***	15.2***	9.6***	

Notes
a This proportion is reported in italics when it is superior to the proportion of genetic variance explained by differences between populations within linguistic groups.
Significance level: n.s. not significant at the 5% level, * 0.05 p 0.01, ** 0.01 p 0.005, *** p 0.005.

Table 15.6 Proportion of the total genetic variation of the GM system that is due to differences within (above diagonal) and between (below diagonal) ST groups[a] compared two by two

	NTB	NC	WSM	SC	STB
NTB		0.5*	1.1*	1.1*	3.0*
NC	2.5*		0.7*	0.8*	1.2*
WSM	8.6*	2.2*		1.3*	2.1*
SC	26.5*	14.2*	5.9*		2.4*
STB	24.0*	12.5*	4.8*	n.s.	

Notes
a See legend to Figure 15.3 for codes to ST groups; and see text for the composition of these groups.
Significance level: n.s. not significant at the 5% level, * p 0.005.

system (approximately 12 per cent, Table 15.4) is mainly attributable to the differentiation of ST from all other linguistically-defined groups.

However, this result is challenged by the MDS analysis on GM data (Figure 15.3), which does not reveal a clear clustering of ST populations. Rather, the MDS suggests some degree of genetic structure within the ST group itself. Indeed, as highlighted in Figure 15.3, and further supported by two-level hierarchical ANOVA analyses (Table 15.6), the ST group can be subdivided into four partially overlapping groups: a northern TB group (i.e. Tibetans and Bhutanese), a northern Chinese group (i.e. Hui and Han samples composed of speakers of Jin and all Mandarin dialects except for Southeastern Mandarin), a Han group of Southeastern Mandarin and Wu speakers, and finally a southern group which comprises both Han speakers of southern Chinese languages (i.e. Xiang, Gan, Hakka, Min and Yue) and southern TB (i.e. Kachari, Sonowal, Lahu, Mikir, Tujia and Yi). This latter group displays close genetic affinities with populations from the Southeast Asian language families.

Correlation between linguistic and genetic distances

Another approach in the study of the relationship between genetics and linguistics is to test for a possible correlation between the degree of genetic similarity (or dissimilarity) between populations and the degree of linguistic similarity (or dissimilarity) between the languages they speak. Genetic dissimilarity between populations, or genetic distance, is a classical measure in population genetics, and several statistics have been developed to quantify it. Here, as for the MDS analyses, genetic distances were computed as coancestry coefficients based on populations pairwise F_{ST} (Reynolds et al. 1983).

We then used phylogenetic classification to infer measures of evolutionary distance between languages. However, the phylogeny of East Asian languages is disputed, especially with respect to higher-order relationships between language families. Different classification schemes are currently being proposed (see the introduction to this volume). In view of this, we have used three different hypotheses for East Asian languages, which we have called, respectively, hypotheses 1, 2 and 3 (Figure 15.4). Hypothesis 1 (Figure 15.4a) is based on a conjecture by Sagart (1994), according to which all the language families of East Asia, south of Altaic, developed from the language of the first domesticators of rice, c.10,000 BP. In the version used here there are three branches: a northern branch consisting of ST plus AN including Tai-Kadai (see Sagart's contributions to this volume, Chapters 9 and 10) and two southern branches, that is HM and AA. For a similar conjecture, with a different internal subgrouping, see Starosta (Chapter 10, this volume). Hypothesis 2 (Figure 15.4b) is represented in such works as Ruhlen (1987) and Peiros (1998) which envision an 'Austric' macro-phylum ('Greater Austric' in the introduction to this volume) and a distinct ST family, intrusive in East Asia, with genetic connections to north Caucasian and Yenisseian, following Starostin's Sino-Caucasian theory (Starostin 1984 [1991]). Hypothesis 3 (Figure 15.4c) states that no phylogenetic relationships exist between the main language families of East Asia.

For each of these hypotheses, the linguistic distance between any two languages was equated with the postulated age of the most recent node (i.e. common ancestor) in which they coalesce. When the hypothesis under consideration supposes no genetic relatedness between two languages, the linguistic distance separating them was equated with an arbitrarily high age, to which we refer as the 'maximum linguistic distance' (MLX). A description of the dating of ages of nodes in the three hypotheses is given in the legend to Figure 15.4. Here we stress the fact that these three hypotheses differ mainly in that part of the phylogeny nearest to the root (i.e. in the primary branches); lower levels in the phylogenies are less controversial.

Once a matrix of linguistic distances between all pairs of languages was obtained, it was compared to the matrix of genetic distances between all pairs of populations speaking those languages, in order to test the significance of the resulting correlation coefficient (r). Repeated computations of r were run with

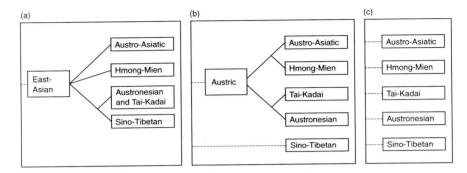

Figure 15.4 Three hypotheses on the phylogenetic relationships among languages considered in this study. In a, hypothesis 1 postulates the existence of an East Asian linguistic macro-family that comprises the AA, HM, Tai-Kadai, AN and ST families (Sagart 1994). Nodes' ages at the level of accepted language families were defined by LS on the basis of estimates by specialists: W. Ostapirat (p.c. 2001) for Tai-Kadai, G. Diffloth (p.c 2001) for AA, and LS own views, especially for Chinese, AN and HM. Datings of higher-order nodes correspond to archaeological events that LS associates with the upper part of the phylogeny: PEA with the domesticaton of rice, Proto-Sino-Austronesian (ST, AN and Tai-Kadai) with the domestication of millet, and Proto-Hmong-Mien with the appearance of iron metallurgy. In b, hypothesis 2 postulates the existence of an Austric macro-family, which relates AA, HM, Tai-Kadai and AN. The dates in this phylogeny follow Starostin (1984 [1987], for the root) and Peiros (1998) and are based on glottochonology. Because the Chinese and AN clades are not dealt with in Peiros (1998), the Chinese and AN internal classifications and datings used in hypothesis 1 were applied to hypothesis 2. The same strategy was applied when detailed statements to construct the classifications dominating specific populations samples included in this study could not be found in Peiros (1998), i.e. central Mon-Khmer, Tai proper and Lolo-Burmese. In c, hypothesis 3 (upon a suggestion raised by R. Blench during the Périgueux workshop) postulates that all the linguistic families considered are unrelated. Here we used, alternatively, the classification and dating schemes of hypotheses 1 (except for Tai-Kadai which is treated as a separate family, not as a branch of AN) and 2. Finally, in a, b and c, nodes for which ages were not directly available were assigned dates through equidistant interpolation.

date values of MLX increased from 15,000 to 50,000 BP, to account for the effect of the value assigned to the MLX on the correlation coefficient. All of the three linguistic hypotheses lead to significant correlation coefficients ($p < 0.001$) in East Asia, with values increasing with the value of MLX: respectively, from $r = 0.19$ to $r = 0.31$ for the RH system, and $r = 0.38$ to $r = 0.45$ for the GM system.

However, populations that are linguistically related tend to occupy geographically adjacent areas. If genetic and linguistic distances are correlated, then this correlation could be due to the fact that these distances are correlated through geography. Indeed, genetic distances are significantly correlated with geographic distances in East Asia: $r = 0.24$ ($p < 0.001$) for RH and $r = 0.35$ ($p < 0.001$) for GM. To address this fact, we computed partial correlation coefficients between genetic and linguistic distances controlled for geography, that is residual correlation coefficients between genetic and linguistic distances once the correlation of both distances with geographic distance has been accounted for (Figure 15.5).

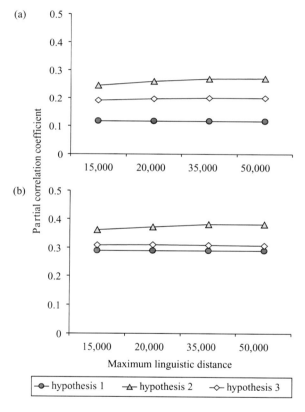

Figure 15.5 Partial correlation coefficients of genetic with linguistic distances, controlled for geography. (a) RH data. (b) GM data. The three hypotheses of language classification are those of Figure 15.4. To test for the effect of the MLX on the partial correlation with genetic distances, the value assigned to it was varied from 15,000 to 50,000 years. For hypothesis 3, the correlation coefficients reported are those inferred by using the intra-family classification and dating scheme of hypothesis 1 (see legend to Figure 15.4). These coefficients differ from those inferred by using the intra-family classification and dating scheme of hypothesis 2 only at the third decimal (results not shown). All coefficients are statistically significant ($p < 0.001$).

For both the RH and GM systems we observe, first, that all three linguistic hypotheses lead to a significant positive partial correlation coefficient between genetic and linguistic distances controlled for geography. Thus, part of the genetic variability among populations observed for both systems is related to the linguistic variability of the languages spoken by these populations. Second, hypothesis 2 leads to a slightly higher partial correlation coefficient (from $r = 0.28$ to $r = 0.30$ for RH data and from $r = 0.36$ to $r = 0.38$ for GM data) than both hypotheses 1 and 3. This is because hypothesis 2 postulates that ST is unrelated to the other linguistic families, in agreement with the observation, both for RH and GM, of a significant genetic differentiation of the ST group from the other Southeast Asian groups (Table 15.5). However, we cannot assume that the rather small differences in r observed between the three hypotheses are significant because a statistical tool to test for such an assumption is not yet available.

Discussion

Patterns of genetic diversity among East Asian populations

Both the RH and the GM polymorphisms reveal a significant level of genetic structure in East Asia (Table 15.2). This level is quite low for the RH system, in agreement with the fact that only a few haplotypes are inferred from serology (Sanchez-Mazas 1990), and one of those (R^1) dominates the genetic makeup of East Asian populations (Plate Va). Conversely, although the polymorphism of the GM system is also tested here by serology, its variation is more informative[2] and it reveals substantial genetic differentiation among the populations in East Asia (Plate Vb). For comparison, the level of GM genetic differentiation observed in this continent (14.32 per cent) is very similar to that observed among Sub-Saharan African populations (14.96 per cent, based on 51 population samples). This genetic structure seems generally related to the linguistic classification of the languages spoken by East Asian populations since we observe a significant level of variance in genetic diversity among populations from distinct linguistic families (Table 15.4). This seems also to be the case with HLA diversity in continental East Asia (Sanchez-Mazas et al., Chapter 16, this volume), and a similar observation is reported in a recent study of Y-chromosome specific biallelic markers (Karafet et al. 2001).

At first sight, these results could appear to be compatible with the hypothesis that the populations of a language family share a common genetic origin. By this assumption, distinct models of evolution can be inferred from the comparison of levels of divergence among populations (F_{ST}) from a linguistically-defined group to levels of diversity within these populations (h), as shown in Table 16.2 of Sanchez-Mazas et al. (Chapter 16, this volume). According to RH and GM, this comparison suggests roughly three distinct types of evolution in East Asia (Table 15.3). First, the relatively high levels of both internal diversity and inter-population divergence observed among STs can be explained either by assuming an ancient divergence of ST populations from a common ancestor, or by substantial incoming gene flow from differentiated sources into STs, for instance, from populations located north and south of their geographic extension. Second, probably because of small population sizes and/or relative geographic isolation, strong genetic drift would characterise the evolution of AA populations from a relatively ancient common origin. This would explain both the relatively low internal diversity and high level of inter-population divergence observed among AA. Finally, because the AN group is characterised by both low internal diversity and low inter-population divergence, it suggests a recent origin of Austronesians from a rather homogeneous common ancestral population, maybe following a demographic bottleneck. Such an evolution can also be assumed for Tai-Kadai populations. Interestingly, Tai-Kadai is considered as a daughter-group of AN under the hypothesis of an East Asian linguistic phylum (Figure 15.4a). For the AN, however, the patterns of intra- and inter-population variation (i.e. h and F_{ST}) inferred from HLA (Sanchez-Mazas et al., Chapter 16, this volume) are quite different to those inferred from RH and GM, suggesting either that RH and GM are not as informative as HLA, or that other evolutionary factors, such as selection, could be playing a role here.

More generally, these evolutionary interpretations are challenged by the observation that the genetic relationships among East Asian populations do not show a clear clustering pattern of linguistically-defined groups. For both genetic systems, populations tend to display genetic similarities according to their linguistic relatedness, but also according to geographic proximity. Indeed, we observe non-significant levels of differentiation between several linguistic groups considered two by two (Table 15.5), substantial overlapping of linguistically defined groups in the MDS analyses (Figures 15.2 and 15.3), and similar correlation coefficients of genetic distances with linguistic and geographic distances. In fact, according to both RH and GM polymorphisms, the populations differentiate progressively, along one major axis, from ST samples down to their Southeastern neighbours, that is HM, Tai-Kadai, AA and AN, all these latter groups sharing close genetic affinities. This pattern of differentiation very roughly corresponds to a longitudinal axis, and it parallels the frequency increase of haplotypes R^1 (Plate Va) and GM*1,3;5* (Plate Vb) from the north towards the south of the continent.

Actually, the ANOVA analyses of differentiation among linguistic groups (Table 15.5) indicate a significant genetic differentiation, for GM, between ST and the other East Asian groups (AA, Tai-Kadai, HM and AN), but this strong divergence is mainly due to the northernmost ST populations (northern Han, Tibetans) (Figure 15.3). ST populations from the south (i.e. Southern Han, TB from India, Burma, Thailand, etc.) present genetic similarities with the populations from the Southeast Asian groups, that is HM, Tai-Kadai, AA and AN, these latter groups being virtually undifferentiated (Table 15.5). However, the differentiation between northern and southern ST populations is not clear-cut: frequency distributions of Han populations from the Wu and Southeastern Mandarin speaking areas (central–eastern China) are intermediate between those observed in northern and southern populations (Figure 15.3 and Table 15.6). For RH, a fine-scale analysis of ST populations was not possible with the available sampling. The only notable differentiation observed with this system is between ST and AN (Table 15.5), but again these two groups include the most differentiated populations in the MDS analyses (Figure 15.2), that is the northernmost ST populations (northern Han, Tibetans) on one hand, and several AN populations of the MP daughter-group on the other hand.

Origin(s) of East Asian populations

At present, two alternative hypotheses have been advanced for the origin of continental East Asian populations. One hypothesis postulates that northern East Asians derive from southern populations (e.g. Chu et al. 1998; Su et al. 1999), whereas the other hypothesis, dubbed the 'pincer model' by Ding et al. (2000) suggests two migration routes from the west into East Asia with subsequent contact (e.g. Underhill et al. 2001).

The idea of two major contributions to the peopling of the Asian continent (the pincer model) has been put forward to explain a marked genetic differentiation between the north and the south of the continent observed in some studies (Cavalli-Sforza et al. 1994; Sanchez-Mazas 1990). However, in agreement with recent analyses of molecular markers (Ding et al. 2000; Oota et al. 2002; Yao et al. 2002), there is little evidence, in our present analyses, for such a clear separation; rather we find a gradual pattern of differentiation. We are aware that our study suffers from the fact that Altaic populations are not represented. However, earlier analyses of GM in East Asia (Sanchez-Mazas 1990) have evidenced continental continuity in changes of frequency distributions, further extending to the north from northern STs towards such populations as Mongolians, Japanese, Koreans and Siberians (e.g. Buriats, Nentzi, Yakuts). The patterns of genetic relationships among populations observed with mitochondrial DNA (Yao et al. 2002b) and Y-specific (Karafet et al. 2001; Su et al. 1999, 2000) polymorphisms further support a continuous differentiation of Altaic populations from their ST neighbours, although the sampling of populations in these studies is more restricted.

Could this general pattern of continuity be simply explained in terms of a process of isolation-by-distance, as suggested by Ding et al. (2000)? Since genetic and geographic distances are correlated, this hypothesis cannot be ruled out, but it might be too simplistic, because genetic and linguistic affinities among populations are also correlated (Figure 15.5). Although our results indicate that the linguistic groups do not correspond to separate genetic clusters of populations, this lack of clustering could be due to substantial levels of gene flow between populations across linguistic borders. Such gene flow would both diminish genetic divergence between linguistic groups and raise it between populations within linguistic groups. From our results we can thus hypothesise that gene flow between linguistically distinct sources has substantially contributed to the genetic makeup of East Asian populations, especially for ST populations.

Advocates of the hypothesis of a southern origin of northern populations claim, among other genetic evidence, that higher numbers of Y-specific haplotypes are observed in the south of the continent (Su et al. 1999). However, caution must be exercised when reasoning on the presence or absence of alleles or haplotypes in samples, as the probability of missing a rare allele or haplotype increases very rapidly as sample size decreases[3] (Sanchez-Mazas 2002). The Y-specific study of Karafet et al. (2001) reported on higher gene diversity (h) in southern populations than in northern ones (although the difference is rather small). To some extent, we observe the opposite pattern with RH and GM, in that ST populations are more heterogeneous than AA, Tai-Kadai, HM or AN populations (Table 15.3). However, RH or GM haplotypes are determined by serology, and any given serological haplotype might include several distinct molecular variants (Dard et al. 1996).[4] Nevertheless, Karafet et al. (2001) also reported on higher molecular diversity among Y-specific haplotypes in the north than in the south, suggesting there were more genetic contributions from distinct sources in northern than in southern East Asia, as in our analyses.

Thus, neither our results nor other studies on molecular markers can discriminate, at present, between the two competing hypotheses on the origin of continental East Asian populations. Actually recent hypotheses tend to reconcile both models into a framework that includes substantial gene flow between populations differentiating in East Asia at various times, as well as an important genetic input from Central Asia into northern East Asia (Ding et al. 2000; Karafet et al. 2001; Su et al. 2000; Wells et al. 2001). Our results are compatible with the hypothesis that AA, Tai-Kadai, HM, and AN populations share a common origin. These groups of populations may have differentiated by settling into geographically distinct areas, eventually coming into secondary contact and thus favouring genetic and cultural exchange. Given the present extension of these linguistic families, it is tempting to assume that these differentiation processes took place in southern East Asia, but we have no evidence to link these groups to the first settlers of the continent. Insights into this matter may be gained in the future by analyses of ancient DNA (Oota et al. 1999, 2001b; Wang et al. 2000).

In turn, at least two scenarios can be envisioned for the origins of ST populations. Either STs differentiated from the same common source as the other East Asian groups, a common source that should be linked to the hypothesis of a PEA linguistic phylum (Figure 15.4a). In favour of this hypothesis, we observe little differentiation of southern STs (either Han or TBs) from other Southeast Asian groups, and in particular from most AN (Figures 15.2 and 15.3). Some ST populations might thus have differentiated through a northwards expansion, where they would have eventually experienced strong genetic inflow from distinct northern, possibly Altaic, groups. Northern Mandarin has indeed been deeply influenced by Altaic languages (Hashimoto 1986). Alternatively, the STs have an independent origin. In this case, a scenario that could fit the genetic data would assume a southwards expansion of STs, where they would have assimilated already settled populations, while imposing their language(s). Under this scenario, substantial gene flow between 'intrusive' STs and already settled Southeastern groups must be invoked to account for the observation of no sharp genetic changes between north and south.

The correlation analyses between linguistic and genetic distances carried out in this study argue in favour of hypothesis 2 (Figure 15.5), that is for a common origin of the populations of the Southeast Asian linguistic families (AA, Tai-Kadai, HM and AN) and a separate origin of STs (Figure 15.4b). The case for this hypothesis is not strong since it leads to correlation coefficients not much higher than those obtained for hypotheses 1 and 3. Moreover, even with the hypothesis that ST populations do share a common origin with the Southeastern groups, hypothesis 2 could still perform better than the others if the divergence of the ST group was accentuated by substantial genetic input from other, differentiated, sources (e.g. from Altaic populations).

Conclusion

In this study, our purpose is not to confirm or invalidate a linguistic hypothesis of genetic relationships among languages with genetic data. Indeed, there is no a priori reason why genetic data could do this. There are several ways by which populations that share a common linguistic and genetic origin might diverge from one another, either genetically, or linguistically, or both. For instance, if linguistically related populations are submitted to strong genetic drift, because population sizes are small, then they can diverge genetically quite rapidly but may retain a strong linguistic relatedness. Alternatively, a population can acquire a new (even unrelated) language, for instance through a process of domination by an elite (see for instance Renfrew 1989), without diverging genetically from their former linguistic relatives.

However, when considering a large set of populations, as was done here, we observe that genetic and linguistic distances are correlated to some extent. We have shown that, among the East Asian groups considered in this study, genetic distances among populations generally increase with the linguistic distances among their languages, although with some variation. Correlation between genetic similarity and linguistic relatedness has also been described for other regions of the world, and other genetic systems (e.g. Sokal et al. 1992). It suggests that there is a relationship between the process of language diversification and that of genetic differentiation of the populations, that is that both processes have occurred through a common cause. If this hypothesis is correct, it implies that the origin of the genetic structure we observe today is to be linked to the origin of language families. In other words, since linguists assume that the ages of East Asian linguistic families are 10,000 years or less, then at least part of the genetic structure of today's populations might originate within that period. Of course the genes (i.e. the genetic variants that we observe) might be much older, but the genetic pools (the frequency distributions observed in the populations) can be much more recent. Indeed, the fact that the vocabulary of domestic crops reconstructs in the proto-languages of several of the East Asian linguistic families considered in this study (Blench, Chapter 2, this volume; Sagart 2003) strongly suggests that the genetic profiles of East Asian populations have been deeply influenced by the demographic (and territorial) expansion that is concomitant with the transition to food-producing economies. Such expansions would both slow down population differentiation through genetic drift and induce conditions to cultural and genetic exchange. If genetic exchange through secondary contact between populations has been the rule rather than the exception in the history of East Asia, then we need to use appropriate statistical tools, such as spatial autocorrelation analyses (Sokal and Oden 1978) and analyses of the impact of linguistic boundaries on genetic structure (Dupanloup de Ceuninck et al. 2000) to discriminate between specific cases of populations differentiating from a common source and cases of convergence through secondary contact.

Acknowledgement

This research was supported by the French CNRS OHLL (Origine de l'Homme, du Langage et des Langues) action to ESP and LS.

Abbreviations

AA   Austro-Asiatic
AN   Austronesian
HM   Hmong-Mien
MLX Maximum language distance
MP   Malayo-Polynesian
PEA Proto-East-Asian
ST   Sino-Tibetan
TB   Tibeto-Burman

Notes

1 'Classical markers' refers here to genetic systems that reveal variation between individuals at the level of the gene product (i.e. the protein), not at the level of the gene itself, as is the case for 'DNA markers'.
2 A worldwide analysis of GM variation reveals one of the strongest levels of population genetic structure observed so far for an autosomal marker (39.14 per cent), and this structure globally corresponds to continental groupings of populations (Dugoujon et al. 2004).
3 For instance, Y-chromosome mutation M95, considered southern-specific by Su et al. (1999), has also been observed in some northern samples (Sino-Tibetan and Altaic) (Karafet et al. 2001; Su et al. 2000; Wells et al. 2001).
4 Actually caution should also be exercised with Y-chromosome haplotypes defined by biallelic markers, because the former could also include further sub-variants.

Bibliography

Cavalli-Sforza, L.L., Menozzi, P. and Piazza, A. (1994) The History and Geography of Human Genes, Princeton: Princeton University Press.

Chu, J.Y., Huang, W., Kuang, S.Q., Wang, J.M., Xu, J.J., Chu, Z.T., Yang, Z.Q., Lin, K.Q., Li, P., Wu, M., Geng, Z.C., Tan, C.C., Du, R.F. and Jin, L. (1998) 'Genetic relationship of populations in China', Proceedings of the National Academy of Sciences USA 95: 11763–8.

Dard, P., Sanchez-Mazas, A., Dugoujon, J.-M., De Lange, G., Langaney, A., Lefranc, M.-P. and Lefranc, G. (1996) 'DNA analysis of the immunoglobulin IGHG loci in a Mandenka population from eastern Senegal: correlation with Gm haplotypes and hypotheses for the evolution of the Ig CH region', Human Genetics 98: 36–47.

Ding, Y.-C., Wooding, S., Harpending, H.C., Chi, H.-C., Li, H.-P., Fu, Y.-X., Pang, J.-F., Yao, Y.-G., Yu, J.-G., Moyzis, R. and Zhang, Y. (2000) 'Population structure and history in East Asia', Proceedings of the National Academy of Sciences USA 97: 14003–6.

Dugoujon, J.-M., Hazout, S., Loirat, F., Mourrieras, B., Crouau-Roy, B. and Sanchez-Mazas, A. (2004) 'GM haplotype diversity of 82 populations over the World', American Journal of Physical Anthropology 125: 175–92.

Dupanloup de Ceuninck, I., Schneider, S., Langaney, A. and Excoffier, L. (2000) 'Inferring the impact of linguistic boundaries on population differentiation: application to the Afro-Asiatic-Indo-European case', European Journal of Human Genetics 8: 750–6.

Hashimoto, M. J. (1986) 'The Altaicization of Northern Chinese', in J. McCoy and T. Light (eds) Contributions to Sino-Tibetan Studies, Leiden: E. J. Brill.

Karafet, T., Xu, L., Du, R., Wang, W., Feng, S., Wells, R.S., Redd, A.J., Zegura, S.L. and Hammer, M.F. (2001) 'Paternal population history of East Asia: sources, patterns, and microevolutionary processes', American Journal of Human Genetics 69: 615–28.

Ke, Y., Su, B., Song, X., Lu, D., Chen, L., Li, H., Qi, C., Marzuki, S., Deka, R., Underhill, P., Xiao, C., Shriver, M., Lell, J., Wallace, D., Wells, R.S., Seielstad, M., Oefner, P., Zhu, D., Jin, J., Huang, W., Chakraborty, R., Chen, Z. and Jin, L. (2001) 'African origin of modern humans in East Asia: a tale of 12,000 Y chromosomes', Science 292: 1151–3.

Lahr, M.M. and Foley, R. (1994) 'Multiple dispersals and modern human origins', Evolutionary Anthropology 3: 48–60.

Lahr, M.M. and Foley, R. (1998) 'Towards a theory of modern human origins: geography, demography and diversity in recent human evolution'. Yearbook of Physical Anthropology 41: 137–76.

Oota, H., Saitou, N., Matsushita, T. and Ueda S. (1999) 'Molecular genetic analysis of remains of a 2,000-year-old human population in China and its relevance for the origin of the modern Japanese population', American Journal of Human Genetics 64: 250–8.

Oota, H., Settheetham-Ishida, W., Tiwawech, D., Ishida, T. and Stoneking, M. (2001a) 'Human mtDNA and Y-chromosome variation is correlated with matrilocal versus patrilocal residence', Nature Genetics 29: 20–1.

Oota, H., Kurosaki, K., Pookajorn, S., Ishida, T. and Ueda, S. (2001b) 'Genetic study of the Paleolithic and Neolithic Southeast Asians', Human Biology 73: 225–31.

Oota, H., Kitano, T., Jin, F., Yuasa, I., Wang, L., Ueda, S., Saitou, N. and Stoneking, M. (2002) 'Extreme mtDNA homogeneity in continental Asian populations', American Journal of Physical Anthropology 118: 146–53.

Peiros, I. (1998) Comparative Linguistics in Southeast Asia, Canberra: Pacific Linguistics.

Poloni, E.S., Semino, O., Passarino, G., Santachiara-Benerecetti, A.S., Dupanloup, I., Langaney, A. and Excoffier, L. (1997) 'Human genetic affinities for Y-chromosome P49a,f/TaqI haplotypes show strong correspondence with linguistics', American Journal of Human Genetics 61: 1015–35.

Renfrew, C. (1989) 'The origins of Indo-European languages', Scientific American 261: 82–90.

Reynolds, J., Weir, B.S. and Cockerham, C.C. (1983) 'Estimation of the coancestry coefficient: basis for a short-term genetic distance', Genetics 105: 767–79.

Rohlf, F. J. (1998) NTSYSpc: Numerical Taxonomy and Multivariate Analysis System New York: Exeter Software.

Ruhlen, M. (1987) A Guide to the World's Languages, London: Edward Arnold.

Sagart, L. (1994) 'Proto-Austronesian and Old Chinese: evidence for Sino-Austronesian', Oceanic Linguistics 33: 271–308.

—— (2003) 'The vocabulary of cereal cultivation and the phylogeny of East Asian languages', Bulletin of the Indo-Pacific Prehistory Association 23 (Taipei papers, vol. 1): 127–36.

Sanchez-Mazas, A. (1990) Polymorphisme des systèmes immunologiques Rhésus, GM et HLA et histoire du peuplement humain, unpublished thesis, Geneva: University of Geneva.

—— (2002) 'HLA data analysis in anthropology: basic theory and practice', in 16th European Histocompatibility Conference, European Federation for Immunogenetics (EFI), Strasbourg, France, 68–83.

Schneider, S., Roessli, D. and Excoffier, L. (2000) Arlequin ver 2.000: A Software for Population Genetics Data Analysis, Geneva: Genetics and Biometry Laboratory, University of Geneva.

Seielstad, M.T., Minch, E. and Cavalli-Sforza, L.L. (1998) 'Genetic evidence for a higher female migration rate in humans', Nature Genetics 20: 278–80.

Sokal, R.R. and Oden, N.L. (1978) 'Spatial autocorrelation in biology', Biological Journal of the Linnean Society 60: 73–93.

Sokal, R.R., Oden, N.L. and Thomson, B.A. (1992) 'Origins of the Indo-Europeans: genetic evidence', Proceedings of the National Academy of Sciences USA 89: 7669–73.

Starostin, S. (1984 [1991]) 'On the Hypothesis of a genetic connection between the Sino-Tibetan languages and the Yeniseian and North-Caucasian languages', translation and introduction by William H. Baxter III, in V. Shevoroshkin (ed.) Dene-Sino-Caucasian, Bochum: Brockmeyer.

Steinberg, A.G. and Cook, C.E. (1981) The distribution of the human immunoglobulin allotypes, Oxford: Oxford University Press.

Su, B., Xiao, J., Underhill, P., Deka, R., Zhang, W., Akey, J., Huang, W., Shen, D., Lu, D., Luo, J., Chu, J., Tan, J., Shen, P., Davis, R., Cavalli-Sforza, L., Chakraborty, R., Xiong, M., Du, R., Oefner, P., Chen, Z. and Jin, L. (1999) 'Y-Chromosome evidence for a northward migration of modern humans into Eastern Asia during the last Ice Age', American Journal of Human Genetics 65: 1718–24.

Su, B., Xiao, C., Deka, R., Seielstad, M. T., Kangwanpong, D., Xiao, J., Lu, D., Underhill, P., Cavalli-Sforza, L., Chakraborty, R. and Jin, L. (2000) 'Y chromosome haplotypes reveal prehistorical migrations to the Himalayas', Human Genetics 107: 582–90.

Underhill, P. A., Passarino, G., Lin, A.A., Shen, P., Mirazon Lahr, M., Foley, R. A., Oefner, P. J. and Cavalli-Sforza, L. L. (2001) 'The phylogeography of Y chromosome binary haplotypes and the origins of modern human populations', Annals of Human Genetics 65: 43–62.

Wang, L., Oota, H., Saitou, N., Jin, F., Matsushita, T. and Ueda, S. (2000) 'Genetic structure of a 2,500-year-old human population in China and its spatiotemporal changes', Molecular Biology and Evolution 17: 1396–400.

Wells, R.S., Yuldasheva, N., Ruzibakiev, R., Underhill, P.A., Evseeva, I., Blue-Smith, J., Jin, L., Su, B., Pitchappan, R., Shanmugalakshmi, S., Balakrishnan, K., Read, M., Pearson, N.M., Zerjal, T., Webster, M.T., Zholoshvili, I., Jamarjashvili, E., Gambarov, S., Nikbin, B., Dostiev, A., Aknazarov, O., Zalloua, P., Tsoy, I., Kitaev, M., Mirrakhimov, M., Chariev, A. and Bodmer, W.F. (2001) 'The Eurasian heartland: a continental perspective on Y-chromosome diversity', Proceedings of the National Academy of Sciences USA 98: 10244–9.

Yao, Y.-G., Kong, Q.-P., Bandelt, H.-J., Kivisild, T. and Zhang, Y.-P. (2002a) 'Phylogeographic differentiation of mitochondrial DNA in Han Chinese', American Journal of Human Genetics 70: 635–51.

Yao, Y.-G., Nie, L., Harpending, H., Fu, Y.-X., Yuan, Z.-G. and Zhang, Y.-P. (2002b) 'Genetic relationship of Chinese ethnic populations revealed by mtDNA sequence diversity', American Journal of Physical Anthropology 118: 63–76.

16
HLA GENETIC DIVERSITY AND LINGUISTIC VARIATION IN EAST ASIA

Alicia Sanchez-Mazas, Estella S. Poloni,
Guillaume Jacques and Laurent Sagart

Introduction

Molecular anthropology – the study of human genetic polymorphisms – is now often used to investigate the accuracy of archaeological and/or linguistic hypotheses. One of the classic examples is the use of genetics in an attempt to discriminate between two alternative models for the spread of agriculture in Europe – the demic and the cultural diffusion models – which finally led to a general approval of the former by geneticists, who regard this spread as possibly linked to the expansion of Indo-European languages (Ammerman and Cavalli-Sforza 1984; Barbujani et al. 1995; Chikhi et al. 2002; Renfrew 1992; Weng and Sokal 1995). More generally, because genetic clines can give evidence for population migrations (Barbujani 2000), the analysis of genetic patterns is particularly interesting for the analysis of early agriculturalist diasporas and their link to the diffusion of human languages (Barbujani and Pilastro 1993; Bellwood 2001). Molecular anthropology can also be useful in estimating the contribution of different gene pools to the make-up of present-day populations, when attempting to ascertain the origin of specific linguistic families (such as the AN family, see further in this chapter); to test the permeability of linguistic boundaries to gene flow (Dupanloup de Ceuninck et al. 2000); or to investigate precise linguistic hypotheses (Excoffier et al. 1987; Poloni et al., this volume; this study), although genetics alone cannot be used to discriminate between alternative linguistic models.

The present work aims at bringing genetic evidence to bear on the vexing question of East Asian linguistic relationships. The phylogenetic links between the main language phyla of this region (ST, AA, Tai-Kadai, AN and Altaic) are still deeply controversial (see the introduction to the volume for a review of the main theories). To investigate these relationships from a genetic point of view, we report here on the results of a population genetics analysis of one molecular polymorphism, HLA-DRB1 The DRB1 locus of the MHC in humans is a cell surface protein-encoding gene, located on the short arm of chromosome 6 and surrounded by other HLA loci. Its allelic variability is amongst the highest known in the human genome thus far, with 418 DRB alleles detected by DNA oligotyping and sequencing techniques (IMGT/HLA sequence database 2003). Besides this high level of polymorphism, the DRB1 locus also has the advantage of having been extensively tested at the DNA level in human populations for at least 15 years (mostly using the HLA International Workshop typing kits), and abundant population data with high-resolution allelic definition are thus available. In this study, we analyse this polymorphism to explore a possible congruence between genetic and linguistic relationships in East Asia.

Material and methods

Populations analysed

We collected population data tested by high-resolution DNA typing for HLA-DRB1 through a thorough review of the literature, adding some samples submitted to the 11th, 12th and 13th HLA workshops and samples obtained through personal communications (Table 16.1). Our aim was to represent all regions of East and Southeast

Table 16.1 Populations considered in this study[a]

#	N	Population	Country	Location	Lat	Long	Language	LF
1	68	Mansi	Russia	Khanty-Mansi	60.2	70.7	Uralic	UY
2	59	Chukchi	Siberia	Several regions	65	185	Chukchi	CK
3	92	Koryak	Siberia	Kamchatka	60	164	Koryak	CK
4	80	Yupik	Siberia	Behring coast	66	185	Eskimo	EA
5	47	Indian	India	North	28.4	77.2	Indo-European	IE
6	53	Nivkhi	Russia	Siberia, Nogliki	51.5	143	Gilyak	GI
7	42	Kazakh	China	Ürümqi	43.4	87.4	Turkic	AL
8	160	Manchu	China	Heilongjiang	45.2	126	Tungus	AL
9	41	Khalkh	Mongolia	Ulaanbaatar	47.5	107	Mongolian	AL
10	201	Khalkh	Mongolia	Kharkhorum	45	100	Mongolian	AL
11	57	Uighur	China	Ürümqi	43.4	87.4	Turkic	AL
12	190	Tuvin	Russia	Kyzyl	51.4	94.3	Turkic	AL
13	44	Tuvin	Russia	Kyzyl	51.4	94.3	Turkic	AL
14	73	Ulchi	Russia	Khabarovsk	54	136	Tungus	AL
15	43	Tofalar	Russia	Nizhneudinsk	54.9	99	Turkic	AL
16	197	Ryukyuan	Japan	Okinawa	26	127	Ryukyuan	AL
17	371	Japanese	Japan	Centre	35.4	139	Japanese	AL
18	916	Japanese	Japan	n.d.	35.4	139	Japanese	AL
19	510	Korean	Korea	Seoul	37.3	127	Korean	AL
20	199	Korean	Korea	Heilongjiang	46	127	Korean	AL
21	91	Chinese	China	Guan County	39.3	116	Sinitic	SI
22	89	Chinese	China	Shanghai	31.1	121	Sinitic	SI
23	59	Chinese	China	Ürümqi	43.4	87.4	Sinitic	SI

(Table 16.1 continued)

HLA GENETIC DIVERSITY OF EAST ASIAN POPULATIONS

Table 16.1 Continued

#	N	Population	Country	Location	Lat	Long	Language	LF
24	162	Chinese	China	Xiamen, Fujian	24.3	118	Sinitic	SI
25	1012	Taiwanese	Taiwan	Tainan	23	120	Sinitic	SI
26	190	Taiwanese	Taiwan	n.d.	24	121	Sinitic	SI
27	70	Buyi	China	n.d.	26.2	106	Tai-Kadai	KA
28	140	Thai	Thailand	Bangkok	13.4	100	Tai-Kadai	KA
29	96	Dai Lue	Thailand	North	17	101	Tai-Kadai	KA
30	106	Dai Dam	Thailand	North	17.6	102	Tai-Kadai	KA
31	100	Kinh	Vietnam	Hanoi	21.1	106	Mon-Khmer	AA
32	81	Muong	Vietnam	Hoa Binh	20.5	105	Mon-Khmer	AA
33	40	Indonesian	Indonesia	Molucca	0	128	Mal.-Pol.	AN
34	49	Indonesian	Indonesia	Nusa Tenggara	9	117	Mal.-Pol.	AN
35	77	Indonesian	Indonesia	Java, Jakarta	6.1	106	Mal.-Pol.	AN
36	77	Malay	Malaysia	n.d.	3.9	101	Mal.-Pol.	AN
37	105	Filipino	Philippines	South Luzon[b]	14.4	121	Mal.-Pol.	AN
38	50	Ivatan	Philippines	Batan islands	20.3	122	Proto-Filipino	AN
39	65	Paiwan	Taiwan	South	23.5	121	Paiwanic	AN
40	51	Paiwan	Taiwan	C. mountains	22.2	121	Paiwanic	AN
41	50	Atayal	Taiwan	C. mountains	24.3	121	Atayalic	AN
42	57	Saisiat	Taiwan	C. mountains	24.5	121	Western Plains	AN
43	88	Bunun	Taiwan	C. mountains	23.2	121	Paiwanic	AN
44	51	Tsou	Taiwan	C. mountains	23.4	120	Tsuic	AN
45	50	Rukai	Taiwan	C. mountains	22.4	120	Tsuic	AN
46	50	Ami	Taiwan	East coast	23.1	121	Sirayan	AN
47	50	Puyuma	Taiwan	East coast	22.4	121	Puyumic	AN
48	64	Yami	Taiwan	Orchid Island	22	121	Proto-Filipino	AN

Notes

a N: sample size; Lat: latitude; Long: longitude; LF: Linguistic family (UY: Uralic-Yukaghir, IE: Indo-European, AL: Altaic, AN: Austronesian, AA: Austro-Asiatic, CK: Chukchi-Kamchatkan, KA: Tai-Kadai, EA: Eskimo-Aleut, GI: Gilyak, SI: Sinitic); n.d.: not determined; Mal.-Pol.: Malayo-Polynesian; C. mountains: Central mountains. References: 1: Uinuk-Ool et al. 2002; 2–4: Grahovac et al. 1998; 5: Rani et al. 1998; 6: Lou et al. 1998; 7: Mizuki et al. 1997; 8: XIIth Workshop data (p.c. to ASM); 9: Munkhbat et al. 1997; 10: Chimge et al. 1997; 11: Mizuki et al. 1998; 12: Martinez-Laso et al. 2001; 13–15: Uinuk-Ool et al. 2002; 16: Hatta et al. 1999; 17: Saito et al. 2000; 18: Hashimoto et al. 1994; 19: Park et al. 1999; 20: XIIth Workshop data (p.c. to ASM); 21: Gao et al. 1991; 22: Wang et al. 1993; 23: Mizuki et al. 1997; 24: Lee 1997; 25: XIIIth Workshop data (p.c. to ASM); 26: Chu et al. 2001; 27: Imanishi et al. 1992; 28–30: Chandanayingyong et al. 1997; 31: Vu-Trieu et al. 1997; 32: XIIIth Workshop data (p.c. to ASM); 33–4: Mack et al. 2000; 35: Gao et al. 1992; 36: Mack et al. 2000; 37: Bugawan et al. 1994; 38: Chu et al. 2001; 39: XIIth Workshop data (p.c. to ASM); 40–8: Chu et al. 2001.
b Typed in USA.

Asia as far as eastern Indonesia. We tried to avoid statistical bias due to low sample sizes, low allelic resolution, or heterogeneous population samples (Sanchez-Mazas 2002). We thus excluded samples with less than 40 individuals, samples with more than 5 per cent 'blank' frequency corresponding to undefined alleles, and samples for which only a generic definition of HLA-DRB1 alleles (HLA 'broad' specificities) was available. We also excluded all samples the linguistic affiliation of which was unclear or ambiguous. These criteria left us with a final list of 46 linguistically well-characterised East Asian populations, defined by a total of 76 DRB1 allele frequencies. We also included two West Asian populations (Mansi and North Indians) to represent the western edge of the area under study.[1] Overall, these 48 populations are represented by a total of 6,613 individuals (Table 16.1).

Linguistic phylogeny

Linguistic phylogenetic trees with absolute differentiation dates were established by one of us (LS) to represent what we consider to be the 'least controversial phylogeny' for each of the phyla under consideration: Koreo-Japonic, Altaic (tentatively accepted here on the basis of shared pronominal paradigms), ST, Tai-Kadai, AA and AN. The trees were established on the basis of the literature, or through consultation with specialists. Because we needed to integrate all the different trees into one so as to obtain separation dates for languages belonging to different families, and in order to avoid the controversial issues of higher subgrouping between these families, each proto-language was directly linked to a root node, the date of which was arbitrarily set at 50,000 BP. The overall phylogeny thus obtained for the present analyses (see the Results section) does not necessarily reflect our own ideas (or anyone else's for that matter), but we believe it integrates largely uncontroversial information concerning the linguistic affiliation of each language, as well as some relatively widely-held views about the internal subgrouping and times of separation within each family, while remaining neutral on higher subgrouping.

Statistical methods

Pairwise F_{ST} indexes among populations (a measure of their genetic variation) were computed from their HLA-DRB1 allele frequency distributions and tested for significance by a permutation procedure (Schneider et al. 2000). A matrix of coancestry coefficients (Reynolds et al. 1983) was used as a genetic distance matrix to plot the populations according to the technique of MDS (Kruskal 1964; Rohlf 2000). Geographic coordinates were determined for all populations, and were used to compute geographic distances based on the arc length of a sphere and transformed to natural logarithms (Nicolas Ray, p.c.). The date of the most recent common ancestor (or proto-language) of two given languages, as given by the linguistic phylogeny that we constructed, was taken as a 'linguistic distance' between the populations speaking those languages (see also the companion chapter by Poloni et al., Chapter 15, in this volume). Correlation coefficients were computed between the genetic, geographic and linguistic distance matrices and assessed for significance by two-way and three-way Mantel tests (Mantel 1967). In three-way tests, the first two matrices are adjusted to take into account their possible covariation with a third matrix (Sokal and Rohlf 1994).

Different fixation indices, F_{ST}, F_{CT} and F_{SC}, were estimated to assess the levels of genetic diversity among populations at different hierarchical levels of subdivision (Excoffier 2001). When a single set of populations is considered, F_{ST} represents the overall genetic variation among these populations. When several groups of populations are considered (linguistically defined groups, for example), one may also estimate F_{CT} and F_{SC} to represent the levels of genetic variation among groups and among populations within groups, respectively. This genetic structure is analysed using an ANOVA framework, where the significance of the statistics is assessed by a resampling procedure (Schneider et al. 2000). We also estimated the gene diversity within each population (h) by its expected heterozygosity (Nei 1987). All resampling and permutation procedures were done with a total of 10,000 runs.

Models of genetic evolution

With the aim of investigating different mechanisms of population differentiation in relation to the history of East Asian linguistic families, F_{ST} and h (h being averaged on all populations considered) were estimated simultaneously within each linguistic family in order to describe the genetic diversity, both among and within populations, of that family. This led us to consider four distinct patterns of genetic diversity (A–D) corresponding to extreme variations ('high' or 'low') of these two statistics taken together. When one of these patterns is identified in a given linguistic family, one or several modes of genetic evolution can be inferred for that family[2] (Table 16.2).

Table 16.2 Main patterns of population genetic diversity and their possible explanations in terms of genetic evolutionary mechanisms

Patterns	Observed genetic diversity		Inferred evolutionary mechanisms
	Among populations (F_{ST})	Within populations (h)	
A	High	High	1 Early differentiation of populations, maintenance of genetic diversity among populations by limited gene flow, maintenance of genetic diversity within populations by large population sizes 2 Intensive gene flow from highly diversified external populations
B	Low	High	1 Intensive gene flow among populations after differentiation from a highly diversified population 2 Recent differentiation from a highly diversified population
C	High	Low	Genetic drift and/or founder effects in small-sized and isolated populations
D	Low	Low	1 Intensive gene flow among populations after differentiation from a population with reduced diversity 2 Recent differentiation from a population with reduced diversity

Results

HLA genetic diversity in East Asian populations

As with most human MHC loci, HLA-DRB1 genetic profiles are generally highly heterogeneous within human populations, that is, they are commonly characterised by numerous alleles at low frequencies. This is what we observe for East Asia (Plate VIII), where, at first glance, genetic profiles do not reveal a clear population structure. Nevertheless, a finer examination shows that some alleles reach relatively high frequencies in specific East Asian populations. This is the case for *1402 and *0401 in Siberians, *1201, *07 or *0301 in Altaic, *0405 in the Japanese, *0901 in the Chinese, *1401, *0803, *1202, *1101, *0403 or *0404 in different Aboriginal populations from Taiwan and *1502 and *1202 in Southeast Asians, with extreme frequencies of the latter alleles in most Austronesians (up to 0.507 for *1202 in Java and up to 0.479 for *1502 in Nusa Tenggara, while *1502 is very rare in Taiwan Aborigines) (Plate VIII). These patterns indicate that some East Asian populations deeply differ genetically from each other, and that a high level of genetic diversity characterises this continental area. This is confirmed by F_{ST} measures. The overall HLA-DRB1 genetic diversity among the 46 East Asian populations considered in this study (thus excluding the West Asian Mansi and Indians) is 4.6 per cent ($p < 0.001$). This is much higher than values estimated for Europe (1.4–2 per cent), and higher than values found in sub-Saharan Africa (3.4–4 per cent), as already suggested on the basis of DRB1 analyses carried out on more limited sets of populations (Sanchez-Mazas 2001; forthcoming).

A two-dimensional scaling analysis (MDS) of the 46 populations, plus the Mansi and Indians, is presented in Figure 16.1a. An overall correspondence is observed between the genetic pattern and geography: continental East Asian populations (Chinese, Japanese, Koreans, Mongolians, Thai, Vietnamese, West Asians and Nivkhi) plus the Puyuma from Taiwan are tightly clustered in the centre of the MDS (dotted box in Figure 16.1a). The Siberians (Koryak, Chukchi and Yupik) segregate at the top, and the Malaysians, Filipinos and Indonesians at the bottom. The Northwest Asian Mansi (Uralic-Yukaghir speakers) and the Indians (Indo-Europeans) are close to the Uighur, the westernmost East Asian population (a non-significant F_{ST} is even found between Mansi and Uighur, see legend for Figure 16.1). We also note that the Aborigines from the central mountains of Taiwan (Atayal, Saisiat, Bunun, Tsou, Rukai, Paiwan) cluster together on one side of the continental East Asians, while those from the east coast (Ami, Puyuma) and Orchid Island (Yami) are more heterogeneous. This correspondence with geography is confirmed by a high and significant correlation between genetic and geographic distances among the 48 populations ($r = 0.279$, $p < 0.001$).

If we now consider the linguistic information in Figure 16.1a, populations belonging to one linguistic group tend to cluster together. However, in many instances, linguistic diversity is not paralleled by genetic differentiations. For example, the three Siberian populations speak languages belonging to different

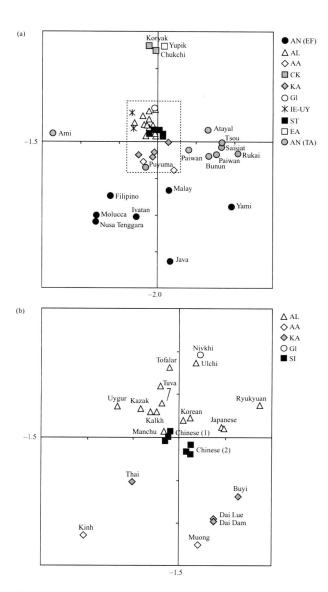

Figure 16.1 MDS analysis of Asian populations based on the HLA-DRB1 allelic polymorphism. (a): 48 populations, stress value = 0.267; (b): 27 populations from the dotted box of Figure 16.1a (excluding 3 IE-UY and AN populations), stress value = 0.291.

Notes
AL: Altaic; AN (EF): Austronesian (Extra-Formosan); AN (TA): Austronesian (from Taiwan); AA: Austro-Asiatic; CK: Chukchi-Kamchatkan; EA: Eskimo-Aleut; GI: Gilyak; IE-UY: Indo-European and Uralic-Yukaghir; KA: Tai-Kadai; SI: Sinitic; ST: Sino-Tibetan (here only Sinitic). Chinese (1): Northern Chinese; Chinese (2): Southern Chinese.

Non-significant F_{STS} (1 per cent level) are found for the following population pairs (see Table 16.1 for population numbers): 1-7, 1-11, 1-13, 2-3, 2-4, 6-14, 7-9, 7-10, 7-11, 8-21, 8-23, 9-10, 9-12, 9-13, 12-13, 13-15, 19-20, 21-22, 21-23, 22-23, 24-26, 25-26, 29-30, 33-34, 33-37, 34-37, 34-38, 39-40, 39-43, 40-42, 40-43, 40-45, 41-42, 41-44, 42-44.

linguistic phyla: Yupik (Eskimo-Aleut), Chukchi and Koryak (both Chukchi-Kamchatkan), but are genetically similar (non-significant F_{ST}s between Chukchi and the other two). Conversely, the AN-speaking populations are genetically highly heterogeneous, despite their linguistic relatedness.

To further investigate the genetic relationships among continental East Asian populations, we performed a second MDS (Figure 16.1b) of 27 populations among those projected in the centre (dotted box) of Figure 16.1a. A general correspondence with geography is again observed, as Nivkhi and Altaic segregate at the top, Chinese at the centre and Southeast Asians at the bottom, with only a few exceptions. Also matching relative geographic locations are the significant differentiation of Japanese and Ryukyuans, the close genetic relationship of Ulchi and Nivkhi (both located in Northeast Russia close to Sakhalin), and the close genetic relationship of northern Chinese and Manchu. Nevertheless, a few examples contradict those findings: the Vietnamese Kinh and Muong are geographically close but genetically distant. The same is true of the Buyi and Chinese in southern China. When linguistic information is taken into account (symbols in Figure 16.1b), we note that, as in Figure 16.1a, linguistic groups do not overlap substantially: this indicates a relatively fine-grained correspondence between genetic and linguistic relationships.

Correlations between genetic, geographic and linguistic distances

We attempted to evaluate the contribution of linguistics and/or geography in the genetic structure of East Asian populations. To this end, we statistically compared genetic, geographic and linguistic distance matrices computed on an identical population data set of 40 populations in our data. Linguistic distances were computed from the linguistic phylogeny shown (as explained earlier) in Figure 16.2. Correlation coefficients and the results of two-way and three-way Mantel tests between the three matrices are presented in Table 16.3.

The correlations between genetics, on the one hand, and geography or linguistics, on the other hand, are low ($r = 0,131*$) and not significant ($r = 0.015^{n.s.}$), respectively,[3] when we include the 40 populations. Results do not differ substantially when the covariation with the third matrix is taken into account ($r = 0.137*$ and $r = 0.042^{n.s.}$, respectively). Conversely, a high and very significant correlation coefficient is found between geographic and linguistic distances ($r = 0.401***$). We conclude that linguistic families are well differentiated geographically in East Asia, but that this structure does not match the genetic structure.

Different results are obtained when AN populations are considered separately from continental East Asians ('non-Austronesians'). As the AN group was found to be genetically highly heterogeneous (Figure 16.1a), we recomputed correlation coefficients for continental East Asians and Austronesians independently (Table 16.3, lines 2 and 3, respectively). For continental East Asians, a high and significant correlation is found between all pairs of distance matrices (genetics–geography, genetics–linguistics and geography–linguistics), even when

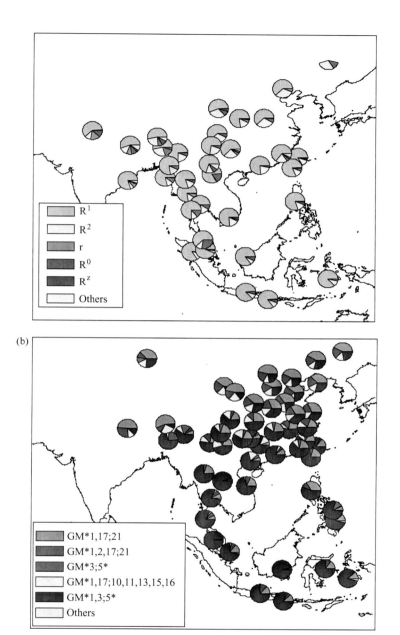

Plate V (a) RH frequency distributions (due to sampling density, only 37 samples are represented). (b) GM frequency distributions (due to sampling density 51 samples are represented).

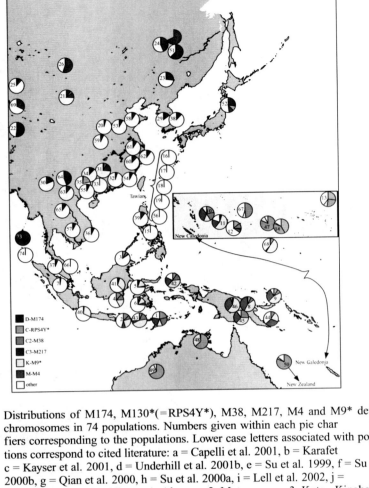

Plate VI Distributions of M174, M130*(=RPS4Y*), M38, M217, M4 and M9* def chromosomes in 74 populations. Numbers given within each pie char fiers corresponding to the populations. Lower case letters associated with popula tions correspond to cited literature: a = Capelli et al. 2001, b = Karafet c = Kayser et al. 2001, d = Underhill et al. 2001b, e = Su et al. 1999, f = Su 2000b, g = Qian et al. 2000, h = Su et al. 2000a, i = Lell et al. 2002, j = et al. 2003. Identifiers: 1_Alor_a, 2_Mataram_a, 3_Kota Kinabalu_a 4_Banjarmasin_a, 5_Palu_a, 6_Toraja_a, 7_Pekanbaru_a, 8_Mandang_a, 9_Ne Ireland_a, 10_Vanuatu_a, 11_Fiji_a, 12_Tonga_a, 13_French P 14_Atiu_a, 15_Philippines_a, 16_Paiwan_a, 17_Bunun_a, 18_Ata 19_Ami_a, 20_N. Han_b, 21_Hui_b, 22_Tibet_b, 23_Manchu_b, 24_Chines Evenk_b, 25_Uygurs_b, 26_Mongolia_b, 27_Sib Evenk_b, 28_Bur 29_Koreans_b, 30_Yi_b, 31_Tujia_b, 32_S. Han_b, 33_She_b, 34_Miao_b 35_Yao_b, 36_Vietnam_b, 37_Malaysia_b, 38_Korea_c, 39_Philippines_c 40_Java_c, 41_S. Borneo_c, 42_Moluccas_c, 43_Nusa Tenggara_c, 44_T Is_c, 45_NG Coastal_c, 46_NG Highlands_c, 47_Cook Is_c, 48_Australia land_c, 49_Australia Sandy Desert_c, 50_Maori_d, 51_Mongolian_ 52_Japanese_e, 53_N.Han_e, 54_S. Han_e, 55_Zhuang_e, 56_T 57_Cambodia_e, 58_Shandong Han_f, 59_Henan Han_f, 60_Zhejiang Han_ 61_Jiangsu Han_f, 62_Shanghai Han_f, 63_Yunnan Han_f, 64_T Khamba_g, 65_N and NE Thai_h, 66_Malay_h, 67_Samoan_h, 68_Micronesia_ 69_Siberia Tuvan_i, 70_Ulchi/Nanal_i, 71_Kamchatka Koryak_i, 72_Siber Eskimo_i, 73_Onge/Jarawa_j, 74_Nicobar_j.

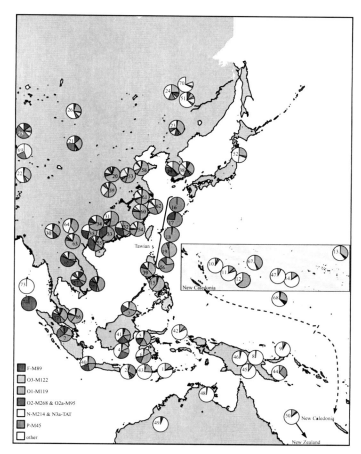

Plate VII Distributions of M89, M122, M119, M268, M214 and M45 related chromosomes in 74 populations. Numbers given within each pie chart are identifiers cor ding to the populations. Lower case letters associated with populations cor to cited literature: a = Capelli et al. 2001, b = Karafet et al. 2001, c = Kayser 2001, d = Underhill et al. 2001b, e = Su et al. 1999, f = Su et al. 2000b, g = Qian al. 2000, h = Su et al. 2000a, i = Lell et al. 2002, j = Thangaraj et al
Identifiers: 1_Alor_a, 2_Mataram_a, 3_Kota Kinabalu_a, 4_Banjar 5_Palu_a, 6_Toraja_a, 7_Pekanbaru_a, 8_Mandang_a, 9_New Ireland_a, 10_Vanuatu_a, 11_Fiji_a, 12_Tonga_a, 13_French Polynesia_a, 14_Atiu_a, 15_Philippines_a, 16_Paiwan_a, 17_Bunun_a, 18_Atayal_a, 19_Ami_a, 20_N Han_b, 21_Hui_b, 22_Tibet_b, 23_Manchu_b, 24_Chinese Ev 25_Uygurs_b, 26_Mongolia_b, 27_Sib Evenk_b, 28_Buryats_b, 29_Koreans_b, 30_Yi_b, 31_Tujia_b, 32_S. Han_b, 33_She_b, 34_Miao_b, 35_Y 36_Vietnam_b, 37_Malaysia_b, 38_Korea_c, 39_Philippines_c, 40_Java_c, 41_S. Borneo_c, 42_Moluccas_c, 43_Nusa Tenggara_c, 44_Trobriand Is_c, 45_NG Coastal_c, 46_NG Highlands_c, 47_Cook Is_c, 48_Australia Arnhem land_c, 49_Australia Sandy Desert_c, 50_Maori_d, 51_Mongolian_e, 52_Japanese_e, 53_N.Han_e, 54_S. Han_e, 55_Zhuang_e, 56_Taiwan_e, 57_Cambodia_e, 58_Shandong Han_f, 59_Henan Han_f, 60_Zhejiang Han_f, 61_Jiangsu Han_f, 62_Shanghai Han_f, 63_Yunnan Han_f, 64_Tibetan-Khamba_g, 65_N & NE Thai_h, 66_Malay_h, 67_Samoan_h, 68_Micronesia_h, 69_Siberia 70_Ulchi/Nanal_i, 71_Kamchatka Koryak_i, 72_Siberia Eskimo_i, 73_Onge/Jarawa_j, 74_Nicobar_j.

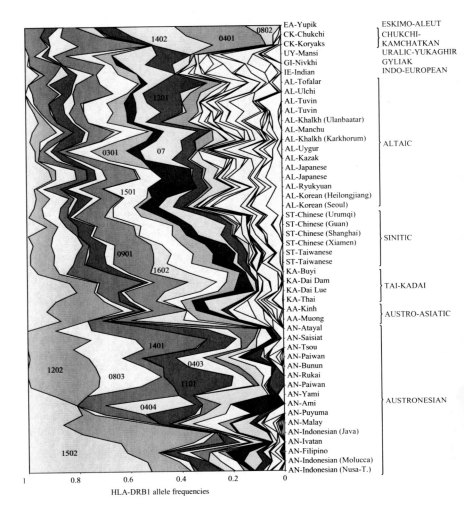

Plate VIII HLA-DRB1 allele frequencies in 48 Asian populations ordered by families. The most frequent alleles (frequency > 14 per cent in at least one population) are represented with bright coloured areas. AN: Austronesian; AL: Altaic; AA: Austro-Asiatic; CK: Chukchi-Kamchatkan; KA: Tai-Kadai; GI: Gilyak; IE: Indo-European; UY: Uralic-Yukaghir; ST: Sino-Tibetan (here only Sinitic); EA: Eskimo-Aleut

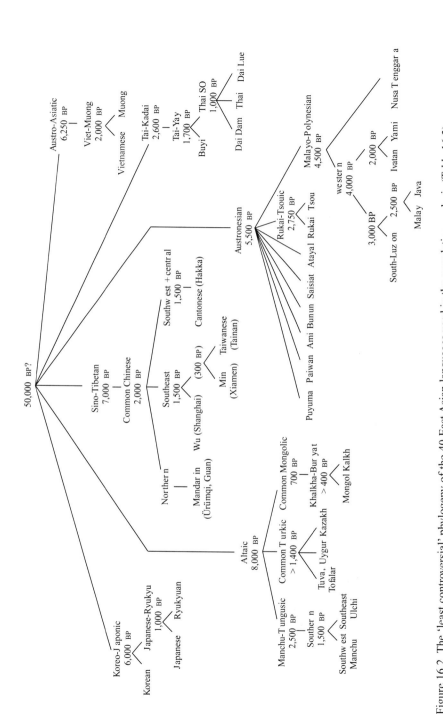

Figure 16.2 The 'least controversial' phylogeny of the 40 East Asian languages used in the correlation analysis (Table 16.3).
Notes
This tree has been reconstructed on the basis of linguistic and archaeological information (see text). Absolute divergence dates are given in years before present (BP).

Table 16.3 Correlation coefficients among genetic (GEN), geographic (GEO) and linguistic (LING) distances in East Asia

	Group size	$r_{GEN,GEO}^{a,b}$	$r_{GEN,LING}^{a,c}$	$r_{GEO, LING}^{a}$
All populations	40	0.131* (0.137*)	0.015$^{n.s.}$ (0.042$^{n.s.}$)	0.401***
Continental East Asians	25	0.352*** (0.288***)	0.333*** (0.264***)	0.270***
Austronesians only	15	0.340* (0.357*)	0.110$^{n.s.}$ (0.158$^{n.s.}$)	0.112$^{n.s.}$

Notes
a ***: $p < 0.001$; *: $0.01 < p < 0.05$; n.s.: not significant.
b In parentheses: partial correlation coefficients between genetics and geography controlled for covariation with linguistics.
c In parentheses: partial correlation coefficients between genetics and linguistics controlled for covariation with geography.

Table 16.4 Amounts of HLA-DRB1 genetic diversity observed among (F_{ST}) and within (h) populations within each East Asian linguistic group

Linguistic group	Group size^a	F_{ST} (%)^b	h (s.d.)^c
Altaic	14	1.70***	0.941 (0.016)
Altaic-proper	9	1.27***	0.946 (0.014)
Koreo-Japonic	5	0.88***	0.932 (0.016)
Sinitic	6	0.50***	0.931 (0.001)
Tai-Kadai	4	2.39***	0.906 (0.007)
Austro-Asiatic	2	5.38***	0.891 (0.019)
Austronesian	16	9.72***	0.815 (0.054)
Formosan	9	7.10***	0.845 (0.042)
Extra-Formosan	7	8.98***	0.776 (0.055)

Notes
a See Table 16.1 for a list of populations and linguistic groups.
b ***: $p < 0.001$.
c The gene diversity has been averaged over the corresponding number of populations; s.d.: standard deviation.

covariation with the third matrix is taken into account (0.270*** < r < 0.352*** for all coefficients). For Austronesians, the correlation between genetics and geography is also high, although less significant (r = 0.340*–0.357*), but neither genetics nor geography are correlated with linguistics (r = 0.110$^{n.s.}$ to r = 0.158$^{n.s.}$, for genetics and r = 0.112$^{n.s.}$, for geography). These results suggest that continental East Asians and Austronesians followed very different modes of evolution, as discussed in the following section.

Genetic diversity within and among linguistic groups

We further conducted ANOVA analyses on the 40 populations considered earlier, in order to assess the levels of genetic diversity within (Table 16.4), and among (Table 16.5) linguistic families. Table 16.4 indicates that the AN group is the most

Table 16.5 Amounts of HLA-DRB1 genetic diversity observed among linguistic groups (F_{CT}), and among populations within linguistic groups (F_{SC}) in East Asia

Linguistic groups[a]			F_{CT} (%)[b]	F_{SC} (%)
Altaic	vs	Sinitic	0.6*	1.3***
		Tai-Kadai	1.8***	1.8***
		Austronesian	3.5***	3.7***
Sinitic	vs	Tai-Kadai	1.4**	1.0***
		Austronesian	2.4*	4.9***
Tai-Kadai	vs	Austronesian	0.5[n.s.]	7.8**
Altaic-proper	vs	Koreo-Japonic	14.5***	1.0***
Formosan	vs	Extra-Formosan	4.8**	7.3***

Notes
a Group sizes: Altaic = 14, Sinitic = 6, Tai-Kadai = 4, Austronesian = 16, Altaic-proper = 9, Koreo-Japonic = 5, Formosan = 9, Extra-Formosan = 7. Linguistic groups with less than four populations represented have been excluded.
b ***: $p < 0.001$; **: $0.001 < p < 0.01$; *: $0.01 < p < 0.05$; n.s.: not significant.

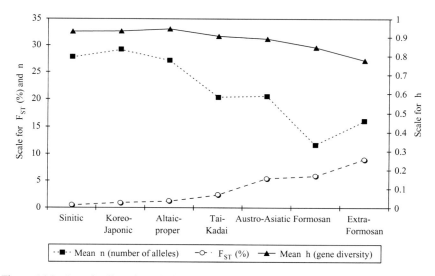

Figure 16.3 Genetic diversity within (h) and among (F_{ST}) populations (see Table 16.4), and mean number of HLA-DRB1 alleles detected (n) within the main East Asian linguistic groups considered in this study. Group sizes: Sinitic = 6, Koreo-Japonic = 5, Altaic-proper = 9, Tai-Kadai = 4, Austro-Asiatic = 2, Formosan = 9, Extra-Formosan = 7.

diverse genetically (high F_{ST} of 9.72 per cent). Among Austronesians, EFs are slightly more diversified than Taiwan Aborigines (Formosan) (F_{ST} = 8.98 and 7.1 per cent, respectively). At the opposite, the Chinese (Sinitic) constitute the most homogeneous group (low F_{ST} of 0.5 per cent), and the Altaic, Tai-Kadai and AA groups are intermediate between the Chinese and the Austronesians

(F_{ST} = 1.7, 2.39 and 5.38 per cent, respectively). For each linguistic family, we also estimated the average gene diversity within populations (h). The lowest value is observed in the Austronesians (0.815), and the highest in the Altaic (0.941) and Sinitic (0.931). These statistics are plotted in Figure 16.3, together with the average number of detected alleles (n) in each linguistic group. A drastic reduction in the number of alleles is observed in Austronesians (mostly Formosans), while this number is above 25 in Sinitic and Altaic (both Koreo-Japonic and Altaic-proper). We checked that these results are not due to a sample size effect (not shown).

Thus, from a genetic point of view, the Austronesians represent a highly heterogeneous group of homogeneous populations (pattern C in Table 16.2), while the Sinitic, and, to a lesser extent, the Altaic, represent homogeneous groups of heterogeneous populations (pattern B in Table 16.2) compared to the former. The other linguistic groups show intermediate characteristics.

Finally, linguistic families were compared genetically two by two[4] (Table 16.5). In only one case does the genetic diversity due to a difference between groups (F_{CT}) exceed the genetic diversity due to a difference between populations within groups (F_{SC}). This case is the pair Altaic-proper–Koreo-Japonic (14.5 per cent for F_{CT}, against 1.0 per cent for F_{SC}). At the opposite, Tai-Kadai is not significantly differentiated from AN (F_{CT} = 0.5 per cent, not significant), whereas a high level of differentiation is found between populations within these groups (F_{SC} = 7.8 per cent). Also, Altaic and Sinitic, and, to a lesser extent, Sinitic and AN, are only weakly differentiated ($0.01 < p < 0.05$). In fact, several Altaic and northern Chinese populations are genetically undifferentiated from each other, as indicated by non-significant F_{ST}s (see legend for Figure 16.1). The remaining pairs (Altaic–Tai-Kadai, Altaic–AN, Sinitic–Tai-Kadai and Taiwan Aborigines (Formosan)–EF) exhibit highly significant differentiations, both among groups and among populations within groups.

Discussion

Linguistic hypotheses considered through HLA genetic analyses

This study reveals complex relationships between the processes of genetic and linguistic differentiations in East Asia. At first sight, HLA genetic diversity among populations is geographically structured, as found with most classical systems (Cavalli-Sforza et al. 1994; Dugoujon et al. 2004) as well as with some DNA polymorphisms (Karafet et al. 2001). In some instances, however, the observed genetic patterns fit specific linguistic relationships, and may lend some support to one of several competing linguistic hypotheses.

The Altaic family

In mainland Asia, a highly significant differentiation of populations into Turkic-Mongolic-Manchu-Tungusic-(Altaic-proper), on the one hand, vs Koreo-Japonic, on the other hand, is observed (Table 16.5). This is consistent with theories that view the two groups as unrelated, or as distantly related within a large macro-Altaic or Eurasiatic phylum. The Altaic-proper group itself does not exhibit a clear genetic subdivision into linguistic families (Turkic, Mongolic, Manchu-Tungusic). For example, Ulchi (a Tungusic population) are genetically closer to Nivkhi (a Gilyak linguistic isolate) than to Manchu (also Tungusic), and the Mongolian Kalkh are very close to some Turkic populations (Kazakh, Tuva) (Figure 16.1b). Gene flow between neighbouring populations depending on specific environments (like steppe or mountainous areas) as well as language shifts due, for example, to territorial invasions by dominant empires (like shift of Buryat from Turkic to Mongolian, following the Mongol invasion (Pakendorf et al. 2003)) probably resulted in intricate relationships between genetic and linguistic patterns. A remarkable result of our study is the very high level of internal genetic diversity (h) observed within Altaic (mainly Altaic-proper) populations (Plate VIII, Table 16.4). It indicates that intensive contacts among populations and/or with external groups played a significant role in the evolution of this family. The genetic legacy of multiple migrations or recolonisations (e.g. Turks, Mongols) in Northeast Asia would thus be reflected in the present heterogeneous Altaic profiles.[5]

The Altaic–Sinitic linguistic border

Compared to Altaic, Chinese populations exhibit more similar HLA-DRB1 genetic profiles (Plate VIII, Table 16.4). Nonetheless, significant differences are found between northern and southern Chinese; northern Chinese are genetically undifferentiated from several Altaic populations (Manchu and Mongolian). Following Hashimoto (1986), some linguists consider that northern Chinese dialects have been 'altaicised' due to recurring episodes of domination of northern China by Altaic-speaking peoples, especially Mongolians and Manchus, followed by shift to Chinese of large numbers of these speakers. Such gene flow into Chinese would then explain the genetic closeness between Altaic and northern Sinitic speakers; the observed genetic differentiation between northern and southern Chinese populations would be a direct consequence of Altaic influence in the North, or of different influences on northern and southern Chinese.

Northern–southern East Asian differentiation

Geneticists are currently debating patterns of genetic differentiation between northern and southern East Asian populations. According to one view, all East Asian populations share a unique origin in mainland Southeast Asia, with a further migration to the North (Jin and Su 2000; Su et al. 1999). Revised versions of this theory state that northern populations differ genetically from those located further South due to late genetic contributions from Central Asia (Chu et al. 1998; Jin and Su 2000; Karafet et al. 2001), but the time and magnitude of these contributions are not clear. A second view, known as the 'pincer model', more explicitly invokes two independent migrations into East Asia along a southern and a northern route, with the influence from the Central Asian gene pool being predominant in the North (Ding et al. 2000).

In the present study, we find a high correlation between genetic and geographic distances (Table 16.3) and a continuous pattern of genetic differentiation, which roughly follows a North–South geographic axis (Figure 16.1a and 16.1b). Actually, this pattern is compatible with both models mentioned earlier. However, the HLA genetic profiles of northern populations (as discussed earlier for Altaic) are more diverse (higher h) than those of southern populations, which is also true for RH and GM (Poloni et al., Chapter 15, this volume; Sanchez-Mazas 1990). This argues against the hypothesis of a unique southern origin whereby northern genetic profiles are a subset of southern ones. Also, Northeast Asians are genetically closer to the Indians and Mansi on the western edge of the region (Figure 16.1A). Such genetic continuity is in keeping with historical relationships established along a northern route.

Proto-East Asian and Austric hypotheses

At the southern edge of China, populations are in genetic continuity (albeit with large genetic distances) with Tai-Kadai and, to a lesser extent, with AA speakers, on the one hand, and Taiwan Aborigines (except the Amis), on the other (Figure 16.1a and 16.1b and Table 16.5). Such results do not favour any specific linguistic hypothesis linking ST to Southeast Asian linguistic phyla (e.g. the Sino-AN hypothesis advocated by Sagart in this volume), or the 'Greater Austric' hypothesis proposed by Benedict (1942), Ruhlen (1987) and Peiros (1998). On the other hand, Benedict (1942) argues that Tai-Kadai and AN subgroup together as the two branches of the Austro-Tai phylum, and Sagart (2001 and this volume) claims that Tai-Kadai is originally an AN language from Taiwan having been partly relexified by a Southeast Asian language. Here we show that Tai-Kadai and AN populations do not differ significantly from each other for HLA (Table 16.5), in agreement with both these theories.[6] Moreover, in Sagart's view, the AN language ancestral to Tai-Kadai belongs to a primary branch of PAN to which all EF languages and Amis also belong: it is noteworthy, from this point of view, that high frequencies of allele *1502 characterise that set of populations (Tai-Kadai, Amis and EFAN, in addition to Puyuma, but not central-mountain Taiwanese), as discussed later. Unfortunately, a deeper analysis of Southeast Asian population relationships is not possible due to a lack of representative samples in our data (e.g. only two AA, no HM, and no TB populations are represented). At this point, we can simply state that Southeast Asian populations are highly differentiated from each other compared to 'continental' groups located further North, in agreement with results recently obtained for mtDNA (Oota et al. 2002).

The remarkable HLA diversity of Taiwan Aborigines

The results of a recent HLA analysis of nine Aboriginal tribes from Taiwan (Chu et al. 2001; Lin et al., Chapter 13, this volume), are worth discussing in detail. As shown earlier (Figure 16.1a), a rough distinction can be drawn between the aboriginal populations from the central mountains (Atayal, Tsou, Saisiat, Rukai, Paiwan and Bunun) and those located on or off the east coast (Amis, Puyuma and Yami) of the island. In fact, the coastal populations are genetically highly heterogeneous. The Yami live on Orchid (or Lan Yu) Island where they probably settled after migrating from Bataan Islands (northern Philippines), since their language is closely related to the Batanic languages of the northern Philippines (Chen 1967). This isolation would explain their genetic divergence from other Taiwanese and EF populations. The Puyuma live together with native Chinese in a few villages around the city of T'ai-Tung (Chen 1967), raising the possibility of some degree of gene flow, as recently suggested by mtDNA analyses (Trejaut et al. forthcoming); although this may be the case generally for Taiwan Aborigines living in the plains.

The Amis exhibit a highly peculiar HLA-DRB1 genetic profile (Plate VIII) with high frequencies for some uncommon alleles (*0404, *0405) and a very reduced genetic repertoire (only seven alleles detected, compared to averages of 20.6 for the total set 48 populations and between 11.6 and 29.2 in the different linguistic groups, see Figure 16.3). The uniqueness of the Amis is observed with several other genetic systems: for example, haplotypes R^1 of the Rhesus system, and GM*1,3;5* of the immunoglobulin-associated GM polymorphism, reach frequencies of 90 and 95 per cent, respectively, in this population (Lin and Broadberry 1998; Schanfield et al. 2002; Sewerin et al. 2002). Schanfield et al. (2002) explain this GM profile by a selective effect linked to resistance to malaria in lowland populations; Lin and co-workers suggest a relationship between the Amis and both Papuans from New Guinea and Australian Aborigines, based on a common segregation of these populations in HLA neighbour-joining trees (Chu et al. 2001; Lin et al. 2000; Lin et al., Chapter 13, this volume) and Sewerin et al. (2002) notice a genetic similarity, based on 6 point mutation loci, between the Amis and native Americans.

Our own explanation is that the Amis underwent a founder effect and rapid genetic drift due to isolation. Mabuchi (1954) suggests that a group ancestral to them and to the Ketagalans and Kavalans migrated from the west to the east coast of Taiwan, with an intermediate period of settlement on an undetermined island off the east coast. This period of isolation could correspond to a bottleneck leading to an impoverishment of their genetic repertoire and accidental genetic convergences with genetically homogeneous populations from other continents. On the other hand, isolation at higher altitudes caused the Aboriginal populations located in the central mountains to evolve independently from coastal tribes, also through rapid genetic drift.

Genetic drift and linguistic variation along the route to the Pacific

Two main alternative models have been proposed to explain the expansion of the Austronesians in the Pacific. These models are popularly known as 'the express-train to Polynesia', proposing a rapid expansion from Taiwan (Bellwood 1978; Diamond 1988), and 'the entangled bank' (Terrell 1988), assuming a more complex history of interactions between Polynesians, Melanesians and Southeast Asian populations. The first model has been supported by mtDNA, nuclear DNA, and HLA genetic studies (Melton et al. 1995, 1998; Zimdahl et al. 1999), but the speed of the AN spread across the Pacific may not have been as fast as previously assumed: according to the 'slow-boat' hypothesis (Kayser et al. 2000), various contact phenomena occurred between Polynesian ancestors and Melanesians. Despite recent alternative views (Hurles et al. 2002; Jin and Su 2000; Richards et al. 1998; Su et al. 2000), both scenarios agree that the AN expansion started in Taiwan and/or nearby East Asia about 6,000–5,000 BP, and reached Polynesia by migrating southwards and eastwards through the Philippines, Indonesia and coastal and islands Melanesia.

If we consider this migration theory, the tentative scenario proposed later would account for the observed HLA-DRB1allelic distribution shown in Plate VIII.

The PANs, originating somewhere in mainland China, were characterised by relatively even HLA allelic distributions (i.e. rather low frequencies for all alleles), as currently observed in continental East Asia.

Migration of these PANs to Taiwan was followed by a main differentiation between coastal and central mountain tribes. The central mountain tribes virtually lost allele *1502 and acquired high frequencies of alleles *1202 and *0803 by genetic drift. At the same time, the east coast tribes, here represented by the Amis and the Puyuma, acquired a higher frequency of allele *1502. The Amis diverged to a greater extent due to a bottleneck, losing allele *1202 and acquiring a high frequency of *0404, very rare elsewhere.

The EFs began to differentiate from the rest of the Austronesians on the east coast, where *1502 was frequent, and the frequency of this allele increased rapidly during their migrations southwards to Indonesia, eastwards to the Pacific, and also back to the mainland where they would form the first Tai-Kadai nucleus.

Overall, as also concluded for Amerindians on the basis of HLA studies (Monsalve et al. 1999; Sanchez-Mazas forthcoming), AN populations would have experienced rapid differentiations through genetic drift, both within Taiwan, and as soon as they expanded away from this island. Contrary to continental East Asians, the AN genetic pool is indeed characterised by high genetic variation among, and low genetic variation within populations (pattern C in Table 16.2, Table 16.4 and Figure 16.3), as well as a low number of detected HLA-DRB1alleles (n = 13.6 in average) compared to other linguistic groups (from 20.3 to 29.2). Their allelic repertoire has thus been impoverished during successive founder effects, in agreement with the hypothesis of isolation and migrations in insular environments. It is even more reduced in island Melanesia, with only 9–14 alleles detected at the DRB1 locus (Hagelberg et al. 1999; Zimdahl et al. 1999), indicating that the founder effect/genetic drift processes continued during the colonisation of the Pacific. Moreover, the dispersal of small and endogamous[7] population groups across insular Southeast Asia (and the Pacific) may explain why so many different languages are identified within the AN phylum (some 1,262 languages (Grimes and Grimes 2000)[8] – about one-fifth of the total number of human languages). Supposing that genetic and linguistic change are random and independent processes, genetic variation presumably ceased to reflect linguistic relationships in this area. On the other hand, gene flow maintained a certain amount of genetic relatedness among neighbouring populations without necessarily slowing down the linguistic differentiation process, as shown by Zimdahl et al. (1999) for some populations of the Solomon Islands. This may be the reason why geography still explains 12 per cent of the AN genetic variation, and linguistics less than 2 per cent (according to determination coefficients (Sokal and Rohlf 1994) estimated by the square of the correlation coefficients given in Table 16.3), while geographic and linguistic differentiations explain an equivalent amount of genetic variation in continental East Asia ($r^2 = 12$ and 11 per cent, respectively).

Inferring mechanisms of population differentiation within language families

In this study, we have sought to emphasise the role of different evolutionary mechanisms in shaping the patterns of genetic variation within linguistic families. F_{ST} and h were taken as two complementary measures of genetic diversity (among and within populations, respectively) allowing the description of four different patterns from which evolutionary processes might be inferred (Table 16.2). For each linguistic family under study, we reported these two statistics on a graph, together with the average number of detected alleles (n) (Figure 16.3). This approach allowed us to identify two main patterns in the HLA-DRB1 data: pattern C (high F_{ST} and low h), observed in Austronesians, was explained by genetic drift; pattern B (low F_{ST} and high h) was observed in Sinitic and Altaic, where either intensive gene flow occurred among populations, or each group as a whole underwent a recent differentiation from a highly diversified population. Different mechanisms can also be inferred for the remaining patterns (A and D), although they were not observed in our study. Pattern D (low F_{ST} and low h, or 'genetic undifferentiation') can be due either to a very recent common origin, or to intensive gene flow between populations. Pattern A (high F_{ST} and high h, or 'high differentiation/high diversity') can suggest at least two contrasting explanations: a remote ancestry of populations, with large population sizes and reduced gene flow maintaining genetic diversity within and among populations, respectively, or intensive gene flow from external and genetically diverse populations. The latter situation could occur, for example, at different linguistic boundaries of a given family (e.g. the Altaic and Tai-Kadai on the boundaries of Chinese).

The approach described in the preceding paragraph should prove very useful in investigating the evolution of populations belonging to different linguistic phyla, given that numerous populations are tested in each group. Moreover, its application to several independent genetic systems (such as RH and GM) or the different HLA loci would allow us to distinguish between patterns resulting from the genetic history of populations – if congruent results are obtained for all systems – and those resulting, for example, from selective effects, or even from methodological biases – if discordant results are obtained (Sanchez-Mazas et al. 2003).

Conclusion

In this study, we used a large set of molecular *HLA-DRB1* data (48 populations represented by 6,613 individuals) to investigate the genetic structure of East Asian populations in relation to some currently debated linguistic hypotheses. We looked at the data through several complementary statistical approaches (correlation analysis between genetic, geographic and linguistic distances, F_{ST} significance among populations, ANOVA across linguistic groups and MDS analysis) not with a view to *prove* or *disprove* linguistic hypotheses, but to explore the compatibility between genetic and linguistic relationships in the continent.

While the HLA polymorphism reveals a complex genetic structure in East Asian, and especially AN populations, some of our findings confirm, or support, various aspects of linguistic classification. First, although Japanese, Korean and Altaic-proper (Mongolic, Manchu-Tungusic and Turkic) are included by some authors into such macrophyla as Altaic and Eurasiatic, few, if any, regard Koreo-Japonic and Altaic-proper as linguistically very close. Not surprisingly, we observe a major genetic differentiation between Koreo-Japonic on the one hand and Altaic-proper on the other hand. Second, we find a high degree of genetic proximity between populations on both sides of the Altaic–Sinitic linguistic boundary, paralleling the linguistic evidence for 'altaicisation' of northern Chinese (Hashimoto 1986). While very few linguists would argue for a genetic connection between Chinese and Altaic, the Altaic features in northern Chinese dialects clearly are of the type resulting from imperfect learning of Chinese by Altaic speakers, suggesting that Altaic speakers in northern China have been shifting to Chinese *en masse* in historical times: our genetic observations support Hashimoto's altaicisation hypothesis. Third, we find evidence of a genetic continuity between AN (especially EF) and Tai-Kadai. This finding is compatible with the hypothesis of an AN origin of Tai-Kadai. Fourth, the results of the present investigation are congruent with a Taiwanese homeland of AN: we propose a tentative historical scenario for the AN expansion, in which EF originated on the east coast of Taiwan. We also drew a parallel between the high level of genetic differentiation among Austronesians and their high number of different languages, both probably resulting independently from the rapid dispersal of small population groups in an island environment. Finally, we have proposed a simple but efficient way of inferring the modes of evolution of different linguistic families through the computation of two statistics. This has also allowed us to contrast the evolution of continental East Asians and that of insular peoples. Of course, as in other disciplines, the conclusions reached by genetic studies strongly depend on the quantity and quality of the data and on the methods used. Our present interpretation of the HLA-DRB1polymorphism in East Asia should therefore be considered tentative.

Acknowledgements

This work was supported by the French CNRS (OHLL grant to ESP and LS) and the Swiss FNS (grant 3100-49771.96) to ASM.

Abbreviations

AA	Austro-Asiatic
AN	Austronesian
ANOVA	Analysis of variance
EF	Extra-Formosan
EFAN	Extra-Formosan Austronesian
HM	Hmong-Mien
MDS	Multidimensional scaling
MHC	Major histocompatibility complex
MP	Malayo-Polynesian
mtDNA	mitochondrial DNA
PAN	Proto-Austronesian
ST	Sino-Tibetan
TB	Tibeto-Burman

Notes

1 Missing from this list are TB and HM populations; AA populations are limited to Kinh (= Vietnamese) and Muong, two closely related languages of the Vietic branch of Mon-Khmer. Our three Tai-Kadai populations come from the Thai branch, and we do not have any Kra populations from South China or Li populations from Hainan. For the AN family, we looked at the western part, especially Taiwan where the family underwent its primary diversification. There is only one Central MP population (Nusa Tenggara) and no Oceanic: this is because we have concentrated our attention on the region where a majority of linguists consider the AN homeland to be located.
2 These models apply to linguistic families considered a priori monophyletic.
3 The correlation between genetics and geography drops from 0.279 to 0.131 when 40 instead of 48 populations are considered, probably because of the exclusion of three Northeast Siberian populations (Chukchi, Koryak, Yupik), which are both genetically and geographically very distant from all other populations.
4 AA was not considered because it included only two populations.
5 The evolution of the HLA polymorphism is possibly influenced by selective pressure maintaining a high level of diversity in human populations (Meyer 2002; Meyer and

Thomson 2001). We thus checked the possibility of a departure from selective neutrality in all populations considered in this study, and we found that seven out of 48 population samples (thus 15 per cent) were significantly deviant towards an excess of heterozygotes at the 1 per cent level, namely Manchu (p = 0.004), Khalkh (p = 0.008), Tuvin (p = 0.004), Japanese (two samples, p = 0.001 and p = 0.002) and Koreans (two samples, p = 0.0006 and p < 0.0001). As all these populations belong to the Altaic family, it is reasonable to suppose that historical events like gene flow, rather than selection, maintained such high levels of genetic diversity.

6 Note, however, that this test was not applied to AA speakers as these are here represented by only two populations.
7 Endogamous here refers to the fact that the genetic pool of isolated populations is generally more homogeneous than in outbred populations due to a higher kinship between individuals.
8 http://www.ethnologue.com/ (accessed July 2003).

Bibliography

Ammerman, A.J. and Cavalli-Sforza, L.L. (1984) The Neolithic Transition and the Genetics of Populations in Europe, Princeton, USA: Princeton University Press.

Barbujani, G. (2000) 'Geographic patterns: how to identify them and why', Human Biology 72: 133–53.

Barbujani, G. and Pilastro, A. (1993) 'Genetic evidence on origin and dispersal of human populations speaking languages of the Nostratic macrofamily', Proceedings of the National Academy of Sciences USA 90: 4670–3.

Barbujani, G., Sokal, R.R. and Oden, N.L. (1995) 'Indo-European origins: a computer-simulation test of five hypotheses', American Journal of Physical Anthropology 96: 109–32.

Bellwood, P. (1978) Man's Conquest of the Pacific: The Prehistory of Southeast Asia and Oceania, Oxford: Oxford University Press.

—— (2001) 'Early agriculturalist population diasporas? Farming, languages and genes', Annual Review of Anthropology 30: 181–207.

Benedict, P.K. (1942) 'Thai, Kadai and Indonesian: a new alignment in Southeastern Asia', American Anthropologist, n.s. 44, 576–601.

Bugawan, T.L., Chang, J.D., Klitz, W. and Erlich, H.A. (1994) 'PCR/oligonucleotide probe typing of HLA class II alleles in a Filipino population reveals an unusual distribution of HLA haplotypes', American Journal of Human Genetics 54: 331–40.

Cavalli-Sforza, L.L., Menozzi, P. and Piazza, A. (1994) The History and Geography of Human Genes, Princeton, New Jersey: Princeton University Press.

Chandanayingyong, D., Stephens, H.A., Klaythong, R., Sirikong, M., Udee, S., Longta, P., Chantangpol, R., Bejrachandra, S. and Rungruang, E. (1997) 'HLA-A, -B, -DRB1, -DQA1 and -DQB1 polymorphism in Thais', Human Immunology 53: 174–82.

Chen, K.-C. (1967) Taiwan Aborigines, A Genetic Study of Tribal Variations Cambridge, MA: Harvard University Press.

Chikhi, L., Nichols, R.A., Barbujani, G. and Beaumont, M.A. (2002) 'Y genetic data support the Neolithic demic diffusion model', Proceedings of the National Academy of Sciences USA 99: 11008–13.

Chimge, N.O., Tanaka, H., Kashiwase, K., Ayush, D., Tokunaga, K., Saji, H., Akaza, T., Batsuuri, J. and Juji, T. (1997) 'The HLA system in the population of Mongolia', Tissue Antigens 49: 477–83.

Chu, C.C., Lin, M., Nakajima, F., Lee, H.L., Chang, S.L., Juji, T. and Tokunaga, K. (2001) 'Diversity of HLA among Taiwan's indigenous tribes and the Ivatans in the Philippines', Tissue Antigens 58: 9–18.

Chu, J.Y., Huang, W., Kuang, S.Q., Wang, J.M., Xu, J.J., Chu, Z.T., Yang, Z.Q., Lin, K.Q., Li, P., Wu, M., Geng, Z.C., Tan, C.C., Du, R.F. and Jin, L. (1998) 'Genetic relationship of populations in China', Proceedings of the National Academy of Science USA 95: 11763–8.

Diamond, J.M. (1988) 'Express train to Polynesia', Nature 336: 307–8.

Ding, Y.-C., Wooding, S., Harpending, H.C., Chi, H.-C., Li, H.-P., Fu, Y.-X., Pang, J.-F., Yao, Y.-G., Xiang Yu, J.-G., Moyzis, R. and Zhang, Y.-P. (2000) 'Population structure and history in East Asia', Proceedings of the National Academy of Sciences USA 97: 14003–6.

Dugoujon J.-M., Hazout, S., Loirat, F., Mourrieras, B., Crouau-Roy, B. and Sanchez-Mazas, A. (2004) 'GM haplotype diversity of 82 populations over the world suggests a centrifugal model of human migrations', American Journal of Physical Anthropology 125: 175–92.

Dupanloup de Ceuninck, I., Schneider, S., Langaney, A. and Excoffier, L. (2000) 'Inferring the impact of linguistic barriers on population differentiation: application to the Afro-Asiatic/Indo-European case', European Journal of Human Genetics 10: 750–6.

Excoffier, L. (2001) 'Analysis of population subdivision', in D.J. Balding, M. Bishop and C. Cannings (eds) Handbook of Statistical Genetics, Chichester: John Wiley & Sons, Ltd.

Excoffier, L., Pellegrini, P., Sanchez-Mazas, A., Simon, C. and Langaney, A. (1987) 'Genetics and history of Sub-Saharan Africa', Yearbook of Physical Anthropology 30: 151–94.

Gao, X.J., Sun, Y.P., An, J.B., Fernandez-Vina, M., Qou, J.N., Lin, L. and Stastny, P. (1991) 'DNA typing for HLA-DR, and -DP alleles in a Chinese population using the polymerase chain reaction (PCR) and oligonucleotide probes', Tissue Antigens 38: 24–30.

Gao, X., Zimmet, P. and Serjeantson, S.W. (1992) 'HLA-DR, DQ sequence polymorphisms in Polynesians, Micronesians, and Javanese', Human Immunology 34: 153–61.

Grahovac, B., Sukernik, R.I., O'hUigin, C., Zaleska-Rutczynska, Z., Blagitko, N., Raldugina, O., Kosutic, T., Satta, Y., Figueroa, F., Takahata, N. and Klein, J. (1998) 'Polymorphism of the HLA class II loci in Siberian populations', Human Genetics 102: 27–43.

Grimes, B.F. and Grimes, J.E. (eds) (2000) Ethnologue: Languages of the World, Dallas: SIL International (http://www.ethnologue.com).

Hagelberg, E., Kayser, M., Nagy, M., Roewer, L., Zimdahl, H., Krawczak, M., Lió, P. and Schiefenhövel, W. (1999) 'Molecular genetic evidence for the human settlement of the Pacific: analysis of mitochondrial DNA, Y chromosome and HLA markers', Philosophical Transactions of the Royal Society of London B354: 141–52.

Hashimoto, M.J. (1986) 'The altaicization of Northern Chinese', in J. McCoy and T. Light (eds) Contributions to Sino-Tibetan studies, Leiden: E.J. Brill.

Hashimoto, M., Kinoshita, T., Yamasaki, M., Tanaka, H., Imanishi, T., Ihara, H., Ichikawa, Y. and Fukunishi, T. (1994) 'Gene frequencies and haplotypic associations within the HLA region in 916 unrelated Japanese individuals', Tissue Antigens 44: 166–73.

Hatta, Y., Ohashi, J., Imanishi, T., Kamiyama, H., Iha, M., Simabukuro, T., Ogawa, A., Tanaka, H., Akaza, T., Gojobori, T., Juji, T. and Tokunaga, K. (1999) 'HLA genes and haplotypes in Ryukyuans suggest recent gene flow to the Okinawa Islands', Human Biology 71: 353–65.

Hurles, M.E., Nicholson, J., Bosch, E., Renfrew, C., Sykes, B.C. and Jobling, M.A. (2002) 'Y chromosomal evidence for the origins of Oceanic-speaking peoples', Genetics 160: 289–303.

Imanishi, T., Akaza, T., Kimura, A., Tokunaga, K. and Gojobori, T. (1992) 'Allele and haplotype frequencies for HLA and complement loci in various ethnic groups', in K. Tsuji, M. Aizawa and T. Sasazuki (eds) HLA 1991, Vol. 1, Oxford: Oxford University Press.

IMGT/HLA sequence database (2003) Online. Available http://www.ebi.ac.uk/imgt/hla/intro.html (accessed 27 August 2003).

Jin, L. and Su, B. (2000) 'Natives or immigrants: modern human origin in east Asia', Nature Reviews Genetics 1: 126–33.

Karafet, T., Xu, L., Du, R.F., Wang, W., Feng, S., Wells, R.S., Redd, A.J., Zegura, S.L. and Hammer, M.F. (2001) 'Paternal population history of East Asia: sources, patterns, and microevolutionary processes', American Journal of Human Genetics 69: 615–28.

Kayser, M., Brauer, S., Weiss, G., Underhill, P.A., Roewer, L., Schiefenhövel, W. and Stoneking, M. (2000) 'Melanesian origin of Polynesian Y chromosomes', Current Biology 10: 1237–46.

Kruskal, J.B. (1964) 'Nonmetric multidimensional scaling: a numerical method', Psychometrika 29: 28–42.

Lee, J. (1997) 'Chinese normal', in P. I. Terasaki and D.W. Gjertson, (eds) HLA 1997, Los Angeles: UCLA Tissue Typing Laboratory.

Lin, M. and Broadberry, R.E. (1998) 'Immunohematology in Taiwan', Transfusion Medicine Reviews 12: 56–72.

Lin, M., Chu, C.C., Lee, H.L., Chang, S.L., Ohashi, J., Tokunaga, K., Akaza, T. and Juji, T. (2000) 'Heterogeneity of Taiwan's indigenous population: possible relation to prehistoric Mongoloid dispersals', Tissue Antigens 55: 1–9.

Lou, H., Li, H.C., Kuwayama, M., Yashiki, S., Fujiyoshi, T., Suehara, M., Osame, M., Yamashita, M., Hayami, M., Gurtsevich, V., Ballas, M., Imanishi, T. and Sonoda, S. (1998) 'HLA class I and class II of the Nivkhi, an indigenous population carrying HTLV-I in Sakhalin, Far Eastern Russia', Tissue Antigens 52: 444–51.

Mabuchi, T. (1954) 'Takasagozoku no ido oyobi bumpu (part 2)', Minzoku Gaku 18, 4.

Mack, S.J., Bugawan, T.L., Stoneking, M., Saha, M., Beck, H.-P. and Erlich, H.A. (2000) 'HLA class I and class II loci in Pacific/Asian populations', in M. Kasahara (ed.) Major Histocompatibility Complex, Evolution, Structure, and Function, Tokyo: Springer Verlag.

Mantel, G. (1967) 'The detection of disease clustering and a generalized regression approach', Cancer Research 27: 209–20.

Martinez-Laso, J., Sartakova, M., Allende, L., Konenkov, V., Moscoso, J., Silvera-Redondo, C., Pacho, A., Trapaga, J., Gomez-Casado, E. and Arnaiz-Villena, A. (2001) 'HLA molecular markers in Tuvinians: a population with both Oriental and Caucasoid characteristics', Annals of Human Genetics 65: 245–61.

Melton, T., Peterson, R., Redd, A.J., Saha, N., Sofro, A.S.M., Martinson, J. and Stoneking, M. (1995) 'Polynesian genetic affinities with southeast Asian populations as identified by mtDNA analysis', American Journal of Human Genetics 57: 403–14.

Melton, T., Clifford, S., Martinson, J., Batzer, M. and Stoneking, M. (1998) 'Genetic evidence for the proto-Austronesian homeland in Asia: mtDNA and nuclear DNA variation in Taiwanese Aboriginal tribes', American Journal of Human Genetics 63: 1807–23.

Meyer, D. (2002) 'Studies on selection and recombination in human major histocompatibility complex genes', unpublished thesis, University of California, Berkeley.

Meyer, D. and Thomson, G. (2001) 'How selection shapes variation of the human major histocompatibility complex: a review', Annals of Human Genetics 65: 1–26.

Mizuki, N., Ohno, S., Ando, H., Sato, T., Imanishi, T., Gojobori, T., Ishihara, M., Goto, K., Ota, M., Geng, Z., Geng, L., Li, G. and Inoko, H. (1998) 'Major histocompatibility complex class II alleles in an Uygur population in the Silk Route of Northwest China', Tissue Antigens 51: 287–92.

Mizuki, N., Ohno, S., Ando, H., Sato, T., Imanishi, T., Gojobori, T., Ishihara, M., Ota, M., Geng, Z., Geng, L., Li, G., Kimura, M. and Inoko, H. (1997) 'Major histocompatibility complex class II alleles in Kazak and Han populations in the Silk Route of northwestern China', Tissue Antigens 50: 527–34.

Monsalve, M.V., Helgason, A. and Devine, D.V. (1999) 'Languages, geography and HLA haplotypes in Native American and Asian populations', Proceedings of the Royal Society of London B266: 2209–16.

Munkhbat, B., Sato, T., Hagihara, M., Sato, K., Kimura, A., Munkhtuvshin, N. and Tsuji, K. (1997) 'Molecular analysis of HLA polymorphism in Khoton-Mongolians', Tissue Antigens 50: 124–34.

Nei, M. (1987) Molecular Evolutionary Genetics, New York: Columbia University Press.

Oota, H., Kitano, T., Jin, F., Yuasa, I., Wang, L., Ueda, S., Saitou, N. and Stoneking, M. (2002) 'Extreme mtDNA homogeneity in continental Asian populations', American Journal of Physical Anthropology 118: 146–53.

Pakendorf, B., Wiebe, V., Tarskaia, L.A., Spitsyn, V.A., Soodyall, H., Rodewald, A. and Stoneking, M. (2003) 'Mitochondrial DNA evidence for admixed origins of central Siberian populations', American Journal of Physical Anthropology 120: 211–24.

Park, M.H., Kim, H.S. and Kang, S.J. (1999) 'HLA-A, -B, -DRB1 allele and haplotype frequencies in 510 Koreans', Tissue Antigens 53: 386–90.

Peiros, I. (1998) Comparative Linguistics in Southeast Asia, Camberra: Pacific Linguistics.

Rani, R., Fernandez-Vina, M.A. and Stastny, P. (1998) 'Associations between HLA class II alleles in a North Indian population', Tissue Antigens 52: 37–43.

Renfrew, C. (1992) 'Archaeology, genetics and linguistic diversity', Man 27: 445–78.

Reynolds, J., Weir, B.S. and Cockerham, C.C. (1983) 'Estimation for the coancestry coefficient: basis for a short-term genetic distance', Genetics 105: 767–79.

Richards, M., Oppenheimer, S. and Sykes, B. (1998) 'MtDNA suggests Polynesian origins in Eastern Indonesia', American Journal of Human Genetics 63: 1234–6.

Rohlf, F.J. (2000) NTSYSpc: Numerical Taxonomy and Multivariate Analysis System New York: Exeter Software.

Ruhlen, M. (1987) A Guide to the World's Languages. V.1, Classification, London: Edward Arnold.

Sagart, L. (2001) 'Comment: Malayo-Polynesian features in the AN-related vocabulary in Kadai', Paper presented at the International Meeting Perspectives on the Phylogeny of East Asian Languages, Périgueux, August 2001.

Saito, S., Ota, S., Yamada, E., Inoko, H. and Ota, M. (2000) 'Allele frequencies and haplotypic associations defined by allelic DNA typing at HLA class I and class II loci in the Japanese population', Tissue Antigens 56: 522–9.

Sanchez-Mazas, A. (1990) Polymorphisme des systèmes immunologiques Rhésus, GM et HLA et histoire du peuplement humain, unpublished thesis, University of Geneva, Switzerland.

—— (2001) 'African diversity from the HLA point of view: influence of genetic drift, geography, linguistics, and natural selection', Human Immunology 62: 937–48.

—— (2002) 'HLA data analysis in anthropology: basic theory and practice', Paper presented at the 16th European Histocompatibility Conference of the European Federation for Immunogenetics (EFI), Strasbourg, March.

Sanchez-Mazas, A. (forthcoming) 'HLA genetic diversity of the 13th IHWC population data relative to worldwide linguistic families', to appear in J.A. Hansen and B. Dupont (eds) HLA 2002: Immunobiology of the Human MHC, Seattle: IHWG Press.

Sanchez-Mazas, A., Poloni, E., Jacques, G. and Sagart, L. (2003) 'Processus de différenciation des locuteurs des grandes familles de langues est-asiatiques: hypothèses de la génétique', Paper presented at the annual meeting of the Société d'Anthropologie de Paris, Museum National d'Histoire Naturelle, Paris, January.

Schanfield, M., Ohkura, K., Lin, M., Shyu, R. and Gershowitz, H. (2002) 'Immunoglobulin allotypes among Taiwan Aborigines: evidence of malarial selection could affect studies of population affinity', Human Biology 74: 363–79.

Schneider, S., Roessli, D. and Excoffier, L. (2000) Arlequin ver 2.000: a software for population genetics data analysis, Geneva: Genetics and Biometry Laboratory, University of Geneva.

Sewerin, B., Cuza, F.J., Szmulewicz, M.N., Rowold, D.J., Bertrand-Garcia, R.L. and Herrera, R.J. (2002) 'On the genetic uniqueness of the Ami aborigines of Formosa', American Journal of Physical Anthropology 119: 240–8.

Sokal, R.R. and Rohlf, F.J. (1994) Biometry, New York: W.H. Freeman and Co.

Su, B., Jin, L., Underhill, P., Martinson, J., Saha, N., McGarvey, S.T., Shriver, M.D., Chu, J., Oefner, P., Chakraborty, R. and Deka, R. (2000) 'Polynesian origins: insights from the Y chromosome', Proceedings of the National Academy of Sciences USA 97: 8225–8.

Su, B., Xiao, J., Underhill, P., Deka, R., Zhang, W., Akey, J., Huang, W., Shen, D., Lu, D., Luo, J., Chu, J., Tan, J., Shen, P., Davis, R., Cavalli-Sforza, L., Chakraborty, R., Xiong, M., Du, R., Oefner, P., Chen, Z. and Jin, L. (1999) 'Y-Chromosome evidence for a northward migration of modern humans into eastern Asia during the last Ice Age', American Journal of Human Genetics 65: 1718–24.

Terrell, J. (1988) 'History as a family tree, history as an entangled ban: constructing images and interpretations of prehistory in the South Pacific', Antiquity 62: 642–57.

Trejaut, J.A., Loo, J.H., Li, Z.Y., Lee, H.L., Chang, H.L., Chu, C.C. and Lin, M. (forthcoming) 'Mitochondrial DNA diversity in nine Taiwan indigenous tribes', (in preparation).

Uinuk-Ool, T.S., Takezaki, N., Sukernik, R.I., Nagl, S. and Klein, J. (2002) 'Origin and affinities of indigenous Siberian populations as revealed by HLA class II gene frequencies', Human Genetics 110: 209–26.

Vu-Trieu, A., Djoulah, S., Tran-Thi, C., Ngyuyen-Tanh, T., Le Monnier de Gouville, I., Hors, J. and Sanchez-Mazas, A. (1997) 'HLA-DR and -DQB1 DNA polymorphisms in a Vietnamese Kinh population from Hanoi', European Journal of Immunogenetics 24: 345–56.

Wang, F.Q., Semana, G., Fauchet, R. and Genetet, B. (1993) 'HLA-DR and -DQ genotyping by PCR-SSO in Shanghai Chinese', Tissue Antigens 41: 223–6.

Weng, Z. and Sokal, R.R. (1995) 'Origins of Indo-Europeans and the spread of agriculture in Europe: comparison of lexicostatistical and genetic evidence', Human Biology 67: 577–94.

Zimdahl, H., Schiefenhövel, W., Kayser, M., Roewer, L. and Nagy, M. (1999) 'Towards understanding the origin and dispersal of Austronesians in the Solomon Sea: HLA class II polymorphism in eight distinct populations of Asia-Oceania', European Journal of Immunogenetics 26: 405–16.

17

A SYNOPSIS OF EXTANT Y CHROMOSOME DIVERSITY IN EAST ASIA AND OCEANIA

Peter A. Underhill

Introduction and caveats

While reflective of a single history of our species, archaeology, evolutionary population genetics and historical linguistics measure separate parameters. Since these often span different temporal and spatial scales, inconsistencies between them can occur. Furthermore, the complicating and homogenising factors of cultural borrowing, language shifts and gene flow operate in all human contexts creating potentially misleading parallelisms (Bellwood 2001). Therefore, the recovery of the history of populations from a comparison of archaeology, genetics and language cannot be a matter of proof but rather the balance of evidence for a hypothesis through correlation.

The absence of recombination and haploid nature of the Y chromosome permits the reconstruction of an unequivocal haplotype phylogeny based on the geographic distribution of the Y chromosome binary chromosomes, an approach known as 'phylogeography' (Avise et al. 1987; Underhill et al. 2001b). The term haplotype was introduced by Ceppellini et al. (1967). A haplotype is an array of specific alleles on a single chromosome. An allele is any one of multiple DNA sequence character states possible, typically a substitution of one of the four possible nucleotides, an insertion or a deletion. Generally for these types of data usually only two alleles are observed, either the ancestral allele or a derived allele. What is central is the assumption that the derived allele arose once in human history, and all males that display a particular mutant allele descend from a common paternal ancestor on which the mutation first appeared. The sequential accumulation of such mutational events across the generations can be readily determined and displayed as a genealogy. Informally, the last known mutation to occur on a particular chromosome can be used to define a particular lineage. Thus, when I refer to a particular mutation event or M marker number, I am actually often discussing a specific chromosomal lineage (or haplotype). In order to keep terms simple for non-geneticists, I will substitute the term 'chromosome' for haplotype.

Thus I discuss a specific chromosome by a mutation designation. In a similar manner, mitochondrial DNA (mtDNA) provides the analogous female record, although its inherently higher mutation rate causes greater recurrence and thus more noise in the underlying pattern of maternal relationships. A lower effective population size for the Y chromosome, which can be further reduced by male specific non-random mating patterns, translates into increased levels of population subdivision respective to other DNA sequences (Shen et al. 2000). The rarity of back and recurrent mutations further contributes to the property of displaying the strongest geographic correlation and greatest diversity amongst, rather than within, populations.

Despite the increasing knowledge concerning the genetics of living populations, it is important to recognise the following

1. Such facts provide only proxy data for actual pre-historical events;
2. There is no a priori reason for a 1:1 correlation between the evolution of a DNA molecule and other non-genetic evidence;
3. Different population histories can generate the same genetic landscape and;
4. Earlier demographic episodes may be hidden or replaced by more recent events.

Nonetheless, the consistent hierarchical nature of the newly resolved Y chromosome genealogy (Underhill et al. 2000; Underhill et al. 2001b) provides an independent and robust framework for interpreting archaeological and language complexity that is intrinsically more decentralised. The availability of both slow and fast evolving polymorphic markers on the human Y chromosome exposes the male genetic history of human populations at different time scales. Also, extensive Y chromosome data contradicts the possibility that early hominids contributed significantly, if at all, to the gene pool of anatomically modern humans of the region (Capelli et al. 2001; Ke et al. 2001).

The relevant aspects of human history and the Y chromosome genealogy to be addressed in this summary include

1. The earliest successful colonisation of Asia as suggested by the arrival of anatomically modern humans in Australia perhaps 60,000 years ago (Stringer 2000).
2. The impact of climatic change, contraction, the area and extent of isolation and subsequent re-dispersal(s). The inference of putative 'homelands' of lineages should be possible, as well as deducing their subsequent dispersal routes, by localising regions of highest associated diversity.
3. The transition to agriculture. What is needed is greater sampling density since relationships between food production and language flow may only be recognisable in a genetic context when studied on a micro-geographic scale.

The primary aim here is to summarise the current knowledge of Y chromosome affinity and diversification. This rendition of East Asian Y chromosome heritage provides an independent counterpoint to theories of prehistoric events and resemblances based upon material culture, linguistic and other genetic information.

Populations and methods

Populations

The Y chromosome frequency data summarised in this review involves 74 populations and 3,762 samples, derived from a series of peer-reviewed papers published by various international research groups from 1999 to 2003 (Table 17.1). I alone am responsible for any omissions, errors and inadvertent misinterpretations of published data. In most cases, unless stated otherwise, a threshold of at least n = 25 individuals per population (or pooled regional populations) was applied to justify inclusion in this synthesis. Readers are referred to the original papers for specific details.

Table 17.1 Populations considered in this study

#	Populations	N	Reference
1	Alor	50	Capelli et al. (2001)
2	Mataram	24	”
3	Kota Kinabalu	51	”
4	Banjarmasin	33	”
5	Palu	36	”
6	Toraja	52	”
7	Pekanbaru	44	”
8	Mandang	90	”
9	New Ireland	86	”
10	Vanuatu	41	”
11	Fiji	41	”
12	Tonga	51	”
13	French Polynesia	86	”
14	Atiu	38	”
15	Philippines (unspecified)	28	”
16	Paiwan	53	”
17	Bunun	50	”
18	Atayal	50	”
19	Ami	53	”
20	N. Han	44	Karafet et al. (2001)
21	Hui	54	”
22	Tibet	75	”
23	Manchu	52	”
24	Chinese Evenk	41	”
25	Uygurs	68	”
26	Mongolia	147	”
27	Siberian Evenk	95	”

(Table 17.1 continued)

Table 17.1 Continued

#	Populations	N	Reference
28	Buryats	81	,,
29	Koreans	74	,,
30	Yi	43	,,
31	Tujia	49	,,
32	S. Han	40	,,
33	She	51	,,
34	Miao	57	,,
35	Yao	60	,,
36	Vietnam	70	,,
37	Malaysia	32	,,
38	Koreans	74	,,
39	Philippines Ilocano	39	Kayser et al. (2001)
40	Java	53	,,
41	S. Borneo	40	,,
42	Moluccas	34	,,
43	Nusa Tenggara	31	,,
44	Trobriand Island	54	,,
45	Coastal New Guinea	31	,,
46	Highland New Guinea	31	,,
47	Cook Island	28	,,
48	Arnhem Land Australia	60	,,
49	Sandy Desert Australia	35	,,
50	New Zealand Maori	28	Underhill et al. (2001a)
51	Mongolia	24	Su et al. (1999)
52	Japan	29	,,
53	N. Han Chinese	82	,,
54	S. Han Chinese	280	,,
55	Zhuang	28	,,
56	Taiwan 4 pooled aboriginal populations	49	,,
57	Cambodia	26	,,
58	Shandong Han	32	Su et al. (2000b)
59	Henan Han	28	,,
60	Zhejiang Han	50	,,
61	Jiangsu Han	55	,,
62	Shanghai Han	30	,,
63	Yunnan Han	27	,,
64	Tibetan-Khamba from Yunnan	27	Qian et al. (2000)
65	Pooled N. and N.E. Thailand	40	Su et al. (2000a)
66	Malaysia	27	,,
67	Samoa	36	,,
68	Micronesia 7 pooled populations	73	,,
69	Siberian Tuvana	40	Lell et al. (2002)
70	Lower Amur Ulchi/Nanal	53	,,
71	Kamchatka Koryak	27	,,
72	Siberian Eskimo	33	,,
73	Onge/Jarawa	27	Thangaraj et al. (2003)
74	Nicobarese	11	,,

Inference of haplotypes

The task of unifying diverse published data sets is difficult because different markers and several unrelated and non-systematic nomenclatures for Y-chromosomal binary haplogroups are used. However, considerable progress concerning phylogenetic knowledge and recent cooperative work amongst laboratories to formulate a standard nomenclature (The Y Chromosome Consortium 2002) has made such a task feasible. Fourteen markers, their phylogenetically equivalent counterparts or other markers associated with more derived lineages were used to infer related chromosomes for each of the various data sets. Table 17.2 summarises inferred relationships amongst the variously defined lineages in the different studies. Readers are referred to the original papers for specific details concerning chromosome definitions. I use a recently proposed convention for Y chromosome nomenclature (The Y Chromosome Consortium 2002). The * symbol is used to designate lineages that are not yet currently defined on the basis of subsequent derived characters and thus are potentially paraphyletic. Three such regionally important lineages are M9*, M130* and M214*. The rationales and assumptions applied regarding the translation of each data set to any one of the 14 lineages discussed in this summary are given in the Appendix to this chapter.

Results and discussion

The phylogenetic relationships of the 14 relevant inferred chromosomes defined by 14 mutations within a simplified hierarchical maximum parsimony phylogeny containing an additional 12 mutations marking important bifurcations in the overall global tree is shown in Figure 17.1. The geographic locations of the 74 populations involving 3,702 individuals taken from the various publications summarised in this review and their haplotype frequency charts are shown in two companion plates (Plates VI and VII) for clarity. All observed lineages in East Asia descend from a M168 common ancestor that subsequently evolved into three distinctive primogenitors, defined either by the YAP, M130 or M89 mutations. These data are consistent with the same tripartite relationship observed in a study of over 12,000 East Asian chromosomes (Ke et al. 2001). The original founders diversified into important lineages that display an irregular geographic distribution. These geographic patterns of genetic affinity and diversification provide intriguing clues into the history of East Asia and Oceania, especially the population dynamics associated with migration, population subdivision, fluctuations in population size and more recent gene flow episodes. The relevant East Asian and Oceanic M130, YAP and M89 associated lineages are discussed in the following text.

The M130 (= RPS4YC711T) component

It has been postulated that M130 probably arose in Asia on an unresolved M168* lineage sometime after an early departure event prior to the arrival of modern

Table 17.2 Cross reference of various haplotype designations between published data sets and the combinations used to collapse data into 12 chromosome group summary. The assumptions used to deduce inferences are described in the Appendix.

References	M174	M38	M130*	M217	M89	M9*	M122	M119	M268 M95	M4	M214 TAT	M45
Su et al. 1999, 2000a,b, 2001 and Qian et al. 2000	H2-H3	H1 inferred	H1 inferred	H1 inferred	H4	H5	H6-H8	H9-H10	H11-H12	H17	Inferred	H13-H16
Kayser et al. 2000 and 2001	Inferred	RPS4YT DYS390.3 del	RPS4YT DYS390.1 del	RPS4YT Inferred	Inferred	M9G DYS390.3 del	M122C	M119C	inferred	M4 and M5	Inferred	Inferred
Capelli et al. 2001	hg A	hg C Inferred	hg C	hg C Inferred	hg B	hg F	hg L	hg H	hg G	hg E	Inferred	hg D
Karafet et al. 2001	h11, h12	Inferred	h16	h17	h20-h24	h27-h28	h29-h31	h32	h33-h36	h37	h25, h26	h40-h45
Underhill et al. 2001	M174	M38	M130	M217	M89	M9	M122	M119	M95	M4	M178	M45
Lell et al. 2002	YAP	inferred	S4Y-T	S4Y-T M48	M89	M9	Inferred	M119	Inferred	Inferred	7C TAT-C	M45 M17 M3
Thangaraj et al. 2003	M174	None	None	None	None	None	None	None	None	None	None	None

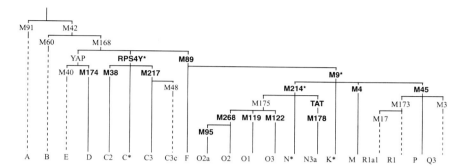

Figure 17.1 Phylogenetic relationships of East Asian and Oceanian Y chromosome binary lineages. The bold font and solid lines indicate the 14 either experimentally or inferred chromosomes used in the data set comparisons. Dashed lines reflect other extant chromosomes shown to provide phylogenetic context. The tree is rooted with respect to non-human great ape sequences. The * symbol indicates chromosomes that are not yet currently defined further on the basis of subsequent mutations. M130 = RPS47C711T.

humans in Sahul (Underhill et al. 2001b). The M130 mutation has not yet been detected in Africa. Archaeological data indicates that modern humans occupied coastal East Africa and exploited marine resources during the last interglacial about 125,000 years ago (Walter et al. 2000). This has been interpreted as a support for an early out of Africa migration via a coastal route to southern Asia, eventually reaching a destination in Australia (Stringer 2000). The distribution of M130 lineages is consistent with this scenario. The M130 mutation defines a cluster of lineages that has a geographically pronounced subdivision, between M130* and M217. Principal amongst these is the M217 derived subclade of lineages. These are the predominant representatives of the M130 clade in East Asia and Siberia (Karafet et al. 2001; Lell et al. 2002) with representatives in North America (Bergen et al. 1999; Karafet et al. 1999) being M217 chromosomes (Underhill et al. 2001b). Results from Siberian populations indicate the high prevalence of M48 chromosomes, which is a subset of M217 (Underhill et al. 2001b). Interestingly, M217 derived lineages are absent in the M130 lineages seen in insular Southeast Asia (Underhill et al. 2001a) and Yunnan (Karafet et al. 2001). Although M130 has been reported at low frequency in Southern India (Bamshad et al. 2001; Ramana et al. 2001; Wells et al. 2001), the allelic status of the M217 mutation was not reported. Subsequently it was determined (unpublished results) that the M217 mutation was not associated in the Indian M130 lineages reported in Wells et al. (2001) nor in the relevant Bamshad et al. (2001) M130 lineages (see Redd et al. 2002). Recently, it has been reported that 17 out of 367 samples (4.6 per cent) from India carried the M130 mutation but lacked the M217 mutation (Kivisild et al. 2003). The persistence of M130* lineages in India provides intriguing indirect support for the model of an early coastal migration route via southwest Asia to insular Southeast Asia and Oceania. Several studies have shown the presence of M130 chromosomes in Melanesia, Australia and Polynesia (Karafet et al. 1999; Kayser et al. 2000; Capelli et al. 2001; Kayser et al. 2001). Although M217 was not genotyped in these studies it is possible to infer, from an unusual fixed DYS390 microsatellite allele, that many of the Melanesian populations in Kayser et al. (2001) are derived at M38 and thus do not display positive character state at M217. Since there is an absence of M217 within the M130 lineages observed in south India (unpublished results) and along the Indonesian archipelago (Underhill et al. 2001a) and throughout Oceania (Redd et al. 2002; Kayser et al. 2003), these two categories of M130 related chromosomes imply an important population subdivision, namely between M130* and M217. Notable is the absence of any M130 related lineages in Taiwan aboriginal populations. M217 has been observed in Han Taiwanese populations at less than 10 per cent frequency (Karafet et al. 2001). However, actual M217 experimental data from more aboriginal Taiwanese and Philippine populations is needed. The phylogeography suggests that some of the earliest male colonisers of Oceania were M130* descendents. While M130* lineages occur at considerable frequency in Oceania, it occurs at lower frequencies in Southeast Asia, consistent with a relic distribution in which other evolved lineages have achieved higher frequency via the consequences of population dynamics. The relatively high frequency of M217 in Siberia (Karafet et al. 2001; Lell et al. 2002) is consistent with a northerly dispersal following the Last Glacial Maximum. This interpretation has also been deduced from mtDNA studies (Forster et al. 2001). Interestingly, while M217 chromosomes have been observed in Japan (unpublished results), one M130 lineage, without M217 and defined by M8, has also been observed in Japan. Deciphering this relationship will have to be held in abeyance until further studies of the M8 lineage in Japan and Asian mainland populations are conducted. However, one clue regarding which populations to consider sampling would involve Himalayan populations, since Japan shares another unrelated haplotype (defined by M174) with Tibet.

The YAP/M174 component

Based upon phylogeography and diversity knowledge, it has been postulated that YAP probably arose in Africa from a M168* ancestor (Underhill and Roseman 2001). Later some of these YAP descendents departed Africa during an early dispersal event (Underhill et al. 2001b). These migrants subsequently evolved into the M174 clade that persists at low frequencies throughout East Asia, except in peripheral locations like Tibet and Japan where significant frequencies have been observed, most likely because of founder effects. Recently, molecular analyses of 4 extant Jarawa and 23 Onge males from the Andaman Islands revealed that they all belonged to the M174 defined D haplogroup (Thangaraj et al. 2003). The presence of distinctive M174 lineages in the Andaman Islands, Japan and the Asian mainland indicates that these populations have been isolated geographically for a considerable time. The M174 data bolster the coastal migration model of the dispersal of anatomically modern humans from Africa during Pleistocene episodes of lower sea level. It is plausible that the M174 lineages arrived in Japan with the Jomon people before 10,000 BP. The appearance of M174 lineages throughout East Asia (albeit at relatively low frequency) is informative since these surviving M174 chromosomes also display a relic distribution. Also notable is their apparent absence in Oceania and India. These chromosomes either never migrated through these regions or their descendents subsequently went extinct. The apparent absence of M174 or any surviving precursor lineages in Southwest Asia including India makes deduction of the original migratory pathway from Africa uncertain although the presence of M174 in the Andaman Islanders is consonant with a coastal route. What is clear from the phylogeography is that the M174 lineages are representative of the early successful colonisers into Asia from Africa, which for the most part have been subsequently displaced to geographic margins by pressures from ensuing peoples. While both the M130* and M174 related lineages have different frequencies and geographic distribution patterns, (Plate VI) they both are reflective of the early formation of non-African heritage, often with an outlier status. These populations could potentially become the focus of investigations of possible remnant shared linguistic relationships.

The M9*, M4 and M214, TAT components

The M9 C to G transversion mutation occupies a major internal node within the M89 clade. This mutation occurs at considerable frequencies in all non-African populations. Most significant is the fact that the M9 mutation lies at the root of a spectrum of lineages present throughout Eurasia, the Indian subcontinent, Europe, America and Oceania. The assemblages of M89 derived lineages that lack the M9 mutation occur mainly in North Africa, Europe, the Mediterranean, West and South Asia. The phylogeographical data regarding M9* related lineages strongly suggests that the M9 mutation arose on a M89 ancestor somewhere outside Africa relatively soon after an early migration event (Underhill et al. 2001b). Several of the data sets summarised here report chromosomes resolved only to the M9 level at significant frequencies. These data were sub-divided into either M9* only or as combined M214* and TAT lineages using the inference criteria outlined above. While the precise boundary or overlap between M9* and the M9 differentiated M214* and TAT lineages remains uncertain, their distribution implies two different independent demographic histories in East Asia and Oceania. The preponderance of data indicates that the M9* only chromosomes occur in Australia, New Guinea, Melanesia and Polynesia as well as the eastern Indonesian archipelago. The M4 lineage is a major component of the M9* group in Melanesia and Polynesia but not Australia (Kayser et al. 2001). The associated high microsatellite diversity reported by Capelli et al. (2001) and Kayser et al. (2001) implies a considerable period of time has elapsed since original colonisation of these territories and subsequent isolation. It is tempting to speculate that both M130* and M9* lineages reflect the upwards to 50,000 year period when Australia and Papuan populations had a potential shared geography (i.e. the Sahul landmass). The divergences observed between Australian and New Guinean populations reflected as M38 (Underhill et al. 2000) or DYS390.1 del (Kayser et al. 2001) defined chromosomes associated with M130 and M4 related M9* lineages (Underhill et al. 2000) in Melanesia only (Kayser et al. 2001) are best explained as novel sub-division events since their isolation, no later than 8,000 BP, when sea levels rose. Conversely, the LLY22g and TAT frequency and distribution data from Karafet et al. (2001) and unpublished data regarding M214* indicate that these chromosomes are informative in East Asian and Siberian populations. The low microsatellite diversity reported for TAT defined chromosomes indicates the occurrence of a bottleneck and subsequent demographic and range expansion (Zerjal et al. 1997). The presence of M214* lineages in East Asia suggest that they may have originated here and then dispersed northward on trajectories reaching the Baltic region. An East Asian origin of M214 is reinforced by the fact that it is a sister clade of the M175 clade that comprises the majority of East Asian lineages. Confirmation of the apparent temporal and spatial dichotomy between the M9* lineages in the various data sets will potentially manifest itself with the possible future discovery of an as yet unidentified binary marker that potentially unites many of the Oceania-specific lineages, but not those in East Asia and Siberia. While this is admittedly a tentative scenario, current knowledge best supports this proposed framework of population substructure. Hence it is prudent to consider mtDNA and non-genetic evidence in the context of Oceanian related M9* lineages as possibly having an older and distinctive demographic history (Plate VI) than those M9 Asian, Siberian counterparts not defined by M175 or M45 (Plate VII). One such M9 related lineage is defined by M11 that is informative in Southwest Asia populations (Underhill et al. 2000) including tribal populations (Ramana et al. 2001).

The M175 components

Chromosomes associated with the M175 common ancestor occur at considerable frequency in East Asian populations but to a lesser extent in Oceania (Plate VII). The current data indicate that at least three major sub-lineages characterise the M175 clade, namely M119, M122 and M268 (unpublished) of which M95 defines a major subclade. The most common in East Asia are M122 related lineages (see the series of Su et al. papers for further haplotype subdivision of both M122 and M119 lineages). While these lineages occur in some Melanesian and Polynesian populations, their distribution suggests that while some may have arrived in the Philippines from Taiwan, they probably did not disperse across Oceania from there, but rather from a mainland source. Thus, the Y chromosome data suggests that the colonisation of Polynesia is more consistent with a deep genetic contribution of Melanesian ancestry (i.e. the M130 derived but not M217 related and M9* lineages) associated with a subsequent contribution from the Southeast Asian mainland (i.e. the M175 related lineages). While the associated binary marker diversity within the M175 clade is considerable, indicative of considerable time depth and/or effective population size, it is plausible that many of these lineages participated to a large extent in the transition to agriculture; eventually displacing earlier M174 and M130 related lineages in East Asia. Other lineal participants in a possible climatic and/or agriculturally catalysed demographic expansion include some of the M214 related and M217 lineages.

M89 and M45 components

While these lineages do not usually occur at high frequencies in East Asia and Oceania, they do in Europe (Semino et al. 2000), Central Asia (Underhill et al. 2000; Wells et al. 2001) and Pakistan, India (Ramana et al. 2001; Underhill et al. 2000), representative of additional demographic episodes. The ability to catalogue European specific M89 and M45 related lineages indicates that their presence in Oceania is a consequence of recent gene flow. Conversely, their presence in mainland Asia is more suggestive of demographic events associated with earlier expansions into Central Asia and the Indian subcontinent (Ramana et al. 2001; Wells et al. 2001). The capability to further evaluate these lineages at numerous other diagnostic markers that allow further informative resolution now exists and awaits further study.

Conclusions

This review has catalogued 14 different Y chromosomes among 74 East Asian populations, totalising 3,762 individuals. The reconstructed phylogeny shows that all 14 chromosomes descend from a unique origin (M168) further subdivided into 3 different clades, YAP, M130 and M89. The YAP lineages, probably originating in Africa, would be representative of the early colonisers into Asia. They are observed at low frequencies throughout East Asia, except in Tibet, Japan and the Andamanese where they are more common. This suggests that they were initially present in the region but pushed to peripheral regions by new migrants carrying other lineages. The M130 and M89 mutations, not detected in Africa, may have arisen in Asia, but prior to the arrival of modern humans in Sahul. These clades further subdivide into several related lineages that are widely distributed in East Asia, for example M217 in northern regions as far as Siberia (and North America), and M130* in southern regions and further east in Polynesia, thus reflecting wide population expansions. Although the interpretation of Y chromosome lineages is complex, this study shows that they can be tentatively related to major events of East Asian peopling history. Future studies fractionating these 14 lineages into further resolved sublineages using both additional binary mutations and associated faster mutating Y short tandem repeat loci will expose important patterns of micro-geographical substructure of population differentiation.

The task ahead

The recovery of complex prehistoric scenarios can be approached via a triangulation of independent disciplines. The task ahead requires continued effort to find an integrative consensus despite issues associated with the different scale of measurements. The additional factors of cultural borrowing, gene flow and language shifts also create complications, creating confusion and controversy. Nonetheless, all evidence should be reflective of an overall history and some correlation should be expected. This review provides one such perspective by integrating recent knowledge from the Y chromosome, which is now the most useful haplotyping system known. Only a small fraction of the Y chromosome has been surveyed for informative DNA sequence variants. Thus, considerable expansion of the bandwidth of chromosome types can be anticipated in the future. Also, only a fraction of populations have been surveyed. While perhaps not transformative, the recent progress in deciphering the Y chromosome structure in contemporary populations provides new impetus for re-evaluating non-genetic views of pre-historical affinity and diversification. Experts in archaeology, historical linguistics and other fields of human prehistory are encouraged to consider more direct joint investigative relationships with evolutionary geneticists in the formulation of specific testable hypotheses as well as possible population DNA sampling opportunities.

Appendix: Translation of the data published in different sources into the 14 Y chromosome lineages discussed in this study

Su et al. (1999, 2000a,b) and Qian et al. (2000) data

Their unresolved haplotype H1 was assumed to represent M130 (= RPS4Y) derived chromosomes based upon Bergen et al. (1999), Underhill et al. (2000) and Kayser et al. (2000) results. The inferred M217 defined sub-cluster of H1 was deduced based upon Karafet et al. (2001) and Underhill et al. (2001a,b) results. The assumption that their H2 (YAP) defined chromosomes were indeed M174 derived was deduced from M174 and M15 results summarised in Su et al. (2001). The H5 (M9) lineages in the various data sets were further sub-divided into unresolved M9* and differentiated M214, TAT lineages by inference using insights gleaned from M9 and M175 data in Kayser et al. (2001), Capelli et al. (2001), Underhill et al. (2001a) and M175, LLY22g and TAT data reported in Karafet et al. (2001). The LLY22g mutation is a surrogate for the M214* lineage.

Kayser et al. (2001) data

These data are tabulated based upon experimental results involving markers M130, M9, M175, M122, M119, M4, DYS390 and the following assumptions. The frequency of M38 was inferred from DYS390.3del/M130 data since these have been shown to be essentially phylogenetically equivalent (Underhill et al. 2001a). The 10 per cent of reported M130 lineages in the Philippines are tentatively assumed to be derived M217 chromosomes based upon the prevalence of M217 lineages in many East Asian populations (Karafet et al. 2001). The 1 per cent undifferentiated lineages are assumed to belong to the M89 defined haplotype, although it is conceivable that some may be defined by M174 instead. The inference that all lineages reported as undifferentiated M9* is based upon their M175 results and the distribution of related data for insular Southeast Asia and Oceania (Capelli et al. 2001). The frequency of M95 was inferred from comments made in the manuscript concerning M175 and results reported for M95 in Su et al. (1999), Capelli et al. (2001) and Karafet et al. (2001).

Capelli et al. (2001) data

This compilation is based upon experimental data involving markers M130, M9, M4, M175, M122, M119, M95 and 92R7. The 92R7 mutation is a surrogate for M45. The 4 chromosomes from Taiwan that were just defined by M175 were excluded because of their uniqueness. The few (approximately 1 per cent) lineages characterised as just derived for SRY10381.1 are assumed to be M89 related chromosomes. Although some of these could be M174, this is less likely, since other data (Hammer et al. 1997) regarding YAP suggests that it is absent in these regions. All reported M130 (RPS4Y) lineages are assumed to lack the M217 derived haplotype based upon results from Indonesia in Underhill et al. (2001a) and Melanesia in Kayser et al. (2000). Since neither M38 nor its mimic DYS390.3del/M130 were typed by Capelli et al. (2001), the degree of sub-division is uncertain. However, since such lineages occur at about 50 per cent from similar geographic regions (Kayser et al. 2001; Underhill et al. 2001a) this synopsis assumes that 50 per cent of the reported M130 lineages are derived for M38. All reported M9 only lineages are assumed to probably be undifferentiated chromosomes with respect to M214, TAT since LLY22g and TAT lineages have not been observed in Oceania (Zerjal et al. 1997). Also the M9* associated microsatellite diversity is highest in Melanesia (Capelli et al. 2001).

Karafet et al. (2001) data

These comprehensive data were relatively straightforward to condense and merge with other data since many of the relevant markers or their phylogenetic equivalents were typed (e.g. LLY22g ≈ M214*, TAT ≈ M178, PN27 ≈ M45).

Underhill et al. (2001a) data

The Maori data involve most of the markers pertinent to this synthesis and exclude lineages attributed to European gene flow. The M214* chromosome was not observed (unpublished results).

Lell et al. (2002) data

The following markers provided polymorphic data: M3, M9, M17, M48, M89, M119, M130, M173, YAP, DYS7C, TAT. In addition, the following markers were tested but were reported as 'essentially' monomorphic: M7, M40, M50, M88, M95, M103, M111, M122. The following assumptions have been made to normalise the data: All M130 related lineages are considered to be M217 based upon phylogenetic knowledge associated with M48 and the DYS7C deletion. M48 is a sub-lineage of M217 chromosomes (Underhill et al. 2001b). Although DYS7C is recurrent (Jobling et al. 1996), it is informative when used in context with the M130 and M9 mutations. The one reported YAP chromosome was assumed to be M174. The assignment of M214* was based upon knowledge relating to TAT and DYS7C. The 8 samples from Ulchi that were defined as just M9 derived were tentatively assumed to be M122, although some could be M95 or even M214* without TAT. The M45 haplotype includes M17 data in Siberian Tuvana while the M45 lineage in Siberian Eskimos includes the common Native American M3 haplotype.

Thangaraj et al. (2003) data

The singular presence of M174 derived chromosomes was observed in 4 Jarawa and 23 Onge samples from the Andaman Islands. All 11 samples from Nicobar Island assigned to the M95 lineage.

Acknowledgements

I thank L. Luca Cavalli-Sforza for helpful comments and formal reading of the draft. I thank Kristina Prince for expert assistance with the graphic illustration. The author was supported by NIH grants GM 28428 and GM 55273 to L.L.C-S.

Bibliography

Avise, J., Arnold, J., Ball, R.M., Bermingham, E., Lamb, T., Neigel, J.E., Reeb, C.A. and Saunders, N.C. (1987) 'Intraspecific phylogeography: the molecular bridge between population genetics and systematics', Annual Review of Ecology and Systematicsl 8: 489–522.

Bamshad, M., Kivisild, T., Watkins, W.S., Dixon, M.E., Ricker, C.E., Rao, B.B., Naidu, J.M., Prasad, B.V., Reddy, P.G., Rasanayagam, A., Papiha, S.S., Villems, R., Redd, A.J., Hammer, M.F., Nguyen, S.V., Carroll, M.L., Batzer, M.A. and Jorde, L.B. (2001) 'Genetic evidence on the origins of Indian caste populations', Genome Research 11: 994–1004.

Bellwood, P. (2001) 'Early agriculturalist population diasporas? Farming, languages, and genes', Annual Review of Anthropology30: 181–207.

Bergen, A.W., Wang, C.Y., Tsai, J., Jefferson, K., Dey, C., Smith, K.D., Park, S.C., Tsai, S.J. and Goldman, D. (1999) 'An Asian-Native American paternal lineage identified by RPS4Y resequencing and by microsatellite haplotyping', Annals of Human Genetics 63: 63–80.

Capelli, C., Wilson, J.F., Richards, M., Stumpf, M.P., Gratrix, F., Oppenheimer, S., Underhill, P., Pascali, V.L., Ko, T.M. and Goldstein, D.B. (2001) 'A predominantly indigenous paternal heritage for the Austronesian-speaking peoples of insular Southeast Asia and Oceania', American Journal of Human Genetics 68: 432–43.

Ceppellini, R., Curtoni, E.S., Mattiuz P.L., Miggiano, V., Scudeller, G. and Serra, A. (1967) 'Genetics of leukocyte antigens. A family study of segregation and linkage', in E.S. Curtoni, P.L. Mattiuz, and R.M. Tosi (eds) Histocompatibility Testing 1967, Copenhagen: Munksgaard.

Forster, P., Torroni, A., Renfrew, C. and Rohl, A. (2001) 'Phylogenetic star contraction applied to Asian and Papuan mtDNA evolution', Molecular Biology and Evolution 18: 1864–81.

Hammer, M.F., Spurdle, A.B., Karafet, T., Bonner, M.R., Wood, E.T., Novelletto, A., Malaspina, P., Mitchell, R.J., Horai, S., Jenkins, T. and Zegura, S.L. (1997) 'The geographic distribution of human Y chromosome variation', Genetics 145: 787–805.

Jobling, M.A., Samara, V., Pandya, A., Fretwell, N., Bernasconi, B., Mitchell, R.J., Gerelsaikhan, T., Dashnyam, B., Sajantila, A., Salo, P.J., Nakahori, Y., Disteche, C.M., Thangaraj, K., Singh, L., Crawford, M.H. and Tyler-Smith, C. (1996) 'Recurrent duplication and deletion polymorphisms on the long arm of the Y chromosome in normal males', Human Molecular Genetics 5: 1767–75.

Karafet, T., Xu, L., Du, R.F., Wang, W., Feng, S., Wells, R.S., Redd, A.J., Zegura, S.L. and Hammer, M.F. (2001) 'Paternal population history of East Asia: sources, patterns, and microevolutionary processes', American Journal of Human Genetics 69: 615–28.

Karafet, T.M., Zegura, S.L., Posukh, O., Osipova, L., Bergen, A., Long, J., Goldman, D., Klitz, W., Harihara, S., de Knijff, P., Wiebe, V., Griffiths, R.C., Templeton, A.R. and Hammer, M.F. (1999) 'Ancestral Asian source(s) of new world Y-chromosome founder haplotypes', American Journal of Human Genetics 64: 817–31.

Kayser, M., Brauer, S., Weiss, G., Underhill, P.A., Roewer, L., Schiefenhövel, W. and Stoneking, M. (2000) 'Melanesian origin of Polynesian Y chromosomes', Current Biology 10: 1237–46.

Kayser, M., Schiefenhövel, W., Underhill, P.A. and Stoneking, M. (2001) 'Independent histories of human Y chromosomes from Melanesia and Australia', American Journal of Human Genetics 68: 173–90.

Kayser, M., Underhill, P., Shen, P., Oefner, P., Tommaseo-Ponzetta, M. and Stoneking, M. (2003) 'Extreme reduction in Y-chromosome, but not mtDNA, diversity in human populations from West New Guinea', American Journal of Human Genetics 72: 281–302.

Ke, Y., Su, B., Song, X., Lu, D., Chen, L., Li, H., Qi, C., Marzuki, S., Deka, R., Underhill, P., Xiao, C., Shriver, M., Lell, J., Wallace, D., Wells, R.S., Seielstad, M., Oefner, P., Zhu, D., Jin, J., Huang, W., Chakraborty, R., Chen, Z. and Jin, L. (2001) 'African origin of modern humans in East Asia: a tale of 12,000 Y chromosomes', Science 292: 1151–3.

Kivisild, T., Rootsi, S., Metspalu, M., Mastana, S., Kaldma, K., Parik, J., Metspalu, E., Adojaan, M., Tolk, H.V., Stepanov, V., Golge, M., Usanga, E., Papiha, S.S., Cinnioglu, C., King, R., Cavalli-Sforza, L., Underhill, P.A. and Villems, R. (2003) 'The genetic heritage of the earliest settlers persists both in Indian tribal and caste populations', American Journal of Human Genetics 72: 313–32.

Lell, J.T., Sukernik, R.I., Starikovskaya, Y.B., Su, B., Jin, L., Schurr, T.G., Underhill, P.A. and Wallace, D.C. (2002) 'The dual origin and Siberian affinities of Native American Y chromosomes', American Journal of Human Genetics 70: 192–206.

Qian, Y., Qian, B., Su, B., Yu, J., Ke, Y., Chu, Z., Shi, L., Lu, D., Chu, J. and Lin, L. (2000) 'Multiple origins of Tibetan Y chromosomes', Human Genetics 106: 453–4.

Ramana, G.V., Su, B., Jin, L., Singh, L., Wang, N., Underhill, P. and Chakraborty, R. (2001) 'Y-chromosome SNP haplotypes suggest evidence of gene flow among caste, tribe, and the migrant Siddi populations of Andhra Pradesh, South India', European Journal of Human Genetics 9: 695–700.

Redd, A.J., Roberts-Thomson, J., Karafet, T., Bamshad, M., Jorde, L.B., Naidu, J.M., Walsh, B. and Hammer, M.F. (2002). 'Gene flow from the Indian subcontinent to Australia', Current Biology 12: 673–7.

Semino, O., Passarino, G., Oefner, P.J., Lin, A.A., Arbuzova, S., Beckman, L.E., De Benedictis, G., Francalacci, P., Kouvatsi, A., Limborska, S., Marcikiae, M., Mika, A., Mika, B., Primorac, D., Santachiara-Benerecetti, A.S., Cavalli-Sforza, L.L. and Underhill, P.A. (2000) 'The genetic legacy of Paleolithic Homo sapiens sapiens in extant Europeans: a Y chromosome perspective', Science 290: 1155–9.

Shen, P., Wang, F., Underhill, P.A., Franco, C., Yang, W.H., Roxas, A., Sung, R., Lin, A.A., Hyman, R.W., Vollrath, D., Davis, R.W., Cavalli-Sforza, L.L. and Oefner, P.J. (2000) 'Population genetic implications from sequence variation in four Y chromosome genes', Proceedings of the National Academy of Science USA 97: 7354–9.

Stringer, C. (2000) 'Palaeoanthropology. Coasting out of Africa', Nature 405: 24–5, 27.

Su, B., Xiao, J., Underhill, P., Deka, R., Zhang, W., Akey, J., Huang, W., Shen, D., Lu, D., Luo, J., Chu, J., Tan, J., Shen, P., Davis, R., Cavalli-Sforza, L., Chakraborty, R., Xiong, M., Du, R., Oefner, P., Chen, Z. and Jin, L. (1999) 'Y-Chromosome evidence for a northward migration of modern humans into Eastern Asia during the last Ice Age', American Journal of Human Genetics 65: 1718–24.

Su, B., Jin, L., Underhill, P., Martinson, J., Saha, N., McGarvey, S.T., Shriver, M.D., Chu, J., Oefner, P., Chakraborty, R. and Deka, R. (2000a) 'Polynesian origins: insights from the Y chromosome', Proceedings of the National Academy of Science USA 97: 8225–8.

Su, B., Xiao, C., Deka, R., Seielstad, M.T., Kangwanpong, D., Xiao, J., Lu, D., Underhill, P., Cavalli-Sforza, L., Chakraborty, R. and Jin, L. (2000b) 'Y chromosome haplotypes reveal prehistorical migrations to the Himalayas', Human Genetics 107: 582–90.

Su, B., Ramana, G.V., Lu, S.H., Wen, B., Deka, R.J., Underhill, P., Chakraborty, R. and Jin, L. (2001) 'Abstract 1244. Y chromosome polymorphisms indicate an ancient migration from the Himalayas to Japan', American Journal of Human Genetics 69 (supplement): 395.

Thangaraj, K., Singh, L., Reddy, A.G., Rao, V.R., Sehgal, S.C., Underhill, P.A., Pierson, M., Frame, I.G. and Hagelberg, E. (2003) 'Genetic affinities of the Andaman islanders, a vanishing human population', Current Biology 13: 86–93.

The Y Chromosome Consortium (2002) 'A nomenclature system for the tree of human Y-chromosomal binary haplogroups', Genome Research 12: 339–48.

Underhill, P.A. and Roseman, C.C. (2001) 'The case for an African rather than an Asian origin of the human Y-chromosome YAP insertion', in L. Jin, M. Seielstad and C. Xiao (eds) Recent Advances in Human Biology, Vol.8, Genetic, Linguistic and Archaeological Perspectives on Human Diversity in Southeast Asia, New Jersey: World Scientific.

Underhill, P.A., Shen, P., Lin, A.A., Jin, L., Passarino, G., Yang, W.H., Kauffman, E., Bonne-Tamir, B., Bertranpetit, J., Francalacci, P., Ibrahim, M., Jenkins, T., Kidd, J.R., Mehdi, S.Q., Seielstad, M.T., Wells, R.S., Piazza, A., Davis, R.W., Feldman, M.W., Cavalli-Sforza, L.L. and Oefner, P.J. (2000) 'Y chromosome sequence variation and the history of human populations', Nature Genetics 26: 358–61.

Underhill, P.A., Passarino, G., Lin, A.A., Marzuki, S., Oefner, P.J., Cavalli-Sforza, L.L. and Chambers, G.K. (2001a) 'Maori origins, Y-chromosome haplotypes and implications for human history in the Pacific', Human Mutation 17: 271–80.

Underhill, P.A., Shen, P., Mirazon Lahr, M., Foley, R.A., Oefner, P.J. and Cavalli-Sforza, L.L. (2001b) 'The phylogeography of Y chromosome binary haplotypes and the origins of modern human populations', Annals of Human Genetics 65: 43–62.

Walter, R.C., Buffler, R.T., Bruggemann, J.H., Guillaume, M.M., Berhe, S.M., Negassi, B., Libsekal, Y., Cheng, H., Edwards, R.L., von Cosel, R., Neraudeau, D. and Gagnon, M. (2000) 'Early human occupation of the Red Sea coast of Eritrea during the last interglacial', Nature 405: 65–9.

Wells, R.S., Yuldasheva, N., Ruzibakiev, R., Underhill, P.A., Evseeva, I., Blue-Smith, J., Jin, L., Su, B., Pitchappan, R., Shanmugalakshmi, S., Balakrishnan, K., Read, M., Pearson, N.M., Zerjal, T., Webster, M.T., Zholoshvili, I., Jamarjashvili, E., Gambarov, S., Nikbin, B., Dostiev, A., Aknazarov, O., Zalloua, P., Tsoy, I., Kitaev, M., Mirrakhimov, M., Chariev, A. and Bodmer, W.F. (2001) 'The Eurasian heartland: a continental perspective on Y-chromosome diversity', Proceedings of the National Academy of Science USA 98: 10244–9.

Zerjal, T., Dashnyam, B., Pandya, A., Kayser, M., Roewer, L., Santos, F.R., Schiefenhövel, W., Fretwell, N., Jobling, M.A., Harihara, S., Shimizu, K., Semjidmaa, D., Sajantila, A., Salo, P., Crawford, M.H., Ginter, E.K., Evgrafov, O.V. and Tyler-Smith, C. (1997) 'Genetic relationships of Asians and Northern Europeans, revealed by Y-chromosomal DNA analysis', American Journal of Human Genetics 60: 1174–83.

INDEX

Note: Page numbers in italics indicate illustrations.

9-bp deletion 204, 215

ABO 232, *235*; *see also* blood
Achang 248
Admiralty Islands 208, 211, 213
adze 7, 24, 63, 68, 69, 71, 98, 195; stone 63, 73
Africa: humans in 303, 307; migrations from 11, 96, 250, 303, 305
agriculture: language and 1, 11–12; language dispersal and 17–31, 87–9, 99, 278; origins of 51–4; spread of 55–61, 87, 91, 202, 273, 276; *see also* millet agriculture, rice agriculture
Ainu 44, 208, 211, 215, 216
allele 297
Alor 221, 291
Altaic 1, 18, 20, 253, 261, 266–9, 276, 278–86, 289–90, 292
Ami 10, 65, 231–6, 238–42, 275
Andaman Islands 304, 310
Angkor 37
anthropology, physical 201–24; *see also* craniometric studies
Asia: human colonisation of 202, 213, 289, 298
Assam 78, 98, 101, 189, 190, 192, 194
Atayal 65, 120, 168, 170, 188, 207–8, 211, 213, 223, 231–6, 275, 278, 287
Atiu 299
Australia 186, 204, 206–7, 211–12; Aborigines 215, 235, 242, 287; human colonisation 212; New Guinea and 186, 242, 287
Australoids 67

Austric 4, 5, 11, 24, 42; current status of 132; genetics and 282; lexical evidence for 133–50; morphosyntactic evidence for 146–50; rice terms 43; spread of 173
Austro-Asiatic (AA): Austronesian and 194, phonological correspondences 133; Chinese and 290; family tree 86; genetic studies and 80, 96, 230, 243, 288, 291; geographical distribution 91; Hmong-Mien and 26–7; languages of 3; morphemes 3; morphology 3; origins 24, 25, 125; phylum 5; rice and 41; spread of 37, 41, 273; word order 3; *see also* Mon-Khmer
Austronesian (AN): age 23; Austro-Asiatic and 191–3, phonological correspondences 152–6; Chinese and 4, 6, 174; genetics and 282, 297, 261; Kra-Dai and 107–28; languages of 3–4, 147; morphology 4, 147, 161–2, 168, 172–3, 183; origins 24–6, 63–72; phonology 151–8; pre-history 91; reconstructions 134, 137; rice terms 39–44; Sino-Tibetan and 83–6, 101, 150, 161–74; spread of 43, 101, 173; subgrouping 108, 161, 162; Tai-Kadai and 177–80; Taiwan 25, 61, 185–6; Tibeto-Burman and 101; tones 122–8; vocabulary 108–11, 164–6; word order 4
Austronesian Ancestor of Kadai (AAK) 174, 193, 195
Austronesian (AN) people 172, 202, 213
Austronesians xvi, 8, 10, 45, 55, 72, 101, 173, 185–6, 265, 278, 282–4, 288–90
Austro-Tai xxi, 5, 6, 11, 24, 101, 103, 107, 125, 127, 132, 178, 180, 188, 286

315

INDEX

Bachuc Village 215
Bag-skad 86
Bahing 169
Bahnar 147–8, 150–2, 154–8
Bai 248
Bai Yue 185, 191
Bangladesh 18, 27, 35, 78, 101
Banjarmasin 299
Barnes, Gina 185
Bataan Islands 287
Batanic languages 287
Beixin culture 172
Bellwood, Peter xvi, 7–8, 11, 18–27, 64, 67, 71, 126, 173, 182, 186
Benedict, Paul 3, 5, 25, 85, 88, 107, 119, 125, 162, 169, 175, 177, 186, 193
Bhutan 2, 86, 100
Biak Island 211, 212
bilingualism 12
biodistance studies 203–4
Bismarck Archipelago 204, 211
blood: groups 203, 232, *234*, alleles/frequencies 240–4; samples 234; red blood cell (RBC) *234*; polymorphisms 240, Taiwan's *243*; red cell enzymes 232
Blust, Robert 4, 37, 126, 159, 179
Bodic languages 39
Bodo-Garo 169
Bontok 134, 147, 149
Borneo 192, 194, 196, 206–7, 211
Boro 170
bottleneck 99, 268, 291, 292, 312
Brahmaputran languages 91, 101
Brazil 239
Bronze Age cultures 23
Brown, Nathan 84
Bulang 248
Bunun 65, 161, 170, 171, 231, 234, 241–2, 278, 287
Burma 2, 3, 78, 190, 192
Buryats 300
Buyang language 118
Buyi 120, 280

Cachar Hills Zone 192
Cambodia 35, 37, 79, 192, 194, 207, 215
Caroline Islands 208, 211–13, 216
Caucasian 261
Celtis sinensis 70
Central Asia 22, 23, 249, 267, 270, 285–6, 290, 307, 313; cereals and 23
Chab-mdo culture 100

Chamorro 37, 42, 43
Chang, K.C. 22, 63–4, 65, 67, 68, 175
Changguogou culture 172
Changpin Culture 64, 245
Chepang 171
chicken 21, 128, *167*, *168*, *169*
China: agriculture in 20–6, origins of 20, 22; anthropological studies 230; Bronze Age 51; DNA banks 248; DNA polymorphism 248; ethnolinguistic composition 97; genetics and 248–50, 290, 291–2; Human Genome Diversity Project 97, 248; language geography, Neolithic 24–7; language minorities 32–4; languages: dispersal 17, 201, numbers of 248; microsatellite markers 249; Neolithic cultures 26; northern and southern 291; populations: homogeneity 45, 241, increase 21, minority, genetic analysis 248–50, officially recognised 249, southern and northern 291; Y chromosome markers 249
Chinese 86, 123, 125, 148, 162–5, 165–8, 262, 290; writing 188, 190; *see also* Middle Chinese, Old Chinese
Chrau 147
Chu 3, 190, 191, 193
Chukchi 278, 280, 281
Cishan 21, 52
Cishan-Peiligang culture 9, 52, 172
Colebrooke, Henry Thomas 83
Cook Islands 300
Corded Ware culture *see* Tapenkeng culture
cord-marked pottery *see* pottery
craniometric studies 203; discussion of 212–15; divisions produced by 211; genetic component and 204; map of locations 205; materials and methods 204–12; multivariate statistical studies 203–6
crop cultivation 12

Dadiwan 21, 25, 58, 189
Dai 248
Dai Dam *275*, *279*
Dai Lue *275*, *279*
Daic 84–5, 101, 102, 104; rice terms 39–42
Dapenkeng culture (DPK) 185, 191; *see also* Tapenk'eng, Tapenkeng culture
Dawenkou culture 172, 175
De'ang 248
Dian culture 192

316

Diller, A. 107
Di people 248
DNA (deoxyribonucleic acid):
  analysis 269; molecules 298;
  polymorphisms 12, 250, 288; *see also*
  mitochondrial DNA
Dulong 248
Dyen, Isidore 64–5

East Asia: anthropological studies
  230–44; climate 58; cranial studies
  206, 217; genetic studies 96, 288–9;
  human settlement 252, 287; migrations
  into 286; north/south genetic
  differences 285; populations, origins
  of 201, 267
East Asian languages: agriculture and
  261; classification of 4–7, 261;
  dispersal 20–7; genetics and 12, 18,
  254–72, ANOVA analyses 60, 77, 82,
  259, 265, discussion of 264–8;
  diversity 252, 264, evolution 277, gene
  flow 266, 267, 273, 285, GM system
  253–7, 259–60, 262, 264–8, 286–7,
  HLA diversity 264–5, 273–91,
  populations analysed 274–7, RH
  system 253–66, 286; geography and
  280–2, 289; homelands 20, 26, 27, 265;
  macrophyla 4, 5, 11, 12; materials and
  methods of studies 253, 274, 276–7;
  multidimensional-scaling (MDS) 256,
  260, 276, 278, 280; multivariate
  analysis 254–7; origins of 20, 26, 27,
  265; phyla 1–2, 273, unifying 6;
  phylogenies, complex of 4–7, 62, 261,
  273, 276, 280; relationship 20; results
  of studies 254, 256, 259–67, 276–86;
  statistical methods 276–7
East Asiatic 7
East Coast Linkage (Formosan; ECL)
  161, 180
Eastern Austro-Asiatic (EAA) 134, 147
Entangled Bank model 292
Eskimo 274, 300
Europe 305, 307
Evenk 299

Farming/Language Dispersal Hypothesis
  25, 27
Fengpit'ou 63, 64, 68, 70
Ferrell, R. 65, 66
Fiji 211, 212, 299
Formosan languages 41, 82

founder effect/genetic drift 237, 240, 268,
  271, 272, 280, 291–3, 310
Fujian 24, 126

Gan 260
Gansu 21, 22, 23, 99, 100
Gene: diversity 261, 270, 280, *286*, *287*,
  288; flow 240, 244, 268, 269, 270, 276,
  280, 289, 291, 293, in East Asia and
  Oceania 301, 305, 313, 314, 315;
  frequencies 240, 255; *see also* blood
Genetic: clines 276; continuity 290, 294;
  distances 242, *243*, 256, *259*, *260*,
  264–7, 268, 271, 279, 290; diversity
  236, 240, 243, 267–9, *see also* HLA;
  drift *see* founder effect/genetic drift;
  evolution 236, 252, 254, 255, 267, 268,
  280, 288–9, 293–4; history 254, 294,
  302; relationships 242–3, 254, 256,
  268, 269, 271, 284; structure 254, 255,
  259–61, 262, 263, 267, 271, 284, 294;
  variability 255, 256, 259, 260, 262, 267
genetics: agriculture spread and 273;
  archaeology and 1, 297; improvements
  in study of 96; linguistics and 12, 17,
  91, 261, 280, 297
Gilyak 274
glottochronology 20, 24
GM 10, 254, 255 *passim*, *258*, 259, 260,
  261, *262*, 263, 265–7, 268, 270, 290,
  294; polymorphisms 265, *257*, 267,
  268, 291
grass seeds, gathering 51–2, 54
'Greater Austric' hypothesis 10, 286
Guam 213
Guangdong 24, 126, 128, 161,
  180, 193
Guangxi 24, 128, 161
Guizhou 24, 128
Gyarong 169, 170

Hainan Island 3, 128, 211, 214, 215
Hakka 260
Han 248, 260, 265–6, 299, 300, 304
Hani 248
haplotype 297, 301
Haudricourt, André-Georges 84–5, 178
Hayes, L.H. 132–4, 137–9, 150, 154,
  155, 159
Hemudu 54, 184
Henan Han 300
Heng Duan Mountain area 248
Heterozygosity 261, 280

317

INDEX

Higham, Charles 185
Himalayas 97, 100, 189
Himalayo-Burman 189–90
HLA 232, 236, 237, 240, 244, 246, 255, 267, 268, 290; diversity 276–9, 281–4, 286–8, 289, 293; haplotypes 237, 240, 244; HLA-DRB1 235, 236, 237, 238–9, 244, 276, 277, 278, 279, 281, 282, 283, 286, 287, 289, 291, 292, 293, 294, 295; polymorphism 234–40, 294
Hlai 114, 116, 118, 124, 126, 128
Hmong-Mien: Chinese and 2–3, 11; genetics and 261; languages of 2–3; origin of 24; spread of 190; see also Miao-yao
Hmong-Mien peoples 188
HNA-1 see Human neutrophil antigen
Homozygosity 236
Hong Kong 56, 71, 239
Huai He Valley 57, 173
Huanghe Basin 21, 22
Huanghe Neolithic 25
Huanghe Valley 1, 6, 20, 172, 173, 184, 185, 188
Huang Shih-chiang 68
Human neutrophil antigen (HNA-1) 232, 235, 242, 243
Human platelet antigen (HPA) 242, 243
Humboldt, Wilhelm von 83
Hunan 21, 36
hunter-gatherers 18, 19, 34
Hutouliang 52

India 303–7; genetic studies 96; languages of 2, 86, 91
Indian Eastern Neolithic 98
India, northern 3, 91, 274
indigenous Melanesian origin 202
Indo-Chinese 83–5; renamed 85; see also Sino-Tibetan
Indo-European languages 22, 23, 273; spread of 273
Indo-Malaysian Archipelago 214
Indonesia 212–13, 242, 275, 278, 304, 305, 309
Inner Mongolia 171
irrigation 34, 35, 37
isolation-by-distance 269, 290
Ivatan 235, 239, 242, 278

Japan 211, 242, 300, 304, 305, 307; see also Japanese, Japonic
Japanese 274, 280

Japonic: rice terms 43–4
Java 300
Javanese 3
Jiahu 20, 26, 35, 54, 57, 58
Jiangsu Han 300
Jiangxi 21
Jin 260
Jingpo 248
Jinuo 248
Jomon people 305

Kachari 260
Kachin 171
Kadai 193–4
Kam 115, 126
Kamarupan 189
Kam-Sui 113, 114, 116, 117, 118
Kam-Tai 3
Karen 85, 190; word order 2
Karuo culture 172
Kashmir 100, 188
Katu 147
Kavalan 65, 287
Kazakh 274, 285
Kern, Hendrik 101
Ket 6
Ketagalans 287
Khalkh 274, 285
Khasi 3, 146, 190, 192
Khasi corridor 189, 192
Khmer 3
Khmu 146
Khmuic 3
Khok Phanom Di 34
Kinh 275, 280
Kiranti 169
Klaproth, Julius Heinrich von 81–3, 85, 86
Kol 84
Korea 211, 214
Korean 274
Korean people 300
Koreo-Japonic 284, 290
Koryak 274, 278–80, 300
Kota Kinabalu 299
Kra-Dai (Kd): Austronesian and 107–29; genetics and 127–30; homeland 128; language family 111; phonology 114–27; pre-history 128–30; present distribution 129; tones 124–7; vocabulary 110–13; see also Tai-Kadai
Kunming culture 191
Kuo-yeh 68, 69, 71
Kyushu 211

Laha 126
Lahu 260
language dispersal: agriculture and 17–27, 87, 101, 273; foundation 17–19
languages: evolutionary distance between 261; linguistic distance 261, 276; reconstruction 12, 19; see also agriculture, East Asian languages, Southeast Asian languages
Lan Yu Island 287; see also Orchid Island
Laos 2, 3, 37, 190, 192, 215
Lapita cultural complex 201, 213
Last Glacial Maximum 310
Lepsius, Carl Richard 82, 86
Lesser Sunda Islands 211
Leyden, John 83–4
Lilou 54
linguistics: genetics and 261, 280, 282, 289
Lisu 248
loanwords 34
Longqiuzhuang 173
Longshan culture 101, 184, 185
Luce, George Hannington 85
Lungshanoid culture 66, 67, 126, 185

Macro-Austric 6
Macro-Sino-Tibetan 4, 5
Madagascar 3
Mahalanobis' generalised distance statistic 204, 210–12, 214
Majiabang culture 184, 191
Mal 146
Malagasy 3, 194
malaria 239, 287
Malay 3, 171
Malayic 146, 148
Malayo-Polynesian 4, 108, 159, 173, 178–80, 186, 194, 275
Malay Peninsula 192, 194, 214
Malay people 275, 278
Malaysia 300
Manchu 274, 280, 285, 299
Manchuria 211
Mandang 299
Mandarin 260, 265
Mansi 274, 278, 286
Mantel tests 279, 284
Maori people 211, 212, 235, 300
Marianas 37, 42
Marquesas 211, 212
Marshall-Kiribati Islands 211–13
Mason, Francis 84

Maspero, Henri 85
Mataram 323
Mekong River 32, 192, 216
Melanesia 202, 204, 207, 211–17, 288–9, 304–6, 309
MHC see HLA
Mi III 235, 240, 241, 244
Miao 300
Miao-Yao 2–3, 39, 40, 42, 58, 126, 128; rice terms 40; see also Hmong-Mien
Micronesia 204, 208, 211–13, 300
microsatellites 99, 232, 234, 243, 252
Middle Chinese 174, 191, 195
Mikir 260
millet agriculture: in Austronesian culture 184; China 20, 22, 25, 51; origins of (in East Asia) 1, 57; Panicum miliaceum (broomcorn, common) 21–2, 23, 51, 55, 58, 82, 100; Setaria italica (foxtail) 20, 21, 24, 51, 54, 56, 60, 100; spread of 55, 56; Taiwan 56, 59, 60, 61, 71, 172, 173
Min 257, 260
mitochondrial DNA 225, 266, 291, 298
MNS 235, 240, 243
Moken 42
molecular anthropology 273
molecular markers 254, 269, 270
Moluccas 207, 208, 211, 212, 215, 300
Mon 3, 77, 78
Mongolia 206, 208, 223, 274, 278, 299, 300
Mongolian 211, 235, 248, 299, 285
Mongoloids 214
Mon-Khmer 77, 78, 84, 193, 195, 262
Mons 192
morphemes 2
most recent common ancestor (MRCA) 279
Munda 3, 34, 41, 45, 46, 77, 134, 148, 192
Muong 275, 280
mutations 298, 301

Nan-kuan-li 24, 56, 57, 59, 69–71
Nanzhuangtou 52
Naxi 248
Near Oceania 201, 204, 212, 213
Neolithic: European 21–2; term 185; see also agriculture
Nepal 2, 86
neutrophil antigens 243
New Guinea 3, 32, 204, 207, 211–13, 287, 305, 306; Australia and 242
New Ireland 207, 211–14

INDEX

New Zealand 211, 212, 300
Nicobarese 41, 146–9, 194, 300
Nicobar Islands 192, 194
Niulandong 52
Nivkhi 274, 278, 280, 285
non-Austronesian speakers (NAN) 225
North Asia 203, 214, 215
Nu 248
Nusa Tenggara 278, 300

Oceania 252, 297, 301, 304–7, 309; rice in 42
Old Chinese 47, 102, 161, 162, 165, 167, 170, 174, 195
Old Khmer 146
Onge/Jarawa 300
Orchid Island 278; see also Lan Yu Island
Oryza 20, 35; see also rice
Ostapirat, W. 11, 40, 107–8, 111, 180
'Out of Asia' hypothesis 202

Pa-chia-tsun 68, 69
Pacific: anthropological studies 201–24; colonisations of 201
Pacoh 147
Paha 118
Paiwan 65, 162, 170, 171, 231, 232, 235, 238, 239–42, 278, 287, 299
Paiwanic 65, 66, 275
Pakistan 307
Palu 299
Panicum miliaceum 21, 45, 54, 102, 167, 168, 174, 175; see also millet agriculture
Pan-Sino-Austronesian 4, 6
Papua New Guinea 186, 235; Highlanders 235, 242
Pazeh 65, 149
PCR-RFLP/SSP 242
Pearic languages 79–80
Pearl River Delta 57, 71
Peiligang 22, 25, 52, 54
Peiligang culture 20, 54, 58, 172
Pekanbaru 299
Pengtoushan 37, 51, 54
Philippines 32, 37, 194, 207, 214, 215, 235, 242, 288, 299, 300, 306, 309; languages 42, 46, 161, 276, 287
phylogeography 297, 304–5
Picrasma quassioides 70
Pictet, Adolphe 82
pig 21, 56, 70
'pincer model' 269, 290
Plasmodium falciparum 241

platelet 232, 242, 243
Polynesians 186, 201, 202, 212, 213, 215, 216, 288; homeland 212–13, 216
population: agriculture and 18; genetics 264, 276, 301; movement 18–19; samples 256, 257, 259, 260, 267, 278; size 268, 271, 280, 293, 302, 305, 313; subdivision 302, 305, 310
pottery: agriculture and 52; cord marked 63, 65, 66, 68, 69, 71, 100, 102, 175, 184, 186, 187, 191, 193
Pre-Austronesian 25, 59, 173, 184–6, 187, 188
prehistory: reconstructing 91–100
pre-Mundas 192
Proto-Atayalic 120
Proto-Austric 150, 193
Proto-Austro-Asiatic (PAA): age 3; Proto-Austronesian and 135–6, 138, 150–6; Proto-Malayo-Polynesian and 140, 141, 150; reconstructions 133–9; rice terms 41, 78
Proto-Austronesian (PAN): agriculture and 184; Chinese and 162, 173; faunal terminology 41–3; genetics and 291; homeland 24–5, 186; Huang He migration 185; morphology 168; origin of 24–5, 186; Proto-Austro-Asiatic 135–9, 138, 150–4; Proto-Eastern Austro-Asiatic 154–6; Proto-Malayo-Polynesian and 141, 142; reconstructions 137, 138, 148, 161, 162; rice terms 41–3; sounds 118, 125, 126, 165, 168–9; spread of 173
Proto-Austro-Tai 177
Proto-Daic 40
Proto-East Asian (PEA): languages of 182; language spread and 182–94; phylum hypothesis 265
Proto-Eastern Austro-Asiatic (PEAA) 134, 138, 139, 141, 150, 154
Proto-Filipino 275
Proto-Hlai 113
Proto-Hmong-Mien 3
Proto-Japonic 44
Proto-Kadai 161, 194
Proto-Kra-Dai (PKd) 108, 111, 116, 119, 121, 122, 124–6
Proto-Loloish 170
Proto-Malayic 146, 148
Proto-Malayo-Polynesian (PMP) 126, 134, 137–46, 150, 161–2, 178–80; rice terms 42

320

INDEX

Proto-Miao-Yao: rice terms 40
Proto-Mon-Khmer 193
Proto-Munda 193
Proto-Polynesian 186
Proto-Rukai 186
Proto-Sinitic 188
Proto-Sino-Tibetan-Austronesian (PSTAN) 172–3
Proto-Tai 112, 113, 114, 115
Proto-Tibeto-Burman 26
Przyluski, J. 85
Pumi 248
Puyuma 65, 171, 234, 235, 238, 239, 241, 242, 278, 287, 288

Qiangic 189
Qiang nation 188
Qiang people 248
Qin people 188, 189, 191, 248

reaping knife 69, 71
Red Corded Ware culture 68–9
Remote Oceania 201, 204, 212
Rhesus (RH) 235, 240, 254, 255, 256, 257, 258, 259, 260, 261, 262, 263, 265, 266, 267, 268, 269, 270, 290, 291, 294
rice: ancestor of domesticated 54; consumption 35; domestication 35; origin myths and 37; *Oryza rufipogon* (wild) 52, 54; research 34–5; terms for 38–44; *see also* rice agriculture
rice agriculture: Cambodia 35, 37; China 20–4, 35, 36, 38, 51–61; deepwater 35; India 35, 37; Indonesia 34; Japan 34, 56; lowland 35, 37; origins of (in China) 20–4, 57; origins of (in East Asia) 1, 51; Southeast Asia 34, 35, 36, 37; spread of 34, 35, 37, 56–61; state systems and 36–8; Taiwan 36, 56, 59, 71, 172, 173; upland 35, 42; *see also* rice
Ruc 147
Rukai 65, 231, 232, 234, 235, 238, 239, 241, 278, 287
Ryukyuan 274, 281
Ryukyu Islands 211

Sacy, Silvestre de 83
Sagart, L. 4, 6, 9–11, 39, 138, 147, 182, 184, 261, 286
Sahul 303, 306, 307
Saisiat 231, 234, 235, 238, 241, 242, 278
Salween River 192
Samoa 300

Sanxingdui 189
Schlegel, August Wilhelm von 83
Schmidt, Wilhelm 84
secretor 232, *234*
Sedeq/Seediq 65, 149
serological markers 255
serum proteins 232
Setaria italica (foxtail millet) 20, 73, 102, *167*, *168*, 174; *see also* millet agriculture
Setaria viridis (green foxtail millet) 21, 22, 54
Shafer, Robert 85, 89
Shandong 300
Shāng 88
Shanghai Han 300
short tandem repeats (STRs) 98, *243*, 313
Siamese 114, 123
Siberians 266, 278
Sichuan 25, 26, 95, 189, 190, 192
Sikkim 100
Sinitic languages 25, 85, 187–8, 274; age 34; Bodic and 100; rice terms 39–48; spread of 37, 39
Sino-Austronesian 6, 24, 101; argument for 161–73; linguistic evidence 162–72
Sino-Bodic 39, 86, 88, 89, 91, 100, 101, 187
Sino-Caucasian 5, 6, 22, 98, 261
Sinodonty 214
Sino-Tibetan (ST): Austronesian and 5, 6, 8, 9; genetics and 261, 271; homeland 48, 294; languages of 30, 38, 105; macrophylum and 6; morphology 173; naming of 85; origins 105, 131; Proto-Austronesian and 164; proto-language 2; Taiwan 65, 185–6; validity of 164; *see also* Tibeto-Burman
Sino-Tibetan-Austronesian (STAN) 6, 162, 167, 168, 173
Sino-Tibetan (ST) people: Austronesian people and 174
Sino-Tibetan-Yangzian 7, 184, 186–8
skeletal remains 205; study of 203
slash-and-burn agriculture 34
'slow boat' hypothesis 292
SNPs *306*, 307, 312, 313
Solomon Islands 201, 203–4, 207, 211–14, 218, 226, 289
Sonowal 260
Sora 146, 148, 151–3, 156, 157
Southeast Asia: anthropological studies 203–26; demography, historical 32–4; distinction from East/North Asia 212;

INDEX

Southeast Asia (continued):
island 203–4, 213, 216; language phyla 45; mainland 49, 77, 103, 204, 285; population displaced 227; populations highly differentiated 286
Southeast Asian languages: dispersal 34, agriculture and 34, 36; ethnolinguistic geography 7, 103; geographical pattern 19, 34; origins 266, 270
SPQR (Starosta, Pawley and Reid) 174, 195
Starosta, S. 172, 174, 185, 195 n.1, 261
Starostin, Sergei 6
stone adze see adze
stone tools 99
STRs see short tandem repeats
Strahlenberg, Phillip von 82
Sui 117
Sulu 211–12
Sumatra 192, 194, 206–7
Sundadonty 214, 229
swamp agriculture 32

Tagalog 2, 3, 169, 171
Tai languages 14, 24, 114, 192
Tai-Kadai 279; age of 3; Austronesian and 6, 134, 175, 179–82, 288, 290; Chinese and 271; genetics and 255, 259, 261, 262, 264, 268, 279; languages of 3; macrophylum and 4; origins 290; populations speaking 311; Proto-Austronesian and 291; see also Daic, Kra-Dai
Tainan 68–9
Taiwan: aboriginal languages 66; agriculture 19; anthropological studies 230; Austronesians 65; Austronesian-speaking 225; Chinese people 207; deeply buried agriculture 23; earliest inhabitants 64; east coast peoples 233, 235–42; genetic diversity 234, discussion of 243–6, populations studied 231, results 234–43; Hakka 231; HLA polymorphism 234–40, 244; indigenous peoples 56, 59, 61, 230, 231, 235, 238, 304, blood groups 245, Chinese and 207, divisions 237, genetics and 246, origins of 246, red blood cell polymorphism 238, secretor status 239; insular Southeast Asia and 230, 240, 242, 244; island status 242; language minorities 34; mainland connection 244–5; map 70, 245;

migration to 61, 240–1; millet cultivation 7; Minnan group 233; Mountain people 232, 234, 235, 238–42; people's origins 24, 65, 232, 244; Plains people 231; prehistoric activity on 246; Proto-Austro-Asiatic (PAA) 27, 47; Proto-Austronesian (PAN) 27, 61; rice terms 41–2 Sinicised people 231; see also Tapenkeng culture
Tamshui river valley 186
Tangut-Bodish 188–9
Tangut-Himalayan 188
Taoih 149
Tapenk'eng 64; see also Dapenkeng culture, Tapenkeng culture
Tapenkeng culture (TPK): Austronesian origins and 63, 64; characteristics of 63–4; date 73; homeland 69; Proto-Austronesian and 175–6; sites 63–4, 65, 67, 69; subsistence base 63; see also Dapenkeng culture, Tapenk'eng
Tarim Basin 22
Tasmania 212, 215
Thai 3, 241; Chinese and 5
Thailand 3, 192, 214
Thai people 64, 67, 71, 278
Thurgood, G. 108, 112–15, 117, 131, 148, 160, 181, 197
Tibet 86, 100, 172, 304, 307
Tibetan 171, 173, 191
Tibetan-Khamba 300, 304, 308, 309
Tibeto-Burman (TB) 5, 26, 27; Austronesian and 103; China and 101, 105; family tree 89; genetics and 102, 263; homeland 99, 100; migration and 105; morphology 162; Northern/Southern split 102; prehistory 88, 96; rice terms 47; sounds 165, 168; spread of 88; ST theory replaced by 85; study of (history) 88; subgroups outlined 86, 101; vocabulary 161, 162; western 92
Tibeto-Burman people: migrations 97–9
Tocharian languages 22–4
Tofalar 274
Tonga 299
Toraja 299
Trobriand Island 300
Truong Mountains 192
Tso-chen Man 245
Tsou 234, 235, 238, 242, 278, 279
Tsouic 65, 186, 281
Tujia 260, 300

322

INDEX

Tungus 274, 285
Turanian 83
Turkic 274
Tuva 285
Tuvana 300
Tuvin 274

Uighur 274, 278
Ulchi 274, 285
UPGMA 212
Uralic 274
Uygurs 299

Vanuatu Islands 214
Vayu 169
Vietnam 3, 192, 194, 207, 211; languages 42, 147, 190, 193
Vietnamese 3, 84–5
'Voyaging Corridor' model 204

Wa 248
Wei river basin 184
wheat 23
Wu 260

Xiachuan 52
Xiang 260
Xingjiang 21
Xiongnu people 248
Xi River 194

Yami 234, 235, 238, 239, 242, 275, 281
Yangzi Basin 21
Yangzi culture 101, 190
Yangzi River 190
Yangzi Valley: agriculture in 35, 36, 37, 43, 51, 52, 54, 55, 57, 58, 184; middle 20, 24; Proto-Hmong-Mien and 3
Yangzian 6, 7, 190–2
Yao 300
YAP 251, 252, 252, 305, 306, 307, 310–11, 313, 314, 315, 316
Y chromosome: diversity in East Asia and Oceania 297–310, haplotypes 301, populations 299–300, results 301–9, sources 308–10; markers 96
Yellow River Basin 21, 25, 88, 93, 97, 99, 100, 101, 102
Yellow River Valley: agriculture in 51–4, 55–6, 57, 58, 59, 60, 99
Yenisseian 261
Yi 184, 260, 300
Yimeng 171
Yue 191, 260
Yunnan 189, 190, 191, 192, 248, 303
Yunnan Han 300
Yupik 274, 279, 280

Zhejiang Han 300
Zhou 88, 188
Zhuang 300

Index 233

Ten-Year Program of Action, 1980 10
tomboi, 104–5
Toye, R.
 Churchill's Empire, 207n. 1
triangulation, 6, 130, 132–6, 139–40, 144–6, 148
 of Western exceptionalism, 7–8, 118–25, 130, 132, 140, 149, 154, 208n. 5
Turner, B. S., 23, 30, 31, 44, 193n. 5, 194n. 8

Vakulenko, A., 192n. 11
Vanita, R., 201–2n. 6
Van Wichelen, S., 207n. 3

Wahab, A., 203n. 19
Waites, M., 24, 54, 81, 82, 142, 197n. 23, 206n. 2, 207n. 14, 208n. 5
Walker, A.
 In Search of Our Mothers' Gardens, 9
Weber, M., 29–30, 32
Weeks, J., 6, 95–7, 99–102, 126, 190n. 3, 204n. 1, 3–4
The World We Have Won, 96
Weiss, M. L., 91, 208n. 5
Welzel, C., 60–1, 64
Western exceptionalism, 3, 6, 28, 42, 45, 47, 51, 63–4, 69, 72, 92, 100, 114, 116, 117, 118, 135–6, 139
 democracy as, 34–7
 embracing through homocolonialism, 149–54
 triangulation of, 7–8, 118–25, 130, 132, 140, 149, 154, 208n. 5
Whannel, G., 206n. 6
Wilcox, C., 46
Williams, W. L., 87
womanist, definition of, 9
Wong, Y., 204n. 6
World Values Survey (WVS), 56, 57, 59, 60, 63, 197n. 23, 199n. 15

Yip, A. Kam-Tuck, 110–11
Yogyakarta principles, 53, 198nn. 7–8
YouGov poll, 58
Young, I. M., 207n. 13

Printed in the United States
By Bookmasters